Praise for *Stonehenge*

'From 2003 to 2009, the archaeologist Mike Pearson led the Stonehenge Riverside Project that studied Stonehenge ... His book is a detailed account of that archaeological survey, expressed in a genial style that invigorates the story of the groundwork'
Iain Finlayson, *The Times*

'*Stonehenge* has both the taste and the content of an authentic archaeological log-book, and without doubt will become an essential academic source. What sets it apart is the almost painstaking patience with which Pearson is prepared to break down even the most complex of scientific processes'
Daisy Dunn, *Joint Association of Classical Teachers*

'Parker Pearson's book is the fullest account to date of what is known about Stonehenge and its surroundings; it should be essential reading'
Steve Marshall, *Fortean Times*

'The book we have all been waiting for ... *Stonehenge* fizzes with new ideas that will give archaeologists much to argue about'
Current Archaeology

'The book describes one of the outstanding archaeological projects of recent years. It is accessible, original, carefully researched and important. But, above all, it is exciting'
Richard Bradley, *Professor of Archaeology at Reading University*

'This is brilliantly-written scholarship. The book combines old ideas about the circle with the unexpected revelations of today. It is a triumph'
Aubrey Burl

STONEHENGE

EXPLORING THE GREATEST STONE AGE MYSTERY

by

MIKE PARKER PEARSON
and the
STONEHENGE RIVERSIDE PROJECT

**SIMON &
SCHUSTER**

London · New York · Sydney · Toronto · New Delhi

A CBS COMPANY

First published in Great Britain by Simon & Schuster, 2012
This paperback edition published by Simon & Schuster UK Ltd, 2013
A CBS COMPANY

1 3 5 7 9 10 8 6 4 2

Simon & Schuster UK Ltd
1st Floor
222 Gray's Inn Road
London WC1X 8HB

www.simonandschuster.co.uk

Simon & Schuster Australia, Sydney
Simon & Schuster India, New Delhi

A CIP catalogue record for this book is available
from the British Library.

ISBN: 978-0-85720-732-6
ISBN: 978-0-85720-733-3 (ebook)

Typeset in Baskerville by M Rules
Printed and bound by CPI Group (UK) Ltd, Croydon, CR0 4YY

CONTENTS

ACKNOWLEDGEMENTS

My co-directors of the Stonehenge Riverside Project were Josh Pollard, Chris Tilley, Julian Thomas, Colin Richards and Kate Welham. We were joined for specific projects in later years by Mike Allen, Wayne Bennett, Charly French, Chris Gaffney, Paul Garwood, Jacqui McKinley, Mike Pitts, Julian Richards, (California) Dave Robinson, Clive Ruggles, Rob Scaife and Armin Schmidt. The long excavation seasons were made possible by the team of supervisors – Becca Pullen, Hugo Anderson-Whymark, (Manchester) Dave Aspden, Ben Chan, Ian Heath, Neil Morris, Bob Nunn, Jim Rylatt, Ellen Simmons and Anne Teather – who were joined by many hard-working site assistants each year. Amongst these, I need to mention Lizzie Carleton, Chris Caswell, Ralph Collard, C.J. Hyde, (Farmer) Dave Shaw, Susan Stratton and James Thomson, who started as novice undergraduate diggers and ended up training others.

The geophysical surveys and data processing depended on Mark Dover, who managed the digital resource throughout the first stage of the project; from among the many Bournemouth students who undertook the surveys, Lawrence Shaw and Charlene Steele continue to work on aspects of the project. All of the above, especially Hugo, also contributed to the success of some indescribable campsite parties, for which Alistair Pike provided glow-sticks; I imagine there are photographs on Facebook, but I have never dared look.

The student diggers came primarily from the universities of Sheffield, Manchester, Bournemouth, UCLAN, Birmingham, Cardiff, Kalmar, Leicester, Exeter, Plymouth and UCL: they cannot be named individually of course, because we probably trained over 500 undergraduates over the life of the project. As is usual with archaeology students on excavations, the majority enjoyed themselves enormously, a handful appeared to hate the whole experience and a lucky few came back for more year after year. Some of the students took part in visitor guiding and public outreach, an integral part of a project such as this, managed by Megan and David Price and then by Pat Shelley. Adam Stanford of Aerial-Cam took many essential – and stunning – photographs throughout the project. Helen Wickstead co-ordinated the artists in residence, who are thanked for bringing a new dimension to the project.

The main staffing problem in the later years of the project was having to turn people away – we could never accommodate everyone who wanted to volunteer. For those who did, I again cannot mention all by name, but Jane Downes, Duncan Brown, Denise Allen, Win Scutt, David Durkin and all the other volunteers know that their work was much appreciated. Three important volunteers throughout the project's life have been Eileen Parker, Lesley Chapman and Jane Ford, all mature students of archaeology in Sheffield, who continue to dedicate their time, patience and skills to the post-excavation process.

All the landowners and tenant farmers were unfailingly helpful and patient, allowing us access to the sites sometimes over several seasons: we owe a debt of thanks to Sir Edward Antrobus, Richard Bawden, Ian Baxter, Stuart Crook, Mr E. Hann, Billy King, Hugh Morrison, Stan and Henry Rawlins, the Rowlands and Rob Turner in Wiltshire and Huw Davies, the late Iorwerth Williams and the late Hyacinthe Hawkesworth, Lady Marcher of Cemaes, in Pembrokeshire. Chris Gingell and Martin Papworth ran the National Trust side of the necessary permissions, and Amanda Chadburn and Rachel Foster of English Heritage had the unsung task of managing all the paperwork and meetings generated by our research proposals every year; English Heritage also funded two seasons' of visitor outreach, co-ordinated by Kath Graham and Lerato Dunn. Dave Field and Martyn Barber at English Heritage have been endlessly helpful and willing to share their research ideas. MoD archaeologists Richard Osgood and Martin Brown are thanked for making arrangements for work on Royal School of Artillery land.

Thanks go to Wessex Archaeology for providing equipment, and support for the flotation programme. Reg Jury provided mechanical excavators, some huge trout and an enormously generous contribution to the diggers' beer fund. The Woodbridge Inn in North Newnton housed us every year, the Masseys provided an essential ex-Army marquee, and Rushall Village Hall and Corsham Scouts helped out with domestic equipment. Archaeological projects rely on such local goodwill, and we are tremendously grateful to all concerned.

We also rely on our funding bodies who, we hope, are pleased with the results of this project that they supported for so many years. The major project funder was the Arts and Humanities Research Council, with further grants and awards for different aspects of the overall project provided by the National Geographic Society, the British Academy, the Royal Archaeological Institute, the Society of Antiquaries, Google, the Robert Kiln Trust, Andante Travel and the Royal Society of Northern Antiquaries of Copenhagen. Naomi Nathan, Jo Mirfield and Chris Grimbley in Sheffield were driven to distraction at times by the problems of administering these multiple grants, and Karen and I thank them for their patience in helping sort out our bundles of muddy, dog-eared receipts every year, and in putting together our hired vans and fieldwork equipment.

My director's site diary will end up in the project archive at some point in the future; as well as recording the technical details of what was going on on site each day, it often mentions visitors to the excavations. We were encouraged and heartened by the interest that other archaeologists took in our work, and it was a pleasure to have so many come to visit the sites. I think we managed to prove that a multi-director team was not just feasible but genuinely productive, especially since we are still working together.

For their archaeological advice or other contributions, I particularly wish to thank Louise Austin, Jenny and Bill Britnell, Dave Buckley, Tim Darvill, Peter Drewett, Julie Gardiner, Alex Gibson, Mark Gillings, Phil Harding, Mats Larsson, Ben Laurie, Neil Linford, Andy Payne, Alison Sheridan, Paul Tubb and Geoff Wainwright. In addition, a large team of specialists – too numerous to list here – continues to work on the post-excavation aspects of the project.

My wife Karen has been in the background, managing the project, from its inception, and has dealt with everything from van-driving and fancy-dress outfits to sewage disposal and impetigo, as well as taking on time-consuming post-excavation tasks back in Sheffield. As she spent each summer cooking for hundreds of people, she rarely had time to see the excavations in action, so her editing work on this and all past and future project publications is her chance to finally see what we found out (or so I keep telling her, as I hand her yet another draft . . .).

The new illustrations prepared for this book are by Peter Dunn (several of them being sponsored by Pat Shelley's Salisbury & Stonehenge Guided Tours) and Irene de Luis.

Bill Hamilton of A.M. Heath & Co., Monica O'Connell, and Mike Jones of Simon & Schuster brought the book to publication.

1

INTRODUCTION

For millennia Stonehenge has stood alone on Salisbury Plain, a mysterious legacy of a vanished culture. Today it is flanked by two busy roads and its visitor centre attracts almost a million tourists a year from all around the world. Yet only fifty years ago it was still a quiet and empty place, reached by lonely roads and tracks over the high plain. A visiting Dutch archaeologist described it in 1957: 'There was no fence nor were tickets sold at Stonehenge, and there were no other visitors, the car was just parked on the grass and you could just walk around the stones and touch them.'[1]

The myth of Stonehenge in seclusion is a powerful one. Many have tried to understand Stonehenge on its own, without thinking greatly about its surroundings on the windswept plain, or the people of its wider world. Astronomers, mathematicians, engineers and all manner of scholars and enthusiasts have pored over plans and drawings of this great stone circle, extracting significance from myriad possible interpretations of its design. In the modern era, many of those interested in the monument have certainly hoped that some secret code to its meaning might somehow be broken – if only we knew how.

If we could travel back in time, some 4000 or 5000 years, we would find that Stonehenge was not an isolated marvel. It was one of many monuments in this part of Salisbury Plain. Some were built of timber, and lasted only a few centuries. At least one monument of stone standing on the bank of the nearby River Avon was dismantled by ancient people only a few centuries after it was put up. The banks and ditches of large earthwork enclosures lasted much longer, but millennia of ploughing and erosion have reduced them to mere humps and bumps that are barely visible today. Stonehenge in its heyday was thus not alone, being part of a landscape teeming with construction and activity. For those studying Stonehenge, therefore, the stone circle is not in itself the puzzle but rather just one piece of a complex jigsaw.

For more than 300 years people have been trying to find that puzzle's missing pieces. In 1666 John Aubrey, the king's antiquary, discovered that there was an 'avenue' leading from Stonehenge towards the River Avon, which runs to its east. In the 1720s the antiquarian William Stukeley recorded many details about Stonehenge and its surrounding burial mounds or 'barrows'. Eighty years later, local landowner Richard Colt Hoare, the excavator of many of these barrows, mapped a huge earthwork enclosure known as Durrington Walls that is situated some two miles northeast of Stonehenge. The pace of discovery quickened during the twentieth century, as the 'footprints' of long-vanished timber circles at Durrington Walls and the nearby site called Woodhenge were excavated by teams of expert archaeologists.

In archaeology context is everything. As a rule, an artefact or a monument studied in isolation is out of context and as such any interpretation of it will always be partial and flawed. If we can understand a monument in terms of what it related to, who made it, how they lived, and what else they did, we stand a better chance of understanding the thing-in-itself as the product of wider forces. But the process of piecing together the past can be compared with assembling a jigsaw puzzle only so far. We may be able to see *what* fits together but this will not necessarily reveal *how* it fits together. There must be a deductive insight – a flash of perception – that explains the hows and whys. This is where we need theories and hypotheses – the starting points of all scientific endeavour, whether we're attempting to explain relativity or the causes of the Second World War.

Theories provide new ways of seeing, new understandings of the facts, and new lines of evidence to be sought out. Theories are not articles of faith or belief; they are there to be tested to breaking point. When we discover that an existing hypothesis doesn't explain new findings, that hypothesis must be discarded or modified. Consequently the history of knowledge is strewn with the debris of rejected theories. In archaeology the most powerful theories are those that match and explain evidence produced by new discoveries; if the new evidence doesn't support the theory's predictions then the theory is wrong.

This book is about the relationship of Stonehenge to its surrounding landscape and to the people who built it. We have tried throughout to explain why some theories about Stonehenge are better than others. Our knowledge has changed dramatically as a result of the Stonehenge Riverside Project, which started in 2003 and ran for seven years, to 2009, during which time forty-five archaeological excavations were opened throughout the Stonehenge World Heritage Site's 26.6 square kilometres. During the first two years of the project, as its overall leader, I gathered a team of expert archaeologists to be co-directors – Colin Richards, Josh Pollard, Kate Welham, Julian Thomas and Chris Tilley. Together we then recruited teams of university students, local volunteers and professional archaeologists from across Britain and Europe on what became one of the world's largest archaeological projects of its day.

Our investigations not only explored locations at and around Stonehenge itself but also focused on the nearby great henge enclosure of Durrington Walls. At the heart of our research was the possibility that Stonehenge and Durrington Walls were not separate monuments, as everyone had thought, but two halves of the same complex. In other words, to understand Stonehenge we had to understand its relationship to Durrington Walls.

Most people have never even heard of Durrington Walls. Named after the present village of Durrington, a stone's throw to its northeast, this is a neglected but internationally important part of the Stonehenge World Heritage Site. A major road runs through the middle of this prehistoric circular earthwork or 'henge'. Just beyond it to the north lies the Stonehenge Inn, where coachloads of Stonehenge visitors stop off for pub lunches, oblivious to the enclosure's existence. And who can blame them? The earthworks of Durrington Walls are visible only to the trained eye. Next to it, on its south side, is the site of Woodhenge, the remains of a timber circle whose excavated postholes have been filled with concrete cylinders to mark the positions of the long-gone timber posts that once stood in them. Another two Stonehenge-sized timber circles – known as the Northern and Southern Circles – were discovered inside the circular earthworks of Durrington Walls in the 1960s, during excavations when the main road was built, but these now lie buried and unmarked beneath the road embankment.

The size of Durrington Walls is impressive. Covering an area of 17 hectares, the earthen banks of this enormous enclosure once stood more than 3 metres (10 feet) high, with a ditch inside the bank some 5.5 metres (18 feet) deep. Today there is little more to see on the surface than a panel informing visitors that this was once the largest of Britain's henges.

Henges were built only during the Neolithic*, Copper Age and Bronze Age (starting at around 3000 BC) and they are found only in Britain. The word 'henge' does not refer to a circular structure of stone or wood, as is commonly thought, but is actually the name given to an earthen enclosure in which the ditch is situated on the inside of the bank – as if keeping something inside it rather than keeping people out. It just so happens that many of these inside-out enclosures have the remains of structures inside them. Paradoxically – and despite lending its name to this type of prehistoric monument – Stonehenge itself is not technically a henge: its own ditch lies outside its bank.

Before the enclosing ditch and bank were constructed at Durrington Walls, some 4500 years ago, this was also the largest settlement of its day in northern Europe. Our excavations have revealed that this was a landscape filled with small wattle-and-daub houses; it must have been alive with the sounds of thousands of people gathering from miles around to celebrate and worship at the two great timber circles. Archaeologists have often wondered whether lots of people lived at Stonehenge, because its stones obviously required a huge number of people to 'dress' them (to shape and smooth them), and to put them up. The builders must have lived somewhere, in large groups for a long period of time, and we know that prehistoric people usually left traces of their presence – things such as broken pots, flint tools, animal bones, burnt grain, houses and storage pits dug into the ground. Archaeologists, including myself, have looked for traces of a builders' camp in the vicinity of Stonehenge but without success. Settlement remains are largely absent

---

* 'Neolithic' means New Stone Age; it follows the Old Stone Age (Palaeolithic) and the Middle Stone Age (Mesolithic). Neolithic peoples used stone tools, made pottery and kept domestic animals.

from Stonehenge and its immediate surroundings. So it seems that the people who lived in the village which we discovered at Durrington Walls built both Stonehenge and Durrington Walls. We now know from our new findings at Durrington Walls that large gatherings of Neolithic people could create huge quantities of waste, even during a period of occupancy lasting less than a few decades. New studies of DNA and isotopes tell us something about who these Neolithic people were, including where they came from, what they ate and how they lived.

Had the timber circles and houses of Durrington Walls been built of stone, they might have survived for people to appreciate today. It would also have been self-evident that Stonehenge was part of a larger complex and should be understood in such terms. There are other reasons why earlier archaeologists failed to understand the link between the two sites. It was thought that Stonehenge and Durrington Walls were built at different times in prehistory and so could not have been in contemporaneous use. The radiocarbon dates for Durrington Walls appeared to be several centuries earlier than those for Stonehenge; as a result, until as late as 2008 (when we reinterpreted the whole chronology of Stonehenge and Durrington Walls), some archaeologists argued that the stones of Stonehenge were put up much later than the Durrington Walls timber circles. Perhaps, as my university teachers suggested thirty years ago, Stonehenge was a stone copy of the timber circles, created after they'd fallen into decay? Until our recent findings changed the story quite radically, the radiocarbon dates misled archaeologists into thinking that the timber circles of Durrington Walls and Woodhenge would have been in ruins by the time the stones were erected at Stonehenge.

Even so, there were always unappreciated clues that Stonehenge and the Durrington Walls timber circles might be related. For centuries it has been common knowledge that Stonehenge's builders employed features derived from carpentry. The lintels* are secured to the tops of the uprights by tenons (carved knobs projecting from the top of the stone) that fit into cup-shaped mortise holes on the undersides of the stone

---

* The lintels are the horizontal stones that rest on top of the upright stones of the circle. Most of them have been taken away over the millennia, but some are still in their original position; others are now lying in the grass around the feet of the upright stones.

lintels. The ends of each lintel are slightly curved so that each nestles snugly against the next in a simple form of tongue-and-groove jointing. It's unlikely that the stonemasons considered these to be practical requirements – the sheer weight of the five-ton lintels made this mortise-and-tenon jointing unnecessary – so their inclusion must represent a stylistic nod towards timber architecture.

For me a flash of insight came from sharing ideas with a colleague from Madagascar. Many archaeologists had assumed that the choice of materials – stone for Stonehenge and wood for the Durrington Walls timber circles – was of no particular significance. My colleague Ramilisonina saw things differently. When he visited the monuments of Wessex* with me for the first time, he explained that in his country, before the arrival of the missionaries, stone had been reserved for the tombs of the ancestors while timber was used for the houses of the living. Might not this be the case here in Neolithic Britain? Could the choice of materials be as important as the architecture itself?

This was a radical idea. Some archaeologists thought it an exciting possibility but others greeted it with mild derision. It was a theory but we needed to find out some crucial information. *If* Stonehenge and Durrington Walls really were contemporary, and *if* there were burials at Stonehenge and none at Durrington Walls, and *if* there were some way of showing how Stonehenge and Durrington Walls were physically connected, *then* there was a case for arguing that timber and stone symbolized the living and the dead respectively. A new idea wasn't enough: we needed more information.

This all seemed a lot to investigate. We knew there were cremation burials at Stonehenge, dug up in the 1920s but since reburied, but none had been dated so there was no certainty about how they fitted into the monument's history. Before our project began, no evidence of any

---

* The term Wessex has three major meanings. It is originally the name of the Kingdom of the West Saxons in southwest England, whose king was Alfred the Great and last earl (until modern times) King Harold. The name was used by Thomas Hardy for a (very large) fictional county in his novels set in Dorset and the southwest; Hardy's revival of the term is the source of most modern uses of the word (e.g. Wessex Water, the regional supplier). The name is used most frequently by archaeologists, as useful shorthand when referring to the southern English counties of Dorset, Wiltshire and parts of Somerset, Berkshire and Oxfordshire during the prehistoric period.

dwellings had been found at Durrington Walls by previous archaeologists, so it would be up to us to find out whether it was a place of the living or not. We suspected that the link between Stonehenge and Durrington Walls was provided by the River Avon, which flows past Durrington Walls and then meanders to the east of Stonehenge before heading towards the English Channel. This river is linked to Stonehenge by a long, linear pair of earthen banks called the Stonehenge Avenue. But no one had ever found any evidence of an equivalent avenue linking Durrington Walls to the river. We would have to do a lot of digging to get new information and start to answer our new questions about the two monuments.

The results of our geophysical surveys and excavations were beyond our wildest expectations. The more we worked in the landscape in and around Stonehenge and Durrington Walls, the more we learned about how Stonehenge was part of a larger complex. We also came up with new evidence casting light on some of the more perplexing questions about Stonehenge. Ramilisonina's insight about places of the living and places of the dead was just the first step on what would turn out to be a long journey of discovery, taking us far beyond the initial theory of stones being associated with ancestors.

As for Stonehenge itself, we had to tackle some big questions about the date of the monument and its sequence of construction. Although Stonehenge's big stones were put up around 2500 BC (4500 years ago), archaeologists have known for a while that the circular ditch and bank around Stonehenge were constructed about 500 years earlier, around 3000 BC. When we started work, nobody knew whether there had been any circles of standing stones or timber posts at that early date. Another really tricky problem centred on the stones themselves. Among the smaller standing stones at Stonehenge today are numerous 'bluestones' of various types of rock that derive from the Preseli Hills, about 180 miles away in west Wales. What are these doing at Stonehenge, so very far from home? When were they brought to Wiltshire and when were they first erected?

Another question – one which we never expected to resolve – was why Stonehenge is where it is. Salisbury Plain is covered with prehistoric monuments but most of these lie close to the rivers and streams that provided water for prehistoric farmers and their animals. So why is Stonehenge located over a mile from water, near the top of a rather desolate ridge? What was so special about that particular spot that prehistoric people brought stones here from so far away? And why did they expend so much effort – literally millions of man-hours – in quarrying, shaping, pulling, dressing, erecting and lifting the huge stones to form a stone circle that imitated wood? Through a combination of carefully thought-through research hypotheses, tightly drafted research designs, very hard work by all concerned (and a modicum of luck), we have discovered new sites and made new interpretations of existing information; this book presents the results so far of seven years' work in the field and in the laboratory.

2

THE MAN FROM MADAGASCAR

In 1998 – fourteen years ago at the time of writing – I was involved in the making of a BBC documentary, *Stonehenge: Ancient Voices*. The programme's producer decided to bring in and interview someone with experience of erecting standing stones. Malagasy archaeologist Ramilisonina knew all about such things: his family still follows ancient traditions of moving and raising large stones to commemorate the dead. So, in February that year, Ramilisonina braved the British winter and came to Wiltshire to take part in filming.

Ramilisonina and I had already been working together for years. Previously he had taken me to lots of interesting tombs and monuments in the spiny deserts of southern Madagascar; now I took him to Avebury. Ramilisonina was transfixed by this stone circle, which stands about twenty miles north of Stonehenge. Its stones are bigger than anything he has ever handled – so huge that he had to ask me whether the people who erected them had used tractors. If not, he mused, they must have been put up by magic. I told him that the stone circle was more than 4000 years old – so no tractors – and that I honestly didn't believe that stones could be moved by supernatural means.

As we wandered among the Avebury stones in the fading afternoon light, I explained that we didn't know what the standing stones were for. Now it was Ramilisonina's turn to look at me in amused disbelief. How could I not know? To him it was obvious. It seemed that even after many seasons of fieldwork in Madagascar I hadn't really grasped the significance of stone: it is an everlasting material with which one honours and

commemorates the dead. There in Madagascar, perishable materials –
wood, fabric, plant materials – are used only for the living, to clothe and
house them during the brief span of human life, before they spend the
eternity of death in a stone tomb. Stone monuments are for the ancestors – for Ramil, this explanation was self-evident.

My first reaction was to laugh. Contemporary Madagascar and prehistoric Britain are so disconnected, both geographically and historically,
that it was surely a bit absurd to suggest that these two completely separate cultures could share any motivation for putting up megaliths.
Nevertheless, at Stonehenge for the filming the next day, I found myself
thinking about what Ramilisonina had said, wondering if it might not be
so far-fetched. I knew that archaeologists had found many human burials at Stonehenge[1] – it certainly had some sort of association with the
dead. And less than two miles away from the great stone circle there once
stood the timber circles inside and outside the massive Durrington Walls
enclosure.[2]

As a student I'd been taught that these three timber circles in and
near Durrington Walls pre-dated Stonehenge and were probably its prototypes. Some thought that they'd once been roofed to make giant
circular buildings – and that Stonehenge was a stone copy made after
they'd fallen into ruin. If Ramilisonina's instinct was right, then the relationship between the stone circle and the timber circles wasn't a question
of prototypes, of one style replacing another. The wooden and stone
monuments would have played different roles in the lives of their
builders. Perhaps wood was juxtaposed with stone for a purpose, to
create a complex of monumental structures associated with the transition from life to death. If the timber circles were monuments for the
living, as opposed to stone monuments for the dead, then there should
be evidence that these structures at Durrington Walls were actually contemporary with Stonehenge.

If the stone and timber circles *were* all part of one system, then what
joined them together? I knew without looking at the map that the answer
was the River Avon. Stonehenge has an avenue, flanked by ditches and
banks, that leads from its entrance towards the river;[3] two miles upstream
from Stonehenge, Durrington Walls lies very close to the Avon. Perhaps
this river was significant as a route between the circles of timber and the

circle of stone, playing a part in a transition from life to death. Eighteen miles north of Stonehenge and Durrington Walls, the stone circles and avenues of Avebury,[4] too, could have been designed as part of a larger wood-and-stone complex. Archaeologists had recently discovered the remains of a series of enclosures surrounded by wooden palisades along the Kennet river, a mile from Avebury.[5] Maybe Avebury was also built as a place for the ancestors, separated by water from the land of the living.

That day at Stonehenge, Ramilisonina answered questions for the cameras. By the dark and freezing evening, when we finally got inside the stone circle, I was already looking at it with new eyes. Could a link between wood and stone explain why Stonehenge's builders had shaped the stones in ways reminiscent of carpentry?

Back at home I discussed the archaeological evidence with Ramilisonina. Over the next three days we wrote an academic paper in which we described the meanings of standing stones in Madagascar and drew an analogy with Stonehenge and Avebury.[6] All archaeology (and in fact all social and historical studies) relies on analogy. An analogy is an equivalence, or a parallel, and we use analogies all the time, even at the most basic level of identification – when we decide to call an ancient stone or metal object with a particular type of sharp edge 'an axe', for example, we are employing the simplest sort of analogy. In more complex attempts to deduce the motivation behind people's actions, we draw on analogies to explain what we see and find.

The problem with analogy is that we must have a broad range of possibilities with which to draw comparisons. If we limit our horizons to our own lived experiences, in the urbanized Western world, we risk imposing our own preconceptions on what we find, and can even fail to recognize the most simple of objects if they are beyond our personal frame of reference. For archaeologists it is essential to draw on as wide a knowledge as possible of cultural diversity and the different ways of explaining human action.

As we wrote, Ramil and I talked about 'materiality' – the use of physical materials to express intangible meanings. I explained to Ramil that even in Britain today we have complex material symbolism associated with death. The funeral itself often involves impermanent, perishable materials – displays of cut, dying flowers, for example, and the marking of a recently dug grave by a wooden cross, perceived as temporary. For us, the funerary process requires stone to reach its conclusion: a gravestone is erected months after an interment, to ensure the permanent memory of the dead. We regard such things as practical, pragmatic actions, but there's usually much more to human behaviour at such important moments.

At various times and in many different places around the world, architecture has been used to express notions of permanence. Building in stone communicates solidity and eternal values, often invoking the words or deeds of ancestral figures. An illustration of this can be seen in Washington DC, which has striking ceremonial architecture. Here colossal edifices house awe-inspiring images of such national ancestors as Lincoln and Jefferson; the overwhelming scale of the statues in their temple-like buildings embodies the immensity of their 'meaning' for the nation – these are monumental figures, in both the precise and the metaphorical senses. The materials with which we surround ourselves can and do affect us. As Winston Churchill once observed, first we build the buildings and then they build us.

The permanence of stone can be used to express concepts of eternity in contrast to life's temporality, as seen in ancient Egypt, ancient China and many other civilizations. The sixth-century BC sage Lao Tzu expressed the concept clearly in *Tao Te Ching*:

> A man is supple and weak when living, but hard and stiff when dead. Grass and trees are pliant and fragile when living, but dried and shrivelled when dead. Thus the hard and the strong are the comrades of death; the supple and the weak are the comrades of life.

Even earlier, from the eighth century BC, we have a written reference to the souls of the dead being set in stone:[7] archaeologists working in southeastern Turkey in 2008 found a stele – a carved and inscribed standing stone – commemorating the death of a man named Kuttamuwa. This is thought to be the first written reference to the soul, and the inscription also includes the words: 'my soul that is in this stele'.

In our article Ramil and I pointed out that this association of stone with the eternal was neither shared just between contemporary

Madagascar and prehistoric Britain, nor an innate human universal found in all times and all cultures. Our cultural metaphors change as our surroundings change: today we commonly draw upon technology to provide metaphors – comparing the human brain with a computer, for instance – but such analogy was simply unavailable to any earlier culture. Stone has no inherent meaning that identifies it with the eternal, the dead or the ancestors. Instead, its meanings are always historically contingent and subject to change according to social context. Even so, the cultural association of stone with permanence, and perishable materials with transience, seems to have been a commonly followed strategy in many different times and places, drawing on some of the most basic metaphors of human life and death.

In prehistoric societies working with stone and wood, these material properties of permanence and perishability would have been self-evident. But of course the meanings ascribed to the materials cannot be assumed to be the same as ours. I wondered how one could find evidence that stone and wood incorporated meanings that invoked permanence and transience, or life and death, for the people who built Stonehenge.

Our idea that Stonehenge was built as a place of the ancestors was not entirely new. In the late nineteenth century two of the finest archaeological minds of their time had come to similar conclusions. In 1880 William Flinders Petrie, later the greatest Egyptologist of his era, declared Stonehenge to be more monumental and sepulchral than religious or astronomical.[8] Five years later Arthur Evans, the excavator of the Minoan palace of Knossos on Crete, wrote that Stonehenge was built to honour the departed ancestors of a whole prehistoric tribe.[9] In 1957 the prehistorian Vere Gordon Childe wrote in the sixth edition of his masterwork *The Dawn of European Civilization* that Stonehenge was built as a monument to the establishment of peace and unity. These interpretations had, however, been forgotten or ignored by most archaeologists.

During the late 1980s and 1990s similar ideas began to resurface. In 1987 in his book *The Stonehenge People* Aubrey Burl wrote that Stonehenge was a house of the dead.[10] Ten years later archaeologists Barbara Bender, Alasdair Whittle and Josh Pollard were all putting new ideas into print about the importance of the Stonehenge builders deliberately having chosen stone to signify permanence.[11]

As a break from thinking about Stonehenge, I took Ramilisonina to my other research area, in the Outer Hebrides off the west coast of Scotland. Even in summer the rain and wind can be extreme and, that February, it was predictably stormy. Although he admired the farming lifestyle, accompanied by all the mod-cons that are still lacking in most of Madagascar, Ramilisonina found South Uist appallingly cold and wet. As a storm blew in from the Atlantic and threatened to rip the roof off our rented caravan, he was convinced that he was about to die and would soon be joining his ancestors.

Four months later our paper was published in the academic journal *Antiquity* and caused a bit of a storm of its own. Some scholars thought it was just the kind of fresh thinking needed to explain Stonehenge and its surrounding monuments. Others thought it was just terrible. (One postgraduate student even asked whether I'd had a particularly bad day when I wrote it.) There were those who didn't like the use of analogy – arguing that Neolithic Britain was a unique society so any comparison was inadequate. Others still said the article was mechanistic and structuralist – that binary oppositions (such as stone:wood) were too simplistic to explain the complex actions and events surrounding Stonehenge's construction and use.[12]

We wrote a reply, setting out predictions of what archaeologists should find in the Stonehenge landscape if the theory were valid, and where to look.[13] If the theory was on the right track, we said, the timber circles at Durrington Walls and Woodhenge should be associated with a 'domain of the living'. The burials at Stonehenge should be part of a 'domain of the ancestors', not just a fleeting and temporary moment of use of the site as a cemetery. If we were right about the role of the River Avon in linking two parts of a ritual landscape, there should also be the remains of an avenue leading from Durrington Walls to the Avon, in the same way that the Stonehenge avenue leads from the Avon to the stone circle.

The debate went round and round, and it was all about theory. For some academics, what mattered was theoretical correctness – structuralism had been fashionable in the 1960s and 1970s but had been replaced by post-modernism. Others felt that archaeology simply couldn't answer such questions. No one seemed particularly interested in going out and collecting new evidence, to see if our idea could be challenged and rejected. All any of us had to work with were some poorly recorded data from old excavations by dead archaeologists. Trial by theory was not a satisfactory resolution – someone needed to get out there and find out whether our predictions had any reality on the ground. If the ideas didn't hold up, then the theory was flawed and we could all move on, and try some different explanation of what Stonehenge is all about.

It often surprises people to learn just how little archaeological investigation has been done at and around Stonehenge. Whenever a new discovery is made there's general amazement that there is anything left to find. Yet the truth is that most of Stonehenge and the land around it have never been investigated. Even the twentieth-century digs within Stonehenge itself explored only half of it. There are also problems with the records of these previous excavations.

Despite the shortcomings of our knowledge about Stonehenge, however, we know a lot about the people who lived in Britain at the time that it was built. They were farmers who lived off crops (such as wheat and barley) and domestic animals (pigs, cows and sheep) as well as gathering and hunting wild foods. They used clay pots for cooking and storing their food, but they roasted meat as well as boiling it. Their diet may have been predominantly vegetarian and dairy-based, interspersed with special occasions when animals were slaughtered and eaten. Judging by finds from elsewhere in Europe, their clothing was made of leather, fur and vegetable fibres such as flax (used to make linen).[14] The Neolithic people of Britain reared sheep but we have no evidence that they had yet invented spinning or weaving of wool. Nor is there any evidence that they had invented the wheel. Horses, too, may well have been unknown; although horses were being used for riding in eastern Europe and the steppes of central Asia, it seems that they had not yet been brought across the Channel.

Stonehenge was built at the end of the Stone Age, so most of the people's tools were made of flint – arrowheads, scrapers for cleaning hides, strike-a-lights for making fire, and a tool-set of other specialized awls, burins, knives and saws. Their axes were made of flint or of igneous rock, polished and then hafted on to remarkably modern-looking axe handles. By 2500 BC, though, the first metal tools (copper axes) were beginning to appear in northwest Europe. Some may have been brought to Britain and Ireland or even made here; there are stray finds of early types of copper axe but these cannot be closely dated. It also seems likely that the earliest copper tools would have been too valuable to put into the ground for archaeologists to find – and they had the advantage over flint axes in being recyclable. We have fewer remains of perishable organic equipment but we do know that people used birch-bark containers, cord made from sinews, rope made from lime bast or from honeysuckle, wicker baskets and leather bags, arrow quivers and belt pouches.

Neolithic people seem not to have lived in villages, except in a few special areas such as the islands of Orkney off the northern coast of Scotland. Across most of Britain their dwellings were single farmsteads or hamlets. Before about 3000 BC a typical farm might have consisted of a rectangular house, normally around 12 metres long and 5 metres wide. Some rectangular houses were rather larger and can be called 'halls' but no one knows if these were domestic dwellings or community buildings. After 3000 BC, house forms adopted a square plan of about 5 metres across. Remains of Neolithic houses are difficult to find because they were usually made of wood and the shallow holes in which their posts were set have only rarely survived later ploughing. Nonetheless, archaeologists are fairly certain that the limited spreads of worked flints found in ploughed fields derive from hamlet-sized settlements.

This apparently isolated pattern of living contrasts with what we know of Neolithic gathering places, where people assembled periodically in large numbers. During the fourth millennium BC the building of large, communal tombs required the collective efforts of many families coming together. Even larger numbers congregated at causewayed enclosures, a type of gathering place that was especially popular in the thirty-seventh century BC. Later on, after 3600 BC, the Neolithic inhabitants of Britain built other large monuments that required many hands, a labour force no doubt drawn from farmsteads scattered over wide areas. Archaeologists often talk of mobility among these populations – meaning that they moved seasonally from place to place with their animals rather than living all year round in one spot. The early farmers

Reconstruction of a Neolithic house of the fourth millennium BC.

of Britain appear to have been more similar in these terms to their hunter-gatherer ancestors than to the early farmers of mainland Europe – who were much more sedentary, living in large longhouses and occupying the same plot of land for centuries.

The periodic gatherings were moments when Neolithic people encountered others from some distance away and at such occasions arte-facts and no doubt animals were traded or exchanged. One of the most archaeologically visible trade items was the axe. Polished-stone axes from the distinctive igneous rocks of Cornwall, Wales and the Lake District ended up hundreds of miles from their quarries, no doubt passed from hand to hand many times. Even pottery was traded. Distinctive pots made from clays found only on the Lizard peninsula in Cornwall made their way to the chalklands of central-southern England, perhaps brought along the coast in boats. So the little settlements of Neolithic Britain were not entirely self-sufficient and self-reliant communities: they were tied in to long-distance networks of kin groups and exchange part-ners across Britain, travelling by land along forest paths, by water in small boats, and meeting up at seasonal gatherings.

Their crops and domesticated animals were part of a 'farming pack-age'.[15] The whole package originated about 10,000 years ago in the area that is now Syria, Iraq and southern Turkey. Much ink has been spilt by archaeologists discussing whether the first farmers then migrated out of the Near East, taking their domesticates with them, or whether the crops and animals merely passed slowly down the line westwards, traded onwards to neighbours who still lived from hunting and gathering. Whichever, the British did not invent farming for themselves – it all comes from 'the cradle of civilization' in the Middle East.

Britain's early farmers also exploited the forests around them. There were edible roots and tubers, stems, shoots and greens, as well as seeds, nuts and fruits. The burnt remains of hazelnuts, crab apples, hawthorn fruits and blackberries are regularly found in Neolithic pits. Britain was also home to wolves, bears, wild boar and a now extinct species of wild cattle, the aurochs (*Bos primigenius*). This hefty beast, standing 1.8 metres high, was found throughout Europe and survived in Britain until at least the Bronze Age. It finally went extinct when the last one died in Poland in 1627. Analysis of the DNA of these massive animals shows that aurochsen were not interbred with domestic cattle, which arrived in Britain around 4000 BC and whose ancestry lies in the Middle East. Recent work on the DNA of Neolithic pigs also shows that, although there could have been interbreeding with European and British wild boar, these too were offspring of animals with similarly Middle Eastern origins.[16]

What happened during the transition from the Mesolithic to the Neolithic – that is, the arrival of agriculture from its place of origin in the Middle East, and the change from a mobile to a settled way of life – is one of the big debates in archaeology.[17] Even today there is fundamental disagreement as to whether the indigenous Mesolithic hunter-gatherers of Britain took up farming by getting hold of the 'package' through cross-Channel trading with farmers on the Continent, or whether domesticates were introduced by Neolithic colonizers who brought animals and crops to Britain in their small boats, perhaps wiping out the indigenous peoples in the process.

Studies of modern and ancient DNA can give us some idea of who Britain's earliest farmers were, and thus reveal something of the ancestry of the people who built Stonehenge. Modern DNA can be used to speculate on the likely periods when new genetic material was introduced into resident populations.[18] It seems that most people in northern Europe today derive the majority of their genes from a time long before farming – the period known as the Upper Palaeolithic, when hunters first moved back into northern Europe and Britain, around 14,700 years ago, as the northern ice sheets of the last Ice Age began to retreat. A small proportion of our genes are likely to have originated from south-west-Asian populations at some point in prehistory, but it is not clear when. While some scholars have considered these genes to be the relict traces of the earliest farmers, others link their introduction into the European gene pool to migrations westwards from the Near East much later on, in the Bronze Age.

Recent studies of ancient DNA from skeletons of central Europe's earliest farmers (7500–7000 years ago) have shown that only a few of these people had ancestors from the Middle East.[19] Most of them were descendants of the hunter-gatherers whose ancestors had settled in Europe during the Upper Palaeolithic. There is growing scientific evidence that Europe's earliest farming communities were melting pots of genetic and cultural diversity in which local hunter-gatherers took up the farming way of life.

Analysis of the ancient DNA of hunter-gatherers and early farmers in Britain is still in its infancy but studies of modern DNA have hinted at the probability that, while most of today's population is derived from hunter-gatherer ancestors already in northern Europe, there are also genes resulting from a large-scale movement of people along the Atlantic seaboard from Spain and Portugal – a movement that could well correlate with the arrival of farming in Britain.[20] The hunter-gatherer ancestors were not necessarily long-term residents in Britain; they could also include former hunter-gatherers in France who had converted to farming and then crossed the English Channel to settle – their genetic signatures, as surviving in modern DNA, would be indistinguishable from indigenous hunter-gatherers within Britain. Whatever the case, the earliest farmers in Britain were most probably ethnically diverse, originating in different parts of Europe's Atlantic zone.

It is unclear just what happened when farming eventually reached the Atlantic edge, having spread across the whole of Europe. In the Netherlands and southern Scandinavia, local communities initially carried on hunting and gathering and adopted only some of the trappings of farming. In northern France, it seems, agriculture was a far more attractive proposition. Almost certainly farming required more work: studies have shown that hunting and gathering are less time-consuming than agriculture, leading social anthropologist Marshall Sahlins to call prehistoric hunter-gatherers 'the original affluent society'.[21] As well as possessing domesticated plants and animals, farmers along Europe's Atlantic coast used fired-clay pots, polished-stone axes and arrows tipped with leaf-shaped flint points; from 4000 BC onwards people were using these distinctive items right across Britain and Ireland.

Alison Sheridan, Head of Early Prehistory at the National Museums of Scotland, has identified groups of Early Neolithic pottery in Ireland, western Scotland and England that she thinks are comparable with styles used by farming communities in northern France and Brittany.[22] Perhaps these were traditions of pottery-making brought by settler farmers who not only made the short hop across the English Channel but also sailed right up the west coast of Britain in search of suitable land to colonize.

The earliest stone monuments in Britain are called closed chamber tombs and simple passage tombs; these were built in stone and appear to derive from styles of tomb building employed in the Morbihan region of Brittany in France, where such tombs date to between 4300 and 4000 BC.[23] Examples at Carreg Samson in west Wales and Achnacreebeag in Scotland are thought to have been erected soon after the arrival of farming in Britain shortly before 4000 BC. Whilst these early megalithic tombs may document the arrival of farming in western Britain and Ireland, there are signs that farming might have arrived in eastern Britain via a different and shorter route – the 22 miles across the English Channel from Calais to Dover. At Coldrum in Kent there is a megalithic tomb built out of sarsen, coincidentally the same type of rock used to construct the great stone circle at Stonehenge; bones of the people buried within the Coldrum tomb have been dated to shortly after 4000 BC.

There is another tantalizing clue about cross-Channel links in the earliest days of farming. One of the most precious tools widely distributed across western Europe at that time was a type of stone axe made out of polished jadeitite.* This shiny green rock was quarried high up in the Alps. An international team of archaeologists has not only established exactly where these quarries were but has also worked out when the axes were made.[24] Those that reached Britain were made after 6000 BC but before 4000 BC, so they must have entered circulation before farming came to Britain. Whereas other types of stone axes were used as tools, it seems that these beautiful and delicate objects had more than just a practical purpose. Alison Sheridan thinks that they were brought across the Channel as already ancient heirlooms by farming colonists. But others have a different explanation. Julian Thomas reckons that these jadeitite axes crossed the Channel soon after they were made, as long-distance exchanges between British hunter-gatherers and Continental farmers; perhaps they accompanied some of the first transactions by which the inhabitants of Britain began to obtain cattle and cereal crops.

The answer to this conundrum should lie in where these extraordinary axes have been found in Britain. If they are found in the campsites of hunter-gatherers, then they were brought across the Channel very early and Julian may be right; if they turn up in Neolithic contexts, then Alison is probably correct. Unfortunately the vast majority of the forty or so jadeitite axes found in Britain are stray finds and come from uncertain contexts. The most secure find-spot is for an axe found in the Somerset Levels, next to a Neolithic trackway known as the Sweet Track, not far from the mid-third millennium BC trackway where a crudely carved wooden 'god-dolly' was found.[25] Prehistoric wooden trackways across swamps and marshes are wonderful archaeological remains because organic materials sometimes survive remarkably well in bogs as a result of remaining perpetually waterlogged. We can also date the tree rings of the timbers felled to make the Somerset trackway – a dating method known as dendrochronology. From this, we know that the Sweet Track was built in the winter of 3807 or spring of 3806 BC, so the jadeitite axe was clearly deposited by early

* Jadeitite consists almost entirely of jadeite, the name by which jadeitite axes were formerly known.

A pair of Neolithic stone axes from the quarries at Langdale in the Lake District. These polished axes are nearly a foot long. While some axes were used for practical purposes, others show no signs of wear so appear to have had a ritual or symbolic value.

farmers, not by Mesolithic hunter-gatherers. Another such axe was found at Durrington, an area where there are traces of Early Neolithic farmers as well as previous hunter-gatherers. The evidence is unsatisfactory but I suspect that most jadeitite axes didn't reach Britain until 4000 BC, so they were already old, if not antique, objects when they were brought here.

There are plenty of theories about the coming of agriculture to Britain but very little evidence of how it affected the island's indigenous population. A scenario of complete ethnic replacement of British hunter-gatherers by Continental farmers is not favoured by archaeologists. In a few instances Neolithic sites sit on top of Mesolithic remains, suggesting some form of continuity. If the growing evidence from mainland Europe is anything to go by, then it seems most likely that the ancestors of the Stonehenge people were a mix of indigenous hunter-gatherers and immigrant farmers, a small proportion of whom had roots as far east as southwest Asia. Yet the radiocarbon dates for Mesolithic hunter-gatherer encampments fade away around 4500 BC, a good 500 years before the first traces of farming in Britain. Could it be possible that the natives had virtually died out before farmers arrived from the Continent?

Study of ancient DNA from the skeletons of Mesolithic hunter-gatherers and Neolithic farmers would enable us to tell whether these were two genetically separate populations or whether the first farmers were the acculturated descendants of indigenous hunter-gatherers. Unfortunately, whatever the British Mesolithic funerary rites may have been, they have left very little trace for archaeologists to find. Although there are few skeletal remains to work with, an ancient DNA project is now underway to compare populations in Britain from before and after the advent of farming.

In the Stonehenge area there are very few traces of the earliest farmers. Hunter-gatherer groups definitely used the Avon valley for their campsites up to the fifth millennium BC: their presence is recognizable from distinctive, long flint blades and tiny stone tools known as microliths. One of these Mesolithic campsites was at West Amesbury, where a stone circle was built more than a thousand years later.

Bizarrely, the oldest suspected cow bone from Britain – and potentially the earliest evidence for farming in Britain – comes from Stonehenge itself. When scientists radiocarbon-dated a long bone of a cow-sized animal from the packing deposit of one of the stones in the sarsen circle at Stonehenge, they were amazed to discover that it dated to within the period 4360–3990 BC.[26]* Given that the sarsen circle was not actually erected until some 1500 years later, this bone is clearly problematic. It could have been an 'antique' brought to Stonehenge when the sarsens were put up but it is more likely that it had become buried below the grass on this spot before 4000 BC and then ended up incorporated into the hole dug for the sarsen. Until future research can confirm that this anomalous bone really is from a domesticated cow as opposed to an

* This is Stone 27 according to the Flinders Petrie numbering system.

aurochs or a large red deer, it remains a tantalizing find. Even if this bone had been lying around for hundreds of years before it eventually ended up in a sarsen stonehole, the possible presence of a cow in the area at such an early date raises the prospect of people having visited this particular spot when farming first came to Britain.

We know that, later on, some early farmers had a party near

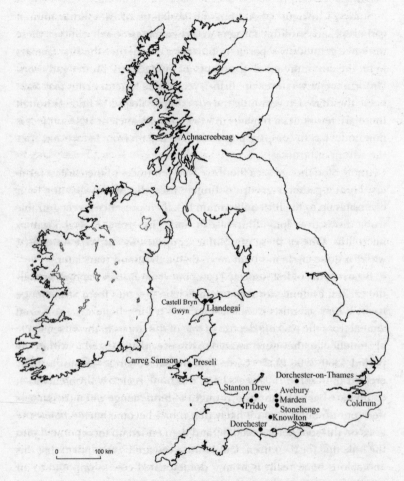

Map of Avebury, Stonehenge and Preseli, with other henge complexes and related Neolithic sites.

Stonehenge. On a hill to the east, high above the Avon valley on the chalk ridge of Coneybury, a group of people congregated around 3800 BC to bury the remains of a feast in a large circular pit.[27] They had eaten eight cattle, roe deer, red deer, pigs and even beaver, having prepared and served the meat in more than twenty different pots, some of which were large enough to provide twenty servings each.

As a student, my project colleague Colin Richards of the University of Manchester had worked on Julian Richards' (no relation) excavation of this remarkable find at Coneybury and was intrigued by the blackness of the soil in which these bones and potsherds lay. This was caused by the high organic content of the deposit, indicating that ash and food residues had been buried to decay here. The quantities of meat-bearing bones found at Coneybury show that this feast could have fed several hundred people. The freshness of the potsherds when they went in the ground indicates that the pit must have been dug close to where the feast was held. Why did all these people gather here, at such an early date, to eat on this hilltop? From Coneybury they would have been able to look southeast towards the river and northwest towards the future site of Stonehenge, just half a mile away.

The Coneybury pit tells us something very important about the new way of life. Taking up farming had crucial advantages over hunting and gathering. Storage was now possible, either in granaries or on the hoof in terms of herds and flocks, to ensure survival through the lean periods of the year. Farmers could also produce more than enough food to go round; after key moments such as harvest they could go for long stretches of time without having to find food. They could also devote this over-production to supporting lavish feasts involving kin and neighbours in their hundreds or more – as demonstrated by Coneybury. In other words, the transition to agriculture presented the possibility of creating surplus. That surplus could be used to support individuals in large-scale projects such as building the huge tombs that are a common feature of the British Neolithic. Since the people of Neolithic Britain might have been more reliant on the size of their herds and flocks than on the size of their wheat fields, their cattle, sheep and pigs served as capital, currency and commodities.

In bare economic terms, the possibility of building Stonehenge depended entirely on the ability to create a sufficient level of surplus production that could be harnessed and managed so that a large enough group – comprising many thousands of people – could be mobilized, fed, clothed and supplied for long enough to enable the stones to be quarried, moved and erected. For whatever reasons, it took a thousand years before these early farmers attained the requisite levels of organization and food-surplus production to make it possible. Why they chose to build Stonehenge, what they intended it to be, and how they managed to build it are rather more complex problems.

3

A BRIEF HISTORY OF STONEHENGE

There are shelves and shelves of books about the history of research at Stonehenge. While I don't want to trot out yet another version, I do think it relevant to include a brief thumbnail account because much of what the Stonehenge Riverside Project has found out about Stonehenge itself has come from re-analysing and re-interpreting the records made by previous investigators.

The most noticeable structure that we see at Stonehenge today is a circle of upright sarsens with some surviving horizontal lintels perched on top of them. The sarsens are large slabs of sandstone-like rock that were probably obtained from the Avebury area, in contrast to the bluestones, smaller stones of dolerite and other geologies that originated in west Wales. The sarsen circle encloses a circle of smaller bluestones, inside which are five large sarsen trilithons arranged in a horseshoe. A trilithon is a pair of upright stones with a lintel joining them. At the centre of Stonehenge is a small, horseshoe-shaped arrangement of bluestones. Some of the stones of these various structures have fallen down, others have been broken up and taken away, and several have been re-erected since the seventeenth century. The sarsen circle is about 30 metres in diameter, but it sits at the centre of a much larger circle, about 100 metres across, formed by the bank and ditch of an earthen enclosure.

People have been digging around in Stonehenge for at least 400 years, on and off.[1] Its above-ground remains have also been surveyed, at differing levels of precision, many times. Yet a huge amount of research still remains to be done or has only recently been initiated. Only in 2009 did

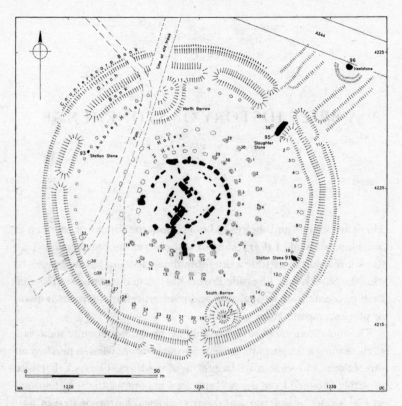

Plan of Stonehenge, showing the ditch, bank, Station Stones and Avenue.

archaeologists carry out a detailed survey of the ground-surface contours of Stonehenge[2] and, two years later, a laser-scanning survey of the standing stones. Only about half of the area within Stonehenge's earthen enclosure has ever been excavated,[3] and many basic matters of fact about its constructional sequence still remain to be established. Gaining permission to dig within Stonehenge is no easy matter, so the opportunities to resolve some fundamental problems may be a long way off in the future.

In 1620 the Duke of Buckingham got his men to dig a big hole in the centre of Stonehenge. We don't know where his trench's edges were;

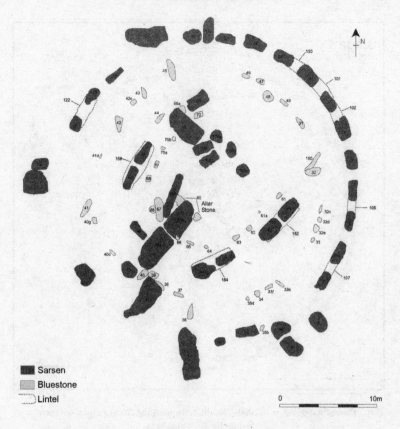

Plan of Stonehenge, showing the numbering of the bluestones and sarsens.

however, almost fifty years later the diarist and antiquarian John Aubrey reported that it was as large as two saw pits, and marked its centre on a plan of the stones.[4] Saw pits have to be deep enough for a man to stand in – this man being the 'underdog', as opposed to the 'top dog' who held the upper end of the saw – so this huge pit must have been more than 1.5 metres deep. The duke's workmen either dug through chalk bedrock, unaware that it would contain no finds, or dug into a filled-in pit from some earlier period (as we will later see, we have recently discovered that there is a large prehistoric pit in the middle of Stonehenge).

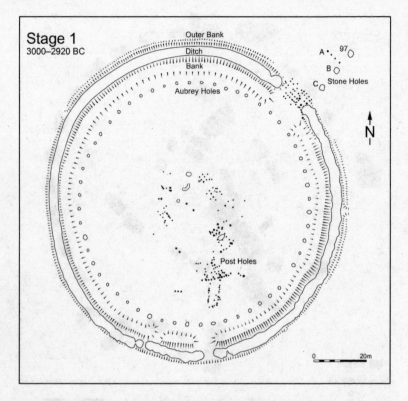

Plan of Stonehenge Stage 1 (3000–2920 BC), showing the Aubrey Holes and postholes inside the ditch and bank.

Buckingham's men found skulls of cattle 'and other beasts' and noted great quantities of 'burnt coals or charcoals' within the stone circle and in several parts of 'the court surrounding Stonehenge' – in other words within its circular enclosure. Sadly for them there was no treasure to be had.

We can dismiss Buckingham's project as totally haphazard, or wish he hadn't done it, but it was taken seriously at the time – Stonehenge was already something worth exploring. Others who were intrigued by this strange monument were William Harvey, the physician who discovered the human circulatory system, and Inigo Jones, the celebrated architect. Jones drew the first reasonably precise plan of Stonehenge.

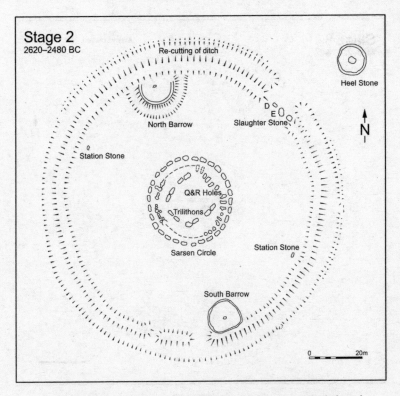

Plan of Stonehenge Stage 2 (2620–2480 BC), showing the sarsen circle and
Q & R Holes.

In the early eighteenth century the owner of Stonehenge, a Reverend
Hayward, found more skulls of cattle and other animals. From 1719 to
1740 William Stukeley surveyed the monument, identifying its avenue and
what he thought were holes along the avenue for standing stones.[5] He dug
into some of the Bronze Age round barrows around Stonehenge and had
a trench dug against the middle of the recumbent stone known as the
Altar Stone, which he discovered lay on solid chalk 'which had never been
dug'.[6] The Altar Stone is made of Welsh sandstone and lies almost at the
centre of Stonehenge, pinned beneath a fallen upright from the great
trilithon, the largest of Stonehenge's five trilithons. Its shaped end shows
that, at some point in Stonehenge's past, it was probably a standing stone.

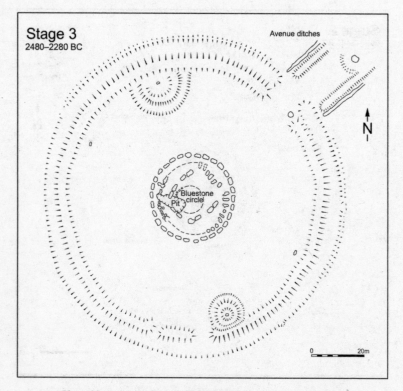

Plan of Stonehenge Stage 3 (2480–2280 BC), showing the Avenue
and re-arranged bluestones.

Barrow-digging went on all over Britain, a cross between a gentle-
man's hobby, a sport and serious research. In 1802 a famous
barrow-digger called William Cunnington dug a pit 2 metres deep by the
Altar Stone, close to Stukeley's trench.[7] Halfway down he found Roman
pottery but close to the bottom there were pieces of charred wood, prehistoric pottery and pick-axes made from red-deer antlers. Without
realizing, Cunnington too had blundered into the mysterious prehistoric
pit in the middle of Stonehenge. In 1803 and 1810 he dug against the
recumbent Slaughter Stone, establishing that it had originally stood
upright.

In 1839 a naval officer, Captain Beamish, dug out an estimated 114

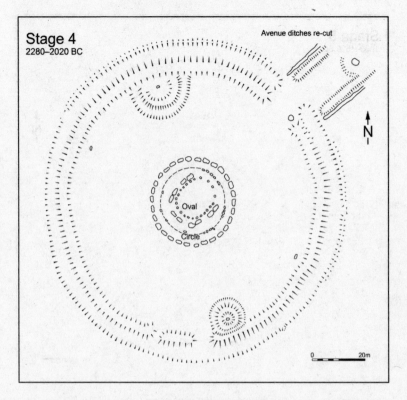

Plan of Stonehenge Stage 4 (2280–2020 BC), showing the bluestone oval and circle.

cubic metres (400 cubic feet) of soil from the front (northeast) of the Altar Stone, much of which was probably chalk bedrock.[8] Captain Beamish's big hole was probably the final blow for any prehistoric features – pits, postholes, stoneholes or ephemeral hearths – that once lay at Stonehenge's centre. Whatever was there was almost certainly utterly destroyed by these early investigations.

The famous Egyptologist Sir William Flinders Petrie began his archaeological career with a survey of the stones between 1874 and 1877; he was keen to produce something accurate to improve on the plans produced by earlier antiquarians John Wood and Sir Richard Colt Hoare. Petrie's main legacy was a numbering system for the sarsens and

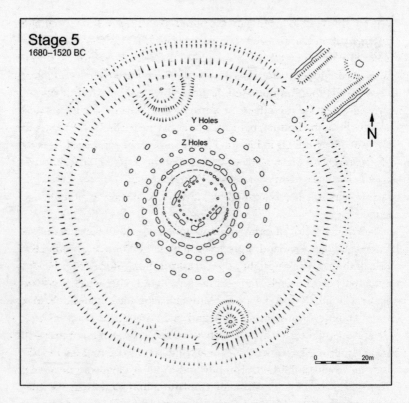

Stage 5
1680–1520 BC

Y Holes

Z Holes

N

0   20m

Plan of Stonehenge Stage 5 (1680–1520 BC), showing the Y & Z Holes.

bluestones that archaeologists still use today.[9] Petrie was a great archaeologist; he never dug at Stonehenge but was nevertheless the first to work
out that the henge ditch and bank were constructed before the sarsen
circle and trilithons. He also pointed out that the sarsen circle, with its
ring of horizontal lintels resting on the upright stones, had possibly
never been finished, because one of its stones (Stone 11) is too short –
perhaps the builders couldn't get enough large sarsens to finish the
circle.

In 1877 Charles Darwin took his family on a picnic to Stonehenge.[10]
He and the children dug two small holes, one against the fallen upright
of the great trilithon and the other against another fallen sarsen, not to

look for finds but to investigate the power of earthworms to move huge stones. Darwin had realized that earthworms not only convert organic material into soil but also sort the soil so that even large stones, as well as small components, are moved vertically downwards. When we look at a soil profile that has not been disturbed by ploughing for many centuries, we can see the effects of worm-sorting because the stones and pebbles lie at the bottom, beneath a layer of fine earth. In 1881 Darwin published his findings in his other great book, *The Formation of Vegetable Mould through the Action of Worms, with observations on their habits.* Although he was not particularly interested in archaeology, Darwin's work on earthworms still has relevance for anyone excavating at Stonehenge today.

The first director of excavations at Stonehenge in the twentieth century was William Gowland, a professor in his sixties, who dug around the base of the surviving upright of the great trilithon (Stone 56).[11] He did this as part of an exercise to re-set the sarsen monolith, which was leaning heavily and likely to fall down. Although a mining engineer, chemist and metallurgist by training, Gowland had a background of amateur archaeological research in Japan, where he had excavated more than 400 ancient tombs. The work on the great trilithon* was carried out in 1901 and the results published promptly and in great detail the next year. Though his trench was only small, Gowland found more than 100 artefacts – mostly worked flints and sarsen hammerstones. His recording was meticulous – sections† were drawn of the stone sitting in its stonehole, a plan was made of the trench, and the major finds were plotted in three dimensions. He could have had little idea that his records would be essential for working out the chronology of Stonehenge over 100 years later.

---

* Trilithon means 'three stones' and is used to describe a pair of uprights supporting a horizontal lintel.

† An archaeological 'plan' shows all the things that can be seen in the ground – changes in soil colour, shapes of pits and postholes, and large objects – and is drawn by standing over the excavation trench looking down at the ground. A 'section' is a drawing of the edge of a trench as seen from the side. It shows a slice through all the layers of soil, from top to bottom. A 'plan' is therefore a horizontal drawing, and a 'section' is a vertical drawing. These scale drawings on waterproof paper are the most important of all excavation records; today they are digitized during post-excavation. After an excavation is published, the originals are sent to secure storage (usually in a museum) where they can be consulted by the next generation of archaeologists.

Professor William Gowland (kneeling centre) supervising
excavations at Stonehenge in 1901.

In 1918 Stonehenge was given to the nation.[12] The Office of Works
realized that more stones were leaning dangerously and that there would
have to be a modest programme of restoration. Gowland was too old to
carry out the excavations that the repairs would necessitate so the job was
given to Lieutenant-Colonel William Hawley. Petrie had wanted to excavate Stonehenge himself – with this in mind, he had even intended to buy
it from its last private owner, Cecil Chubb – but Hawley was Director of
the Society of Antiquaries, the archaeological body advising the Office of
Works, and got the job. Over the next eight years Hawley excavated not
just the holes of the stones to be restored but almost half of the entire
monument.[13] Many archaeologists have since bemoaned this twist of fate.
Petrie was the greatest archaeological excavator of his age, whereas
Hawley's abilities were later described as regrettably inadequate.[14]

Hawley had served in the British army and was a keen amateur archaeologist who had dug at Old Sarum (the old Medieval town of Salisbury,
nestled within the ramparts of an Iron Age hillfort). Already widowed,

Colonel Hawley was sixty-nine when he started work on Stonehenge in 1919.

Apart from during the stone repairs, which were carried out by workmen employed by the Office of Works, Hawley mostly worked alone over long annual seasons, between spring snowstorms and autumnal gales, occasionally helped by Robert Newall, a local enthusiast. Most days he walked the five miles from his lodgings in the old mill at Figheldean, and occasionally lived on site at Stonehenge in an Office of Works hut.

Colonel William Hawley (seated right) with his team of workmen
at Stonehenge in 1919.

He and his team dug trenches in various areas, from Stonehenge's external ditch to the central settings of sarsens and bluestones. Across much of the interior he found nothing but bare chalk. However, the ditch that encircles the stones was full of Neolithic deposits. Inside this ditch there was once a bank of soil standing 2 metres high (now less than a metre high). Just inside the bank Hawley found a circle of fifty-six pits, known as the Aubrey Holes. These are named after the antiquarian John Aubrey.

Hawley excavated thirty-two of these Aubrey Holes, digging out the soil and artefacts that filled them. In both the surrounding ditch and in this circle of pits he found lots of cremation burials – small heaps of burnt human bones that, he surmised, had been deposited in long-since rotted leather bags. Hawley dug every year at Stonehenge from 1919 to 1926 (by which time he was seventy-six years old). His methods were thorough and he recorded his observations daily in a notebook. At the end of each season he delivered a lecture on his findings to the Society of Antiquaries, who published it in their annual journal. Although Hawley lived to a ripe old age (into his nineties), he never published an overall account of his work; today Salisbury Museum takes care of his notebooks.

There's no doubt that Gowland and Petrie were better excavators: Hawley failed to draw many of the plans or sections that we would expect from modern excavations, and his section drawings in particular are often too schematic to be of much use. And not only did he fail to publish a book on his discoveries but also he seemed never to develop any working hypotheses or research questions to test in his excavations. At the end of his work he admitted to being at just as much of a loss about the purpose of Stonehenge as he'd been when he began.[15]

In some ways, however, Hawley has had a bad press. We know what he found and roughly where he found it. Between his diary and his interim reports there's enough to be able to re-explore and re-interpret some of the more tangled problems created by his digging. There are some very detailed accounts of the fillings of the Aubrey Holes and the Stonehenge ditch, for example. Working through his reports has proved to be an exciting 'armchair excavation', almost as much fun as carrying out the excavation itself, discovering important clues that have been missed by previous researchers.

After the Second World War, a group of three archaeologists – Atkinson, Piggott and Stone – agreed with the Society of Antiquaries that they should write a full report on Stonehenge and carry out some limited excavations to resolve some of the problems thrown up by Hawley's work. In 1950 they began with two Aubrey Holes. By 1964 their 'limited programme of fresh excavations' had turned into more than forty trenches within Stonehenge and its avenue.[16] Atkinson returned in 1978 for a final season with a Cardiff colleague, environmental archaeologist John Evans, and Alexander Thom.

When he began working at Stonehenge, Richard Atkinson was a young and dynamic lecturer at the newly created archaeology department of Cardiff University and his methods were revolutionary, using skilled archaeologists working with trowels and making careful observations of soil and stratigraphy. Even as late as the 1950s the actual digging in archaeology was usually left to unskilled labourers; in his textbook on field archaeology Atkinson not only outlined a better way of going about things but he also put it into practice.[17] From his first dig of two Aubrey Holes in 1950 to his last excavation (of the circular ditch in 1978), he brought into common use new methods and skills.

Atkinson was helped in the Stonehenge excavations by Stuart Piggott, professor of archaeology at Edinburgh University, and by J. F. S. 'Marcus' Stone, an amateur archaeologist who worked nearby as a scientist at Porton Down, the Ministry of Defence research centre. Atkinson published his team's Stonehenge excavation results in 1956, and in 1979 he added a few pages to a new edition of this important book on Stonehenge, but he never published the full details of his findings, so it has been hard for others to evaluate his work and results.[18] Paradoxically, he criticized Hawley's work for the same reasons: 'a regrettable inadequacy in his methods of recording his finds and observations and, one suspects, an insufficient appreciation of the destruction of archaeological excavation per se, has left for subsequent excavators a most lamentable legacy of doubt and frustration.'[19] Unlike Hawley, Richard Atkinson seems not to have written much at all in the way of field notes.

In any archaeological project, excavation is the quickest and easiest part of the process; the post-excavation work on finds and plans takes years to complete, often without any funding or dedicated research time. In his later years Atkinson was distracted from writing-up his excavations by administrative duties and illness. He died in 1994, and it seems that little in the way of excavation records was found when his papers were cleared out. Atkinson's students remember him saying that everything was in his head and today no one knows what records he kept of his fieldwork. Stuart Piggott certainly put some things down on paper: he was an accomplished draughtsman and drew many of the plans and sections during Atkinson's excavations.

So in 1956 Atkinson published his book on Stonehenge, describing the monument in detail and setting out what seemed to be a likely sequence in which it was built.[20] He worked out that the first phase of construction was the circular bank and ditch and the ring of pits called Aubrey Holes. Then, he thought, a semicircular arc of bluestones was added. This was followed by the erection of a circle of upright sarsens, all joined together by lintels, and the trilithons inside the circle (with the bluestones being rearranged, also inside the sarsen circle).

At the time Atkinson was writing radiocarbon dating was in its infancy, so he had no real dates to work with and his estimation of when Stonehenge was built was out by quite a bit. We know now that most of it was built during the Neolithic but Atkinson thought that it must have been constructed during the Bronze Age (that is, the second millennium BC), the period after the Neolithic when metals were first introduced to Britain. Because Atkinson thought Stonehenge belonged to the Bronze Age, he thought it might have been built by an architect from ancient Greece – where a civilization was flourishing at Mycenae during the Bronze Age.

For the remainder of the twentieth century no excavations were carried out at or around Stonehenge except in advance of developments such as the car park, the visitor centre, road improvements, cable trenches and the visitor footpath. The most productive of these small investigations was Mike Pitts' excavation in 1980 of a cable trench along the road immediately outside Stonehenge's northeast entrance.[21] Mike was curator of Avebury Museum at the time and had to step in very swiftly when he realized that no one in authority had made any provision for archaeological work in advance of the Post Office laying new cables. During this excavation Mike discovered that the Heel Stone was once one of a pair of stones.* He found the hole for a second stone (Stonehole 97) next to it, and this hole was dug into the soil that had filled an even larger hole.

For a while, archaeologists speculated that the Heel Stone and this

---

* The Heel Stone is a large and unworked sarsen that stands by itself to the northeast of Stonehenge at the beginning of the avenue.

Professor Richard Atkinson (kneeling centre) supervising the re-erection of Stone 53 at Stonehenge in 1964; Professor Stuart Piggott is standing fourth from the left.

previously unknown, vanished stone had formed a 'gunsight' for prehistoric worshippers looking down the Stonehenge avenue: they would have seen the sun rise between the two stones at the midsummer solstice. This idea turned out not to work particularly well. The new stonehole is slightly offset from the Heel Stone so that the pair was not perpendicular to the line of the avenue. Its position is more convincingly explained as being the end of a row of equally spaced stones* within the entrance and leading out from the Slaughter Stone.

* These stones survive only as stoneholes; two of them, known as Stoneholes B and C, were found by Hawley.

As for the large pit that Mike Pitts found beneath Stonehole 97, Atkinson had seen the southern part of this same feature during his excavation of the Heel Stone ditch in 1956. This pit was more than 5 metres long, and Mike wondered if it was actually the natural hollow left by the removal of a very large stone. Perhaps a sarsen had lain here until it was discovered and erected in Stonehole 97 by Neolithic people? This stone might then have been moved to a new position, set within its own circular ditch – the sarsen now called the Heel Stone.[23]

Mike Pitts' cable-trench dig also revealed masses of sarsen chippings in this area outside Stonehenge's entrance. Hawley had also found a large dump of them near the Heel Stone. These areas outside Stonehenge seem to contain greater quantities of sarsen chippings than do the areas that have been excavated inside. In contrast, Atkinson and other excavators working within Stonehenge's interior had found many more Welsh bluestone chippings than Mike found outside Stonehenge. Stone chippings show where a stone has been 'dressed' (worked into shape). The distribution of the chippings shows that the bluestones were dressed inside the circle at some point in time, and that the sarsens were worked outside the ditch and bank.

In the 1980s, English Heritage (the government body responsible for archaeology in England – today's successor to the old Ministry of Works) commissioned a local commercial archaeology company, Wessex Archaeology, to employ a team of young specialists to make sense of Hawley's and Atkinson's excavation records and publish the results as a definitive book on the archaeology of Stonehenge. Although they got little help from either Atkinson or Piggott, this team, led by Ros Cleal (now curator of Avebury Museum), produced in 1995 an authoritative but necessarily second-hand account of the twentieth-century excavations.[24] What makes this report particularly important is that it includes the results of a carefully planned programme of radiocarbon dating and statistical analysis, in which certain finds from the old excavations were dated in order to establish Stonehenge's different phases of use.

The only way we can date Stonehenge is by using radiocarbon dates obtained from items of organic material that were deposited there when it was being built, and re-built – for our generation of archaeologists, there is no way to accurately 'date' a stone (but who knows what techniques will be developed in the future). The stones at Stonehenge have been moved about and re-erected many times. Stonehenge is full of pits where stones once stood; the stones themselves have since vanished, either shifted to a different spot or removed completely. These pits, called stoneholes, and the ditch around the stone circle, contain the dating evidence.

The ditch that encircles the standing stones has been the easiest thing to date, as more than twenty antler picks were left on the bottom of the ditch by the Neolithic workers who dug it out. Dated together, and taking into account dates from articulated animal bones from higher up in the soil that fills the ditch, these antler pick-axes from the ditch produced a combined date now refined to 3000–2920 cal BC (calibrated years Before Christ)* at 94.5 per cent probability. Thus, the Stonehenge ditch was dug out at some point during this eighty-year period within the thirtieth century BC, when people in Britain had already been farming for a thousand years. The ditch then started to silt up, becoming filled in during the period 2560–2140 cal BC.

Compared to dating the various arrangements of standing stones, dating the Stonehenge ditch was easy for Cleal's team. Richard Atkinson's excavations in the centre, building on Hawley's discoveries, revealed a semicircular double arc of holes for bluestones that once stood near the centre of the stone circle. Atkinson named these the Q and R Holes and he thought that the bluestones that once stood in them must have been in position before the large sarsens were erected. He excavated more than twenty of these Q and R Holes but sadly no antler picks (pick-axes) were found.

In the outer circle of large sarsens, one stonehole excavated by Hawley did have an antler pick in a layer of chalk rubble that had once been packed around the stone. This pick produced a date of 2640–2485 cal BC. More antler picks came from around the sarsen trilithons that stood within the sarsen circle, enclosed by it. The dates for these varied from 2850–2400 cal BC to 2470–2200 cal BC. Since a layer must always be dated by the latest artefact left in it, the date for the trilithons is apparently more

---

* BC is still standard terminology. Dates are sometimes given as 'years BP', meaning 'before present' (which is 1950). BCE (Before the Common Era) is sometimes substituted for BC.

recent than the date for the outer circle of stones. It seemed as if the trilithons were erected more than a century *after* the outer circle. These were the dates that Ros Cleal's team had to work with. It all depended on whether Atkinson and Hawley were right about the layers in which they found the antlers and hadn't made any mistakes interpreting the complex stratigraphy, in which pits frequently intercut each other.

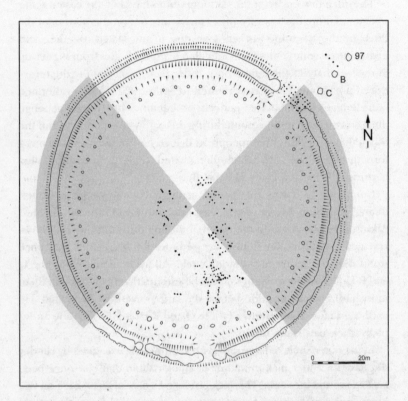

Schematic plan of astronomical alignments at Stonehenge – Stage 1 (3000–2920 BC). The post settings in the northeast entrance were aligned approximately on the northern major moonrise; Stone 97 provided a sightline from the centre of the circle to the midsummer solstice sunrise. Together with Stones B and C, it provided an approximate alignment on the northern major moonrise. Some of the post settings in the centre of the circular enclosure were aligned approximately on the southern major moonrise to the southeast. The area shaded grey shows the range of moonrise (east) and moonset (west) at major standstill.

Ros's team did a good job of making sense of it all – the pits, the stones, the perpetual rearrangements. Using all the old excavation records they could find, together with the new radiocarbon dates, they worked out a new chronological sequence for Stonehenge's use. There were still some anomalies but it seemed it was the best that could be done on the available evidence. At the time English Heritage were pulling together this big report, it seemed highly unlikely that anyone was going to be digging at Stonehenge to get any new dating evidence. To put things in context, the report was being prepared during a period when Stonehenge was at the centre of real conflict – the country was in the midst of what sociologists call a 'moral panic' about New Age travellers, and Stonehenge had been the scene of violent confrontations between the police and the 'peace convoy'. Potentially contentious excavations were not on the agenda.

In general, archaeologists accepted that the Stonehenge radiocarbon dates just had to be right but this left a big problem in the construction sequence. How could the builders have put up the trilithons in the centre of Stonehenge if the outer sarsen circle was already in position? There simply isn't enough room. Perhaps the outer circle was never finished – with a big gap in the outer ring, it would have just been possible to manoeuvre the inner stones into position. This was a real puzzle for archaeology, as the sequence didn't seem to make sense. Perhaps the dates were misleading – maybe some of them came from extremely old antler picks that had been antiques when they were buried? It was not until years later that the mystery was unravelled.

Ros Cleal and her team were careful to present the facts – accurate plans and detailed descriptions. It would be left to others to mull over the astronomical orientations and opportunities that Stonehenge presented. Ever since William Stukeley noted Stonehenge's orientation towards the midsummer solstice sunrise,* there has been fascination with Stonehenge's astronomical possibilities.[25] At the end of the nineteenth century the astronomer Norman Lockyer attempted unsuccessfully to

---

* The solstices are the longest and shortest days of the year, at midsummer and midwinter. They are not to be confused with the spring and autumn equinoxes, when night and day are of equal length.

date Stonehenge on the basis of its solstice orientation: slow changes in the tilt of the earth's axis cause the sun's cyclical movement to change very slightly over time (about one seventieth of a degree every hundred years). It was not until the 1950s and 1960s, however, that astronomy came to play a dominant role in many new interpretations of Stonehenge.

In 1963 an American astronomer, Gerald Hawkins, shook the archaeological establishment by proposing that Stonehenge was used not just as a complex calendar but also as a predictor of solar and lunar eclipses.[26] His claims ushered in a new era of regarding Stonehenge as something more than a temple of the sun – an idea that had been current for over 200 years, ever since William Stukeley had declared it a druids' temple. Hawkins' bestseller, *Stonehenge Decoded*, was published in 1965 and was read by a public in awe of the newly invented computer, an important tool in Hawkins' investigation.

Gerald Hawkins' main idea was a simple one. The fifty-six Aubrey Holes could have been used to hold markers moved on a regular basis to plot the movements of the moon and thereby mark and predict the occurrence of eclipses. It seemed a possibility but Richard Atkinson and other archaeologists were certainly not convinced. If this was a society of sky-watching astronomers, why was the necessary number of fifty-six holes not found on any other monument? There are plenty of pit circles of this period elsewhere in Britain but no other has Hawkins' magic number of fifty-six pits.

The retired British astronomer Fred Hoyle also weighed in on the eclipse theory with his book *On Stonehenge*, claiming to have proved Hawkins' point.[27] Twenty years later, John North, a retired professor of the history of science, wrote an impressively complex book on the role of sun, moon and stars as explanations for the shapes and alignments of many of the prehistoric monuments on Salisbury Plain.[28] The archaeologists were under siege and not for the first time. Back in the late 1950s a retired professor of engineering, Alexander Thom, had conducted a wide-ranging study of British megalithic sites, claiming among other things that astronomer-priests of Neolithic Britain laid out their monuments using a Megalithic Yard of 2.72 feet.[29] Later on, he directed his attention to Stonehenge, identifying the diameter of the sarsen circle as 37 megalithic yards.[30]

Atkinson, Piggott and their colleagues Glyn Daniel and Colin Renfrew, who were to be successive professors of archaeology at Cambridge University, had no time for Gerald Hawkins' claims, even though his ideas were taken up enthusiastically by many among archaeology's public. It was only in the 1980s that archaeologists and astronomers began to think the whole problem through together and to establish rigorous methods and procedures for investigation and inference. The biggest problem had been that astronomers knew little about the archaeology and archaeologists were largely ignorant of astronomy. What was needed (and indeed

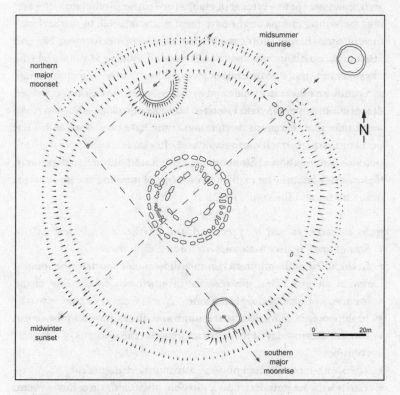

Plan of astronomical alignments at Stonehenge – Stage 2 (2620–2480 BC). The axis of midwinter sunset/midsummer sunrise was marked by the great trilithon within the sarsen circle. The Station Stones also provided an alignment on this solstice axis as well as a further alignment with the southern major moonrise and northern major moonset.

then evolved) was a new subject of 'archaeoastronomy', practiced by people who were expert in both fields. Astronomical claims could then be grounded in archaeological knowledge.

In the few years after Ros and her team's book was published, Clive Ruggles, a professor of archaeoastronomy at Leicester University, began researching the astronomical alignments of Stonehenge. He was in no doubt that most of the previous work by Hawkins, Hoyle, Thom and North, while extremely inventive and challenging, had gone well beyond the evidence. Not only did Clive know his astronomy but he was also an archaeologist. He was critical of claims for eclipse prediction – the fact that such observations might have been made possible by the architecture of Stonehenge didn't mean that they were performed. He and other archaeoastronomers were interested in looking at the social role of astronomy in pre-industrial societies, rather than seeing Stonehenge as a primitive observatory manned by astronomer-priests. Clive reasoned that prehistoric people didn't need to build a huge stone edifice to make astronomical observations. Such things could have been done with a few wooden markers much more easily and effectively.

In his investigation of Stonehenge, Clive found only a few alignments that can satisfactorily be explained in terms of marking the movements of the moon and the sun:

- As researchers had long noticed, the northeast–southwest axis of Stonehenge is closely aligned on solstice directions.
- In the third millennium BC on the midsummer solstice (the longest day of the year), the sun rose in the northeast on the line of the avenue, just west of the Heel Stone.*
- In the opposite direction, to the southwest, the midwinter solstice sun (on the shortest day of the year) set between the uprights of the great trilithon.
- The south entrance had no such astronomical alignment.
- The northeast entrance had a possible alignment on a lunar event.

* The tilt of the earth's axis ('the obliquity of the ecliptic') has moved slightly in relation to the sun since the third millennium BC, and the solstice alignment at Stonehenge today is therefore not the same as it was.

The initial position of the ditch terminals† and nine rows of post-holes set within this entrance were oriented towards the rising moon's northerly limit, reached roughly once a month. The exact position varies from month to month and over an 18.6-year cycle, however, and the postholes, which line up just east of the overall lim-iting direction ('major limit'), were only imprecise markers. (The ditch terminals, incidentally, were later shifted to align with the mid-summer sunrise.)

- Clive was also satisfied that the four Station Stones were astronomically aligned.* To the northeast they lined up with the midsummer sunrise. To the southeast they corresponded roughly with the southerly major limit of moon rise. To the northwest they were roughly aligned on major northern moon set.[31]

It may seem that Clive's conclusions supported the notion that Stonehenge was used at many different times of the year for making sightings of the sun and moon. However, Clive pointed out that these various lunar observations would have been most dramatic when the moon was full in midwinter and midsummer. So, observing the rising or setting moon's northerly limit was best achieved when the moon is full in midwinter, while the southerly limit of moon rise (or set) coincides with full moon in midsummer. This was corroborative evidence that Stonehenge incorporated astronomical elements emphasizing the two periods of midwinter and midsummer in the calendric year.

In Clive's view, Stonehenge was not an observatory but a monument in which the timing of biannual ceremonies was expressed in material form. But if the astronomy is only part of understanding Stonehenge's purpose, what might its principal use have been?

† The end of a ditch is always called a 'terminal' in archaeology.
* Two out of four Station Stones survive; they were laid out in a rectangle whose corners were on the circle of the Aubrey Holes. The Station Stones were erected in the stage after the Aubrey Holes were in use.

4

STARTING THE PROJECT

Stonehenge and its surrounding landscape form one of the most heavily protected areas of archaeology in the world. Not only is the area a World Heritage Site, but each of its hundreds of visible monuments (and many others not visible above ground) is also protected by the state. A plethora of organizations is involved – English Heritage, the Department of Culture, Media and Sport, the National Trust, the Environment Agency, the Ministry of Defence, Wiltshire County Council and even the Ministry of Justice. They all have responsibilities for the rich and unique archaeological heritage of Salisbury Plain, and all employ people to ensure that the archaeology is protected and conserved. It might seem strange that their remit includes limiting and even preventing archaeological excavations.

We needed answers to our questions, and digging was the only way we would get them. We wanted to know whether Durrington Walls really was a domain of the living, just when and how Stonehenge had been used as a burial ground for the dead, and whether the two places were linked together by the River Avon. We needed our excavations to be big enough to answer these questions while, at the same time, disturbing as little as possible in order to leave intact as much as we could for archaeologists of the future.

Archaeology has been likened to a historian reading the last surviving copy of an ancient book and then tearing out and burning every page. When we dig, we disturb the ground irreversibly, removing soil and finds and destroying the context in which they have lain for thousands of years. Techniques improve all the time, and every generation of archaeologists curses the work of those before them. If only they had left well alone, or had had access to the sophisticated analytical methods of today. Half of Stonehenge was dug up during the twentieth century alone; one day, there may be nothing left undisturbed for archaeologists of the future.

One way of dealing with this is to forbid any further digging. We can learn a certain amount by 'non-invasive' methods such as geophysical survey – and maybe, in the distant future, archaeologists will be able to find out all they need to know without putting a spade in the ground. It would be pretty ironic if previous archaeologists had dug it all out by then.

But stopping all excavation – preservation only, at all costs – is not viable. Sometimes excavation is essential, usually when development takes priority over heritage preservation – Stonehenge's proposed road-tunnel scheme, for example, would have destroyed around 100,000 square metres (10 hectares) of the World Heritage Site. In cases where there is no development threat, the problem of preservation is intellectual rather than economic. The present generation is enormously interested in archaeology, but without new work we cannot learn more about our past. The argument that the main aim of archaeological resource management should always be preservation rather than excavation unfortunately means giving up trying to find things out for ourselves in favour of keeping things hidden for unspecified and distant-future generations. This is sometimes hard to swallow: if archaeology cannot produce new and exciting discoveries today, then it may well not have a tomorrow. It is never better to live in enforced ignorance.

Of course, there is a balance to be struck. Good conservation combines active research with management of the archaeological 'resource'. The disturbance of hitherto untouched remains is balanced against the acquisition of new knowledge and a better understanding of what exactly that 'resource' consists of. In Britain today no archaeologist digs a site just because it might be interesting. Excavations have to be closely targeted on answering clearly formulated research questions, excavating just enough to be sure of getting answers. That doesn't mean digging only tiny trenches – 'keyhole excavations', as archaeologists call them, can sometimes do more harm than good, as the archaeologist sees so little that they cannot interpret the layers and features glimpsed through the keyhole. That method leads to archaeological damage without providing understanding. Excavations have to be appropriate to the questions being asked: the methods must fit the research.

How was I going to persuade the various conservation organizations that new fieldwork was needed in the Stonehenge area? Under English Heritage's watchful eye there had been no new digs at Stonehenge and the surrounding monuments for almost twenty years. They had had firm justifications for turning down any new proposals until the previous digs at Stonehenge had been written up and a research framework for the Stonehenge area was in place. These were now published, so the time was ripe. My idea for a project was going to require geophysics and other forms of above-ground survey but we were also going to have to dig; a lot of what we would be looking for was beyond the capabilities of non-invasive research. Spades and trowels would reveal answers to the key questions.

This would also have to be the biggest project that I'd ever undertaken. I'd worked with large teams when digging in the Outer Hebrides, but this was going to require something more. I started by ringing Colin Richards, a lecturer in archaeology at Manchester University. We've known each other since we were students, and I'd dug for him on his excavation of a Neolithic settlement at Barnhouse in Orkney.[1] Orkney is famous for its Neolithic remains – especially the village of Skara Brae, which was built before Stonehenge.[2] Once the prehistoric inhabitants of Orkney had chopped down all their trees, they had to resort to building houses, and furniture, out of stone – the houses at Skara Brae have stone box beds, dressers and storage units that would certainly have been made of wood in landscapes with trees and forests. At Skara Brae, the house walls still stand to full height in places, whereas at Barnhouse centuries of stone-robbing and ploughing had left only the floor plans of the houses. Even so, Colin's dig revealed two very large houses, much bigger than those at Skara Brae.

Colin's career in archaeology had started at evening classes, where his first project was a study of Durrington Walls. Walking across its grassy

The interior of House 7 in the stone-built Neolithic village at Skara Brae, showing the stone dresser and central hearth.

interior more than thirty years ago, he saw that there were tiny pieces of what looked like Neolithic pottery in the soil of the molehills.

Back in 1967, Geoff Wainwright directed a massive project at Durrington Walls, what was then the largest excavation undertaken in Britain. He had to deal with a 50-metre-wide strip driven right through the middle of this huge henge, in advance of a new road. In the henge ditch, under the henge bank, and in the holes for the posts of the two timber circles, Geoff's team had found lots of pieces of pottery.[3]

Peterborough Ware was a style of Middle Neolithic pottery used throughout most of Britain in 3400–2600 BC.

This Neolithic pottery is decorated in a very distinctive style. It's covered in patterns of grooves or incisions, and almost looks like an imitation of basketry. Styles of ancient pottery are always given names – archaeological shorthand that lets specialists talk about pottery without having to describe it every time they have a conversation. Pottery is often named after a 'type site', such as a widespread type of Neolithic pottery called Peterborough Ware. Sometimes it's named after its shape, such as the Beaker pottery of the early Bronze Age. And sometimes it's given the simplest name imaginable – the Neolithic pottery found at Durrington Walls has grooves, so it got called Grooved Ware.[4] Another linguistic quirk is that the clay of the pot is called its 'fabric' – this has nothing to do with cloth.

The soft, black fabric of Grooved Ware looks to the untutored eye like coal or charcoal. Looking back, Colin realizes that what he thought were tiny sherds of Grooved Ware in those molehills at Durrington Walls were actually pieces of not-so-ancient coal or coke from Victorian steam-ploughing. But he'd caught the archaeological bug. Not only did Colin have a passion for Grooved Ware, but he was also fascinated by the

Grooved Ware was a style of Late Neolithic pottery used throughout Britain in 2800–2200 BC, probably originating in Orkney around 3200 BC. It is the style of pottery used at the Neolithic village of Durrington Walls.

mysterious people who used it – these are the people who built the henges and standing stones more than 4000 years ago. Working for Colin at Barnhouse, where the Neolithic inhabitants had also used Grooved Ware, I could see how he was revealing their everyday lives through his excavations of the remains of their houses.

If our project was going to get off the ground, we would have to do a lot of work at Durrington Walls, above all to find out whether it was linked to the River Avon by a ceremonial avenue, as predicted in our article published four years earlier. By huge luck, we were in the right place at the right time. Durrington Walls lies mainly on private land and everyone had heard that the farmer really wasn't keen on archaeologists. As Colin and I made plans, however, we learnt that the land had been sold; we crossed our fingers and contacted the new farmers, Stan and Henry Rawlins. When we turned up to have a look at their field, they were a bit wary at first – just how much of their untouched pasture did we want to dig up? – but they let us get on with it. We explored the field, starting at an entrance through the henge bank and ditch, and then moving eastwards down a slope towards the River Avon.

Few archaeologists had ever looked down by that part of the river. The steep bank between the river and the field was covered in brambles, stinging nettles and blackthorn but Colin and I could see that there was a large, deep gully leading down to the river from the east entrance of the henge. Was this the remains of an artificial incline constructed by Neolithic builders to provide access to the river?

We arranged a site meeting with staff of English Heritage, adjourning to the nearby Plume of Feathers at Shrewton to discuss the possibility of starting a project. Durrington Walls and its environs down to the river are scheduled as an ancient monument. This means that it's protected by law and that any works which affect it by breaking the ground surface require consent from the Secretary of State for Culture, Media and Sport. The minister makes her decision on the advice she receives from English Heritage, whose archaeologists must decide whether any proposal for an excavation on a scheduled ancient monument is acceptable. If they were unhappy with what we wanted to do at Durrington Walls, then the project would be a non-starter.

Unfolding maps and plans between the beer mats on a pub table, Colin and I outlined our ideas for a Stonehenge Riverside Project, to investigate the possibility that this stretch of the River Avon was a significant key to understanding the two henges – Durrington Walls and Stonehenge – as parts of a single complex. The feedback was positive. If we could raise enough money and resources to run a project to the best archaeological standards, then there was a chance that our project might actually happen. English Heritage certainly were not going to pay for the research but they could help with some of the geophysical survey and would be prepared to recommend consent if they received a strong proposal.

The next summer, in 2003, we got started. With no money but helped by a team of local volunteers, we cleared the scrub on the slope down to the riverside so we could map the earthworks of the gully. We also brought in a soil specialist, Mike Allen, who has worked on chalklands for most of his professional career. His favourite bit of kit is a petrol-powered auger that drills thin cores of soil and chalk from deep below the ground. We hoped his machine would tell us whether the gully was indeed a prehistoric earthwork and whether there was any trace of a prehistoric road surface leading down to the river. At the same time, English Heritage's geophysics team carried out a magnetometer survey across the field, looking for magnetic variations below ground that might reveal

the locations of buried features such as pits and ditches – what archaeologists call 'magnetic anomalies'.

The augering results were difficult to make sense of. There was indeed
a filled-up gully leading to the river, but whether it was a buried roadway
or just a natural valley was difficult to say. The geophysics had picked up
evidence for a ditch running along one side of it but not the other.
Otherwise there was not much showing outside the henge's east
entrance, apart from two highly magnetic areas.

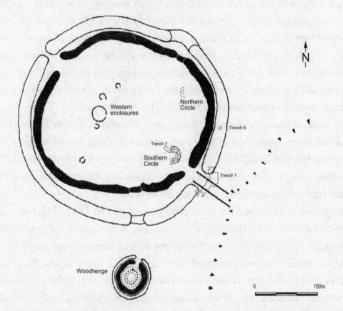

A plan of Durrington Walls showing the bank of the River Avon (right), the avenue
leading through the ditch and bank from the Southern Circle, the Western
Enclosures (centre left) and the positions of some of our trenches. Woodhenge is the
much smaller monument at the bottom.

One of the people who joined us that week was Kate Welham, an
archaeology lecturer at Bournemouth University who had finished her
PhD at Sheffield University just a few years earlier. Her main research
interest is in glass-making in the fifteenth to eighteenth centuries, so prehistory was not exactly her thing, but she came over to Durrington for

the day to help out. With a background in science, Kate had something Colin and I couldn't provide: a thorough grasp of computing, GPS surveying and geophysics. If this was going to be a big project, we would need someone with her abilities to organize the vast amounts of data that would be collected from survey and excavation and to co-ordinate the various kinds of surveys. This was the first time Colin and Kate ever met – we spent the day getting absolutely soaked and eventually left Kate surveying on her own in the rain while we huddled rather guiltily in the car. I don't think Kate held it against us: she and Colin have since worked together on many survey projects from the Western Isles to Easter Island – that nasty wet afternoon in Wiltshire saw the birth of a good team.

Drying Kate out back at the pub that evening, we realized that even three of us would not be enough to direct a project of the size required. We worked out that we were going to need a team of experts, to draw on resources and expertise from many different institutions. There would have to be at least six of us. At Manchester University, Julian Thomas had recently been appointed as professor of archaeology. Julian was not only an expert in the Neolithic of Wessex and southern Britain[5] but had also worked with Colin years before, re-analysing the results of Geoff Wainwright's excavations at Durrington Walls.

Geoff had published his results very promptly in 1971.[6] His team had recovered large quantities of finds – animal bones, flint and bone tools, and pottery – from the topmost layers of soil (the 'upper fills') in the postholes of the long-vanished timber circle known as the Southern Circle. Geoff thought these were chance items that had been propped randomly against the posts, falling into the holes when the posts decayed. In 1984 Colin and Julian, still students at that time, had reinterpreted the patterns of deposition in the holes.[7] They found that the distribution of finds in the postholes was far from random. One pit might have lots of bone pins but no flint tools, for example, while another might be principally full of broken pots. They suggested that the items in each posthole had been selected – that they hadn't ended up in the postholes by chance but were 'structured deposits' put there as part of ritual activities within the decaying timber circle.

Julian was delighted to be asked to join the project. Like Colin, he had always harboured a secret wish to dig at Durrington Walls. The two of them could bring university funding and equipment that would get the project afloat.

Chris Tilley, professor of material culture studies at University College London and one of my student contemporaries, also joined us. Chris had shaken the world of archaeology in the 1980s and 1990s with his radical theoretical approaches. Most recently he had pioneered an approach to understanding prehistoric landscapes, known as phenomenology: this basically entails trying to experience moving through landscapes in the ways that prehistoric people would have used them.[8] Maps, plans and geographical information systems (GIS) are all very well but, in Chris' view, there is no substitute for learning about the Stonehenge landscape on the ground – walking the routes that ancient Britons walked and experiencing the views and vistas that they would have seen.

Modern roads and pathways, hedges and fields completely disrupt our appreciation of how prehistoric people saw and experienced Stonehenge and the monuments around it. Chris wanted to explore the ways that the natural topography was used for approaching the monuments, by following the many small valleys or coombes that lead up from the river, by walking the routes of the Stonehenge avenue and another long, thin earthen monument to its north, called the Greater Cursus, and by exploring the course of the River Avon. He appreciated that the Neolithic was essentially a riverine culture, in which streams and river valleys were the roads and motorways of their day, for both foot and boat travel.

Our other co-director was to be Josh Pollard, then newly appointed as a lecturer in archaeology at Bristol University and now a reader at Southampton University. Josh had excavated Neolithic sites across the Wessex chalklands and was just coming to the end of a project at Avebury.[9] Avebury is Britain's second-greatest stone circle, set within a ditch and bank enclosing almost as big an area as Durrington Walls but with a much deeper ditch. Durrington Walls' ditch is pretty impressive at 5.5 metres (18 feet) deep, but the Avebury ditch is a staggering 8 metres (26 feet) in depth.

Like Stonehenge, Avebury has a complex sequence of use. It was begun about 200 years before Stonehenge and was probably in use throughout the third millennium BC. Two avenues lead out of the henge in different directions, one to a stone setting and ditched enclosure at

Beckhampton and the other to a stone and wooden-post circle, named the Sanctuary by early archaeologists.[10] In 1987, in the valley of the River Kennet, below the Sanctuary, archaeologists had found the remains of a series of large palisaded enclosures at West Kennet. Between these and the Avebury henge lies the huge mound of Silbury Hill, built around 2400 BC.[11] Positioned enigmatically in the valley bottom rather than on a commanding hilltop, this peculiar mound has defied archaeologists' understanding for more than 300 years.

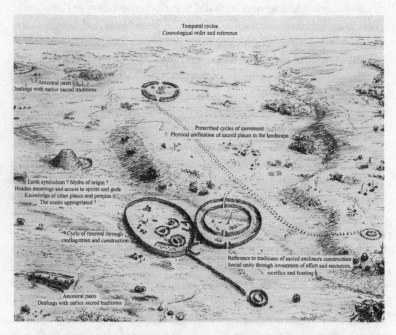

The Avebury stone circles and henge (centre rear) were part of a complex ceremonial landscape that included Silbury Hill (left) and the West Kennet palisaded enclosures (foreground).

Josh could bring not only the resources of his university but also his knowledge of the comparable Avebury complex, as well as many years of experience in digging on chalk. All good archaeologists can work on whatever type of soil comes their way, but experience helps to get one's eye in; you have to be able to recognize stains in the soil that show the presence of pits and postholes, to see the distinctions between different soil layers that have built up over the millennia and to know when to tell your team to dig with paint brushes and when to get out the pick-axes. Although Colin, Julian and I had all been working in Scotland for some years, in peat and sand soils, we had all started our archaeological lives digging on chalk and would be reviving some old skills.

We now had the makings of a great team but there was one big problem. Organizing academics is about as easy as herding cats. Everyone has their own ideas driving them, strong egos are in play, and no one wants to be told what to do. Would we really be able to work together, pooling resources and backing each other up, or would the project's management disintegrate into disagreements and academic fisticuffs? Other archaeologists gleefully predicted that it would end in tears, and wondered if we could install a webcam so they could watch disaster unfold.

We planned our first season of fieldwork for 2004. If all went well, this could be the first of seven years' work. Stan Rawlins agreed to move his cattle for a month so that we could dig up a small part of his field. We applied for permissions to English Heritage, English Nature and the Environment Agency (who had to be consulted on any works within 8 metres of the river's edge). And we also applied for grants. We needed £4000 in addition to the support provided by our various universities. Labour wasn't going to cost much, as this was to be a student-training excavation. Digging on a world-famous Neolithic henge is as good as it gets for student archaeologists, so we knew we'd have no trouble finding a big enough team, but we had to raise money to feed, house and transport them as well as to buy all the necessary equipment. We also needed to pay some supervisors: with so many inexperienced students on site, we had to recruit a handful of unusually patient professional archaeologists to make sure things went smoothly.

Although £4000 would see us through four weeks' digging, it would not be enough to pay for the many months of processing and analysis back in the lab, nor the costs of the fieldwork planned from 2005 onwards. What we really needed was a very large grant so that we could plan well into the future and avoid scrabbling for small pockets of cash every season. Until we got long-term funding, English Heritage would not be satisfied that the project was sufficiently resourced for it to run for more than a season. But what institution would take the risk of providing such funding for a project that hadn't even started? We had a good theory, and a good research design, but no one knew if we'd find anything at all.

Things looked brighter when the Royal Archaeological Institute announced a national competition to award a prize of £100,000 to the best archaeological project proposal. Our brand-new Stonehenge Riverside Project made it through to the final three, but then we received a dismal letter informing us that the RAI found our proposal 'too speculative'. In fact, they decided not to award the money to anybody. We realized that what we were attempting did not have the support of many senior archaeologists. In some experts' minds our plans were clearly wrong-headed: why were we going to dig *outside* the Durrington Walls henge, when surely everyone knew that the place to look was *inside*?

Still, we ignored the disappointment and raised enough money to dig in 2004. That August we excavated a large trench near the henge's east entrance and two smaller trenches on the steep slope leading down to the river. None of the geophysics results or contour surveying prepared us for what we would find. Down by the river, Josh's team hacked deep into layers of sediment accumulated from centuries of plough-movement, only to find that the gully in the riverbank was of comparatively recent origin, created during the last 2000 years. It had nothing to do with access from the Neolithic henge to the River Avon.

Colin and Julian had more luck nearer the henge. Part of their trench had been positioned over the highly magnetic spots picked up by the magnetometer. These turned out to be Neolithic pits filled with animal bones, broken pottery, worked flints and ashes. Even better, there were about forty pits – many more than indicated by the magnetometer results.

Some pits were filled with finds and others were almost empty. The emptier ones were grouped in small clusters, and we realized that they had been dug to extract the chalk sub-soil. We normally picture 'chalk' as a soft white rock whose surface is covered in fissures and cracks. However, these Neolithic pits were dug into a yellow claylike chalk

A pit excavated in 2004 at Durrington Walls. It contained animal bones which are the remains of feasting, as well as flint tools and pottery and a human femur. The black and white photographic rods are used to indicate scale.

residue that had collected within a wide and deep gully more than 20,000 years ago, during the last Ice Age. The glaciers never reached Salisbury Plain but the front of the ice sheet may have been only fifty miles to the north. Conditions on the plain were therefore extremely cold. Within this periglacial environment, areas of chalk were heavily weathered and eroded – turning some of the chalk rock into fine silt and clay, carried away by seasonal meltwater and deposited within newly formed gullies and valleys. This soliflucted chalk is perfect material for making daub, the clay that has been used for millennia together with wattles (wooden rods and branches) to build house walls.

These extraction pits filled the northern half of the trench but, disappointingly, the southern half – where we expected to find signs of an avenue running eastwards between the entrance and the river – had uncovered an area that had been scoured by thousands of years of erosion and ploughing. We found the bottoms of a few pits but little else.

Even the ditch found by the geophysicists turned out not to be one side of an avenue; it was an Iron Age land boundary constructed 2000 years after the henge itself.

Although we were disappointed at not finding an avenue, the huge amount of Neolithic rubbish in some of the pits showed that we were not far away from something intriguing. There were lots of flint arrowheads, of the type known as 'oblique arrowheads'.

Bows and arrows were standard equipment for Neolithic people. They

The fragment of human femur from the pit shown in the previous figure.
Note the impact scar in the centre of the bone (below the 3cm mark in the scale)
caused by a flint arrowhead.

were probably used for hunting but were also used as weapons, together with wooden clubs. Recent analyses of human remains dating to the Neolithic period seem to indicate that more Neolithic people suffered injuries from being whacked on the head than from being shot with arrows; about one in fifteen people buried in tombs of this period had been clubbed on the head, fatally in half the cases.[12] In contrast, we have fewer than a dozen instances across Neolithic Britain of skeletons with arrowheads in them. However, these are probably the tip of the iceberg.

In identifying an individual as having been shot, archaeologists tend to recognize only those cases where the arrowhead fortuitously hit solid bone. More than a hundred arrowheads have been found in Neolithic tombs; many of them might have entered these burial places buried deep in the soft tissues of archery victims rather than as gifts for the dead.[13]

One of our pits, filled with animal bones, contained a battered human leg bone. Unlike the animal bones, deposited fresh as food waste, this femur had evidently been knocking around for some time, possibly a century or more, before it had ended up in the pit. We wondered if it might be a grisly trophy of combat. Its surface was perforated by two small depressions, pronounced by our human bone specialists to be the results of trauma caused by arrow impacts. There were no broken-off tips of flint arrowheads in the wounds but this leg bone was evidence that the Stonehenge people were not entirely peaceful.

As well as providing evidence of warfare and violence, arrowheads are also useful to the archaeologist as indicators of chronology. Their shapes

A chisel arrowhead from Bluestonehenge. This type of arrowhead was in use in the Middle Neolithic (3400–2600 BC).

changed over time. The earliest farmers had different arrowheads to Britain's hunter-gatherers. During the first thousand years of farming, these were leaf-shaped points. From around 3400 BC to 2600 BC people adopted a new fashion of arrowhead with a flat blade, called a chisel arrowhead – these could cause a wider wound than the leaf shapes and would be more likely to remain behind when the arrow was pulled from the body of its victim. Between 2600 BC and 2200 BC these were themselves replaced by 'oblique' arrowheads, with a distinctive asymmetrical, pointed triangular form. One side of an oblique arrowhead is longer than the other, and culminates in a tang. Some are beautifully made, pressure-flaked to produce long ripples across their surfaces.

We found almost 400 oblique arrowheads at Durrington Walls, a surprisingly large number. They were almost as numerous as flint scrapers, normally the most common tool on Neolithic settlements and used for scraping fat and bristle off animal hides. Another surprise was the very small number of bone points for pegging out skins and piercing hides. Instead, there were bone and stone beads and lots of bone pins, several inches long and polished smooth, used to secure either clothing or hair. Clearly this was a different kind of settlement to the norm, since the everyday tool types used in daily farming life were so few. The large sizes of the broken pot sherds and the fact that some of the animal bones had been dumped with soft tissue still holding them in articulation showed that this was rubbish collected up after some sort of feast. The rubbish had been buried soon after each feasting event but, judging by the gnaw-marks on some of the bones and some preserved dog faeces, not until after the dogs had rummaged through the party refuse.

The find that caught most people's attention was a flint phallus. The flint of Wessex formed about eighty million years ago, as seams within chalk, derived from the calcium in tiny animals' bodies decaying at the bottom of a long-vanished tropical sea. It seems that the silicate components of their bodies collected in seams at certain levels within the chalk and formed flint in all kinds of shapes, sometimes flat or tabular, sometimes nodular. It also formed occasional small spheres and elongated knobs. These bizarre shapes have sometimes been further exaggerated during their formation by the impressions of prehistoric

An oblique arrowhead from the ditch of the Stonehenge Avenue. This type of arrowhead was in use in the Late Neolithic/Chalcolithic (2600–2200 BC).

shells and sea urchins.

Prehistoric man (for I suspect it was he rather than she) seems to have had an eye for these natural oddities. Back in the 1920s a local archaeologist and antiques dealer, Mr A. D. Passmore, excavated a round barrow (a Bronze Age burial mound) close to Stonehenge; its central grave pit contained not a prehistoric skeleton but a collection of strangely shaped flint nodules.[14] From the bottom of a Neolithic flint mine in Sussex came an impressively large penis-shaped flint nodule, its glans formed by a fossil echinoid or sea urchin.[15] At other Neolithic sites archaeologists have found phalli carved out of chalk. There is even one from Stonehenge. They are generally unattached, anatomically speaking, but a rare find of a carved wooden figurine – the so-called 'god-dolly' – from a bog in the Somerset Levels portrays a hermaphroditic individual with both penis and vulva.

Our Durrington Walls phallus was a natural nodule whose glans was formed by a fossil shell, with a possibly worked groove at the tip. It might have been nothing more than a chance geological quirk – more in the excavators' imagination than noticed by prehistoric people – except that its context provided evidence for careful selection. This phallic object lay near one end of a narrow Neolithic pit, in close proximity to two testicle-sized, natural flint balls. Close to it, a small flint slab covered another unusual natural flint lying on the sloping side of the pit. This flint had a natural hole through its centre and came to be called the 'pelvis flint' by the diggers because of its shape. Perhaps we had uncovered a prehistoric sex-education lesson.

Phalli are known from many different cultures, ancient and modern.

The flint phallus (and two flint balls) from a pit beneath the avenue at
Durrington Walls.

The Romans, for example, used to provide them with wings and considered them symbols of luck and fertility. Perhaps they were similarly treated as fertility objects in the Neolithic. Back at the campsite our find soon took on the nickname of the 'Durrington Dong', and gave its name to the project's improvised cocktail of the season – gin, Campari and ginger beer.

PUTTING THE TRENCH IN
THE RIGHT PLACE

Working out where we should dig in the next excavation season in 2005 was difficult. All our trenches in 2004 had been in the wrong places. Only the trench halfway between the river and the henge had found Neolithic remains and even that trench was not quite where it should have been. Had we known in advance how severe the erosion was immediately up-slope from the riverside, we would have positioned the trench westwards, further up the slope, where preservation was better. In 2005 we could undo the mistake and put the trench in the right place.

This might be our only chance to look for what we had predicted in our theory about Durrington Walls. We had to open a trench that would produce undisputed evidence of concentrated human settlement. The pits that we found in the first year's digging were full of feasting rubbish but that wasn't enough proof – they could be the remains of some one-off event, like Coneybury. If we didn't find an avenue or better evidence that Durrington Walls had been a place of the living, we'd have to pack up and go home for good.

If there were an avenue or roadway outside Durrington Walls, perhaps a new trench into the better-preserved zone, south of where we had found the pits, would pay dividends. If we found an avenue here then we were on the right track; if not, Ramilisonina's theory could be dismissed. It was also worth extending the trench northwards beyond the group of pits. Kate Welham's geophysics team had found an anomaly in this area. They had detected it using earth-resistance survey, which measures the resistance to electrical current below ground. High resistance is created by dense and dry features, such as walls, whereas low resistance is found in damper areas, such as the 'fills' of ditches and pits. The anomaly north of our 2004 trench was a large circular area of high resistance; it could be a small henge or a round burial mound.

One of the most exciting moments of archaeological excavation is the removal of ploughsoil by mechanical excavator to see what lies beneath. However much research has been done above ground to work out what is there, the mechanical digger always reveals surprises. Machine stripping of topsoil is a delicate task: take off too little and what remains has to be laboriously removed by hand; take off too much and you've destroyed valuable archaeological layers. It all depends on the sharp eyes of the archaeologist and the skilled hand of the digger driver.

The 2004 season had shown us that well-preserved Neolithic remains lay immediately at the base of very shallow ploughsoil, buried as little as 0.15 metres (6 inches) deep. As I watched the hired digger prepare the trenches in the summer of 2005, the driver gently removed the topsoil to reveal a layer of black soil filled with animal bones and potsherds. This was an entire ground surface that had been preserved for more than 4000 years – a complete surprise. Not only was the ground strewn with settlement waste (what archaeologists call 'midden') but it had also survived four millennia of weathering and erosion.

The chalklands of Wessex are famous for their archaeological remains of all periods but normally an excavator sees only the lower parts of features such as pits, ditches and graves that have been cut into the chalk bedrock. The uppermost layers have usually been destroyed over time by natural and man-made processes. Rainwater percolating through soil on to the surface of the chalk reacts with the calcium to form a weak hydrochloric acid that eats away at the upper layers of chalk; meanwhile ploughing not only breaks the surface to accelerate this weathering but also actively erodes the chalk. Most of the uplands of Wessex have been ploughed since prehistoric times and studies have shown that nearly a metre (3 feet) of chalk has been removed. We therefore rarely see a view of the Neolithic at the original ground level – this has vanished completely – but are instead usually looking at things that were once below ground. We now know that even at Durrington Walls parts of the henge interior have lost at least half a metre of chalk since it was first constructed. So how had the ground surface in our new trench been preserved?

Ground-surface preservation can be expected beneath substantial earthworks such as a henge bank, but our new trench was at least 10 metres from the edge of Durrington Walls' bank. It soon became clear that the bank had been quarried into a couple of centuries ago by people in search of chalk to puddle into cob (a traditional material for making walls) or lime (to spread on the more acidic soils of the river's floodplain). The quarrymen, who left behind a button and pieces of their clay pipes, had spread chalk rubble well beyond the edges of the henge bank, inadvertently sealing the Neolithic ground surface beneath.

It was this circular-shaped spread of more recent rubble that had shown up on the resistivity plot. It had provided protection from nine-teenth- and twentieth-century ploughing, but how had the old surface survived earlier erosion? We later discovered that this small part of the field, in front of the henge entrance, had for some reason been spared the ploughing that had commenced in the Iron Age. Evidence of the farming landscape of the Iron Age can still be seen today: the hedge lines of Iron Age fields are preserved at Durrington as lynchets – ridges still visible in grassland today throughout Britain – formed by ploughsoil accumulating against a hedge line on the upslope and by plough erosion against the downslope of the hedge.

As soon as the digger was off the trench, we trowelled off the last of the protective chalk lumps, and could then see a blackened surface that extended beyond the limits of the trench. Within it were heaps of burnt flint, low mounds of piled-up chalk (the up-cast from Neolithic pits) and spreads of ashy soil. The southernmost of these ash spreads extended just as far as the edge of our 2004 trench. As we trowelled over the top of it we could see that the thin layer of ash lay on top of a square area, just over 2 metres across, of solid chalk plaster at the centre of which was a circular depression. So this was where some of the soliflucted chalk extracted from the Neolithic pits we found in 2004 had been deposited. Both Colin and I recognized what we were looking at: this was a house floor, not very dif-ferent from the ones that we'd been digging for the last fifteen years in Orkney and the Outer Hebrides. More than that, it was very similar in size and plan to the Neolithic houses that Colin knew so well from Orkney.

The floor of House 547 at Durrington Walls. The white rectangular area is the
chalk-plaster floor in the centre of the house. Within it, the dark circular area
is the hearth. A line of stakeholes, showing where the wattle-and-daub wall once
stood, surrounds the house.

As we excavated further we realized that this was the centre of a house
measuring about 5 metres by 5 metres. The ash layer and the plaster
floor were surrounded by a line of holes that had held small upright
stakes. These 'stakeholes' showed us where the wattle-and-daub walls of
the house had once stood. There were even small pieces of daub surviving on the floor. Between the wall and the edge of the plaster floor,
the ashy soil had filled in shallow grooves that had once held horizontally
laid logs or planks. These beam slots were all that was left of the furniture – they were the foundations of box beds and storage units like those
crafted in stone in the Orcadian houses. Our 2004 trench had been too
small for us to see that these ephemeral traces were the remains of a
house. By extending and enlarging the trench we could finally appreciate what we were seeing.

Realizing that a single episode of ploughing into the Neolithic
ground surface would have virtually destroyed these house floors, we
now understood just why so few Neolithic houses have ever been found
in England.

Over the next few weeks we found traces of another four houses within the trench; we knew we couldn't rush this and would need more time in future summers to excavate each of them to the highest standard possible. Having spent the best part of two decades excavating prehistoric house floors, Colin and I had developed new methods for studying them. As a student I'd listened to an experimental archaeologist, Peter Reynolds, tell us about his reconstruction of an Iron Age roundhouse.[1] He'd suggested that the evidence in such houses is so minuscule that archaeologists should dig with teaspoons, not trowels and mattocks, in order to understand how they were lived in. I had roared with laughter at the time: this seemed a preposterously obsessive and time-consuming thing to do.

Years later, though, as I dug my first house floor in the Outer Hebrides, I realized he was very nearly right. I was working with some very talented environmental archaeologists, Helen Smith and Jacqui Mulville, and we worked out that the micro-debris and chemical residues accumulated on the floor during the house's occupation could tell us a lot about daily domestic tasks and where they were performed – but it was going to be a major job to retrieve the evidence.

Archaeologists can pick larger finds out of the ground they're working on – those things easily visible in the soil – but it's usual practice to use a 10-millimetre sieve on site (about the mesh size of a normal garden sieve) to ensure nothing gets missed. Smaller sieves are pretty useless because the soil clogs the mesh so quickly. In order to retrieve anything smaller than 10 millimetres in diameter we need to wet-sieve the soil: to wash it through sieve mesh of various sizes in a system of water tanks. It's a long and dirty job, as the soil from each context has to be bagged up in sacks, labelled in minute detail, and usually taken away from the excavation site to a wet-sieving team working in an area with an ample water supply. It slows down the excavation process enormously but the results are worth the effort.

In South Uist we'd carefully wet-sieved the entire occupation layer on top of the floor of a Bronze Age house, which was excavated in half-metre squares. Using a mesh size of just 2 millimetres we'd retrieved minute fragments of animal bone, potsherds, burnt plant remains and broken artefacts and were able to identify the areas of the house where

The remains of four Late Neolithic houses are visible in this main trench at Durrington Walls. I am standing outside the doorway of one of the houses in an area of midden (heaps of domestic rubbish).

cooking and various types of craft-working were carried out. We also took hundreds of small soil samples from the floor, to plot concentrations of chemical elements such as phosphorus and nitrogen, and many further samples to send to a soil micromorphologist – micromorphology being a technique of examining sections through the soil under a microscope, to establish how the floor layers were formed, of what they were composed, and whether floors were re-laid on top of earlier floors.

The Durrington Walls houses needed us to apply these well-honed techniques once again. We knew we had to sample the whole floor of each house in minute detail. We dreaded doing it – because we knew how long it would take and how many sacks of soil we'd have to heave back and forth – but we knew the results would make it worthwhile.

Unlike the Hebridean house floors of soft peat and sand, the Durrington floor surfaces comprised fairly hard chalk plaster. Every time the Neolithic inhabitants had given their house a good sweeping, they'd sent much of the micro-debris of their lives straight out of the door, so it was more difficult for us to reconstruct activity patterns than it had been on the Scottish sites. Nonetheless, the thin ash layer across the floor gave us a moment frozen in time: the moment of the house's abandonment. And, as we were to discover later on, the floors held other clues to unravelling the secrets of Neolithic daily life.

The houses were built on a slope but had level floors. This had been achieved by terracing the hillside, stripping the turf from higher up and laying it in a band lower down. Houses higher up were cut into the bare soil while those lower down the slope sat on a levelled platform of turf. This showed an element of organization and planning that went beyond that of the household. Perhaps this new settlement was larger and more organized than we'd at first expected.

This was not the first time that people had lived here. Buried in the turf were flints, including a leaf-shaped arrowhead, indicating that early farmers had lived here at some point during the fourth millennium BC, at least 500–1000 years before the houses were built.

At the bottom of the slope, within the valley that leads from the interior of the henge towards the river, we finally uncovered what we'd set out to find. By extending our excavation trench 20 metres upslope from the eroded area where we'd dug in the valley bottom in 2004, we discovered that a metre-deep layer of colluvium (soil, loosened by ploughing, that had washed down from higher up the valley) had settled on top of – and hence protected – the prehistoric ground surface. This surface was a thin layer of relict turf and topsoil that covered a flat road surface of packed and broken flints. As the roadway had gone out of use, so grass and weeds had sprung up, eventually creating a thin layer of humus worked into soil over decades by earthworms. Carefully plotting the finds within the prehistoric turf layer covering the road, we discovered that this soil had accumulated over several centuries. Mixed in with the oblique arrowheads and Grooved Ware of the Neolithic were the later styles of barbed-and-tanged arrowheads and pieces of distinctive Beaker pottery from the Early Bronze Age, indicating that there had been activity here long after the Neolithic houses had been abandoned.

Our theory was right – there was an avenue running from Durrington Walls to the river, an avenue so wide that our trench was not big enough for us to see the full width of this Neolithic roadway. In 2005 we found its northern edge, defined by a low chalk bank about 5 metres wide, and in 2006 we found the parallel bank running along the south side. The flint road surface was 15 metres wide and, in its entirety, the avenue was 30 metres (100 feet) across from the outer edges of its parallel banks. It dwarfs the modern A-road built in 1968 through the middle of Durrington Walls: that has a carriageway only 10 metres wide.

The Neolithic road surface was constructed from hard-packed natural, broken flint but it also contained lots of animal bones, pieces of burnt and worked flint and even potsherds that had been incorporated when the road's matrix was laid down. These bits of rubbish mixed into the road construction meant that people were already living here before the surface was laid.

When we stripped off part of the upper surface of the road, we found a lower layer of flints that contained no artefacts at all. Mike Allen and fellow soil specialist Charly French reckoned that this basal deposit was formed by natural agency, a geological deposit of coombe rock. Before the Neolithic, the bare valley floor had become covered with broken flint eroding out of the valley sides. This natural feature had been exploited and re-made by the Neolithic inhabitants of Durrington Walls.

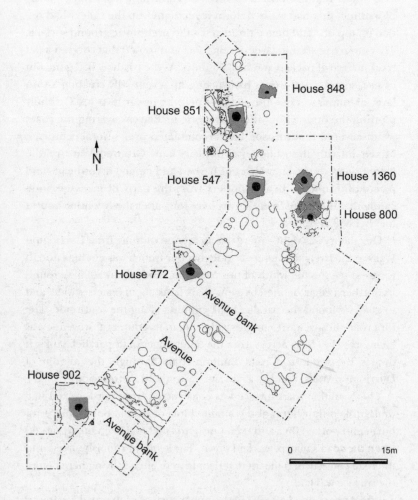

A plan of the main excavation at Durrington Walls showing the plaster floors
of the Neolithic houses (shaded) and their central hearths (black).
The other features are pits and stakeholds.

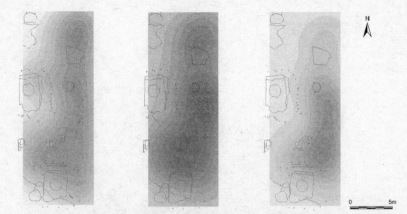

Computer-generated plots showing the relative density in the northern part of the
main trench of animal bones (left), worked flints (centre) and burnt flints (right).
The outline plans of the houses are visible, as is the curving line of
postholes forming a fence that separated two of the houses.

The avenue had yet more information to give us. Clive Ruggles came
to take a good look at the Durrington avenue while it was being excavated, to record its exact orientation. He found that the avenue's
orientation when looking westwards, upslope from the river, was within
a degree of the midsummer solstice sunset during the Neolithic. Clive
already knew that the Southern Circle inside the henge, partially excavated in 1967, had an entrance facing southeast, to the point at which
the sun rose on the midwinter solstice. Since the two directions of midsummer sunset and midwinter sunrise are opposite to each other, there
is usually no way of being sure whether both directions are significant or
only one of them. Our avenue was pretty much aligned with the entrance
to the Southern Circle, but was a few degrees off the precise axis of the
midwinter sunrise. Which mattered most to the avenue's builders – was
the avenue meant to share the same alignment as the timber circle
(towards midwinter sunrise), or was it aligned in the opposite direction
towards midsummer solstice sunset?

Clive worked out that the midsummer solstice sunset was the important direction – the avenue shows a deliberate alignment with the setting
sun, not with the axis of the timber circle. He is convinced that the

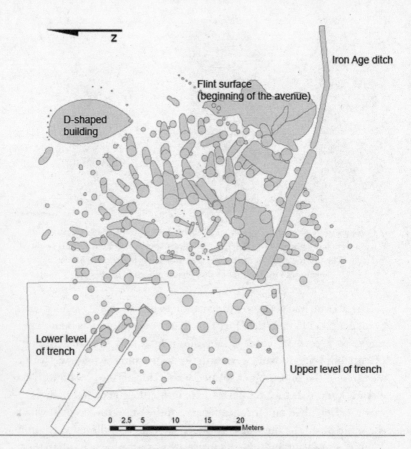

Full plan of the Southern Circle, combining the 1967 and 2005-2006 excavation and geophysics results. The 'cone' shapes are the postholes and their ramps. Julian Thomas' excavation trench is marked to the west. The rest of the circle is now buried beneath the modern road.

builders made sure that the avenue was a few degrees off the axis of the Southern Circle so that it would align with the midsummer sunset. As a consequence, it has an imperfect alignment with the midwinter sunrise. Had the avenue had been constructed simply to lead from the midwinter sunrise to the Southern Circle, it would have missed the alignment with the midsummer sunset. The midsummer solstice alignment is

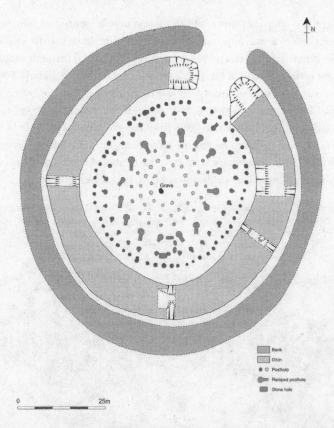

A plan of the Late Neolithic timber circle of Woodhenge. Today the postholes are
marked with small concrete pillars and the bank and ditch are barely visible.
The contents of the grave were destroyed during the Blitz but the burial is
thought to date to the Early Bronze Age.

affected by the topography: the Durrington valley rises quite steeply from
southeast to northwest. The steepness of the valley means that the sun disappears below the horizon sooner than it would on flatter ground, so the
avenue is aligned on the spot where the midsummer sun actually sets.

Ever since Geoff Wainwright's discovery of the rings of postholes that
held the timbers of the Southern and Northern Circles within
Durrington Walls, archaeologists have tried to reconstruct what these
timber circles looked like. The Northern Circle consisted of one or

perhaps two rings of posts enclosing a rectangular setting of four large posts.[2] This circle was approached from the south (from the direction of the Southern Circle) via a post-lined passage that passed through a façade of posts forming a screen on the south side of the rings of timbers. Geoff tentatively ascribed the outer and less convincing of the two post rings (almost 25 metres across) to a first phase of the structure. Since more than half a metre of chalk had gone from the ground surface here by the twentieth century, when he excavated the site, only the deeper features survived. A four-post square setting in the centre of the rings appears to have been oriented eastwards, towards the midwinter sunrise.

A reconstruction of the timber posts at Woodhenge.

The Southern Circle was much more impressive and better preserved; artefacts lying on the Neolithic ground surface around it were still in position.[3] At its centre was a rectangular arrangement of posts enclosing a smaller setting of six posts. Geoff interpreted these posts as belonging to the first phase of construction. They were surrounded by two concentric rings of timbers, and approached from the southeast through a screen of posts.

The timbers of this first phase of the Southern Circle had been left to decay in their holes. When the circle was excavated, the outlines of the rotted timbers survived as 'post-pipes', voids left by the rotted-out wood into which soil had slowly trickled. These posts were around 20 centimetres in diameter, slightly thinner than a telegraph pole. Archaeologists can tell from the soil layers if a pit or posthole has been dug into at some point after its first construction. At the centre of the Southern Circle, one of the postholes in the rectangular setting showed that the post had been replaced twice; two others had been replaced just once. On the basis of the likely lifespan of these timber uprights, Geoff estimated that the first phase of use of the Southern Circle lasted a minimum of sixty years.

This first phase was replaced by six concentric circles of posts whose uprights ranged in size from around 20 centimetres to over a metre in diameter; the outermost ring of posts measured almost 39 metres across. Among the largest posts were the two marking the southeast entrance. These posts too had decayed in their holes. Geoff reckoned that these huge posts probably survived for the best part of 200 years.

All of the Southern Circle's 'Phase 2' posts were so large and tall that the builders had to cut ramps into the chalk to feed the end of each post into its hole before heaving it to a vertical position. In 2006 Time Team built a replica of the Southern Circle, borrowing twenty soldiers from the Larkhill army barracks to try to raise just one of the smaller-sized posts by muscle power. To everyone's surprise it was too difficult – they had to resort to twenty-first-century mechanical means to erect it.

In and around the Southern Circle Geoff found some traces on the surviving Neolithic ground surface of what took place here. A small fireplace was positioned in the centre of the circle, and an enormous fire-pit (5 metres long) outside the southeast entrance was set into a 15-metre-wide surface of broken flint, adjacent to a platform of chalk blocks. Part of the interior of the circle was surfaced with rammed chalk but otherwise it had no proper floor. On the northeast perimeter of the circle was a post-lined hollow whose shallow filling of pottery, bones and other rubbish led Geoff to interpret it as a 'midden'.[4]

Forty years before Geoff Wainwright went to Durrington Walls, Maud Cunnington had excavated a similar timber circle at Woodhenge,

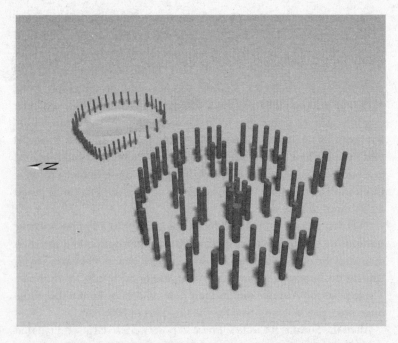

Model of Phase 1 of the Southern Circle as a square-shaped arrangement of posts surrounded by two concentric timber circles, with the D-shaped house to the northeast.

situated on the high ground just south of Durrington Walls, overlooking both the River Avon and the small valley in which the large henge lies.[5] Sitting on top of a ridge and ploughed in recent times, Woodhenge's original ground surface had disappeared long before Cunnington's excavations. This circular timber monument had also consisted of six concentric arrangements of posts, except these were laid out as ovals rather than true circles. The posts, of similar diameters to those of the Southern Circle, had been left in position to decay. The whole structure was enclosed within a ditch and external bank. Cunnington noticed that the long axis of the ovals was oriented on both the midsummer sunrise and the midwinter sunset, as is also seen at Stonehenge itself. At the centre of the timber circles was a cairn of flint nodules beneath which was the skeleton of a child.

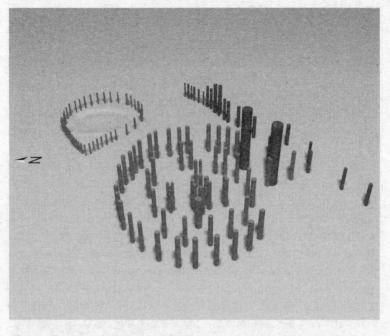

Model of Phase 1/2 of the Southern Circle. In this phase the builders added a timber
portal facing the midwinter sunrise.

Cunnington thought that the child had been sacrificed. She noted
that its skull was split in two, perhaps by a stone axe. Curiously, there is
no mention of this injury in the pathologist's report on the skeleton –
and we can't go back and re-examine the original bones because they
were destroyed during the bombing of London in the Second World
War. Josh Pollard has had another look at Cunnington's records and he
thinks that she may have been mistaken:[6] the skull could have collapsed
naturally along the bone's sutures under the pressure of earth from
above, rather than being damaged by a deliberate blow. He also thinks
that this is a later burial – that the child was not buried here by the
Neolithic builders but was added in the Early Bronze Age, when the
wooden monument would have been decayed ruins.

These three timber circles pose difficult questions. Were they built
at the same time as Stonehenge or were they erected earlier, some sort

of wooden prototype for the ultimate version in stone? Were they roofed? If so, did people live in them? Colin and Julian were also keen to find out more about what was in the postholes – were the animal bones and pottery plain old rubbish, or 'structured deposits' of ritual offerings? The question of how these artefacts had fallen into the postholes was also tricky. Geoff had reckoned that the decay of the timbers had created cone-shaped voids ('weathering cones') into which material stacked against the posts or lying close to them had fallen. Colin and I were not so sure.

During one of our evenings in the Plume of Feathers in 2003 we'd spent hours looking at the drawings of every posthole from the 1967 excavation. It was a Saturday night and the bar was getting crowded and noisy so no one seemed to notice us or our Eureka moment. Colin realized that the so-called 'weathering cones' were actually pits dug into the tops of the postholes after the wood of the posts had completely decayed. But why should anyone have done this? Why was it so important to dig new pits into old postholes, and there deposit groups of artefacts? Was it something to do with marking change and decay? We really needed to look at some of the postholes that hadn't been dug out during the 1967 excavation. Geoff's three-month rescue dig in 1967 had had to stick to the corridor of the proposed new road. Consequently parts of both timber circles remained unexcavated because their edges lay outside the construction corridor.

The 1967 excavations were spectacular, a watershed in British archaeology. Rarely used before, a fleet of mechanical diggers proved their worth in stripping off soil down to the chalk bedrock across the huge area. The use of diggers was considered frankly scandalous by some archaeologists – Geoff had to put up with vicious criticism – but a new generation realized the value of these machines in terms of allowing archaeologists to open up huge areas to investigate, rather than being confined to small, hand-dug trenches. In retrospect, this was one of the biggest revolutions in modern archaeology.

As the digger machines clawed their way across the interior of Durrington Walls, a team of 100 labourers and volunteers followed behind, scraping to the top of the bare chalk and revealing the outlines of postholes. Over a long, hot summer Geoff's workforce toiled on the

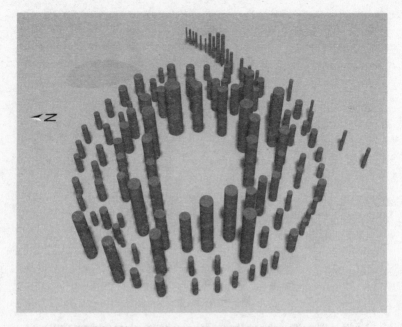

Model of Phase 2a of the Southern Circle. In this phase, a
horseshoe-shaped arrangement of timber posts was erected inside
three concentric circles.

baking chalk to empty out two sections of the henge's enormous ditches
(5.5 metres or 18 feet deep), and to dig out the postholes of the Southern
and Northern Circles. By night the team slaked their thirst in the nearby
Stonehenge Inn, spending their £1-per-day wages on as much beer as they
could drink. The excavation took on a legendary significance. This was
one of the key digs where Geoff recruited an intensely loyal crew of
heavy-drinking, hard-grafting tough guys. Over the next eighteen years
they went wherever Geoff needed them, working in all conditions. By the
late 1970s they'd acquired an official name (the Department of the
Environment's Central Excavation Unit) and a fearsome reputation.
They were the archaeological equivalent of Hell's Angels – other teams
lived in fear of a social visit from the Central Unit because of the
mayhem that would result.

I was keen to ask Geoff and other old-timers about the Durrington

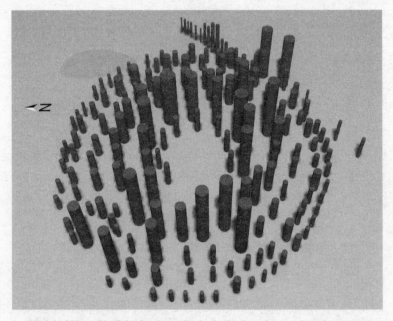

Model of Phase 2b of the Southern Circle. In this last phase, a ring of posts was
added at the centre of the circle and a final ring was added around the outside.

Walls excavation. Although I'd worked with Central Unit diggers before
going to university, and had heard a lot of stories, I wanted to get a sober
version of what happened during the '67 dig. Geoff came to visit in 2004,
taking the opportunity to re-visit the Stonehenge Inn (from which he
had been barred thirty-seven years before). Two of his supervisors, Dave
Buckley and Peter Drewett, both now senior archaeologists, also had stories to tell of the wild parties and the hectic digging. Living conditions
were spartan. The campsite was in the excavation field, with just a single
cold-water tap. Today it just wouldn't be allowed – one Portaloo for every
ten people is mandatory, for example, and students absolutely must be
able to charge their mobile phones.

On site, the '67 team worked hard and dealt with everything Geoff
and the site threw at them. Many among the first swathe of a dozen
supervisors were not up to the job and only four survived to the end of

the season. Peter Drewett, then only nineteen, found himself in charge of most of the day-to-day digging and planning. One-eyed Pedro was another of Geoff's hard-driving supervisors. Peter and Dave remembered a careless dumper-truck once going straight over the edge of the ditch, to be caught by the mechanical arm of a fast-acting digger driver. The excavation finished with the burial of someone's Ford Prefect in the henge ditch.

In August 2005 we had the chance to go back to the Southern Circle and answer questions that had been building up for years. We devised a strategy for excavating just enough of its remaining western arc for our needs, leaving as much as possible still untouched for archaeologists of the future. A narrow trench from the edge of the circle towards its centre would provide a selection of postholes in each of the outer five rings. It was also important to get a full plan but the postholes were buried too deep for conventional geophysics and ground-penetrating radar to work. We therefore carefully removed the top metre of colluvium and carried out the geophysics from that height.

Julian Thomas directed the excavation and was delighted to find one antler pick after another in the postholes, crucial finds for radio-carbon dating. It was clear that the 'weathering cones' were, as we suspected, later pits cut into the tops of the decayed posts. Some of these pits had taken centuries to fill up. Pieces of two human skulls from the fill of one pit dated to around 1800 BC, more than 500 years later than the posts themselves.

Julian also discovered that the circle had a second entrance on its northwest side, formed by two large postholes within the outermost ring. There was also evidence that the circle had been open to the elements. Despite the good preservation of the Neolithic surface, there was no sign of a floor of the sort that would be found inside a roofed building. We are certain that the Southern Circle was never roofed. If there had ever been such an intention, it was never carried through.

We could now see the Southern Circle's full plan. It was remarkably similar to that of Stonehenge itself. The second innermost post 'ring' was actually a horseshoe of uprights, just like Stonehenge's arrangement of trilithons. It faced in the opposite direction to the Stonehenge trilithons, however, towards the southwest and the midwinter sunset. The fourth circle of timber posts was equivalent in its position to Stonehenge's sarsen circle, and had the same number of uprights – thirty in all. The two structures were built virtually from the same blueprint, one in wood and the other in stone, except that the horseshoe-shaped arrangement within each faced in exactly opposite directions.

Geoff's finds have been curated by Salisbury Museum, so it was possible to obtain new radiocarbon dates for antler picks found in some of the Southern Circle's postholes. Although we knew that the main structure (Phase 2) had been put up shortly after 2500 BC, there was no dating for Phase 1. Colin had also pointed out that some of the postholes assigned to Phase 2 were actually earlier, because their holes and construction ramps were cut by other postholes. He also suspected that the innermost ring had been erected after all the others because the ramps for these postholes sloped from inside to outside whereas all the other rings' ramps sloped from outside to inside.

The new dates from the museum's antler picks suggested that there were probably more than two phases of construction. The southeast façade of small posts, previously assigned to Phase 1, was no different in

A computer-generated image of the Southern Circle in its final phase. The image has been created as an overlay on the excavation plan of the postholes and other features. The lintels are hypothetical.

date from the timbers of Phase 2. As Colin had predicted, the innermost ring of posts, dating to 2580–2340 BC, could have been contemporary with Phase 2a but was most probably put up after all the others. Two post-holes – numbered 84 and 85 – were probably put up slightly earlier than the others. Posthole 84 had been dug into by the holes of other large posts and so was earlier by perhaps a few years or decades. Together with posthole 85, it might have held one of a pair of timber uprights that framed the midwinter sunrise, possibly topped by a wooden lintel to form a timber trilithon (or, more correctly, a 'tridendron').

There was an even earlier setting of postholes which were cut by post-holes 84 and 85. These early postholes formed part of a circle, about 20 metres in diameter, of smaller posts just 20 centimetres wide. No antler picks were found in them so they cannot be dated.

We can now expand on Geoff's observation that the Southern Circle was rebuilt more than once. It began with a square setting of posts at the centre of two concentric circles of small posts, probably around 2500 BC (Phase 1). Probably about twenty years later, after the small posts had decayed, the builders put up a pair of large timbers to create a portal facing the midwinter sunrise (Phase 1/2). The main array of a horseshoe of timbers inside three concentric rings of timbers was then erected soon after, in the period 2485–2455 BC (Phase 2). Finally, a ring of small posts was constructed at the centre of the circle in the period 2580–2340 BC, together with a ring of posts around the outside of the circle (Phase 2a). In all, there were probably four phases of construction, spanning a period of less than a century. The pits that were later cut into decayed posts continued to be filled for another 500–600 years.

Had Durrington Walls' Southern Circle been built of stone, it would be recognized today as being just as architecturally magnificent and com-plex as Stonehenge itself. The fact that it was built of timber is, however, of great importance for unravelling the Stonehenge story. It now looks as if the Southern Circle and Stonehenge were very similar monuments, albeit in different materials.

6

THE HOUSES AND THE HENGE

The results of the 2005 excavations were spectacular, revealing that Durrington Walls had once been a huge settlement of 17 hectares (42 acres), filled with small, square houses whose surroundings were clogged with Neolithic trash from feasts that must have involved thousands of people. Its central area was dominated by two timber circles (the Southern Circle and the Northern Circle, found in 1967). In 2006 we discovered that this central area was surrounded by a wide arc of impressive buildings, consisting of fenced-off houses. Later on, the entire settlement was enclosed by a huge, circular bank and ditch – the 'walls' of the site's name – which buried many houses around the settlement's perimeter under deep deposits of chalk. Although thousands had lived here, this was never a town. It lasted decades and not centuries, and most of its inhabitants were probably seasonal visitors and not permanent residents.

With the discovery of the avenue and the unique Neolithic houses, we had verified part of the original theory about Durrington Walls being a place for the living, in a landscape of complementary monuments where wood and stone, the living and the dead, all played a part. We were in a good position to apply for a large grant and by 2006 the project had been awarded nearly £500,000 from the Arts and Humanities Research Council. Although most of this was for salaries and university overheads, it gave us enough to do the unglamorous behind-the-scenes lab work and analysis that are the principal aspects of archaeology.

For every month of digging in the field we were creating about six months of what is called 'post-excavation': the sorting and analysis of finds and samples, the processing of digital data, the production of computerized plans and records, the drawing of finds, and the writing of detailed reports by an army of specialists. We needed experts to work on flint tools, animal bones, human bones, pollen, carbonized plant remains, wood charcoal, pottery, soil chemistry and micromorphology, land snails, and chemical isotopes in animals and humans.

The project was now on a firm financial footing and we could plan ahead. Rather than restrict our efforts to Durrington Walls, we could also investigate crucial sites at and around Stonehenge itself. We proposed another four years' work, at Durrington Walls and Woodhenge, at the Stonehenge Cursus, along the ridge along the riverside south of Woodhenge and at the Cuckoo Stone (a fallen standing stone near Woodhenge), then Stonehenge itself, its avenue and environs, with a final season to wrap up any loose ends. Our money worries were never quite over, though. Since most of the grant was earmarked to pay for post-excavation and compulsory university overheads, there was still not enough money to fund the digging. We were going to have to apply for extra grants every year but the project was no longer 'too speculative' and even international organizations such as the National Geographic Society were excited by our discoveries.

In December 2005 we presented the project's first results to a packed audience at the Theoretical Archaeology Conference in Sheffield. Working from old finds and records, we had a new argument about the dating of Stonehenge (about which more later) and had also taken stock of our own discoveries the previous summer. By studying photographs of the flint surface found in 1967 outside the southeast entrance to the Southern Circle, we could see that this was part of the flint-surfaced avenue that we had unearthed less than 100 metres away. The surface of broken flints had been laid at the same time as or after the Circle's Phase 2 posts were erected. It had initially been interpreted as being a platform on which to make offerings and perform rituals, but was actually the western end of the avenue leading to the Avon.

We were less certain about the other end of the avenue. Erosion had destroyed the avenue nearer the river and the riverbank itself has moved during the last 4000 years, as the river has cut into the solid chalk on its west bank. If there ever was a timber or stone monument at the riverside end of the Durrington Walls avenue, it would have been eroded away long ago.

In 2006 we split the team into four different excavations. I stayed with the houses and avenue at Durrington Walls, Julian dug in the centre of the Durrington Walls henge, Colin went two miles away to the northwest of Stonehenge next to Fargo plantation, and Josh dug two trenches into Woodhenge. One of these Woodhenge trenches was on the external bank enclosing the timber circle; the Neolithic ground surface would be preserved here and we hoped to find evidence of activities from before Woodhenge was built. The other trench was within an area already dug by Mrs Cunnington. At the southern end of the timber circle her workmen had found two holes much shallower than the many postholes. She interpreted them as holes for standing stones, partly because some sarsen chippings were found close by. Josh wanted to know whether she was right and, if so, how the stones had related to the timber posts.

Josh was joined by David Robinson, lecturer in archaeology at the University of Central Lancashire – or, as we know him, California Dave. Although his main interest is in the rock art of California, and the hallucinogens taken by Native Americans to attain trance states for making the art, California Dave is also an expert in the British Neolithic. As a student years earlier, he came on an exchange programme to Sheffield University and has spent many summers digging for Josh and Julian.

As they dug to the bottom of the holes that Cunnington thought had once held stones, Josh and Cali Dave could see that she had been right. Two enormous sarsens once sat in these holes and had left distinctive layers of crushed chalk at their bases. Furthermore Cunnington had missed another two stoneholes. These stones had actually formed a three-sided setting, open to the west; a similar stone setting still stands within the Avebury henge, where it is called a 'cove'. Four standing stones, probably less than 2 metres high, had formed this cove at Woodhenge; they were later removed and replaced around 2000 BC by two large sarsens, standing probably more than 2 metres high. Just where all these stones have gone is a mystery. The last two could have been dragged out and broken up in historical times, but the first four were definitely moved during the Neolithic; perhaps they were taken to Stonehenge or to an unknown spot in Woodhenge's immediate vicinity.

Excavating one of the postholes at Woodhenge. After the posts had decayed, a 'cove'
of sarsen standing stones was erected in the southern part of the monument.

It is most likely that the cove at Woodhenge was erected after the wooden posts had decayed. This process of replacing wooden monuments with stone, known as 'lithification', has been noticed by archaeologists on many megalithic sites.[1] Perhaps it represented the process of hardening in which the transient and decaying was replaced by the eternal. At the centre of the cove, Josh and Dave discovered a hole left by the roots of a blown-over tree. Potsherds and flint blades from its fill were of styles found in the fourth millennium BC, at least 500 years earlier than Woodhenge's timber posts, so this tree might have been growing here long before Woodhenge was erected.

Beneath the henge bank, Josh and Dave found that the builders of Woodhenge had stripped away the turf. In doing so, the henge-builders had exposed another such tree-throw hole, which they had capped with a surface of rammed chalk. Within and around this tree hole there was a small heap of sherds from a pot. The shape of this pot indicated that it came from the beginning of the Neolithic, around 3800 BC. This pot was dumped here more than a thousand years before Woodhenge was built, at around the same time as the Coneybury pit was filled with feasting debris.[2] Although we could not be sure whether the broken pots found in the two tree holes at Woodhenge were of the same type, they could well have been deposited around the same time, when the earliest farmers began clearing the few trees standing on the high chalklands.

In the valley below the east entrance to Durrington Walls we extended our trenches to investigate more houses as well as to obtain a complete cross-section of the new avenue. I'd promised Farmer Stan that this would be the last time we dug up his field but I was hopelessly wrong – it took another year to finish what we'd first started in 2004, far longer than we had expected. Stan wasn't best pleased (the loose soil of our filled-in trenches was attracting rabbits and creeping thistle into his pasture) but he knew that what we were finding was rewriting the Stonehenge story. It was worth the inconvenience.

On the avenue leading from the henge entrance to the river, we discovered a line of pits that had been dug out and filled with animal bones before the final road surface was laid, arranged on a slightly different alignment to that of the avenue itself. On the north side of the avenue we found a group of three holes that – one after the other – had each held a standing stone. Next to them, large chunks of sarsen from a broken-up stone had been buried in a shallow pit. Smaller pieces of this shattered stone covered the area around, lying on the road surface and buried within the soil that had developed over the next few centuries. It's unusual to find evidence for destruction of a standing stone in prehistoric times, but here it was. Maybe the stone stood as a single marker along the avenue, in the same way that the Heel Stone stands alone on the Stonehenge avenue.[3] Alternatively this was one of a row of stones along the avenue's north side. In 2004 we'd found the bottom of a similar pit just seven metres away, close to the 'phallus pit' within the eroded part of the avenue. Perhaps a line of stones had led to the river.

The number of Neolithic house floors we discovered and excavated rose from five to seven. Five of the houses were terraced down the slope overlooking the avenue. The other two sat opposite each other on the avenue's low banks, like a pair of entry kiosks. These were particularly odd structures, and not exactly houses. Each had only three walls, lacking the fourth wall facing southeast down the avenue. Each had a central fireplace but there were no traces of the footings for wooden furniture of the sort found in the other houses. They look more like heated Neolithic bus-shelters than real houses. Yet their floors had been carefully maintained and repaired and the southern building had a large midden on its south side. Perhaps they were places where certain people could gather, protected from the rain and the cold, to watch whatever was happening along the avenue, as processions moved up from the riverside towards the Southern Circle and the blazing fire outside its entrance.

The houses on the slope beside the avenue were all slightly different but were built to a similar specification: always square, with a central hearth and a yellow chalk-plaster floor. The largest house was also the most solidly built. Deeply driven stakes had formed a wattle-and-daub wall whose outer face had been surfaced with a mixture of crushed and puddled chalk that would have looked something like pebble-dash. In technical terms, this is not exactly the traditional building material known as 'cob', which is a mix of crushed chalk and cow dung, but it's close enough. In 2009 I stopped to look at a dilapidated old barn in the nearby village of Winterbourne Stoke. This building had cob walls much the same as those of the Durrington house built more than 4000 years earlier. It seemed extraordinary that some Victorian farmhand had used the same methods and materials as his predecessors 180 generations before.

This large house beside the Durrington avenue had its doorway facing south. Immediately inside the threshold, the plaster floor had been worn away by the comings and goings of many feet. On the left-hand side of the door, in the southwest corner, there was a square storage area, perhaps for coats, bows and arrows, antler picks and all the things one puts down when coming indoors. Along the west wall were the foundations for a wooden box bed, with another one opposite it along the east wall. Colin had studied exactly the same arrangement in the Neolithic houses in Orkney.[4] Chemical tests there had shown that the area around the bed furthest from the door had higher levels of phosphorous, which has been explained as the result of babies and small children wetting the bed.

Against the north wall of the large house, opposite the doorway, were the foundations of a piece of wooden furniture, narrower than the beds, with two end uprights and another in the centre. Thanks to the surviving stone-built Orcadian furniture, we know exactly what this was – a wooden 'dresser' formed of two shelves, one on top of the other, and divided into left and right sides. Perhaps this was where the house's special belongings were kept, or the clothes and fabrics. At the end of the east bed, tucked into the southeast corner, was another square storage area. The ashy layer left on top of this part of the house when it was abandoned was littered with tiny pieces of broken pottery. The plaster floor in this corner was also heavily stained by ash, no doubt from countless rakings-out of the fire. Here was the kitchen area, and this box in the corner must have once contained cooking items and perhaps food supplies.

To cap it all, we found two knee-prints close by, on the south side of the fireplace, where someone had spent long hours kneeling by the fireside, tending the fire and cooking food in flat-bottomed Grooved Ware pots. I initially wondered if these knee-prints might actually be footprints, made by someone squatting on their haunches as people do the world over in cultures where there are no chairs or tables – but there is no doubt that these hollows were shaped by a pair of knees. The house floor had been kept fairly clean and the only complete items we found were an arrow-head and a bone pin that had both fallen behind the furniture and escaped whatever served as a Neolithic broom. In the northwest corner of the plaster floor we found two teacup-sized holes full of the tiniest flint flakes and chippings. Perhaps these little dustbins were used to dispose of unwanted splinters that could inflict deep wounds on bare feet.

A laser scan of the floor of House 851, showing the beam-slot indentations where wooden furniture once stood around the edge of the plaster floor. To the left of the circular hearth a pair of indentations, made by someone's knees, are also visible.

Colin and I had seen this exact layout of furniture before, in the largest house at Skara Brae.[5] In fact, you can overlay the internal plan of Skara Brae's House 7 on the large house at Durrington: they are exactly the same in size, shape and the positions of internal furniture. The only differences are that House 7 was built on a different orientation, its hearth – like all Orcadian hearths – was square and not round, and it had two stone boxes for storing shellfish. But the two houses are more than 500 miles apart – how can they be so alike?

Although Skara Brae was founded before 3000 BC, House 8 was not built until near the end of the village's occupation 500 years later. So the two houses are just about contemporary. Was Durrington Walls built by prehistoric Scots from the Orkney Islands? This is pretty improbable, though the people of the Stonehenge area might have been heavily influenced by fashions that originated in Orkney. It is very likely that Grooved Ware was invented in Scotland, if not in Orkney itself, and then spread southwards.[6] It seems not to have been adopted in Wessex until around 2800 BC, 400 years after it first appeared in Orkney.

Archaeologists have recently uncovered a large settlement in Orkney at the Ness of Brodgar, with hall-like buildings and a thick boundary wall separating it from the Ring of Brodgar, Orkney's version of Stonehenge. This complex was built before 3000 BC, so it predates Stonehenge and Durrington Walls. Perhaps the remote northern islands spawned a religious and cultural reformation that eventually spread across the whole of Britain. Similar square house plans of this period are known from Wales and eastern England. This was probably the standard form of housing across Britain, replacing the long rectangular houses of the previous millennium and itself to be replaced in the Bronze Age by round houses.

Just northeast of the large house at Durrington was a small house, also rectangular, with a proportionately small fireplace. The door of this little house was probably also south-facing, and the scatter of small chalk lumps around it showed that it had 'cob' walls like the other, but there were no holes for stakes to support the walls. At 3 metres by 2 metres this was a tiny building, and the lack of debris on its floor shows that it was a shed or store. This pair of one big and one little house was separated from all the others by a short length of fence, surviving as a curving line of postholes. It is evident that this was a main house with an ancillary out-house, set within their own compound. Turning back to the plan of Skara Brae, we saw that House 7 similarly had its own outhouse, and that this pair of buildings was separated from the other houses by a long passageway. Comparing the plans of the small 'ancillary' structures, we could see that the Scottish outhouse was virtually identical to the one we were digging in Wiltshire.

We found another three houses down the slope from these two. In all of these we identified beam slots for beds set around the central fire-place but no elaborate fittings like those found in the large house. The houses' doorways were difficult to spot but two faced west and the third to the south. This group of buildings provides a glimpse into a society that was not equal in terms of how people lived. The large house was near the top of the hierarchy (literally, too, by being at the top of the slope) and it had all the features of a family dwelling. With floor areas of almost 25–30 square metres, these houses were certainly big enough to each accommodate a nuclear family of parents and children. Perhaps the head family lived in the top house and their relatives or dependants lived in the smaller houses lower down the slope. The piles of broken cooking pots in the rubbish heaps outside these smaller houses form a stark contrast with the almost sherd-free surface of the large house and its compound; perhaps the people in the small houses did the cooking for the residents of the large house. How many more households formed this segment of the community is difficult to tell, but the Skara Brae village seems to have consisted of nine or ten houses as a social unit.

While part of the team concentrated on excavating the delicate house floors, Julian opened two trenches inside the western half of the henge itself. Back in 1996 a team of geophysicists had discovered a group of five ditched enclosures in this part of Durrington Walls. These enclo-sures formed an arc, running north to south, with the largest – about 40 metres in diameter – in the centre. This largest enclosure was circular and its entrance (facing east down the slope) was visible on the geo-physics plot. This enclosure had actually first been located many years before, in the 1920s, from aerial photographs of cropmarks. Were these various features going to be Neolithic, or were they Iron Age like the ditch we had dug in 2004? Positioned on the slopes above the Southern

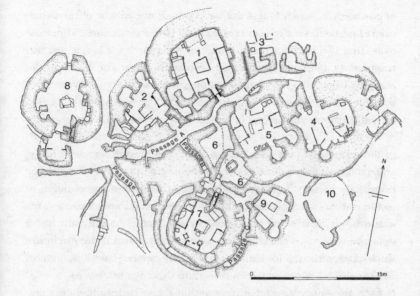

A plan of the Neolithic village of Skara Brae in Orkney. The Durrington Walls houses are very similar in plan and internal organization but were built in wood rather than stone. A photograph of House 7' is shown in Chapter 4.

Circle, whatever they were, they would have had fine views of the valley leading down to the river. We selected the largest enclosure and its southern neighbour for investigation. At the centre of each, the magnetometer showed a small 'hot spot' – would this be a prehistoric burial?

The mechanical excavator removed the topsoil, revealing pits cut into the lower part of the colluvium within the large enclosure. As the students excavated these we could see that they were grain-storage pits containing Iron Age pottery – not the period of prehistory we were looking for, but not a surprising find either, as much of the interior of Durrington Walls was re-used by Iron Age farmers 2000 years after it was built.

Another 30 centimetres deeper, we reached bare chalk. Here the 'hot spots' turned out to be fireplaces in the centres of square houses just like those we had found down the valley beside the avenue. There was a house within each enclosure but their preservation was not good. Here in the interior of the henge, the top of the Neolithic ground surface had been scoured away before the Iron Age and the plaster of the house floors had been eroded – except directly under the hearth, where the heat from the fire had made it as hard as rock. Each house was surrounded by a circular row of holes for fence posts. The house to the south had then also been encircled by a ditch, its entrance to the west, with the chalk deposited outside the ditch. This ditch and bank had turned the house into a mini-henge after its original fence had gone out of use.

The sequence in the large enclosure was slightly different. This house and its surrounding fence were positioned at the centre of a large circular enclosure whose bank had first been positioned inside the ditch, just like at Stonehenge, but had later been moved to outside the ditch when the ditch was dug out again. So although it had initially had a defensive-looking boundary feature (ditch then bank), this enclosure too had been turned into an inward-looking henge (bank then ditch). There were other unusual features within this large enclosure.

First, the entire ground surface within the enclosure had been levelled. We had seen this kind of landscaping elsewhere, associated with the construction of each of the houses on the slope above the avenue and for the Southern Circle itself. Outside the circular fence a pit had been filled with the butchered remains of a whole pig, the remnants of a small feast. Halfway between an opening in the fenceline and the entrance to the enclosure, two huge postholes lay close together. They had held posts almost a metre in diameter. What was odd was that the postholes' bases were at different depths. Julian wondered if this had been a way of making sure that the tops of the posts were at the same height. Perhaps these posts had supported a wooden lintel on their tops to make a trilithon-shape in wood. To their south, and right against the edge of the excavation trench, Julian found another similarly massive posthole. Was this part of another 'tridendron', one of two sets of massive posts flanking the approach to the central house?

Whoever lived here was clearly very important indeed. Although the house's floor area was no bigger than that of the large house further down the valley, it had footings for 1.8-metre-wide posts arranged in a square around its central hearth. These must have given this particular house a far more monumental appearance than the others; perhaps these hefty posts supported a high roof. All the floor deposits had been washed away long ago, so there were few clues to what had happened inside the house. The fills of all the holes for the wall stakes and fence posts were clean as a whistle, completely unlike the black, organic fills in the corresponding features around the houses lower down the valley. Even the fill of the pit with the dismembered pig was much cleaner than equivalent pits associated with those houses. This was a very clean place despite the central hearth having been in long-term use. Whoever kept the fire burning also made sure that very little domestic rubbish was left lying about.

Julian favours this building having been used as a spirit house, a place where the supernatural could be visited by the living. A guardian would have periodically tended the fire but otherwise no one actually lived here. My preference is that it was used as a dwelling by a leading family, who might have received guests here or arbitrated on matters of justice. Perhaps the family's food was brought to them from a cooking area elsewhere, at the back of the enclosure or further away.

Having found houses both inside and outside the henge, we began to wonder if Durrington Walls had been a much larger settlement than we'd first appreciated. What if the entire henge enclosure, all 17 hectares of it, turned out to be a village? Recorded on Kate's geophysics plots, there are hundreds of magnetic 'hot spots' similar to the two that turned out to be hearths – many of these could be the sites of former houses. Sadly, we will never be able to identify whether or not they are all houses without excavation over an enormous area, an impossible task logistically and something that English Heritage and the National Trust (who own most of the Durrington Walls henge) would never permit.

By 2006 it was clear that the houses down by the avenue had been occupied before the ditch and bank of Durrington Walls were constructed. The settlement had been in use before the henge was built, and the earthworks were not a circuit of 'town walls'.*

Since we were certain that the settlement predated the henge bank and ditch, we knew we should find well-preserved occupation evidence on the

* One archaeologist suggested at the time that perhaps the inward-facing earthworks of henges are 'ghost-catchers', designed to safely corral the spirits, keeping them in, away from the outside world.[7]

An elevated view of Julian Thomas' trench showing the central square house and the postholes of its circular palisade fence within the largest of the Western Enclosures.

buried ground surface beneath the henge bank. Turning to the records of previous digs at Durrington Walls, I found what I was looking for. In 1917 a local archaeologist, Percy Farrer, dug a narrow trench through the bank on the west side and found a thick, black layer of occupation debris.[8] In the early 1950s archaeologists monitoring a trench for utilities along the old A345 road running through the henge observed similar deposits where the pipe trench cut the bank at the north and south sides.[9] We ourselves dug five small trenches into and beneath the rampart on the east side of the henge and discovered thick occupation layers.

Inexplicably, there was a lack of such evidence from Geoff Wainwright's wide trenches in 1967, even though these had run through the north and south banks. He had, however, found buried soil under the south bank, both on the roadline and in a narrow pipe trench close to where our own excavations would be.[10] While the mechanical excavators were removing this buried soil, his supervisor Pedro Donaldson found lots of artefacts in it – more than 3000 worked flints and 100-plus potsherds – but there had been no sign of any house floors. The north bank had also preserved a buried soil underneath it but there was very little Grooved Ware pottery. Instead, Geoff and Pedro found a small area of occupation here with an earlier style of pottery radiocarbon-dated by charcoal to around 3300 BC, the best part of a thousand years earlier than the village.

The absence of any evidence for Grooved Ware houses in the buried soil under the north bank was not difficult to explain. A geophysical survey carried out in 2004 made clear that there had originally been an entrance through the north bank, and Geoff's excavation was fortuitously located on what was actually a later blocking ditch that had been dug to close off this entrance.[11] This explained why the northern ditch as recorded by Geoff was unusually shallow and why it produced surprisingly late radiocarbon dates of 2200–1700 BC.[12] The geophysics plot also revealed a similar blocked entrance on the south side, leading to Woodhenge. We can presume that these entrances to the henge were access routes into the settlement, which explains why Geoff's team found no Grooved Ware occupation or houses beneath the north bank.

Geoff is certain that his old colleague Pedro would not have missed any house floors while machining off the buried soil beneath the south bank. He was an extremely experienced archaeologist who had worked on digs all over the world. On this I have to disagree with Geoff; I think that the section drawings and photographs from 1967 show at least two and probably more houses, visible as level, horizontal stripes in the sides of the excavation.[13] One even has a hearth and a small posthole. My guess is that there may have been up to a dozen houses under this part of the south bank, based on the 1967 records and on the density of houses where we dug. I'm not criticising Geoff and Pedro for this probable mistake – no one is infallible and in 1967 not only were they teaching themselves and others how to use mechanical diggers for topsoil stripping, but no one had ever seen a Neolithic house floor; when we began work nearly forty years later, we were standing on the shoulders of giants.

Further confirmation came in 2007, when we dug through the south terminal of the bank at the east entrance to the henge. This bank was made from the upcast from the Neolithic digging of the ditch. Layers of material thrown up from the ditch had been tipped one on top of another, so that the topsoil was covered by chalk rubble. That Neolithic topsoil contained large blocks of cob-type walling, just like that of our large house; we think that there was at least one house in this area, which was demolished and removed by the Neolithic builders in order to dig the henge ditch.

There are two important factors to take into account when comparing our success at finding houses to the apparent absence of houses in the 1967 excavations. Back in the sixties archaeologists had little knowledge of what Neolithic house floors might look like. By sheer chance, Colin and I had developed a very specific knowledge of these very ephemeral surfaces because of their occurrence on the sites in Scotland where we had been working over the previous two decades. Even so, when we started digging at Durrington Walls in 2004 we could easily have machined off the first house floor that we found because it was so slight and so shallow. Fortunately, we had dug some test pits beforehand and knew not to go to the top of the subsoil with the digger bucket. We were also conducting a research excavation with no pressing deadline; if we failed to finish, we simply covered the trench over and came back the next summer. Geoff's team, however, had just three months in which to complete the job. By comparison, it took us four months with a similar-sized (but much more inexperienced) team to dig an area less than a fifth of the size of the 1967 trench – and that's without having to empty any deep henge ditches.

Geoff does agree that one structure found in the 1967 excavations is a house. Set close to the northeast side of the Southern Circle, there is a hollow partly surrounded by small postholes.[14] It was initially interpreted as a midden, filled by rubbish dumped from some unknown activity inside the timber circle. A closer look reveals that it had the same yellow chalk-plaster floor as seen in the houses that we excavated. It was no ordinary house, however, since it had a strange D-shaped plan and no fireplace. Its floor space would also have been four times the size of any of the other houses.

This was more like a large hall, perhaps an indoor space in which a hundred or more people could gather. The people of the Neolithic were certainly capable of constructing very big buildings: similarly large houses have been found in Orkney within the settlements at Ness of Brodgar and Barnhouse.[15] This hall-like building adjacent to the Southern Circle was probably built before the circle's six rings of posts were erected, as part of its Phase 1. In ruins by the time the Phase 2 posts were put up, its hollow would have slowly filled with rubbish over the next few centuries.

This wasn't the first D-shaped building to be found in Wessex. Its plan is very like that of a building with a plaster floor found by Hawley at Stonehenge. Just inside the south entrance to Stonehenge through the bank and ditch, a Station Stone once stood within a small mound known as the South Barrow. Beneath this barrow Hawley found an area of yellow chalk plaster, but did not realize that it was the floor of a building. The stone, which was removed after the mound was built around it, had been set into this floor.[16] Until 2005 no one really understood what Hawley had seen here and what he was trying to describe. Only after we excavated the house floors at Durrington Walls did Hawley's description make sense. We now realize that he found a house floor, actually inside Stonehenge.

This D-shaped structure under the South Barrow within Stonehenge was presumably a roofed gathering place for people entering and exiting the small south entrance; Hawley saw no trace of a fireplace in the house. An Aubrey Hole was sealed beneath the plaster floor, so the building has to be later than Stonehenge's first phase. Hawley could not tell if the plaster floor was the same date or earlier than the Station Stone. If it was the same date, then this southern Station Stone once sat at the centre of this building – the D-shaped structure must have been built around the stone. If the floor was earlier, then the stone might have been put up after the house was ruined.

Other than this D-shaped meeting house, are there any signs of houses at Stonehenge? The various excavations within the monument have uncovered many small postholes, but these do not seem to be the remains of buildings. They are most likely to indicate the presence of passageways, fencing, platforms and scaffolding. Some of the postholes are arranged in recognizable patterns. For example, one group of posts formed a passageway that led from the monument's centre towards the small south entrance through the bank and ditch, a route that passed the D-shaped building and the southern Station Stone.

If the D-shaped building and the post-lined passageway at Stonehenge were contemporary with each other, they could have provided 'backstage' facilities: was this where a special group of officiants gathered, before moving to the centre to greet their audience who had arrived from the northeast via the Stonehenge avenue? Perhaps the passageway – and a wooden screen through which it passed – was earlier than the sarsens? Unfortunately, there is no way of knowing, and the fixing of the Station Stones and this curious D-shaped building within Stonehenge's chronology is only loose.

When our project began not one of the hundreds of postholes at Stonehenge had been dated. All the excavations had shown that, where the postholes intersected with stoneholes, the stoneholes were always later, so it seemed a reasonable hypothesis that all the posts were put up before any stones were erected, during a phase of building in timber. When putting together the Stonehenge volume for English Heritage, Ros Cleal and her team therefore put all the postholes into a second phase of building. This was thought to have occurred about 2900–2400 BC, following the first phase (which consisted of just the earthen bank and ditch) and preceding the cremation burials and the standing stones.

Only one of the several hundred postholes has produced anything dateable – some pieces of pig ribs. We got permission from Salisbury Museum to date one of these bones and the radiocarbon results show that this particular posthole was used during the period 2580–2460 BC, at the end of the supposed 'posthole phase'.[17] Perhaps posts were put up at different times, right from the beginning of work at the site until well after the sarsens had gone up: stone-erection would have needed scaffolding posts, so the confusing mass of postholes at Stonehenge may have been dug on many different occasions over a long period of time.

WAS THIS WHERE THE STONEHENGE BUILDERS LIVED?

Less than 5 per cent of the area of Durrington Walls has been dug by archaeologists. Even so, it's now possible to put together the results of all past excavations and have an idea of what the Neolithic village looked like[1] – and of how it then developed into Britain's largest henge:

- The settlement was probably divided into four quarters, separated from each other by access routes to the south, east, north and west.
- There was an open space in the centre, flanked on its west by an arc of special houses, the middle one being set within its own terraced, circular enclosure with a pair of wooden 'trilithons'.
- On the east side of this open area was the Southern Circle of concentric rings of timber posts and on its north side, approached along a post-lined footpath, the Northern Circle.
- Within each quadrant there were perhaps as many as 250 houses, many of them terraced into the hillsides of the valley in which the settlement lay. With a nuclear family occupying each dwelling, this village could have housed a population of more than 4000.
- The east entrance out of the village, leading from the Southern Circle, was the most formalized, with a broad flint-surfaced avenue flanked by banks on which stood a pair of small pavilions.
- There were also small standing stones of sarsen lining the avenue on its north side, perhaps providing sightlines to the midwinter solstice sunrise.

- The north entrance of the settlement led to a group of flint mines (today underneath the houses and gardens of Durrington village).[2]
- The south entrance led to Woodhenge and a series of three or more timber circles beyond it.
- The west entrance led to the top of a rise called Larkhill. Today a military barracks, Larkhill is a prominent feature in the Stonehenge landscape, on the midsummer sunrise axis from Stonehenge.

In 1974 Alexander Thom and his sons found a small earthwork on Larkhill that they named Peter's Mound in memory of the astronomer C. A. 'Peter' Newham.[3] This was never a large enough landmark to be seen from Stonehenge, and neither is it prehistoric. Today it is infested with rabbit burrows, a dump of twentieth-century date. We wondered, though, whether other long-vanished monuments might have been sited on this hilltop. In 2005 Josh carried out excavations on Larkhill, in the field across the road from the odd mound, to see if this area had been used at the time of Stonehenge. Barring a handful of worked flints, he drew a complete blank. We were disappointed but the Ministry of Defence were pleased: the excavation did uncover early-twentieth-century bits and pieces that proved useful in helping to fill in the history of Salisbury Plain as a military training area.

So when was all this happening – when was the village at Durrington Walls inhabited? By selecting radiocarbon samples from layers whose stratigraphic relationships to each other are known, our dating specialist, Peter Marshall, has been able to use Bayesian statistics to refine the broad ranges of each date.[4] The settlement began in the period 2525–2470 cal BC and ended in 2480–2440 cal BC; it was thus probably occupied at some point within the years 2500–2460 BC. The avenue was built in the period 2505–2465 cal BC and the Southern Circle (in its Phase 2) in 2490–2460 cal BC. The first posts, of the Phase 1 timber circle, would have decayed after about sixty years, so the first timber circle on this spot – together with the adjacent hall – was probably built in the second half of the twenty-sixth century BC. These dates are unusually precise – it's rare to end up with a timespan as short as forty years for the date of any event in prehistory.

It would nonetheless be useful to get an even more precise idea of how long the settlement was in use. There are some clues about the length of time for which each house was inhabited. Each house had a group of nearby quarry pits, from which its occupants dug soliflucted chalk to resurface the floors and repair the walls. In some cases, these pits were dug so close together that a new one clipped the edge of one that had filled in. With up to a dozen such pits in a household cluster, it seems likely that this indicates the number of times that each house was repaired. Perhaps this was seasonal work, taking place once or even twice a year.

There is another clue in the plaster floors. Under the microscope soils expert Charly French of the University of Cambridge could see separate lines of plaster in his micromorphology sections through the house floors. These show separate plastering events – the large house had its floor re-plastered six times. Again, was this an annual event? There is no way to be sure but there is a good chance that each house was occupied for no longer than a decade within the years 2500–2460 BC.

Before the henge ditch and bank were built, someone decided to mark the perimeter of the village with a palisade of posts. Holes for these posts were found on the south side of the henge in 1952; here small posts were put up in a line and then covered by the henge bank.[5] Larger postholes of this palisade were excavated on the north side in 1968. On the east side we found a line of three large postholes, each with a ramp for the post to be inserted. What was odd was that these had never actually held posts. Each hole had a heap of dug-out chalk still sitting next to it; this should have gone back in the hole to pack the post in place but the holes had instead been filled in with a mix of clean chalk and rubbish.

Either the timbers for the east side never arrived or someone changed their mind about what to build here. Instead of erecting posts they dug a deep ditch and piled up the chalk in a bank outside it, so that the outer edge of the chalk bank reached to the line of redundant postholes. The position of the southern bank terminal outside the east entrance was marked by a heap of four antlers. This is a curious deposit – these particular antlers are unlikely to have been used as pick-axes as their curved tines would have made them useless as digging implements.

A group of antler picks deposited by Neolithic builders before they built the henge
bank of Durrington Walls.

The ditch around the henge, with its four openings, was dug out
sometime in the years 2480–2460 BC. The work would have been desperately slow. When you use a pick-axe today, you swing it over your head
and bring it down with huge force. That doesn't really work with an
antler pick. Experimental archaeologist Phil Harding has found that the
best way of digging with an antler pick is not just to hack away indis-
criminately at the solid chalk but to pick away at the small fissures and
lever out the chalk in blocks. A deep, narrow hole can then be enlarged
by undercutting its sides, causing the chalk to collapse. This works well
for the first 10 feet or so. Deeper down, the fissures in the chalk run out
and the rock is completely solid. Here the tip of the tine has to be hammered deep into the chalk until there is enough leverage to pull the pick
handle upwards and flake off an inch or two. We know that the deep
chalk was dug out like this because we have found the holes made by
hammering the tips of the picks into solid rock.

At Durrington Walls this laborious process would have continued for more than 5 metres, down to the bottom of the ditch. Digging this by hand with antler picks was a Herculean undertaking, cutting near-vertical sides down to a depth of 5.5 metres then hauling baskets of shattered chalk up ladders to the top, and then carrying the rubble a further 3 metres up to the top of the bank.

The geophysical survey shows that the diggers dug the Durrington ditch in segments, each about 40 metres long. The segments look in plan like a string of sausages, with narrow strips between wider segments, showing where the work teams had to break through to join up. One ditch segment on the south side was started and then filled back in and re-dug in a slightly different place: another occasion where someone in charge changed their mind, or realized that the diggers had made a mistake.

In 1967 Geoff's team of archaeologists dug right to the bottom of the henge ditch at the east entrance. There was so much soil to move that they needed mechanical help, especially at the start since the uppermost layers had few finds. They even lowered a mechanical digger into the ditch to help remove the lower sediments. The Durrington ditch is so wide and deep that it took more than 2000 years to silt up: at a level about halfway up the filled-in ditch, the archaeologists found the bones of a woman and two children buried there around 300 BC, during the Iron Age.[6]

At the end of the job the Neolithic work gang digging that segment of the ditch at the east entrance had literally downed tools, leaving them in a large heap on the bottom of the ditch. Geoff's team counted 57 antler picks.[7] With one person to hold the pick and another to hammer its tip into the chalk, there must have been at least 114 workers doing the digging, together with an unknown number of basket-carriers removing the rubble, probably using ladders made from notched tree-trunks. Perhaps 200 people had worked in this one segment. Add another 20 for support staff (someone must have been doing the Neolithic equivalent of making sandwiches and getting the kettle on), and we get a grand total of 220 men, women and children. There is space along the henge ditch for about 22 segments. That would suggest that almost 5000 people were engaged, in one way or another, in digging the ditch. Alternatively, it could have been dug sequentially by one gang, or just a few gangs, working their way around the whole perimeter.

During our own excavation we wanted to get a better idea of whether multiple work gangs were involved, so we dug a trench into the chalk bank on its east side at the division between two ditch segments. The group who had worked on the north side of this division had dug their 40-metre-long section of ditch slightly wider than those on either side of them, and had piled up their chalk slightly higher so that their mounded rubble interrupted the uniformity of the henge bank. We nicknamed this the 'maverick' segment. There was also something rather strange on the magnetometry plot. It showed that the mavericks had constructed some kind of enclosure here. There was something beneath the bank and therefore definitely built in the Neolithic, before the ditch-digging started. Whatever it was, its width was the same as the length of this ditch segment – so the two seemed to be related.

As we dug through the soil and rubble that form the henge bank we found many chalk blocks with round holes in them, made by hammering in the tips of antler picks. There was even a piece of a broken pick. We could see how the Neolithic diggers had worked by looking at the vertical sides of our excavation trench. The appearance of these sections, cutting through and exposing all the different layers of soil, told us that the mavericks had started to pile up their chalk before the gang responsible for the ditch segment immediately to their south had even started work. Their head-start had been only small, though: their pile was just waist-high when the other gang started. Clean chalk throughout showed that both groups had worked without break until the job was finished. Had they taken a few weeks off during the work, we would have seen silting lines and erosion surfaces in the bank's layers of heaped-up chalk rubble.

At the bottom of the henge bank we discovered a small, narrow ditch, running perpendicular to the henge ditch. Only 0.6 metres wide and 1.8 metres deep, it was filled with chalk and must have been dug out very shortly before the major ditch-digging began. This seems to have been a marker ditch, to show the boundary between the two segments. Just 2 metres south of it we found the cause of the strong magnetometry response: a bank of wood ash and domestic debris. We were presumably looking at a group – the mavericks – who had heaped up their rubbish against an outside perimeter, thereby defining their own space within the huge village before the ditch was dug.

At the bottom of the henge bank we also found a rubbish pit that had been created by digging into a very large hole left by the falling of a huge, ancient tree. This hole had slowly filled up with soil; in the turf on top of it we found a leaf-shaped arrowhead from the fourth millennium BC. The tree had been standing perhaps a thousand years earlier, before the first farmers. Long after it had fallen, around 2500 BC, the hollow left by its toppling seems to have been used as a boundary marker between two different groups within the village.

When we've been examining the finds from Durrington Walls one of the things we've looked for is any supporting evidence for the village, or the ditch-digging, having been divided into distinct zones or groupings. The potsherds do show a particular distribution pattern. The Grooved Ware pottery from the middens (rubbish heaps) on the south side of the avenue has an unusual style of decoration, in which the grooves form spiral patterns. Though we have found much more pottery north of the avenue, there is not a single piece of spiral decoration from that area.

Spiral-decorated pots were also found in the lower layers of the henge ditch on the south side of the avenue, so this type of pot was in use in the area south of the avenue both before and after the ditch-digging. More intriguingly, the spiral motif is also found on pots deposited into the pits dug into the decayed posts of the Southern Circle almost 200 years later, but only in its south quadrant. If spiral decoration was used by one particular group, this raises the possibility that a group specifically associated with one area of the village (and one segment of ditch-digging) might also have been associated with a particular segment of a monument such as the Southern Circle. Perhaps this also happened at Stonehenge, with different groups responsible for separate sectors – a portion of the outer ring of sarsens, say, and a trilithon or two.

If the ditch-digging was indeed done by gangs working simultaneously, then we have a window into Neolithic labour organization. This helps us think about how Stonehenge itself could have been built. At the ground level were fairly large groups, perhaps organized and co-ordinated by a middle level of 'management'. At the top, decisions must have been taken by a council or even by a chief and his associates.

Choosing the right vocabulary is difficult when talking about prehistoric social organization. In normal usage in anthropology, a 'tribe' usually numbers thousands of people, as does a 'clan'. It is more precise to use the less familiar term 'lineage group'. By this I mean a community that defines itself as the offspring of a single founding ancestor going back five or six generations (about 150 years). That is your grandparents' grandparents' parent or grandparent. If the first and each subsequent generation produces four children per family who themselves all reproduce at the same rate, numbers soon grow. The second generation has four new members, the next generation adds sixteen new members; such a lineage has over 250 members by the sixth generation.

Considering the logistics needed to keep our own fieldwork running smoothly, we could easily see that the Neolithic builders of Durrington Walls, and those of Stonehenge, would have *had* to have been well-organized. We had a digging team of 160 to 180 people, equivalent to one Neolithic ditch-digging work gang. Keeping the team functioning was a huge undertaking: we had six directors, a team of supervisors and their assistants (they called themselves 'middle management'), a back-up crew running domestic affairs and finds analysis at our campsite, and a public-outreach team. Imagine another twenty such teams all involved in the same project.

One of the mysteries of Durrington Walls has always been where everybody lived while they constructed the henge ditch and bank. Although we discovered a previously unknown village, all the settlement areas that we've found were in use *before* the ditch was dug. Perhaps the ditch-diggers lived somewhere else entirely, or perhaps they set up camp further out, beyond the perimeter of the old village. A few years ago archaeologists found a number of Neolithic pits while monitoring the installation of a water pipe along the modern road north of Durrington Walls.[8] Perhaps these pits were part of this later, henge-builders' settlement.

Although the enclosure of the henge covered the houses of the old village under the new ditch and bank, the central enclosed area was still used after the ditch and bank had been built. Although the new bank partly blocked the old avenue, encroaching on to its southern edge, there was continued use of this routeway too, even as its flint surface became overgrown and buried under a thin layer of soil. Around 2400

BC or later, new styles of pottery – known as Beakers – were deposited at the front of the decaying Southern Circle and in the nearby hollow where the large D-shaped building had once stood. We know from scientific analysis that Beakers in many parts of western Europe, including Britain, were used for alcoholic drinks such as mead or ale. Research by chemist Anna Mukherjee has shown that the Durrington Walls Beakers contained lipids (fatty acids) deriving from dairy products.[9] These could have been milk, butter or curds and whey; we cannot rule out the possibility that they were fermented to make an alcoholic drink.

Beakers were first used in Britain about 50 to 100 years after the Southern Circle was erected, but Grooved Ware remained in use. In about 2300 BC – at least 150 years after the posts were erected – the holes of the Southern Circle's decayed posts were dug out so that special deposits of Grooved Ware pottery (together with a few Beaker sherds), worked flints, bone tools and animal bones could be put in each of them. Some of these new pits were quickly filled in but others, such as the one with two human skulls, took hundreds of years to fill.

The radiocarbon dating results show that Durrington Walls in its various stages was in use for three centuries, from about 2600–2300 BC (not

A Beaker pot from a site called Naboth's Vineyard near Cowbridge in Wales. In both shape and decoration, it is like those found at Durrington Walls.

including some ephemeral traces of activity in the area during the previous millennium). What particularly interested us was the brief period of probably less than forty years (within 2500–2460 BC) during which it was the largest settlement anywhere in northwest Europe. Why did so many people come here? Where did they come from? Did they live here full time or did they come just for short stays at different seasons of the year?

We knew we could answer these questions if our excavations produced the right materials to analyse. The bones and teeth of the human skeleton, for example, preserve a record of our lives. Our diet can be reconstructed from microscopic wear-marks on our teeth and from levels of carbon and nitrogen isotopes in our bones.[10] Our tooth enamel forms in childhood: for the rest of our lives we carry in our teeth (until they all fall out) the traces of the geology and environment in which we lived when we were very young. By measuring levels of strontium, sulphur and oxygen isotopes in tooth enamel we can find out if people moved from one region to another after childhood and sometimes where it was that they moved from.

We would be able to do similar analyses on the bones and teeth of the animals that the inhabitants of the Durrington Walls village had eaten there. In certain cases our specialists in animal bones – faunal analysts – could tell us at what time of year the herds were culled. By studying the range of foods consumed and their seasonality, we could also work out whether this was a full-time or seasonal settlement.

All the human bones that Geoff's team found in 1967 have been radiocarbon-dated and have turned out to be much later than the time of the settlement. Our own excavations produced about 80,000 bones but of all these, only three are human. A broken femur (upper leg bone), a skull fragment and a toothless jaw date to the occupation of the village. The femur, belonging to an adult male, has two deep nicks in it.[11] Our human bone specialists, Andrew Chamberlain and Chris Knüsel, have identified these as arrow wounds received around the time of death.

To suffer one leg wound in which the arrow went right to the bone was unfortunate but to get two was really unlucky. I wondered how many other arrows had struck this individual – perhaps he'd been pierced like a pin cushion, a veritable prehistoric St Sebastian. Had he been executed by firing squad? And where was the rest of him anyway? Like the human skull and the mandible, but unlike the animal bones, this battered leg bone had been kicking around for a very long time. Perhaps it was somebody's trophy, kept for years until it was left in a pit with cow and pig bones and other food waste.

Archaeologists are never surprised to find stray fragments of human bone in pits and other contexts on prehistoric sites. It may seem strange to us to keep a bit of human body lying around the house – nowadays we take great care to dispose of bodies as definitively as possible, by burying them or scattering cremated ashes, and find it hard to imagine deliberately chopping bits off to keep. It was definitely different in prehistory. From the Neolithic to the Iron Age, odd pieces of bone and skull turn up in contexts that are nothing to do with burials and funerals, often in rubbish pits and ditches, along with domestic waste and animal bones. Human remains must have been scattered on the ground around houses and villages. Some of these bones do seem to have been kept as special objects, especially skulls and long bones. Human bones weren't 'sacred' in our terms, though they had some sort of meaning for prehistoric people. To find just three human bones from among 80,000 animal bones is surprising. It is actually a very low number for a prehistoric settlement.

Our faunal specialists, Umberto Albarella and Sarah Viner, have much more data to work with. Umberto has gone through the 1967 finds and discovered that most of the young pigs were killed at around nine months old. He can tell this by measuring the growth and wear on the teeth within the mandible. Reckoning that, like today, pigs farrowed only once a year in Britain's temperate climate (during the spring), Umberto has deduced that since the young pigs were killed at nine months, they were therefore killed in midwinter. To his surprise, when examining the faunal remains he found the tips of flint arrows embedded in pig bones: at least some of these animals were shot with arrows.[12] Then the pigs were barbecued or roasted – the ends of many of their limb bones have been scorched by flames while the meat was cooking.

Such arrow injuries might be expected were the pigs in question wild boar, but there wasn't a single wild pig among the 1967 bones – all were domesticates. Umberto knows that in some parts of the world – New Guinea, for example – domestic pigs are shot with arrows at point-blank range when a tribe or village is laying on a feast. His results don't tally with this possible scenario, however, because the wounds on the Durrington pigs are located in all parts of the skeleton, including the limbs and feet. This suggests that perhaps these pigs were shot from a distance. Maybe archers demonstrated their skills by bringing down squealing ranks of porkers in front of a crowd ready and eager for a huge pig-roast.

There is another curious feature of the animal bone remains. None of the animals were very young – no piglets and no calves. Umberto and Sarah have looked at animal bones from many different places and periods and know that bones of new-borns are frequent finds on prehistoric settlements. Such very young animals are not only more likely to die of natural causes, but also provide tender meat – in the form of suckling pig, for instance. This absence of new-borns (or neonates) can only mean that there was no year-round stock-breeding at Durrington Walls. The animals were brought in already grown and did not give birth here. This was a 'consumption site', a place for eating but not for raising animals.

Isotopic analysis of the animals' teeth can confirm this and tell us where the livestock might have come from. Together with isotope scientist Jane Evans, Sarah and Umberto have tested the teeth in 175 cattle mandibles.[13] Given that Durrington Walls and Stonehenge are surrounded by chalkland in every direction for at least twenty miles, they expected the cattle to have values consistent with their having been reared on chalk soils.

The results are fascinating. Very few of these animals had lived on chalk and the others lived fairly eventful lives, for cows. Some were reared in the far west, either in Devon and Cornwall or in west Wales. The others were from the lowlands, either west of Wessex or to its east. By slicing the tooth enamel more finely, Jane tracked their movements as young animals. Many had different histories, coming from different herds.

A similar picture is emerging with the enamel on the pigs' teeth. Although we initially thought that pig-tooth enamel is not strong enough to have remained uncontaminated by the chalk soil in which the animal remains lay, researcher Richard Madgwick working at Cardiff University found that some of the Durrington pigs were also raised off the chalklands. Herding pigs is never an easy business, but these had travelled at least twenty miles to Durrington.

The results so far have been so unexpected and so revealing that we've started a project to look at more of the pig teeth, and the results should be available in a couple of years' time. In the meantime we can conclude that the Durrington Walls village was the hub of a network that stretched across southern Britain to provide supplies to feed an army-sized population possibly bringing some animals from as far away as Scotland. The inhabitants of Durrington Walls would have required huge quantities of resources: antler picks to dig the holes, massive tree-trunks for building the timber circles as well as wood and reed thatch for their houses, ropes for manoeuvring timber posts into position, flint for tools, clay for making pots, reeds and withies for making baskets, skins for making bags, and meat and vegetables to feed everyone.

Some of these could be found locally. Reeds grew in beds along the river, clay could also be found along the river margins, and ropes were made out of lime bast, honeysuckle or twisted animal hides. Local flint mines north of the henge provided nodules of top-quality flint, but other items had to come from further away. Red deer were more numerous in Neolithic Britain than they are today but the number of antler picks required must have been in the thousands. The vast majority were naturally shed – red deer lose their antlers in spring – and would have been collected from the hills where the deer roamed.

We know that there was a certain amount of woodland in the Avon valley at the time that Durrington Walls was inhabited[14] but not the huge numbers of tall, mature trees needed to build the timber circles. These grew in canopy woodland where dense stands of oak, elm, ash and lime competed for light by growing long, straight trunks that branched out only towards their tops. Such woodland would have been found to the north, in the Vale of Pewsey, or further south along the Avon valley. Most of the larger trees must have been brought from at least ten miles away, whether floated down the river or hauled overland.

While pork, beef and dairy products provided animal protein, the

Durrington population also ate a variety of vegetable crops. Prehistoric plant remains can survive for thousands of years but are hard to recover; they survive only in heavily waterlogged places (where they haven't been able to rot) or if they were charred by fire in prehistory. Such remains are usually too small and fragile for the digger to retrieve them directly from the soil. They are usually found by 'flotation': like the wet-sieving for small artefacts and bone fragments, soil samples are washed through sieves (with very fine mesh sizes of 1mm and 300 microns) to catch seeds and other fragments.

Ellen Simmons, the project's specialist in carbonized plant remains (palaeoethnobotany), has found burnt fragments of apples, hazelnuts and tubers on the Durrington house floors and in the yards. The apples would have been small and sour – more of a crab apple than a Cox's Orange Pippin – perhaps best used for making cider. Hazelnuts are found on virtually all Neolithic settlements; they were evidently a dietary staple and might well have been managed in coppiced woodlands as an autumnal crop. Various wild plants, such as pignut, silverweed, dande-lion and burdock, have edible tubers and would have been easily collectable and relatively simple to store and transport.[15] Ellen has also discovered the burnt remains of a starchy 'cake', probably made from crushed fruits of wild species such as hawthorn.

Ellen found burnt grains of wheat within the village. They are from southwest of the avenue; none are from the house floors or yard sur-faces on the northeast side of the avenue. Does this restricted distribution of cereal remains mean that wheat was hardly used at Durrington Walls?

More than twenty years ago archaeologists noted that many Neolithic sites in Britain had much more evidence for wild-plant use than for domesticated cereals.[16] They concluded that cereals were not common and, in this period, people still mostly relied upon wild-plant foods, just as their hunter-gatherer forebears had. Other archaeologists then pointed out that this was all to do with bias of recovery: hazelnut shells are very likely to have been thrown in the fire, with some of them becom-ing carbonized, but cereals get burnt only by accident. So it is only in extraordinary circumstances that we find carbonized prehistoric cereal grains. The state of knowledge at present is that well over a hundred

Neolithic sites in Britain have now yielded carbonized cereal remains, so they are not as rare as previously thought.[17]

The rarity of such crop remains on a site such as Durrington Walls that has been so carefully sampled, with thousands of litres of soil sent off for flotation, is still not unusual compared with other Neolithic settlements. It probably reflects the poor survival of cereals (with few of the precious grains ending up burnt on the fire) for the archaeologist to find. Cereals might well have been more common at this village than appears to be the case.

Another ticklish question concerns the tools that were used at the Durrington settlement. Among 80,000 worked flints Ben Chan, the project's flint specialist, has found just one small fragment of a flint axe. The 1967 team found fragments of just two among almost 10,000 Neolithic worked flints.[18] By comparison with other Neolithic sites with similar quantities of worked flints, there should have been at least sixty axes and axe fragments. There was plenty of carpentry going on at Durrington but there's no visible trace of the axes used to chop and shape the timbers for either houses or post circles. Were axes and their broken fragments carefully collected up and dumped elsewhere? Or were axes used only by people living in other parts of the settlement not yet excavated? Neither of these explanations is at all convincing. There are three pieces of circumstantial evidence that this Stone Age culture had in fact got hold of some new technology.

When people were living at Durrington Walls, copper had already been in use in eastern Europe for thousands of years, since about 5500 BC. That part of Europe has a distinct Copper Age (the Chalcolithic) between the Neolithic and Bronze Age.[19] It has been generally thought that ancient Britons changed from using stone to using bronze without a noticeable intermediate stage, though archaeologists now speak of a brief Copper Age (or Chalcolithic) in Britain between 2500 and 2200 BC.

It took an exceedingly long time for copper metallurgy to spread across Europe. By 3200 BC it had only got as far as the Alps: the man nicknamed Ötzi the Iceman by his finders, who ended up frozen into a high-altitude glacier, had a copper axe. Mysteriously, copper metallurgy then apparently took about 700 years to spread as far as Britain. That is painfully slow progress, only about a mile a year.

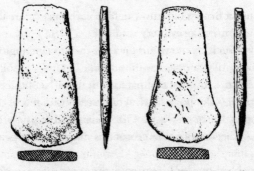

Copper axe-heads from Castletown Roche in Ireland. These are similar to the earliest metal axes used in Britain.

The earliest copper in Britain is found in Beaker burials, a new burial rite that appeared around 2400 BC, and many archaeologists have assumed that copper was introduced by these immigrant Beaker people, who found out after their arrival how rich in deposits of copper ore Britain and Ireland actually were. But perhaps copper tools were already in use before the Beaker immigrants arrived. Copper must have been very valuable at first, so it is unlikely that people would have casually let it fall into the kinds of places where archaeologists would find it. Copper tools would have been both highly prized and recyclable, so there's no reason why they should have ended up in the ground.

Archaeologists have often wondered whether copper axes were actually much use. They are very pretty, shiny objects, but were they any good for practical tasks such as chopping down trees? Unless copper is mixed with tin to form bronze (which doesn't seem to have happened in Britain until about 2200 BC), it's quite soft and its edge blunts easily. Perhaps copper axes and other objects were symbolic items, more like jewellery than tools, made to impress rather than be used.

One of the documentary crews filming our excavations around Stonehenge decided to find out. They gave Phil Harding, *Time Team*'s well-known local archaeologist, a hafted copper axe and a medium-sized tree to chop down. Phil had often used flint axes for felling trees and was suspicious that the copper axe wouldn't be anywhere near as good. To his surprise not only was it easier to use than its flint counterpart, being lighter, but it also cut more quickly. Stone axes have to chop with oblique strokes so the axeman's cut into the tree is very broad, resembling the chewing of a beaver. Copper axes can be used to cut at a more perpendicular angle. You just have to stop every now and again to hammer out the blunted edge.

Archaeologists can get very hot and bothered about exactly when copper metallurgy started in Britain, and there has been a reluctance by some to see it pushed back any earlier than 2400 BC, or fifty years earlier at most. There are few hard facts but some circumstantial evidence now suggests that the use of copper in Britain does go back to before the arrival of the Beaker people. When we dug into Durrington's henge bank we discovered that, while some of the chalk from digging the ditch bears the marks of antler picks, two chalk blocks have long thin, V-shaped cuts into them, as if made by the chopping motion of an axe. Yet the cuts are too thin to have been formed by a stone axe. It seems likely that only a metal axe could have produced such a thin groove. We can date the ditch-digging to 2480–2460 BC so have a clue that someone was using a copper axe slightly earlier than expected.[20]

New research on the metal composition of Beaker copper in Britain also hints at a start about a century or two earlier than 2400 BC. Peter Bray, a researcher at Oxford University working on Britain's earliest metals, suspects that some of the heavily worn copper daggers found in Beaker burials might have been heirlooms already ancient when buried as grave goods. While some daggers and axes were made from copper dug out of the mines at Ross Island in southern Ireland from about 2400 BC onwards, Peter thinks that the manufacture of other daggers and axes with a slightly different chemical composition could have started earlier, perhaps a century or two before.

Another tell-tale clue is the change in the scale of tree-felling after about 2500 BC. Monuments prior to that date were constructed using timbers that were generally no thicker than 30 or so centimetres. After that date, we find monuments built of timbers up to a metre in diameter.[21] This change is perfectly shown in the size difference between the timbers used in the Southern Circle's first phase and those of its second phase. Perhaps what was special about that moment around 2500 BC was that copper axes became available in sufficient numbers in Britain to fell much larger trees with greater ease. A great gathering place such as the Durrington Walls village might have been just the right venue for people from different regions to discuss new innovations, show off their prized new copper tools and swap ideas about new technology. Perhaps it actually helped to spread the use of copper across Britain.

So, can we resolve the question of whether this was a seasonal gathering place or a permanently occupied settlement? Hazelnuts and apples are gathered in autumn but can be stored through the winter. The pig-culling tells us that people were here, feasting on pork, at midwinter – most likely around the midwinter solstice, given the midwinter sunrise orientation of the Southern and Northern Circles.

Was the henge ditch also dug in midwinter, when it would seem too cold to be outdoors? A regular visitor to our dig each summer was Jake Keen, an 'ancient technologist' who has studied traditional rural trades, such as iron-smelting, in Britain and other parts of the world. He knows, for example, how to make ropes from the bast of lime trees. He is also very interested in finding out how Neolithic people dug such deep ditches. Living on the chalkland of Cranborne Chase, south of Salisbury Plain, he has noticed that chalk is softer and easier to work when it is wet. It would have been easier to hammer in those antler picks during wet periods. Perhaps the ditch-digging and henge-building were done in the wetter months of winter, a time of slack in the agricultural year.

While there's definite evidence for gatherings at Durrington in the winter months, there is also new evidence that people came here during the summer too. Umberto's team of animal bone specialists has identified a second peak in pig mortality about six months after the first, indicating that there was feasting in the summertime as well as the winter. Other evidence for this summertime presence is provided by the discovery of chemical residues of dairy fats in the pots. Before our agricultural revolution, cows produced milk in quantity during the spring and summer months only, after calving. So the milk pots deposited at the front of the Southern Circle, at the end of the midsummer-sunset-oriented avenue, are also evidence that people were here in the summertime. It's reasonable to assume that they came to celebrate the midsummer solstice as well as the midwinter solstice.

Why did people come to Durrington Walls? There were the timber circles to erect, feasting and general partying, but perhaps people actually came here to work on a nearby construction site: a great stone circle just downriver. We needed to find out how closely we could date the stages of construction at Stonehenge, and whether any of these stages coincided with the settlement at Durrington Walls.

8

THE GREAT TRILITHON AND THE
DATE OF THE SARSENS

Standing stones can be dated only by what is found in the holes that they stand in. We have to be sure that whatever we're dating was put in the hole before the stone went in, and that it was fresh when it was deposited. The best objects for dating are the antlers used as pick-axes by Neolithic builders, who had the fortunate habit of deliberately leaving behind an occasional tool in the pit they'd just dug.

The radiocarbon dates obtained from antler picks found in the holes for the Stonehenge sarsen circle and the sarsen trilithons have always been problematic because they don't seem to make sense. The date from the great trilithon's hole (2440–2100 BC) is later than the dates (2620–2480 BC) from another trilithon (Stones 53–54) and from the sarsen circle (Stone 1). When in the 1990s Ros Cleal and her team drew together all the available information about Stonehenge, these dates seemed to suggest only two possible scenarios:

- The great trilithon was built *after* the circle of sarsens enclosing it. This would have been possible only if part of the circle was first taken down, or if part of the circle hadn't yet been finished, thereby leaving a big enough gap through which these massive stones could have been manoeuvred into the centre and set upright. No one has ever been comfortable with this explanation because the engineering problem is so huge.

Or:

- The dates can't be trusted. Is there something wrong with the dates for the antler picks found in the sarsen circle and around Trilithon 53–54? Perhaps these antlers were antiques that were no good for digging but had been carefully kept for generations and thus were already old when they were deposited in the stoneholes. This is not as far-fetched as it might sound: there are many prehistoric instances of old objects being kept as curios or treasures.

Most archaeologists thought the latter explanation more likely: the great trilithon just cannot be later than the sarsen circle because of the logic of construction, so therefore the antlers that produced the earlier dates of 2620–2480 BC must have been antiques when they were buried. For those who accepted this argument, the trilithons and sarsen circle were put up in 2440–2100 BC. I'd never been happy with either interpretation, because both meant ignoring dates simply because they were inconsistent and didn't fit expectations. It was time to go back to the records and re-examine where the antler picks in the stoneholes actually came from.

Atkinson found two antler picks near Stone 56, one of the uprights of the great trilithon. This is one of the two longest stones at Stonehenge, set 2.4 metres into the ground. He thought that the antlers came from a 'ramp' sloping down to the stonehole.[1] This ramp, Atkinson argued, would have been used to tip the foot of the stone into its hole before the sarsen was hauled upright. On re-examining the plans, though, we became very doubtful of this interpretation. The other Stonehenge sarsens don't appear to have ramps leading into their stoneholes, so why did this stone have one? (And a sizeable one at that – the area Atkinson called the 'ramp' is more than 5 metres long.)

In addition, Atkinson's explanation of how the stone was put in place using the ramp is extremely convoluted. Megalithic stones can be erected most easily by being brought to the chosen spot on a wooden cradle and then simply hauled and levered upward to the vertical. Atkinson, however, was convinced that this huge stone must have been brought in on its side and then lifted up: that is, raised from its *narrow* side rather than from its *wide* front. At first glance this seems feasible, if awkward, but when I looked more closely at Atkinson's plans it became evident that this scenario would have been impossible.

The 'ramp' is simply too long – it could never have guided the stone into its hole. It supposedly enabled the builders to tilt their stone on the fulcrum of the pit's edge, to tip its foot into the bottom of the hole. But we know exactly how long the stone is and it just couldn't have been tipped down into the stonehole from this ramp: the measurements don't allow this possibility because the ramp's edge is too far away from the stonehole for the stone to tip into it.

More importantly, the ramp doesn't actually lead to the stonehole at all.[2] Atkinson's trench, dug in 1956, did not uncover the stonehole itself – that was dug by Gowland in 1901. Atkinson's trench stopped just 40 centimetres from Gowland's trench and uncovered only the west end of the feature Atkinson calls the 'ramp' in his trench. By matching what he had found to Gowland's account of features found in the earlier trench, Atkinson extrapolated that the ramp should continue to the edge of the stonehole. Unfortunately he didn't read Gowland's account closely enough.

Gowland had indeed picked up the edge of what Atkinson later reckoned to be a 'ramp', but this feature in Gowland's trench didn't lead directly into the stonehole. Atkinson's 'ramp' is off-centre to the stonehole and connects only with the north side of the hole: the stone could not have been erected from the supposed 'ramp'.

It seems that Atkinson mistook the western end of a large and deep pit to be a sloping ramp leading to Stone 56, the west upright of the great trilithon. What Gowland, and then Atkinson, actually found was simply a very large hole.

Someone dug a huge pit into the centre of Stonehenge on the west and north sides of the great trilithon – a pit as deep as the bottoms of its stones. Perhaps this was what ultimately led to their destabilization and caused the great trilithon to fall. Gowland had excavated at the foot of its only surviving upright because it too was expected to topple, and excavation was needed prior to intrusive remedial work.

The antler picks found here are *not*, therefore, associated with the building of a ramp for the great trilithon's erection; they're picks deposited in a large pit dug *after* the trilithon was erected. It is this pit that dates to 2440–2100 BC, not the trilithon stonehole: the picks belong to the pit but the pit *doesn't* belong to the trilithon. We know that this pit was filled back up to the top in prehistory, within a century or so, because a bluestone was later set into it as part of the inner oval of bluestones, dated by an antler pick to 2270–1930 BC.

Why did the Neolithic builders dig this pit? Its north and east edges have never been located (no one has ever dug in that area) but it extended at least as far north as the Altar Stone, where William Cunnington encountered part of a deep hole. This pit must have been

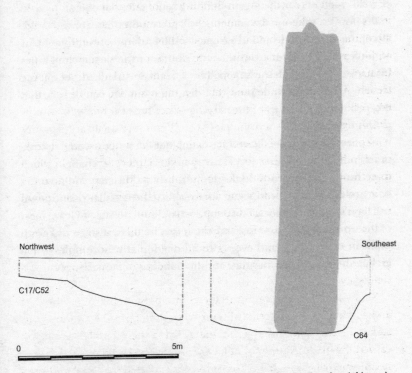

Reconstructed profile of the great trilithon Stone 56 in its pit, showing that Atkinson's presumed 'ramp' is too long to have been a construction ramp for erecting the stone. The numbers refer to Atkinson's and Gowland's trenches.

huge, at least 12 metres long, 5 metres wide and 2.4 metres deep. Its purpose is a complete mystery: it is far too deep to be explained as simply part of the works undertaken by the Neolithic builders during the rearrangement of the small bluestones within the centre of Stonehenge. Its upper fills contained all sorts of later finds, so it was probably dug into millennia later by the Duke of Buckingham's men in 1620 and 200 years after that by Colt Hoare.

The dates from the antler picks have, of course, been used until now to date the great trilithon; the realization that they actually belong to another, later pit means that we can discard those dates from the construction sequence of the sarsen circle and trilithons. Instead, the date of 2620–2480 BC for the sarsen-building is the one that counts.

It's possible that one day someone will get another date for the building of the sarsen circle and trilithons. In 1964 Atkinson found the tip of an antler pick embedded in the side of one of the sarsen stoneholes (Stone 9) – it had evidently snapped off as someone tried to lever out the chalk wall of the pit while they were digging it out. We can be sure that this pick was in use during the digging of the hole for Stone 9.

Unfortunately this surviving piece of antler is very small: at 1.4 grams, it may provide enough collagen for dating but the process would destroy pretty much the whole object. The tip and the piece of chalk in which it was found are currently on display in Salisbury Museum and no one's going to touch them until scientists are able to use smaller quantities of collagen to obtain radiocarbon dates – when it will possible to leave most of the tip intact for future researchers. It may be then, at some unknown point in the future – and even without digging any more holes – that archaeologists get another date for the building of Stonehenge.

9

MYSTERIOUS EARTHWORKS: THE LANDSCAPE OF STONEHENGE

Until the 1970s archaeologists had a tendency to study each site in isolation, rather than looking at landscapes of monuments that should be treated as a whole. Stonehenge was a prime candidate for trying out a new approach to ancient landscapes that paid more attention to the associations between sites. It is surrounded by prehistoric monuments of all kinds and scatters in the plough soil of worked flints and pottery. In 1982 Julian Richards, at that time a project officer for the newly formed commercial company Wessex Archaeology, started a landscape survey called the Stonehenge Environs Project.[1] He hoped to understand prehistoric use of the landscape over time, from the Mesolithic to the Iron Age, by systematically recovering flints and potsherds from ploughed fields around Stonehenge and digging exploratory trenches into a wide range of nearby prehistoric sites in order to date them.

The results were spectacular. Some 102,175 pieces of worked flint were collected from the surfaces of ploughed fields by teams walking in 50-metre-long transects at 25-metre intervals. This is a type of sampling. By spreading a 'field-walking' team at consistent, regular intervals, a survey project picks up only a proportion of the total finds, and cannot accidentally select only the most 'interesting' items from a field. From the quantities picked up, and the surface area sampled, one can extrapolate the total quantity of finds likely to be present in the topsoil.

For the Stonehenge Environs Project the sampling strategy used meant that about a tenth of the total number of surface finds was picked up. Flints on the surface of a ploughed field represent just the tip of the iceberg – amounting to an estimated 2 per cent of the overall number – with many more lying within the soil beneath. Thus the likely total of worked flint in the fields around Stonehenge in 1982 was about 51 million pieces. The survey area stretched from Durrington Walls southwards to Lake, west to Normanton Down and north to Larkhill, covering some 752 hectares. Unlike the landscape surrounding Avebury or other major henge complexes, the Stonehenge landscape was full of the debris of prehistoric activity.

Most of the worked flints found by Julian Richards' field-walking team could not be closely dated. People have worked flint in Britain from the Palaeolithic (up to 10,000 years ago), through the Mesolithic (8000–4000 BC), the Neolithic (4000–2500 BC), the Copper Age (2500–2200 BC), the Bronze Age (2200–750 BC) and even into the Iron Age (750 BC–AD 43). Only the diagnostic items such as arrowheads can be dated to particular periods. There are also changes in flint-making technology, from long blades and microliths (tiny flakes and blades) in the Early Mesolithic to small blades and microliths in the Late Mesolithic. Microliths then went out of use. During the Neolithic, blades were common in the fourth millennium but were made less often after 3000 BC.

Richards could see that there had been a great deal of prehistoric activity in the hills and dry valleys around Stonehenge, with some areas filled with flintwork. Working out when that activity happened was harder. When potsherds are found in association with flints they, like arrowheads, are more closely dateable. Of course, this is not a secure way of dating a flint scatter, since the pottery may derive from activity much later or much earlier than the flint-knapping. Similarly, arrowheads might well have been fired and lost a long way from home.

Two types of flintworking are entirely missing from the Stonehenge Environs Project's recovery. These are the large-blade technologies of the Upper Palaeolithic and Early Mesolithic and the microliths of the Early and Late Mesolithic. There is simply no trace of these hunter-gatherers on the chalk plateau of Stonehenge, either on its hills or in its dry valleys. This is puzzling because we know they were here: the evidence is in the Stonehenge car park.

The Mesolithic posts under the visitors' car park

In 1966 increasing visitor numbers to Stonehenge made it necessary to enlarge the car park. An archaeological dig in advance of the construction work was carried out by Lance and Faith Vatcher. Major and Mrs Vatcher were local archaeologists who conducted seven rescue excavations at and around Stonehenge as well as others elsewhere in Wiltshire. At first sight there seemed to be nothing of much interest in the area of the car-park extension, just a tree-hole and a line of three rather large postholes east of it, in an east–west line. With no finds in these postholes other than a burnt bone and some charcoal, the Vatchers concluded that they probably dated to the time of Stonehenge.[2]

Susan Limbrey, an environmental archaeologist at Birmingham University, examined the charcoal from these postholes in her laboratory and discovered that it was pine. This was curious because pollen analysis shows that pine did not grow on the chalklands of southern England in the Late Neolithic and Bronze Age. There was enough charcoal from two of the postholes for radiocarbon dates and the results confirmed her suspicions. One of the posts dated to 8820–7730 BC and the other to 7480–6590 BC.[3] These posts were erected during the Early Mesolithic, around 4000 years before Stonehenge was built, when the inhabitants of Salisbury Plain would have lived in small, mobile groups with no fixed campsites, hunting game and birds, and gathering wild plants and fruit.

The dates of the Mesolithic posts do not overlap, and it's therefore possible to conclude that the posts were not contemporary with each other. When dating the burnt wood of a tree, however, everything depends on which tree-rings are dated. A pine-tree trunk 0.75 metres in diameter, like the ones in the car park, is likely to have accumulated 200–300 annual growth rings. It looks as though the bases of the two tree trunks were charred before they were erected, so the charcoal could come from rings growing at any point in the tree's life.

In 1988 further work in the car park unearthed another Mesolithic pit, about 100 metres east of the others. This was the same size as the three found in the Sixties and contained pine charcoal dating to 8090–7690 BC, but it may not have held a post. Many layers of soil filled the pit neatly, one after the other, very different from the stratigraphy left by a

A reconstruction of the Early Mesolithic posts (today under the Stonehenge car park where they are marked by white circles on the tarmac) with the solstice-aligned chalk ridges in the background.

decayed post or by a post later removed: if this pit *had* once held a post, then when that post was removed the entire fill of the pit had been dug out and then filled in again. Nonetheless, it was further demonstration that something important was happening here long before Neolithic people started building Stonehenge.

You can read in the textbooks that hunter-gatherers do not and never have built monuments. All over the world the earliest monumentality is associated with agricultural societies. There all sorts of reasons why this is so. Generally, hunter-gatherer societies are less able to produce a surplus that can be used to feed people over the long periods required for monument-building. In contrast, the slack periods in the agricultural cycle, between planting and harvesting, provide dead time when farmers' labour can be mobilized. The experience of clearing cultivable land – felling trees and moving stones – provides the know-how to take on moving big trees and rocks. The need to lay claim to a specific territory is more important for sedentary farmers than for more mobile hunter-gatherers. So the Stonehenge pine posts were a bolt from the blue for archaeologists and anthropologists. As late as 2004 some specialists in Mesolithic-era hunter-gatherers were still arguing that no Mesolithic societies built monuments, despite the fact that the Stonehenge results were published almost ten years earlier.

The Stonehenge posts are also very early in global terms. At places such as Göbekli Tepe and Jericho in the Near East we have the earliest monuments in the world. Jericho has a large stone-built tower around 10,000 years old,[4] whereas the earlier site of Göbekli Tepe in southeastern Turkey consists of large buildings filled with carved standing stones.[5] These date to the late tenth and ninth millennia BC – about a thousand years or so earlier than the eighth millennium, when the posts were put up on Salisbury Plain.

What were the Stonehenge posts for? It has been suggested that they might have been totem poles, perhaps like those of the Northwest Coast of America. The people there were also hunter-gatherers when Captain Cook visited them in the late eighteenth century, although their sedentary lifestyle and organized management of salmon-fishing makes them rather atypical. The Stonehenge posts' east–west alignment might have been referencing the tree-hole to their west, or rather the tree itself. And the posts lined up towards the highest point in the landscape, Beacon Hill to the east.

It would be a bit of a coincidence if the one part of Stonehenge's vicinity to be stripped for building work – the car-park excavation involved an area measuring only 150 metres by 50 metres – were the only spot where these features might be found. Perhaps such pits and post-holes are much more widely distributed around Stonehenge than anyone has realized. Was there something important in the vicinity of Stonehenge that would explain why this place was so special for prehistoric people at such different points in time? And, since they have left few other remains of their presence on Salisbury Plain, where did the Mesolithic builders of these posts live? In later seasons we would find some answers to these questions, but by 2007 we were investigating other monuments in Stonehenge's neighbourhood.

The Neolithic long barrows

After the Mesolithic posts nothing was built in the Stonehenge area until after 4000 BC. The earliest of the Neolithic monuments are the long barrows. Long barrows are mounds constructed of earth and subsoil (chalk, in the case of those on Salisbury Plain) dug out from parallel ditches on

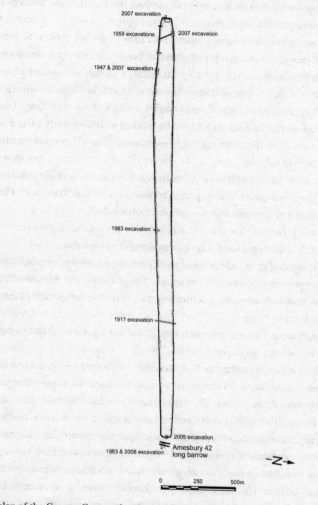

A plan of the Greater Cursus, showing the Amesbury 42 long barrow and the locations of all excavations between 1917 and 2008.

either side of the mound; typically the mound covers a mortuary structure of wood or stone containing the bones of the dead. The tomb of West Kennet, near Avebury, is the largest example in Wessex of just such a stone chamber inside a long mound.

Other long barrows seem not to have contained any structures other than flimsy wattle fences put up to act as barriers between sections of the mound while it was being built. Although long barrows are indubitably tombs for the human dead, it's common to find the skulls and bones of cattle inside, often mixed with the human bones; in a few cases excavated long barrows have turned out to contain no human bones at all. There are more than 2,000 long barrows known in Britain, of which only a fraction has been archaeologically excavated with modern methods. These long barrows mostly date to within the period 3800–3400 BC, the Early Neolithic. There are about fifteen known long barrows around Stonehenge.[6] Unfortunately, we know very little about them because so few have been investigated in modern times. None has yet produced a date earlier than 3600 BC so it may be that this part of Salisbury Plain was late in adopting this island-wide style of tomb.

Robin Hood's Ball causewayed enclosure

The other type of monument built in this early part of the Neolithic was the 'causewayed enclosure'.[7] These are areas of ground, often several hundred metres across, surrounded on all sides by ditches with internal banks. There are many gaps in the ditches, where solid ground leads to and from the interior: these form the 'causeways' that give their name to this type of site.

Early in the first investigations of such sites, archaeologists realized that these enclosures have too many entrances to have served a defensive purpose. Subsequent work on examples such as Hambledon Hill and Windmill Hill (both quite near Stonehenge, one to the southwest and the other near Avebury) has confirmed their use as ceremonial gathering-places.[8] There is one causewayed enclosure in the immediate Stonehenge area, lying almost 3 miles (4 kilometres) to the northwest: the very curiously named Robin Hood's Ball. Very little work has been done on it but dating of old finds indicates that it was in use around 3650 BC, making it among the latest of the causewayed enclosures to be built in Britain.

The Greater Cursus

The largest prehistoric earthwork in the Stonehenge area is known as the Cursus, an unusual monument that was first recorded almost 300 years ago. The antiquarian William Stukeley was a good landscape archaeologist: not only did he survey the avenue leading from Stonehenge, but he also found another avenue-like earthwork half a mile to the north. While he deduced that Stonehenge was prehistoric, Stukeley thought that this long, straight monument must have been built by the Romans. He thought it could have been a racecourse, and therefore named it the Cursus – from the Latin word for a chariot-racing track.

The Cursus is 1.75 miles long, east–west, and consists of two parallel banks and ditches (with the ditch on the outside, unlike a henge enclosure), culminating in banks and ditches at either end. It appears to have had no entrance and its western end was separated from the rest of the Cursus by a ditch running at an angle, northwest–southeast. The west end of the Cursus sits on a high saddle of chalk, from where its route leads eastwards down a gradual incline into Stonehenge Bottom, the dry valley (which might have flooded annually in the form of a 'winterbourne') that runs north–south past the eastern side of Stonehenge. The Cursus continues up the other side of Stonehenge Bottom, terminating at its eastern end on a high ridge where sits a Neolithic long barrow (a monument known to archaeologists by the very uninspiring name 'Amesbury 42').

When our project began, in 2004, the Cursus had been known about for 300 years and still no one had established its date or purpose – though everyone did agree that it had been built during the Neolithic. When Julian Richards excavated two trenches into it in 1983, as part of his Stonehenge Environs Project, there had already been digs by three previous excavators.

Percy Farrer was the first of these, cutting a narrow trench through it in 1917, shortly before he put a trench through Durrington Walls.[9] In 1947 J.F.S. Stone dug a length of the long south side of the Cursus and found an antler pick in what he described as an 'embayment', a possible wide 'niche' in the bank.[10] Much later, Julian Richards had this pick radiocarbon-dated; it was from the same period as Durrington Walls and Stonehenge's main phase, but Julian was not convinced that it dated the Cursus' construction because the embayment was possibly a later pit cut into the silted-up ditch.

Stone's other interesting find was a small chip of Welsh sandstone, similar to a type of sandstone out of which two of the Stonehenge bluestones are formed. Unfortunately Stone could not tell when his sandstone chipping entered the ditch – whether it had been at its construction or much later, when it had filled up – but he knew that other bluestone chippings lay in the field just to the south of the Cursus. William Young had found some on its ploughed surface some years earlier and Stone plotted another seven.

In 1959 Patricia Christie excavated at the west end of the Cursus and discovered that the terminal ditch was 1.5 metres deep, nearly a metre deeper than the side ditches.[11] She found a layer of flint-knapping debris at the bottom of this end ditch but nothing else that could allow it to be dated. Intriguingly, inside the west end of the Cursus she found a pit containing pine charcoal. In retrospect we can be fairly sure that this was another Mesolithic pit, although it has not been radiocarbon-dated.

Julian Richards' trenches in 1983, on the Cursus itself and into the ditch of the long barrow at its east end, were similarly unforthcoming in terms of dateable finds.[12] Although his survey team had found high densities of flints and prehistoric sherds to the north of the Cursus, the monument itself seemed to contain no vestiges of human use or occupation. Julian had more luck with another monument, the Lesser Cursus, which lies just to the northwest of the Cursus.[13] This was identified long after Stukeley's time and is much smaller, being only 400 metres long by 60 metres wide. The main Cursus is often called the Greater Cursus to distinguish it from this smaller monument.

The Lesser Cursus

Like the Greater Cursus, the Lesser Cursus also runs east–west but its east end has no terminal ditch, and it is cut in half by a ditch running north–south across its centre. In his excavation here Julian found antler picks that had been left at the bottom of the ditch and was able to date the construction to the second half of the third millennium BC, between 3600 and 3000 BC. It is older than Stonehenge. But why are there two cursuses so close together? Did one replace the other? Or were they built and used by two different groups?

The eastern ditch of the Amesbury 42 long barrow, excavated by Julian Thomas' team in 2008.

Digging the Greater Cursus and its long barrow

In 2007 and 2008 the other Julian – Julian Thomas – had the opportunity to try his luck with the enigmatic Greater Cursus and its long barrow. From the experience of archaeologists excavating the ditches of cursuses and long barrows elsewhere in Britain, Julian knew that narrow trenches weren't going to produce the required antler picks on the ditch bottom. To stand a reasonable chance of success we needed to dig long sections of ditch. Balanced against this was the necessity to dig as little as possible, thereby leaving as much as we could untouched for the future.

The National Trust owns both sites and for a long time their archaeologists weren't happy with what we proposed; it was too much to sacrifice. After months of wrangling and discussions we finally agreed a compromise: four trenches into the Cursus ditch – the largest to be no more than 10 metres long – three into the Cursus interior, and a single trench, also 10 metres long, into the long-barrow ditch. This was more of a gamble than we wanted to take but we had no option.

None of the smaller trenches produced any antler picks but Julian was lucky with the two larger trenches. The one at the west end of the Cursus appeared very disappointing at first. The upper layers here had been badly disturbed by digging and dumping when there was an army camp in the area during the First World War. From the empty .303 bullet casings dating to 1940 and 1942 it seemed the military presence had continued during the Second World War. As Julian dug lower into the ditch, however, he could see that the layers at the bottom were undisturbed. Then, right in the middle of the trench, he found the broken-off tip of a large antler pick, lying on the very bottom of the ditch. Its radiocarbon date of 3660–3370 BC places the construction of the Greater Cursus in the same date range as the Lesser Cursus.[14]

Re-opening Stone's 'embayment' into the south ditch and extending sideways from it, we could see that it was indeed a later pit; in fact it was one of two pits cut into the partially filled-in ditch. This south ditch had then been cleaned out during the Early Bronze Age and had again filled up with fine silt, presumably deriving from Bronze Age ploughing of the grassland around Stonehenge. On the north side of the Cursus the ditch had also been dug into after it had partly filled up. The angled ditch we found here proved to be a Bronze Age field boundary, partitioning off what was almost a ready-made field demarcated on three sides by the west end of the Cursus.

On the long barrow our scaled-down plans allowed for a 10-metre-long trench into the 60-metre-long ditch on the barrow's east side. We decided to place it immediately north of Julian Richards' 2-metre-wide trench into the ditch,[15] reckoning that this would help to increase the odds of finding an antler pick. Excavation trenches are always refilled when a dig is over. The location of a trench remains visible on the ground surface for some years but, providing the 'backfilling' and re-turfing are done well, it eventually disappears, becoming indistinguishable from the surrounding area. Julian Richards' trench had been dug more than twenty years earlier, so we were relying on a plan to determine where it had once been.

As we started digging we soon discovered a large rectangular pit. We had landed on the edge of Julian Richards' trench. After some pleading with English Heritage and National Trust officials, who had to re-issue the excavation paperwork, we were allowed to re-site our trench to where it should have been and start again. The barrow ditch was massive, 3 metres deep and 3.5 metres wide. As we sieved every bit of soil and chalk we became increasingly disappointed to find that there was nothing in the lower fills of the ditch. Then, right on the bottom of the ditch, Julian found what he was looking for: just 2 metres from the edge of Julian Richards' trench there was a broken antler pick. Its radiocarbon date was almost identical to that of the antler pick from the Cursus ditch.

The radiocarbon dates for the Cursus, Lesser Cursus and long barrow present us with a dilemma. The calibration curve forms a flat plateau for this period, meaning that artefacts cannot generally be dated more closely than 3600–3300 BC. Within this 300-year period, all three monuments could have been built at the same time, or any one of them could have been earlier than the other two. From this dating evidence we'll never know for sure if the long barrow was built first, followed by the Cursus lining up on it, or whether the Greater Cursus replaced the Lesser Cursus. What we can say is that the long barrow would not have been an already ancient monument at the time the Cursus was built.

Are we any closer to understanding what these cursus monuments were for? There are more than 150 in Britain – and they are, like henges, a specifically British monument, not found on the Continent.[16] Julian Thomas has dug on seven of them in England and Scotland and probably knows more about them than anyone else. The Scottish ones are earlier, being built mostly before 3600 BC, whereas the English ones are from broadly the same date as the two at Stonehenge. There are certain recurring themes. Cursuses often have no identifiable access into them: there is no way in, or out, across their ditches and banks. As confirmed by our trenches inside the Cursus, there is generally no sign of activity within them. Many of them either cross a stream or have a watercourse close to one end. They are also often positioned close to one or more long barrows.

The longest of them is the Dorset Cursus, running for seven miles across Cranborne Chase, about twenty miles south of Stonehenge.[17] This is actually two cursuses joined together, with groups of long barrows positioned at each end. The western of these two cursuses is aligned on the midwinter solstice sunset, framed on the horizon by one of the long barrows. The excavators Martin Green and Richard Bradley interpret it as a monumental avenue of the dead, linking the ancestors with forces of nature such as springs and the sun. Back in 1947 J.F.S. Stone interpreted the Stonehenge Cursus as 'the material embodiment of an attempted connecting link between the living and the dead'.[18]

Neither of the Stonehenge cursuses has a solstice orientation, but they do have relationships with long barrows. The barrow at the east end of the Greater Cursus is not much to look at today. Most of the long mound has been destroyed and what little of it survives is underneath a modern track. It must once have been very impressive, originally more than 60 metres long and standing perhaps 3 metres high. It was dug into in the nineteenth century by John Thurnham.[19] He found no human remains in primary positions within the mound, but did recover an ox skull. Our own excavations recovered a stray Neolithic human arm bone.

One of the discoveries made by both Julians – at different times – was a line of pits that had been dug into the side of the mound, just next to the ditch. At some point after the mound was built (and not before, as the 1983 excavation results misleadingly hinted), someone quarried out chalk from these pits dug into the side of the barrow, perhaps to give the mound a makeover by spreading clean, white chalk across its surface. If the Greater Cursus is indeed a later construction than the barrow, then this chalk-digging might have been done when the Cursus was built, to give the impression of newness for both barrow and Cursus.

The Lesser Cursus has a line of Bronze Age round barrows and an undated pit circle off its west end, all of which were most probably built later than the Lesser Cursus itself. However, one of the barrows is a small long barrow – in this case the long barrow lies at the west end of the linear cursus as opposed to the east end, as seen at the Greater Cursus. Perhaps we have a situation not dissimilar to the two Dorset cursuses: the two Stonehenge cursuses might have been constructed as a pair, with the Greater Cursus leading east to the Amesbury 42 tomb and the Lesser Cursus leading west to its own associated tomb.

Julian thinks it is most likely that the Stonehenge cursuses were monuments to former processional routes whose antiquity could have gone back to the Mesolithic. Their position, straddling the watershed between the Avon and its tributary the Till, occupies a natural routeway for people and animals crossing from one valley to another. We know that the upper waters of the Till were an important place for Early Neolithic people: many of its coombes and valleys are overlooked by long barrows. Similarly, there is a significant group of Early Neolithic long barrows to the east, around what would become Durrington Walls and Woodhenge. Perhaps the ditches and banks of the cursuses demarcated routes that had once been used by the ancestors, moving back and forth between the settlement areas in the two valleys.

Julian also has an idea about how the Greater Cursus was laid out. Starting at its west end, the southern ditch runs almost due east, heading for the major landmark of Beacon Hill. For anyone crossing the watershed from west to east, this would have been the skyline feature to head towards. After a few hundred metres, the Greater Cursus ditch then shifts orientation northwards to head for the large long barrow (Amesbury 42). The north side of the Greater Cursus is strangely irregular, as we found when digging our trench into it. Most likely the Neolithic surveyors used the kinked southern ditch as their baseline and then took offsets to establish the line of the north ditch.

Two important points can be made about the Stonehenge cursuses. The first is that they mark not the entire route from the places of the living – down in the valley – to the abodes of the dead, but rather just the second half of that journey to the tomb, a journey which could have started at the riverside. Perhaps the camp sites where the living gathered lie in the valley bottoms awaiting discovery. The second point is that there are more than fifteen Neolithic long barrows in the Stonehenge area but only two of them were considered suitable for the huge labour investment of digging cursus ditches. Was this a time when certain people's ancestors became more important than others?

Like the causewayed enclosure of Robin Hood's Ball, the cursuses' ditches were dug in segments. In both cases the segments are much shorter than those of Durrington Walls henge, so the sizes of the work gangs need only have been tens rather than hundreds of workers. Nonetheless, many hundreds of people were involved in digging and building the Greater Cursus. Perhaps this was the beginning of the complex social arrangements that would culminate in the huge workforces needed to build Durrington Walls and Stonehenge.

The Cuckoo Stone

The Greater Cursus is frequently used as a flight path by the British army's helicopters as they swoop around the Salisbury Plain Training Area. As they fly eastwards along the line of the Greater Cursus, they pass the Amesbury 42 long barrow and continue towards Woodhenge. The pilots probably don't notice the Cuckoo Stone, halfway between the two. This misshapen lump of sarsen lies in a field southwest of Durrington Walls and west of Woodhenge, generally unvisited and largely unknown. Its name may derive from 'cuckold' – for reasons entirely lost to us – and a few centuries ago the stone is supposed to have been standing erect. It would have been a rather stumpy and unimpressive standing stone, as the recumbent sarsen is not much longer than it is wide, about 1.5 metres at its greatest dimension.

In 2007 Colin Richards dug an area around the recumbent Cuckoo Stone to find out where and when it was once erected. Did this small standing stone have something to do with the Cursus, whose axis passes through it, in a line with Woodhenge? Colin had been told that the Cuckoo Stone might have been moved from its original location, so he needed to open a large trench to be sure of finding the hole in which the stone had once stood. In fact the stone has not been moved at all and is lying right next to its stonehole. Colin realized that this pit was cut into a larger depression, a solution hollow that had formed beneath the stone before it was erected. The Cuckoo Stone is therefore a naturally occurring sarsen and has always been here.

People often assume that all the sarsens at Stonehenge and in the surrounding area were quarried elsewhere and moved from their original position. Today most natural sarsens that still remain in the landscape are effectively restricted to the Marlborough Downs, in the area east of Avebury about twenty miles north of Stonehenge. Here some valley bottoms are filled with rivers of stones. The original extent of this geological formation has been reduced by thousands of years of stone-quarrying and removal, so what we see today is not the original distribution of sarsen. There are records of sarsen stones being found across Salisbury Plain, so it is likely that, during the Neolithic, natural sarsens were found as far south as – and possibly beyond – Stonehenge.

After the Cuckoo Stone had been pulled out of its hollow, the prehistoric megalith builders then erected a wooden post in the hollow, rather than raising the stone upright straightaway. We could not tell whether this post was later removed or left to decay *in situ*, but its central position in the hollow shows that it was certainly not a scaffolding post or other such construction device. Mike Pitts reckons he found the same thing happening at Stonehenge, in the hollow beneath his stonehole (Stonehole 97) next to the Heel Stone: the recumbent stone was removed, a wooden post was put up, and then the stone was erected. Was this a symbolic rather than practical act, to 'reanimate' the stone by making it go through the life process of growth, decay and eternal durability, with stone following wood, to mimic the process from decay to permanence?

The Cuckoo Stone's hollow and the two features cut into it – the posthole and the stonehole – were devoid of artefacts; the only finds were flint nodules that had been used to pack the stone upright in its hole. There was no way that we could date the putting up of the post or the stone itself. But there were clues about what happened around the standing stone. Immediately north of the stone, Colin found two pits. One of these contained a roe-deer antler, some cattle bones, worked flints and a piece of Early Neolithic pottery from the time of the Cursus or even before. At some point this stone, whether still recumbent or raised upright, had clearly been a recognized location in the landscape of the Cursus-builders.

The second pit contained animal bones and worked flints as well as an antler pick and a shovel made from the scapula (shoulder blade) of an ox. The tip of the pick was far more worn than it should have been had it been used only to dig the pit in which it was left. Colin wonders if it had first been used to dig the socket in which the stone was set upright. If so, then the pick's date of around 2900 BC gives us the moment when the stone was erected, a few decades after Stonehenge's first phase.

The Cuckoo Stone continued to be a special place. In the Early Bronze Age, after 2000 BC, people brought urns – large ceramic pots – containing the ashes of their dead to bury next to the stone. Early Bronze Age pots are easily recognizable from their very distinctive forms, and antiquarians and early archaeologists gave the different types names that are still used today: Food Vessels, Collared Urns, Cordoned Urns and Biconical Urns. These names will never be changed – again, they are very useful archaeological shorthand – but they don't really fit with what we now know the pots were used for. All four types of pot were used for cooking and storage (not just the 'Food Vessels'); after being used in the kitchen, they were then used as containers for cremated bones. So Bronze Age grandma's ashes were buried in the equivalent of a saucepan. It seems pretty peculiar to us, but was evidently normal to the people of the time.

A new study by geochemist Lucija Šoberl at Bristol University has found that such Bronze Age pots were used mostly for cooking dairy products, with a small percentage used for cooking pork and other meat. Two of Colin's three pots from the Cuckoo Stone are Collared Urns dating to the period 1900–1700 BC. Both are about 30 centimetres high; this style of pot widens out from a narrow base to a rounded belly, with a rim that looks as if it has been folded back on itself to create a wide collar at the top of the pot. The third pot is a Biconical Urn, buried there in the period 1420–1260 BC. The three Cuckoo Stone pots were included in Lucija's study and she found that one had been used to cook either beef or mutton. Placed within the pots were the ashes of three adults.

A Collared Urn (1880–1670 BC) from the Cuckoo Stone. This pot was carefully lifted from the ground so that its contents could be excavated in the laboratory.

Thousands of years after it was erected, the Cuckoo Stone became incorporated into a small Roman village. Towards the end of the Roman period, someone buried two hoards of coins here (later dug up and now in Salisbury Museum). Thanks to volunteer metal detectorist Lee Smeaton, we found another fifteen or so coins in the area. These are different in date to the coins in the two hoards and probably ended up here among the rubbish thrown out from adjacent Roman farmhouses. There was the Roman burial of a child, too, accompanied by the skull of a dog. Colin also found the footings of a large rectangular Roman building with a colonnade of posts along its front.

The Roman village that engulfed the Cuckoo Stone had once been substantial. In the same field, cropmarks to the east reveal the presence of farmsteads, trackways and field boundaries. There was a Roman burial ground further east, cut into a Bronze Age barrow, where Josh and California Dave were digging south of Woodhenge. To the north of the Cuckoo Stone, Geoff Wainwright excavated a much larger area than ours in 1970, and found Late Roman buildings, a corn drier, ditches and pits, close to the southwestern edge of Durrington Walls.

Although Colin and Josh located Early Neolithic features in our Cuckoo Stone and Woodhenge trenches, none were found in 1970 in Geoff's much larger areas of excavation just to the north. He found four pits with Late Neolithic Grooved Ware but nothing from the same early period as the Cuckoo Stone pits. Consequently, we can be fairly confident that the Cuckoo Stone pits were definitely associated with the stone, rather than spread randomly across the landscape. Given the Early Neolithic dates and the pits' positions on the extended axis of the Cursus, it's also possible that they once formed part of an access route east–west across the high ground between the Avon and Till, as Julian had predicted.

The Bulford Stone

Colin's main interest these days is in the origins of standing stones – quarries and access routes have never been well-studied and Colin's work around the world, from the Isle of Lewis in the Outer Hebrides to Easter Island in the South Pacific, is focused on finding out how and why megalithic monuments got to where they are. Colin was keen to chase up the historical records of large sarsen stones in the Stonehenge area.[21] In the early eighteenth century William Stukeley noted a stone in the River Avon at Bulford, and a pair of standing stones in Luxenborough Plantation on Coneybury Hill, to the southeast of Stonehenge. He could well have been referring to Coneybury henge, later excavated by Julian Richards. A late-seventeenth-century engraving of Stonehenge by the artist David Loggan shows a standing stone in the distance, somewhere around the east end of the Cursus, but who can say whether its presence in the picture is pure artistic licence?[22] Colin also found many sarsens marked on the Ordnance Survey map from 1887. All of them have now gone, except for one. This lies in a field southeast of the village of Bulford, on the east bank of the Avon.

Colin went off to look at the stone. It is another recumbent stone, but its tapered ends and large size – 4.6 metres long and 1.7 metres wide – are sure signs that it was once a standing monolith. The stone had no recorded name so Colin had the privilege of choosing a name for the site. He decided to call it the Tor Stone, in honour of Chris Tilley's dog.

The Bulford Stone now lies close to where it once stood, in a field east of the River Avon.

We are lucky that the Tor Stone is still there. It is not a scheduled monument (that is, it is not protected by law from damage or interference) and, some years ago, it was removed from its original position to the edge of the field. Then the farmer tried to bury the stone in a pit in the corner of the field. Fortunately, he didn't go through with it and the stone was subsequently dragged back to where it had come from.

The farmer was happy for us to investigate the area (it had been a good summer and the crop was already harvested) so, in 2005, Colin cleared an area around the stone. From Durrington Walls we could see his team at work in the distance, with Beacon Hill looming above them. Close to the stone itself was a stonehole that contained a row of ten small stakeholes along its western edge. Josh had seen similar features before during his excavations of stoneholes at Avebury; these were anti-friction posts, used to form a barrier for the bottom of the stone to rest against as it was raised upright. Close to it Colin found a solution hollow the same size and shape as the stone. By making a cast of the hollow (fieldwork ingenuity led him to use No More Big Gaps foam filler, in huge quantities), he was able to show that the recumbent stone fitted this hollow perfectly. Here was another instance in which a natural sarsen had been raised as a monolith.

The hollow was full of small chippings of sarsen, broken flints and flint-knapping debris, forming a small cairn in the top of the hole. Beneath was an arrangement of four stakeholes, perhaps the remnants of efforts to remove the recumbent stone. Neither the stonehole nor the hollow provided any clue to the date when the stone was raised, but Colin did discover that it had been encircled by the ditch of a small round barrow, long since ploughed flat. Round barrows are circular burial mounds of the Early Bronze Age (2200–1500 BC), formed by heaping up turf and soil, with a circular ditch dug around the mound.

There was a burial pit beneath the centre of this barrow, just over a metre to the northeast of the hole for the standing stone. Three adults had been buried here, or at least parts of three adults had. Two burials consisted of the cremated bones of adults and the other individual was represented by a handful of unburnt bones. The grave goods (the provisions for the dead) within the pit included some of the most unusual ever found in Wessex.

Against the eastern wall of the burial pit the mourners had placed three antler spatulae (thin strips of antler, perhaps for pressure-working flints), a group of flint flakes, then a group of flint knives, barbed-and-tanged arrowheads and a fabricator (a flint for striking sparks) as well as a hollowed piece of iron pyrites, worn from being used to make sparks for fire-lighting. Then someone had added a small, carved limestone block about 15 centimetres high. Imported probably from the Cotswolds or Mendips (the nearest sources of limestone, almost thirty miles west), it has been carefully squared like a miniature Stonehenge sarsen. It looks like the sort of souvenir that you would have bought from a Bronze Age version of the Stonehenge gift shop! The group was completed by a small Food Vessel.

. This main grouping of grave goods was flanked by other items. On its west side lay a pendant made from a wild boar's tusk. On its south side someone had placed a piece of clear rock crystal. This beautiful piece of stone has been flaked from a larger block, part of whose surface has been polished. Archaeologists sometimes find polished rock-crystal pendants in burials of the Migration Period (the sixth to seventh centuries AD, after the Romans) in Britain. This seems to be the only one from British prehistory. It might well have come from the Alps but we cannot rule out the possibility of more local sources in western Britain.

After all of these objects had been carefully placed in the burial pit, it was filled with soil and some pieces of tabular flint were placed over the grave goods. Then one group of cremated bones, probably from the same person, was put in the centre of the pit and a smaller group was placed in its southwest corner and covered with flint nodules. Then a small hole was dug in the west end of the pit, into which was placed a second cremation burial and a large Food Vessel; this was then packed in place with slabs of tabular flint. When this pot was carefully excavated in the lab it was devoid of finds inside except for a pebble.

The Food Vessel burials at Bulford date to about 1900–1750 BC, so they are from the same period as the Cuckoo Stone's Collared Urns.[23] Yet this was a very different burial – at the Cuckoo Stone Colin found only the urns, without any other grave goods. Here at the Tor Stone not only were there thirty-two grave goods – some of them extremely unusual – in a single grave but also the remains of three people, two of them buried together and the third added later.

The large Food Vessel was not the last deposition. An oval hole was dug against the northern edge of the grave pit, and finally some more cremated bones were buried in what must have been an organic container of which no trace survived. This was the culmination of four acts of deposition in the same spot. Had there been an above-ground marker so that returning mourners knew where to dig? It is very unusual to find an Early Bronze Age cremation burial returned to again and again, so why did this grave get re-used in this way?

The Bulford burial is unique but it does share certain similarities with another burial on Salisbury Plain, from under a round barrow at Upton Lovell, about ten miles west of Stonehenge.[24] This was excavated 200 years ago by Richard Colt Hoare, who found two skeletons, one of which was buried in association with about eighty grave goods. Most of these were bone points, many of them perforated as were a number of boars' tusks. There were also shale beads and a shale ring (from the Dorset coast), as well as ornaments of bone.

Recent re-excavation of Upton Lovell by Colin Shell and Gill Swanton has confirmed that the individual buried here was a man who had also been provided with a bronze awl and a strange array of stone tools: stone battle-axes, polished flint axes, a grooved whetstone, stone rubbers, a 'cushion stone' for fine metalworking, a geode (a hollow nodule with crystals inside) and a rounded stone of white quartz. He has come to be known as the Upton Lovell shaman, an Early Bronze Age ritual specialist whose collection of four antique polished axes – they would have been at least 500 years old when they were buried with him – and the other peculiar stones were part of his equipment. The bone points might have been worn as part of a costume that would have jangled as he danced. The white quartz stone has been considered as his crystal ball.

Perhaps the people buried at Bulford were shamans as well, with a magic crystal of see-through rock, a perforated boar's tusk and a mini-monolith. Both the Upton Lovell and the Bulford graves date to some 500 years after Stonehenge's heyday in the mid-third millennium BC, so if these people had any part to play at Stonehenge it was long after the stones had gone up.

Colin's discoveries at the Cuckoo Stone and the Tor Stone made us think again about this landscape. How many more standing stones had there once been all around this area? We also found stoneholes within Woodhenge and along the Durrington Avenue, where no one had suspected there to have once been standing stones. Perhaps there were many more stone circles and standing stones around Stonehenge than anyone has realized. What has happened to all these stones moved in prehistory? Where have they gone? Perhaps there was frequent moving and repositioning of stones, incorporating them from old sites into new locations. Stonehenge may just be the one stone circle that has happened to survive fairly intact.

MYSTERIES OF THE RIVER

One of the main strands of our investigations was to try to understand the role of the River Avon in this landscape of monuments. We lacked some basic information about how much the river has changed its course since the time of Stonehenge, so we asked Mike Allen and Charly French to go off and find out. Using a hand-powered auger they drilled small holes all over the floodplain to find the routes of ancient river channels, known as palaeochannels.

Over tens of thousands of years, the Avon has cut its own mini-gorge through the chalk plateau of Salisbury Plain. Its path in more recent millennia has been confined to its floodplain, flanked on either side by chalk cliffs. Mike and Charly were able to locate its prehistoric channel to the north of Durrington Walls, west of the present river course. It then flowed directly underneath the modern river, where the Durrington avenue is likely to have met it, and curved eastwards south of Durrington Walls. Here it widened to about 60 metres, with a depth of 1.5 metres (today it is only about 10 metres wide and 0.5 metres deep along this stretch). On its west side is the long north–south river cliff on which Woodhenge sits.

The river then enters more of a gorge near the Countess roundabout (where today it's crossed by the A303 trunk road). It flows west at the foot of the huge chalk cliff of Ratfyn and then meanders through the town of Amesbury until it reaches the high prominence of Vespasian's Camp, an Iron Age hillfort,[1] which it skirts around to the south. Recent investigations by the Open University have revealed that the natural spring close to this hillfort's northeast side may have been used as a shrine in the Roman period. Just a little further downstream is the point where the Stonehenge avenue approaches the river. Here the river channel used to run slightly south and east of where it does today; the river has subsequently encroached upon its ancient north and west banks but, as we were to find when we dug in this area, not so much as to have destroyed what lay at the end of the Stonehenge avenue.

Chris Tilley decided he should float down the Avon from Durrington to Stonehenge, to try to experience the impact that this journey would have had on Neolithic people. On a trial run he launched his Indian canoe off the end of the Durrington avenue. On board were Chris, his colleague Wayne Bennett, Colin, a student and the dog. The canoe was low in the water and those of us waving them goodbye were convinced that disaster lay ahead. In fact all went well, though crossing the various weirs along the river made progress slow. The whole trip from Durrington Walls to the Stonehenge avenue took less than four hours.

A few days later Chris, Wayne and the dog gave it another go, this time floating south past the end of the Stonehenge avenue – right into the heart of English upper-class country living. There are some very exclusive riverside properties south of Amesbury, guarded by electronic security alarms and large, short-haired men. On encountering two of the latter, Chris bridled at being told that he was trespassing on private property – the boss, he was warned, owned not only this stretch of riverside but also this section of the river itself. Chris wanted to know just how anyone could claim to own flowing water that eventually ends up in the sea. Unmoved by this clear-sighted logic, one of the guards addressed Wayne: 'Tell your friend, the next time he tries to come here we'll break his legs.'

Lessons were also learned about the river's prehistoric past. This is the most winding and tortuous stretch of the River Avon on its route to the English Channel. Floating around the river's bends and meanders, Chris and Wayne became completely disoriented. One moment the canoe was heading northwest and the next it had turned through 180°.

Many studies of societies around the world have noted how common it is for those undergoing rites of passage to be deliberately disoriented as they change from one state of being to another. This is very frequently the case during funeral rites; often such ceremonies involve measures to ensure that the dead are confused by their journey, to make certain that they will not return to the living.[2] The dead must be led to the otherworld by such a route that they will not be able to find their way back. I've often seen examples of this during funerals in southern Madagascar: the pall-bearers leave the village with the coffin on their shoulders and twist and turn on the final journey to the tomb, trying to disorientate the vengeful ghost.[3]

If this stretch of the river had been a special place for rituals and ceremonies – what anthropologists call a liminal zone, after the Latin word 'limen' for 'threshold' – held by Neolithic people, then what evidence did they leave along the riverside of this journey from life into death? Is there evidence for passage from the transient world of wood to the permanent world of stone?

During the 1930s and 1940s, amateur archaeologist J.F.S. Stone spent his spare time taking every opportunity to look into holes being dug anywhere in the vicinity of Stonehenge. In 1934 he was contacted by Flight-Lieutenant Somerbough, who had found something in his back garden while putting up a fence. The RAF officer lived at Millmead, a house perched on the high cliff overlooking the Avon at Ratfyn, just north of Amesbury and about a mile southeast of Woodhenge. Two Early Bronze Age skeletons had been found here fourteen years earlier so Stone knew straightaway that something interesting might turn up.

In the garden at Millmead, Stone found four pits containing Neolithic objects.[4] The largest pit was just over a metre deep and had been filled with charcoal packed with more than 500 worked flints, hundreds of animal bones and some scrappy bits of Grooved Ware. Among the flints were two chisel arrowheads, knives and five flakes with edges serrated like saws. The animal bones were mostly of cattle with some pig. There were also some rather peculiar finds: the scapula of a brown bear and pieces of scallop shell. Both of these must have come quite a distance – the shell from the sea (at least thirty miles away) and the bear from some distant forest. Bear bones have turned up with Grooved Ware in two other places, at Wyke Down on Cranborne Chase and at Barholm in south Lincolnshire.[5] This connection with Grooved Ware is interesting because bear bones are hardly ever found on Neolithic sites in Britain.

Perhaps bear-baiting was part of the entertainment at places like Durrington.

Seven years later, in 1941, Stone was called in by the owner of a house called Woodlands on Countess Road North, just 300 metres southeast of Woodhenge, who had also found something strange in his garden. Mr Booth was himself an amateur archaeologist and it was his 'perspicacity and acumen' while gardening that led to this unusual discovery, a pair of Neolithic pits.[6] The first was very odd, having been filled in one go with black earth and wood ash packed with animal bones, worked flints, Grooved Ware and, once again, a scallop shell. Among the flints Stone and Booth found two chisel arrowheads and six saws. The pit had been capped with a cairn of flints, which would originally have been visible above ground level, Stone realized.

There were more saws and chisel arrowheads in the second pit, along with an unused flint axe and a broken stone axe from the Graig Lwyd axe-production site in north Wales. In this pit the wood ash and charcoal formed just a thin layer. Six years later, Mr Booth found another two pits in his garden.[7] The third pit's filling was very similar to the first, and the fourth pit contained just a basket-shaped heap of charcoal and wood ash tipped in and then covered with chalk rubble.

The pits in both gardens sound very strange. We excavated more than fifty Neolithic pits at Durrington Walls and none of them contained these deep layers of ash and charcoal.[8] The bones too are different: among the bones from the first pit at Woodlands were not only those of cattle and pig, but also sheep, dog, fox and chub (a freshwater fish). At Durrington Walls we have found only a few bones of sheep and dog (though their faeces survive) and none of fish or bear. There isn't a single flint saw from Durrington Walls and yet examples of these tools probably for cutting reeds were found in virtually every pit at Woodlands and Millmead. Admittedly, these two sites were occupied probably a few centuries before Durrington Walls (chisel arrowheads date to before 2600 BC) but the time difference doesn't entirely account for the contrast.

The pottery from Woodlands is also very unusual. Although it is Grooved Ware, it has horizontal 'cordons' (strips of applied clay) that are decorated with parallel grooves. The Durrington Walls pottery has both vertical and horizontal cordons but the grooved decoration is found mostly on the surface of the pot rather than on the cordons. Somewhat unimaginatively, archaeologists call these two Grooved Ware sub-styles 'Woodlands' and 'Durrington Walls'.[9] The difference is probably chronological, with the Woodlands style being earlier than Durrington Walls. Some of the pottery from Woodlands is wafer-thin (just 2 millimetres thick); these pots could not have been intended for use more than once.

This 'disposable' pottery, the quantities of ash and charcoal and the bones from an unusually large range of animal species mark Woodlands and Millmead as rather different to Durrington Walls and other settlements of this period. The charcoal and ash were dumped into the pits in a single go, so these deposits are probably the remains of large, open-air bonfires. This is in contrast to the thin layers of hearth ash that we found in the pits around the houses at Durrington Walls. Perhaps the high cliffs overlooking this stretch of the river were used for bonfires and feasting at certain times of the year.

We needed to follow up Stone's work by looking to the south of Woodhenge. Unfortunately, most of this land now lies under a long line of modern houses and gardens along Countess Road North, which runs from Amesbury northwards to Durrington. Any remains are no doubt buried beneath houses, lawns and flowerbeds. We didn't have the heart to knock on doors and ask to dig up gardens on the off-chance that we might find something, but there was one area of open ground, immediately south of Woodhenge beyond the north end of the houses, where we could look.

In 2007 Josh and California Dave opened two large trenches here. They were joined by a colleague of Josh's from Bristol University, Alistair Pike, an archaeological scientist and enthusiastic outdoor chef. At morning tea-break he'd produce fry-ups in a wheelbarrow, and soon everybody on the project was clamouring to be chosen to dig with the 'south of Woodhenge' squad. Maud Cunnington had already dug part of this area in 1928.[10] There used to be three round barrows here but they've all been ploughed completely flat; Cunnington had found post-holes for an unusual building beneath one of the barrows and Josh wanted to take a closer look.[11] He also had a shrewd idea that there might be more than one of these post arrangements.

Cunnington had found a square arrangement of four chest-deep postholes surrounded by a curving but near-rectangular ring of smaller postholes. These formed an enclosure entered from the southeast between two pits. Some Grooved Ware sherds indicated that this enclosure was significantly earlier than the Bronze Age barrow on top of it, and Josh reckoned this might have been a timber circle similar to the Northern Circle.

When Josh opened up his trench he soon found that, over the seventy-nine years since Cunnington's dig, ploughing had almost eradicated the small postholes. He could discern the outlines of some of them, but many had been ploughed away entirely. Some archaeologists thought that Cunnington's structure could have been a house with four large internal posts to support the roof. Josh's investigation showed otherwise.

The smaller postholes around the outside of Cunnington's structure were very like some found by Julian in the centre of Durrington Walls: the postholes of the circular palisades around the two 'special' houses inside the henge. The very large internal postholes of Cunnington's structure were too deep and too wide to have been roof supports. With each of these posts likely to have been more than 50 centimetres in diameter, they would probably have stood at least 5 metres high. Josh realized that the structure was not a house but a tower, surrounded by a fence. The four large posts probably supported a wooden platform. With its entrance aligned on the midwinter solstice sunrise, this tower is likely to have had some ceremonial purpose. The view from its platform, if it had one, would have included grandstand coverage of the river below.

North of Cunnington's structure Josh discovered another, similar array of postholes. Here four postholes formed a square arrangement and had two pits to the east of them; the lay-out was identical to that of the first structure, although slightly smaller, and only a few of the ring of little postholes had survived. The posts of this second structure had been set about 0.5 metres shallower but were nonetheless massive.

These timbers had been left to decay *in situ* and, as with the Southern Circle, pits had been dug into the tops of them and filled with cattle and pig bones – and, in one case, with the skull of a wolf or large dog. One of the two pits at the front turned out to be another posthole. In its fill there was a lump of daub, indicating that the oval enclosure fence had probably been faced with daub like the walls of the nearby houses at Durrington Walls. A radiocarbon date has established that this timber structure was probably of the same date as the settlement at Durrington.

South of Cunnington's structure there was a third arrangement of postholes, this one much smaller and consisting of a square of holes about 2.5 metres apart. There was no sign of a surrounding palisade fence and the fills of these postholes showed that the posts had been pulled out and not left to decay. How many more of these Neolithic timber structures had lined the cliff top above the river? And what were they for?

We don't know what happened to most of the dead during the Neolithic period. During the Early Neolithic some people were buried in long barrows, but certainly not everyone – there are nothing like enough barrows to contain the whole population. There is almost no trace of what happened to the dead of the later Neolithic. Some people were cremated, and the ashes then buried.[12] Perhaps others were scattered after cremation; some groups may have used funerary rites that are unfamiliar to us and that have left almost no archaeological trace. Josh thinks that the timber towers south of Woodhenge were raised platforms for exposing the remains of the dead. Corpses could have been left for their flesh to be picked clean by birds, and the bones then collected up and placed in the river. In that way, the spirits and the bones of the dead could begin their journey downriver towards Stonehenge. Whatever the purpose of the wooden towers, we have no doubt that the people of Stonehenge regarded this stretch of the river as very important in their spiritual as well as everyday lives.

We hoped to find out whether anything had been regularly deposited into the Avon during prehistory. In 2007 we therefore dug a couple of trenches into the palaeochannel below Durrington Walls. Because of the Environment Agency's rule about no disturbance closer than eight metres to the riverbank, we could not examine the bit that we really wanted to get at. We should have liked to investigate the deeper part of the former river channel, where the Durrington avenue would have ended. Anything heavy thrown into the river from here, such as stone artefacts or even pots and human bones, might have sunk into the mud at the bottom of the channel.

We were limited to the eastern edge of the palaeochannel, and here we found only a few burnt sticks and a worked flint. Further downstream, where the channel had widened in prehistoric times to form a reed swamp, there were no artefacts at all in our trench but the deep sequence of layers contained pollen grains that would give us a complete vegetational history of the locality. We could see the bottom layers, formed after the Ice Age when hunter-gatherers lived along the river's margins. Then there were layers of reeds that built up during the Neolithic and Early Bronze Age; these would have provided the roofing material for the Neolithic houses. The reed layers were abruptly terminated by deposits of grey soil, washed into the river from the Middle Bronze Age (about 1500 BC) onwards, as the intensity of farming dramatically increased and rain flushed loosened ploughsoil into the river.

Examining plant pollen is a standard archaeological technique for reconstructing prehistoric vegetational environments. Although the plants themselves rot away, leaving no trace, their pollen can survive for millennia. Ancient pollen survives only in damp places and can sometimes be retrieved by coring a hole through layers of waterlogged soil; pollen is, of course, entirely invisible to the naked eye, so the extracted core of soil is sent for examination by a specialist who identifies the various species present.

Mike and Charly's colleague Rob Scaife has analysed the microscopic pollen grains from the Avon palaeochannel's different layers to find out what species of tree and shrub grew in this area through time. He'd previously studied a sequence from a spot 300 metres upstream from Durrington Walls and these two studies led him to a surprising discovery. The landscape of 8000–7000 BC, inhabited by Mesolithic hunter-gatherers, was only lightly wooded with beech, pine, hazel and oak trees; by the time of the Neolithic and Bronze Age the area was largely devoid of trees and shrubs.[13] Instead, the vegetation was dominated by grasses, with the addition of sedges and marsh plants on the floodplain. Perhaps this vegetational development of Salisbury Plain since the Ice Age – from light woodland to largely treeless grassland – can be put down to woodland clearance by the earliest Neolithic farmers. Mike, Charly and Rob have also found a similar sequence on the high chalkland of Cranborne Chase, twenty miles to the south; here, however, the change probably took place without human interference.

Mike Allen has reached a similar conclusion about the lack of woodland on Salisbury Plain by using a quite different type of evidence. Mike is an expert on snails: when snails are retrieved from archaeological layers, specialists like him can look at which species are present and thereby reconstruct what sort of vegetation was present.[14] When most people think of snails they imagine the big, fat garden variety, a centimetre or more across, but actually the majority of snails are extremely small and have to be identified to species with a microscope.

As far as archaeologists are concerned, there are two types of snail. Some are catholic, in the sense of wide-ranging or broad: these snails are adapted to live in many different and varied habitats, which makes them useless for our purposes. The types of snail that are useful to us are those that are niche-specific; some species can live only in open grassland, others only in shady woodland, and so on. Through years of patient research, examining snails from prehistoric ground surfaces preserved beneath burial mounds, Mike has discovered that during the Neolithic and Bronze Age the area around Stonehenge was not inhabited by woodland-dwelling snails. It looks as if there never was a dense Neolithic forest on the chalk uplands of Salisbury Plain.

After the last Ice Age, growth of trees on the downland began later than in surrounding lowlands, initially with just birch and pine being present. After 8000–7000 BC, the warming climate supported light deciduous woodland of oak, elm and hazel, gradually replacing the cold-temperature species. The woodland thinned out during the millennium before 3000 BC when Stonehenge was built; the open, grassy plain that we see today was already formed 5000 years ago, partly through clearance and grazing by early farmers and their animals, and partly because much of this landscape was already open. Of course, away from Stonehenge, the river valleys, lowlands and lower slopes of the chalk were forested and, even long after the time Stonehenge was built, the Avon's floodplain still supported alder and hazel woodland even though the downlands around it were largely treeless. Only a few stands of woodland or single trees of oak and lime were scattered over this open, chalkland landscape and, as we have learned from our excavations of prehistoric tree-holes, these lone sentinels might well have had special significance for the people of the Neolithic.

11

THE DRUIDS AND STONEHENGE

Anyone planning to dig at Stonehenge has to jump through a lot of hoops. Permission is granted in the name of the Secretary of State for Culture, but the advice given by English Heritage to the Department of Culture, Media and Sport (or 'Arts and Darts', as it's sometimes called) decides the matter. English Heritage's opinion is formed from the views of their regional inspector and regional manager, with input from the management team for Stonehenge. Before their recommendation is sent to DCMS a final decision is taken by English Heritage's chief executive and the English Heritage Advisory Committee (EHAC), which comprises not civil servants but rather the great and the good in matters of historic buildings, ancient monuments and archaeology.

EHAC must have been taken aback when they received not one but two applications for digs at Stonehenge in 2008. The first application was for the work planned by Professors Geoff Wainwright and Tim Darvill. Geoff had retired from his job as Chief Archaeologist at English Heritage and was now President of the Society of Antiquaries. After an illustrious career, including digging on virtually every henge in Wessex other than Stonehenge, he was fulfilling the dream of a lifetime. Tim and Geoff had been working in the hills of west Wales, searching for the source of the Preseli bluestones.[1] Now they planned to dig a trench within Stonehenge to try to date the double arc of bluestones there.[2]

This double arc was thought by Atkinson to be the partial remains of two concentric circles of bluestones. He called the outer arc the Q Holes and the inner arc the R Holes. Atkinson's excavations in 1954 had found that one of the stoneholes in the sarsen circle (Stone 3) cut into the edge of one of the Q Holes (Q Hole 4). Wherever one pit cuts another, we know that the second pit is later than the first. What Atkinson found meant that the Q and R Holes had to be earlier than the sarsen circle. Atkinson had excavated some twenty Q and R Holes but found nothing that could be used to radiocarbon-date their construction. Geoff and Tim hoped they would be luckier.

The Stonehenge Riverside Project made the second of that year's applications. I had invited Julian Richards and Mike Pitts to join us. Julian's Stonehenge Environs Project had made a major contribution to understanding Stonehenge,[3] and he was hugely enthusiastic about the opportunity to dig at Stonehenge itself. Mike also has a considerable amount of knowledge about Stonehenge, having dug there – outside the wire – in 1980 in advance of the cable trench.[4] We wanted to recover a large quantity of cremated human bones dug up by Hawley in the 1920s. These cremated remains were found primarily in the pits known as Aubrey Holes; this circle of fifty-six pits lies inside the Stonehenge ditch and dates to the first phase of activity at Stonehenge. In 1935 these remains had been reburied, for safe keeping, in Aubrey Hole 7 by archaeologists Robert Newall and William Young. It seems that they could find no museum prepared to take the cremated bones, probably because back then, long before the development of today's methods and techniques of analysis, there appeared to be no possibility of ever learning anything from them.[5]

The committee members of EHAC must have had a difficult decision to make: should they refuse both applications, on the grounds that Stonehenge's below-ground remains should never be disturbed, or grant permission to just one project, or agree to both? Fortunately the committee was happy to see both proposals go forward. Each project had a long and fruitful track record over the previous five years, Tim and Geoff in the Preselis and ourselves around Stonehenge. The excavations were supported by meticulous research designs, and would have little impact on preserved remains because of the small sizes of the proposed trenches. Plus, these quite tiny trenches would be placed in or adjacent to areas already dug out by earlier archaeologists.

Tim and Geoff planned to re-open one of Atkinson's trenches, between the sarsen circle and the trilithons, and then extend for about 2 metres into untouched deposits. The trench was positioned in the southeast area of the monument (between Stones 10 and 35; see figure on p. 29), on top of the line of Q Holes, immediately outside the stones of the bluestone circle.[6] Atkinson had recorded half of a Q Hole in the end of his trench here; Tim and Geoff would be able to dig out its other half, and they hoped to find another Q Hole to its west.[7] This end of Atkinson's trench had been full of postholes, so there was a good chance that they might find more of these and be able to date them.

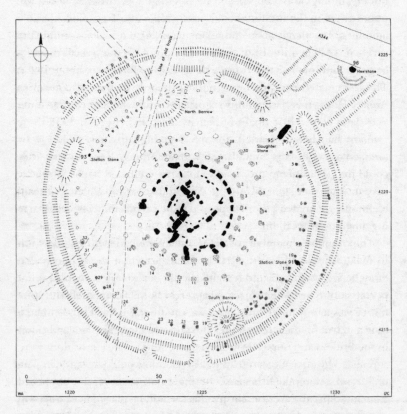

A plan of Stonehenge showing the locations of the excavated cremation burials (black circles) in the Aubrey Holes and ditch.

By 1956 Atkinson had mapped out the extent of the Q and R Holes in the northeast and east areas of Stonehenge.[8] He must surely have looked very hard for a similar double arc of stoneholes on the west and southwest sides, but there is only a single arc in this area. The Q and R Holes, and their place in the story of Stonehenge, can be difficult to follow, particularly because these are stone holes, not stones. Briefly, the Q and R Holes are where bluestones once stood. The bluestones were pulled out of these holes around 2400 BC and then re-erected, in much the same arrangement, as a bluestone circle. The Q and R Holes are mostly underneath where the bluestone circle stands today; nobody knows why the prehistoric builders went to the trouble of removing and then re-erecting these stones.

Some archaeologists think that the rings of Q and R Holes were never finished. Others think that an incomplete double arc was all that was intended. Another possibility, which seems to me more likely, is that as far as the builders were concerned the arrangement *was* complete, with bluestones in a double arc on the northeast side and single stones on the southwest side.

Atkinson's other major discovery was that Q Hole 4 appeared to be cut by the stonehole containing one of the stones of the sarsen circle (Stone 3).[9] Thus the Q and R Holes were thought to be earlier than the sarsen circle, and probably earlier than the sarsen trilithons. Atkinson appeared to have discovered a separate phase of construction at Stonehenge, between the earliest phase of bank and ditch and the sarsen circle. The arrangement of small bluestones belonging to this phase was itself later modified by the erection of the sarsens and the re-arrangement of the bluestones into a bluestone circle and bluestone oval at the centre of the monument. If the Q and R Holes were the first bluestone construction at Stonehenge, then if Tim and Geoff could find dating evidence in one of the Q Holes this would, they reckoned, reveal when the bluestones were brought from Wales.

Their dig started in March 2008, with cameramen jostling to film Tim and Geoff cutting the first sods. There were daily updates on the web, a 'live feed' to a screen in a marquee in the visitors' car park, a blog and web forums. Mike Pitts, Julian Richards and I visited them after their first week's digging. Tim told us that he had spotted that the cuts of the features in the end of Atkinson's trench were not doing what they should have done. He could see that the Q Hole actually cut the hole for the fallen stone of the sarsen circle. According to Atkinson, the relationship between these two pits should have been the other way around. We were all mystified.

Tim and Geoff were unlucky: there was no antler pick in the Q Hole. Given that more than twenty Q and R Holes had already been dug out by Hawley and Atkinson without a sniff of one, it had always been a long shot; it seems it just wasn't Neolithic practice to leave picks in these particular pits. The situation was, however, salvageable. Geoff and Tim hoped to collect enough pieces of charcoal and bone to be able to radiocarbon date groups of such items from particular layers. By the end of the excavation, their hard-working flotation team had accumulated a modest collection of charcoal lumps, along with a few pieces of animal bone and a human tooth.

There was a lot of pottery too. Atkinson's excavation team hadn't sieved the soil and had missed some sizeable sherds of Beaker pottery. What really surprised Tim and Geoff, though, was the quantity of Roman pottery. Just like the Cuckoo Stone, this place had been a magnet for people in the Roman period. They didn't come just to look at the standing stones, but actually dug holes into the site. Even deep in the Q Hole Geoff and Tim found a sherd of Roman pottery. It was no wonder that the stratigraphy was mixed up, as we'd seen on our site visit. These holes had been dug into and re-filled long after they were first used in the third millennium BC.

By the end of the environmental processing Tim and Geoff had enough pieces of charcoal to submit several samples from each context. These came from a sarsen circle stonehole (Stone 10), from two stoneholes belonging to the bluestone circle, and from a Q Hole. Cut by the Q Hole, and therefore earlier than it, were two small postholes. Only one had a piece of charcoal in it. This was the first opportunity in many years to look carefully at postholes in Stonehenge. Like the others found by Hawley and Atkinson, these two were less than 0.5 metre across. Curiously they had no post pipes and no packing, and nor was there any indication that posts had been withdrawn. Their fills were utterly homogeneous. Tim even wondered whether they had really held posts.

Tim Darvill (left), Geoff Wainwright (centre) and Miles Russell (right) excavating at
Stonehenge in 2008.

After a cold few weeks of grey skies and rain (and some unseasonable
snow), Tim and Geoff finished off and filled in their trench. They would
now have to wait months for the results of the radiocarbon dating. Mike
Allen was advising them on this and, well aware of the amount of previous disturbance, set out a strategy to follow:

- First of all, identify the tree species from which the charcoal came, and
  then select only those pieces that derived from small roundwood.
  Dating charcoal formed from heartwood is not much use; if a heartwood sample happens to have come from a large tree, it will have
  been already centuries old when it was burnt. Such a date only tells us
  how old the tree was, not the date of the event at which it was burnt.
- Then submit the roundwood samples for dating.
- The dates from such a strategy can only be considered reliable if pairs
  of dates from the same context are consistent with each other. If
  inconsistent, then the layers have been mixed up at a later date.

- In addition, the dates must be consistent with the stratigraphy: earlier dates should come from layers lower down in the stratigraphic sequence, and later dates should come from the upper layers.
- If the dates were to come out all over the place – completely different dates from the same layer, say, or much older dates from layers above much younger dates – then none of the stoneholes and postholes could be considered as securely dated.

In August 2008 came our turn. We'd be digging Aubrey Hole 7 in order to recover Hawley's finds of cremated bones. Because Tim and Geoff had gone first, digging at Stonehenge was no longer big news so we were spared the press onslaught. Nevertheless, there were going to be thousands of visitors at Stonehenge every day in August, so part of our project design concerned visitor 'management'. We needed a good team to explain to the visitors why we were digging, and what we hoped to find. Pat Shelley, a professional Stonehenge guide who had worked with us at Durrington Walls, ran a small army of trained-up students and National Trust volunteers from a marquee outside the car park, giving guided tours of accessible excavations in a nearby field as well as dealing with visitors gathering inside the monument near the excavation site.

As we set up we noticed a white-robed figure displaying a banner on the fence outside the visitors' entrance to Stonehenge: a Druid, protesting against the Stonehenge entry charge. His banner proclaimed that the site should be open to all, free of charge; the fences should all come down and people should be allowed to walk among the stones whenever they like. It's a nice idea. When I saw Stonehenge as a child, everyone could wander about at will and it was definitely a better experience. Many people find Avebury henge a much more interesting and atmospheric place than Stonehenge, partly because it has unrestricted access, but we have to remember that Avebury is much bigger than Stonehenge and not on the tourist track in the same way.

Whatever we may think about access to Stonehenge, it now attracts almost a million visitors a year and that's a problem in terms of its preservation. English Heritage has decided that the best way to protect the site from erosion is to keep visitors to a fixed path that runs outside the sarsen circle. Anyone wanting to see the stones up close can get inside the circle only as a booked-in visitor outside normal opening hours. The two exceptions are the solstices, when anyone and everyone is allowed in. Currently about 37,000 turn up for the midsummer solstice; the mid-winter solstice is still very much for the hard-core, and usually only a couple of hundred people brave the winter weather for a night in the open. English Heritage and the National Trust have to take responsibility for all the arrangements for the solstices (for which no charge is made): they install Portaloos, sort out the parking and the campsites, arrange first-aid cover and pick up all the rubbish.

The Stonehenge manager had got in touch with his Druid contacts to tell them what we'd be doing. Many different people today call themselves Druids, from members of Friendly Societies established before the twentieth century to twenty-first-century Pagans. The Stonehenge management team has a tough job: they must not just protect the monument, and provide a fulfilling and informative experience for visitors, but also try to stay in touch with the many different interest groups. Our plan being to retrieve human bones from Stonehenge, I could see that some people would find a new grievance to campaign against. Sure enough, it wasn't long before a new placard appeared near the ticket office: 'We the loyal Arthurian warbands and our orders, covens and groves and the Council of British Druid Orders oppose the removal of our ancient guardians: Aubrey Hole seven.' It was going to be an interesting week.

One of the permissions that we'd had to obtain in order to excavate Aubrey Hole 7 was a licence from the British government to remove human remains from their place of burial. This is left over from Victorian times, one of the provisions of the 1857 Burial Act, which proclaims that: 'It is not lawful to remove any body, or remains of any body, which may have been interred in any place of burial, without licence under hand of one of Her Majesty's principal Secretaries of State, and with such precautions as such Secretary of State may prescribe as the condition of such licence.' Such legislation was drafted to address concerns about nineteenth-century grave-robbers – the resurrection men – removing cadavers for sale to medical schools for dissection and to protect the Victorian public from the exhumation of rather fresh corpses in desperately overcrowded cemeteries.[10] It became law well before anyone thought about the role of archaeology.

It used to be that the Home Secretary was the person who signed the licence for archaeological excavation of ancient or prehistoric remains. The licence would specify the archaeological specialists responsible for analysing the remains and the museum in which those bones would be deposited. It would also specify standard conditions about screening the remains from public view while they're in the ground or being lifted (not appreciated by the general public, who are fascinated by skeletons) and notifying the local environmental-health officer (utterly pointless for most skeletons more than 100 years old).

While very large excavations of church cemeteries can be quite startling to the public – simply because of the number of skeletons exposed – visitors to archaeological digs are generally intrigued by burial archaeology. There is another type of excavation, of course, which is almost never seen by the public, this being when a modern cemetery is emptied of dead bodies in advance of development. Such work is often undertaken by professional cemetery-clearance companies, who may have to remove hundreds of coffins and corpses – sometimes of quite recent date.[11] Human remains are most often dug up not for archaeological reasons but as a result of redundant churches being converted (into houses or sports bars, for example) or so that developers may build on old cemeteries. In fact, anyone planning to be buried in a municipal cemetery in Britain should expect to be dug up after about a century, since burial plots are usually 'rented'.

Just prior to our dig in 2008, governmental responsibility for the issue of excavation licences was passed to the newly formed Ministry of Justice. Their lawyers were apparently perplexed by the details of the legislation: initially their view was that the Burial Act was not actually relevant for archaeological excavations and so licences were not required at all. This Ministry of Justice advice changed six months later, when it was decided that licences *were* required and also that all human bones, *whatever their antiquity*, must be re-buried in a 'legal place of burial' after two years of archaeological research. This was an entirely new interpretation of the 1857 Act – such a requirement for the reburial of prehistoric human remains had never been imposed before at any time in the 150 years since the Act was passed; it was a terrible blow to archaeology and most people didn't know that it had happened. The ruling didn't affect archaeological skeletons dug up before 2008, but any new discoveries after that cut-off date – even very, very ancient remains – would be consigned to oblivion. Some of the world's most important archaeological remains were due to be reburied instead of being stored carefully in museums; future generations would have nothing to study and nothing to learn from.

Only in 2011 did the matter come to public and parliamentary attention. In the face of growing pressure from archaeologists, scientists, journalists and the wider public, the Ministry reconsidered their strange interpretation of the law, agreeing to be more flexible and to allow curation of archaeological bones. Yet the matter has left other European archaeologists astonished that such a path could be chosen by a Western European culture (with an indisputable tradition of frequent removal of old burials) that prides itself on its enlightened and scientific heritage.

By 2008 some members of the Druid groups were already calling on museum curators to rebury British prehistoric bones. They perhaps took their cue from indigenous groups in North America and Australia. In these countries the situation is rather different, though. All but the most blinkered scientists accept that there is a difficult moral question surrounding the presence in museums of bones of native peoples collected during the colonial period; many seem to have been acquired in much the same way as 'natural history' specimens were collected. They are a nasty vestige of an inhumane attitude to other races and conquered peoples.

What to do about such human remains in museum collections has been a difficult question to resolve. In general, if a living group of people still exists with a claim to be descended from these long-dead individuals, archaeologists and museums have given up the rights of science (not without a fight) in favour of the rights of very bitter, damaged communities, often nearly annihilated by European colonization, who often wish to bury such remains according to ancient traditions.

The situation in Britain is obviously much more complicated – the remains of the prehistoric inhabitants of these islands 'belong' to all of

us. The majority of British people can have no idea when their own distant ancestors arrived here; we are a complete mixture, descended from
all sorts of people such as early hunter-gatherers, Bronze Age immigrants,
Romans (many of whom were black North Africans, by the way), Saxons,
Jutes, Danes, Normans (who were actually French Vikings), and so forth.
Some of my ancestors probably arrived a long time ago, some of them
may have arrived more recently – I don't know, and I don't care, because
it's just not relevant.

It is a fantasy, too, to think that DNA testing can ever unravel this.
Even in those cases where DNA can be extracted from ancient remains,
to whose modern DNA do you then compare it? Everybody in Britain?
Given modern emigration from Britain, the descendants of any prehis-
toric person could be scattered across the world by now, for all we know.
I think we have to accept that prehistoric human remains in Britain
should be treated either as everybody's ancestors or nobody's ancestors.
We treasure them nevertheless.

A small group of Druids and other Pagans seem to want pre-Roman
human remains to be reburied. As far as I know they are unconcerned
about our other ancestors – the late arrivals, as it were – and I don't think
they've ever commented on the emptying of cemeteries and churches
for development, the displacement of our more recent dead. The small
museum at Avebury was targeted by a small but vociferous group and the
National Trust, the museum's owner, agreed to a national consultation
over whether the museum's prehistoric skeletons should be reburied.
Many months later, English Heritage and the National Trust announced
that there was overwhelming public support for the storage and display
of prehistoric human remains in museums.[12]

At the time of our excavation at Stonehenge in 2008, both the
National Trust and English Heritage were holding the line that prehistoric burials, because of their great antiquity and value for on-going
research, should be retained for future study and education. Neither
organization had yet commented on the illogical position caused by the
Ministry of Justice's change of policy – human remains excavated a long
time ago, sometimes with no information about where they came from,
we keep; remains excavated today, with proper recording and analysis,
we were instructed by the Minister to rebury. And in the middle of this

surreal situation we were hoping to excavate the cremated bones at Stonehenge: our timing was definitely off.

Paganism is an umbrella term that can include Druids, witches, Wiccans, shamans and other belief groups. At the 2001 UK census 30,569 people recorded themselves as Pagans and 1657 as Druids*. This total of about 32,000 people is about one-tenth the number of Sikhs in the UK and about the same number as Spiritualists. (Some 390,000 people said they were Jedi Knights on that same census.) Although some people claim that Paganism and Druidry are ancient religions that survived underground during 1500 years of Christianity, it is a modern invention that seems to draw inspiration from long-abandoned folk beliefs. The term 'pagan' is used to cover a host of religious groups and orders that, as in many other religions, appear to disagree with each other frequently on dogma, rites and rituals and other aspects of belief. By a strange quirk of history, one of modern Druidry's progenitors was William Stukeley, the antiquarian who did so much research on Stonehenge in the early eighteenth century; Stukeley invented his own order of druids.[13]

Stukeley was a clever man – with very little to work on, he was able to deduce that Stonehenge had been built before the Romans arrived. His best available guide to life in prehistoric Britain was Julius Caesar's account of his invasions in 55 BC and 54 BC.[14] In Caesar's time the religious specialists of the ancient Britons were called *druides* (the Latin we translate as 'druids') so Stukeley reasoned that, if Stonehenge was a pre-Roman temple, it must have been something to do with druids. The logic was faultless – except that (obviously) Stukeley had no idea that Stonehenge was built 3000–2500 years before Caesar's druids ever existed. That is more remote in time from Caesar than Caesar is from us today. Is there any evidence that the traditions of Iron Age druids went back thousands of years into British prehistory? It is exceedingly unlikely and all the archaeological and documentary evidence points to their being no more ancient than the Late Bronze Age at best.[15]

* Because today's Druids consider themselves to be adherents of a religious belief-system, the word is now spelt with a capital letter in this context (like Buddhist, Christian etc.); this also usefully distinguishes references to modern Druids from information about Iron Age druids.

William Stukeley's drawing of how he imagined a British druid
of the Roman period to have looked.

Caesar knew a lot about druids. One of his friends, Diviciacus, was a
druid as well as King of the Aedui in central Gaul (now France). Druids
were important ritual specialists who could take up to twenty years to
learn their craft, all of it passed down by oral learning without writing.
According to Caesar: 'The druids officiate at the worship of the gods,
regulate public and private sacrifices, and give rulings on all religious
questions . . . They act as judges in practically all disputes'.[16] Caesar himself served as *pontifex maximus,* high priest of Rome, so he probably had
some interest in comparative religion.

Caesar was one of many Classical authors who wrote about the druids
of Britain and Gaul.[17] Unfortunately these writers do not make the most
reliable of authorities, since most of them never went anywhere near
those barbarian lands and there seems to have been a fair amount of
copying of other writers' tales. Perhaps the author among them who is

most trustworthy – likely more so than Caesar, whose propagandist motives must have affected his writings – was Posidonius, a philosopher and scholar of great renown who travelled in Gaul and other parts of the barbarian world in the early first century BC. Sadly his writings survive only as plagiarized versions by other authors, but he probably witnessed druidical practices with his own eyes.[18] In the first century AD Tacitus wrote graphically in his *Annals* about the Romans' slaughter of the druids on the Welsh island of Anglesey in AD 67: 'their groves, devoted to inhuman superstitions, were destroyed. They deemed it, indeed, a duty to cover their altars with the blood of captives and to consult their deities through human entrails.'[19]

In not one Classical account is there any mention of druids worshipping at stone circles. Authors such as Tacitus mention 'groves', presumably sacred places in forests.[20] Equally the archaeological evidence shows very little activity during Iron Age times in or around the stone circles of the Neolithic. The one period when there was considerable re-use of prehistoric monuments of the Neolithic and Bronze Age was much later, during the Saxon period in the sixth to ninth centuries AD, when these ancient earthworks were often chosen as locations for burials and cemeteries. From Stonehenge itself, there is a single human skull fragment from the Iron Age (dated to 520–360 BC) and other human remains from later periods: a skull fragment dated to AD 340–510, a decapitated skeleton dating to AD 600–680 and a pair of teeth dating to around AD 800.[21]

It is also clear that the Classical writers perceived druids principally as judges and public functionaries, with their religious tasks often being listed almost as an afterthought. To consider them primarily as priests or religious specialists – as many have believed since Stukeley's day – may be to misunderstand their actual roles in Iron Age society.

On the basis of the evidence, archaeologists have to conclude that the association of druids with Stonehenge is an entirely recent invention with no basis in prehistoric reality. Yet, thanks to Stukeley, it has become a modern myth, trotted out again and again by the uncritical. I suspect that many modern Pagans are perfectly well aware that druids never worshipped at Stonehenge; it may be more important that Paganism is a new religion – or, rather, a group of new religions – in which people can make emotional links between the past and the present.

Attitudes to human bones among the many Pagan groups in Britain are very diverse. There is even a group of Pagans for Archaeology, many of whom have no problem with the keeping of bones in museums. Perhaps it is like any cross-section of society, with moderates and an extremist fringe. Anyway, we were soon to meet some people who (I hope) represented the latter minority.

Before we started work on excavation at the Aubrey Hole, the manager of Stonehenge, Peter Carson, invited a small group of Pagans to perform a ceremony of their choice. The same had been done for Geoff and Tim's dig. After years of conflict over the banning of solstice festivals at Stonehenge since 1985, English Heritage had changed their policy in the 1990s: now, instead of confrontation, they seek negotiation. My colleagues and I could see no objection to the peaceful public performance of any religious ritual that anyone cared to undertake (except that we had a tight schedule and needed to get to work); I certainly have no desire to dictate to others what they should or shouldn't believe, and my own beliefs are irrelevant. My personal view is that Druids and other Pagans have a great deal in common with archaeologists – the members of both groups know a great deal about our ancient heritage; they see it as being of inestimable value and care very deeply about what happens to it.

About sixty people turned up in the field outside Stonehenge, wearing what I think was religious costume – a variety of robes and antlers – banging drums and shouting, to the alarm of both the diggers and the visiting public. Two small girls burst into tears and had to be calmed by their parents. Tolerance was apparently a one-sided affair: Julian Richards was publicly condemned with a Druidical curse. Finally, the proceedings calmed down and a Pagan blessing was provided next to the car park by some of the more moderate celebrants.

THE AUBREY HOLES

By the early 1930s mass tourism had reached Stonehenge. There was a pressing need for visitors to have somewhere to park their cars. In January 1935, in consequence, Robert Newall (Colonel Hawley's assistant) and William Young (who had worked at Woodhenge for archaeologist Maud Cunnington in the 1920s) were digging in advance of the construction of this first car park just to the northwest of Stonehenge. They took the opportunity to re-open Aubrey Hole 7 and bury in it all the cremated human bones that had been found by Hawley at Stonehenge. They kept a written record of their work but they didn't record why they chose Aubrey Hole 7 – though its large size and proximity to the road might have been the reason. Young recorded in his diary that they dumped four sandbags of bone in the re-opened hole; so that future archaeologists would know what these bones were – and in case Young's diary did not survive – they also left an inscribed lead plaque in the pit on top of them.

Working out what the Aubrey Holes were originally used for is tricky. Before working at Stonehenge, Atkinson had dug a series of pit circles on the river terrace gravels at Dorchester-on-Thames in Oxfordshire, so he had some experience of this type of Neolithic feature.[1] After digging two Aubrey Holes in 1950, he decided that the Aubrey Holes 'were never intended to hold any kind of upright, either the bluestones . . . or wooden posts'.[2] They were just a circle of pits. Later archaeologists tended not to agree with him. By the time our project started, the usual interpretation given in guidebooks and elsewhere was that the Aubrey

Holes had once held wooden posts. Josh Pollard, for example, could easily interpret the old excavation records and the beautiful sections drawn for Atkinson by Stuart Piggott to see that the compacted chalk rubble found in all the holes was best explained as packing around a central upright.

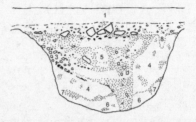

A section of Aubrey Hole 32, drawn by Stuart Piggott, showing the filled-in void where a bluestone once stood (5) and the chalk packing material for the stone (4, 6, 7) from which bones of a cremation burial were recovered (4). To the left (at 3), the side of the pit has been crushed and the packing layer displaced where the stone was removed.

Going back through Hawley's notes and reports of his excavations in the 1920s, I discovered that he had made careful observations about how the Aubrey Holes had been used. He noted that the chalk bottoms of at least two of them had been compacted and crushed. Many more, Hawley wrote, had their edges 'shorn away, or crushed down, on the side towards the standing stones of Stonehenge, this being apparently due to the insertion or withdrawal of a stone, probably the latter'. In 1921 he concluded that 'there can be little doubt that they [the Aubrey Holes] once held small upright stones'.[3]

For some reason Hawley didn't have the courage of his convictions and later changed his mind.[4] In his diary he wrote that Maud Cunnington and her husband had convinced him that the Aubrey Holes were postholes. Their excavation at Woodhenge between 1926 and 1928 had uncovered evidence that part of this Neolithic monument consisted of massive wooden posts, not just standing stones. These Woodhenge postholes were about the same diameter as the Aubrey Holes so superficially looked very similar.

In 2007 I began to wonder if Hawley had been right the first time. In

Our 2008 excavation of Aubrey Hole 7 recovered the cremated bones of about 60 people buried within Stonehenge more than 4000 years ago.

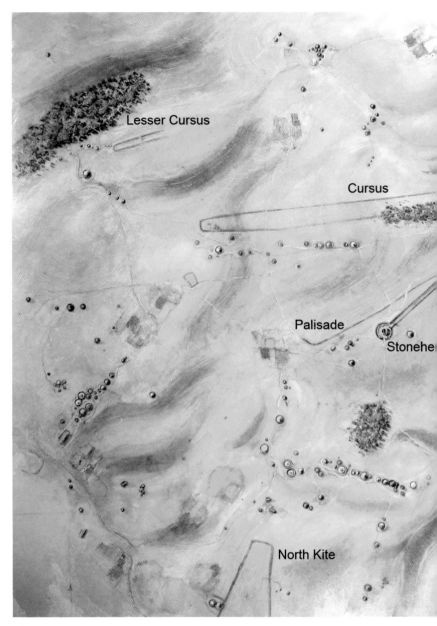

The 26.6 square kilometres of the Stonehenge World Heritage Site, including Durrington Walls, Stonehenge and other Neolithic sites. Clusters of Early Bronze Age barrows encircle Stonehenge.

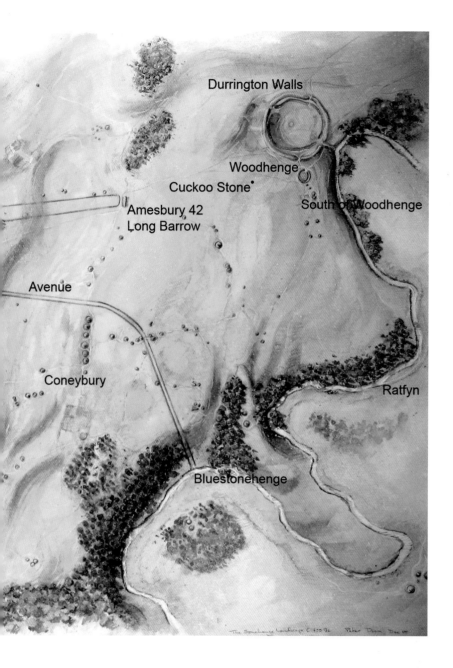

Durrington Walls

Woodhenge

Cuckoo Stone

South of Woodhenge

Amesbury 42
Long Barrow

Avenue

Coneybury

Ratfyn

Bluestonehenge

The Stonehenge Landscape C.1650 BC   Peter Dunn Dec 05

Stonehenge without the tourists.

Sunset through sarsen stones 1 and 30. These form the northeast entrance to Stonehenge, leading to and from the Avenue.

Reconstruction of Stonehenge Stage 1.

Reconstruction of Stonehenge Stage 3.

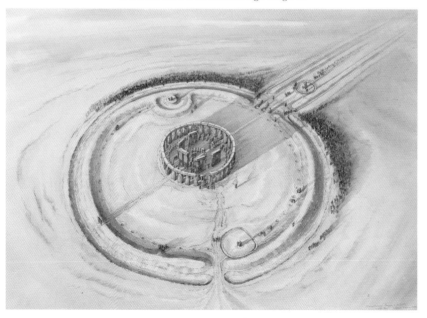

Colin Richards (centre top) excavating one of the Neolithic houses at Durrington Walls.

Trenches around the east entrance of Durrington Walls revealed Neolithic houses (foreground) and the avenue running from the river (visible in the far trench).

The Durrington Walls avenue had a surface of broken flint (darker area in centre), flanked by chalk banks.

Reconstruction of the Southern Circle at Durrington Walls. It is likely to date to the same time as Stonehenge's sarsen circle and trilithons (Stage 2).

The Southern Circle as rebuilt at North Newnton, Wiltshire, in 2006 by *Time Team*.

Reconstruction of the Durrington Walls avenue and surrounding houses.

Reconstruction of the Western Enclosure at the centre of the
Durrington Walls village.

Reconstruction of the Neolithic village of Durrington Walls before the building of
the henge bank and ditch. (© Peter Dunn)

Reconstruction of the Durrington Walls henge bank and ditch.

The discovery of an antler pick at the bottom of the Greater Cursus ditch. This helped us to place the Cursus in the same date range as the Lesser Cursus.

The Cuckoo Stone, near Woodhenge, was erected east of the Cursus.

The Food Vessel burial under excavation at Bulford. This multiple burial, close to the standing stone, contained many grave goods.

At Woodhenge Josh Pollard discovered that a stone 'cove' once stood in the southern part of the site after the timber posts had decayed.

Excavations at Durrington Walls (centre and right) and south of Woodhenge (bottom left).

The remains of a Late Neolithic timber tower overlooking the River Avon, south of Woodhenge. It was subsequently disturbed by the building of an Early Bronze Age barrow.

The completion of the excavation of Aubrey Hole 7.

Reconstruction of Bluestonehenge at West Amesbury, on the west bank of the River Avon.

Reconstruction of the Stonehenge Avenue reaching the West Amesbury henge after removal of the bluestones and construction of a henge bank and ditch.

The busy moments of an excavation. This is Bluestonehenge in 2009.

The periglacial stripes and chalk ridges revealed in our excavation across the Avenue close to Stonehenge in 2008.

Colin Richards (left) and Andrew Chamberlain at the closed chamber tomb or cromlech of Carreg Samson in west Wales.

At Craig Rhosyfelin we found the first clear evidence of bluestone quarrying. The monolith (lower right) left behind in the quarry was detached by prehistoric stone-workers from the outcrop (behind where Ben Chan and I are standing); they then moved the monolith from the rock face along stone 'rails' on which it still rests.

all the discussion and mulling over what the Aubrey Holes could have once held – timber, stone or nothing at all – no one had thought to make a very careful comparison of the dimensions of these intriguing pits with those of known postholes or stoneholes. There are plenty of excavated examples to make such a comparison possible – from Stonehenge itself one can examine the records of excavated sarsen holes, the bluestone Q and R Holes and other bluestone-holding holes. From our own experience at Woodhenge and Durrington Walls and its avenue we knew that stoneholes are much shallower than postholes of equivalent diameter. The stoneholes we had dug also had a thin layer of crushed chalk at their bases, which is something not found in even the largest of the postholes.

The results of a metrical comparison between Neolithic postholes and Neolithic stoneholes are very clear.[5] The Aubrey Holes are too narrow to be pits and too shallow to be postholes. They are, on average, half a metre shallower than postholes of equivalent diameter. They are also narrower than either sarsen holes or, for example, the Neolithic pits found at Dorchester-on-Thames by Atkinson. The Aubrey Holes are, in fact, identical in width, depth and shape to the bluestoneholes located elsewhere in Stonehenge.

One might wonder whether the Aubrey Holes held small, short posts in shallow sockets, thereby contrasting with the normally deep postholes at other Neolithic sites such as Woodhenge and the Southern Circle. But that cannot be the case because such short posts would not have been heavy enough to cause the crushing and compaction that Hawley noted within the Aubrey Holes.

Returning to Piggott's section drawings of the Aubrey Holes I could see how the crushed chalk rubble that fills the holes had been deposited and then displaced. It seems that the chalk 'fill' had initially been packed against the base of a stone in each hole and was then displaced on one side when the stone was pulled out. Looking at the drawings, it is evident that in Aubrey Hole 32, for example, not just the rubble but also the side of the pit itself was crushed by withdrawing a stone, just as Hawley had observed on other examples.[6] From the records and drawings alone a very strong case can be made for the Aubrey Holes having held small upright stones – presumably the bluestones – and for these to have formed a stone circle right at the beginning of Stonehenge's sequence.

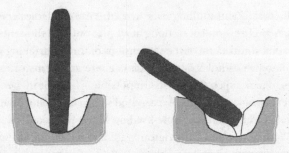

Removing a bluestone from an Aubrey Hole, showing how the shape of a pit is altered when a stone is removed.

I am puzzled as to why Atkinson said that the Aubrey Holes had held no uprights of either wood or stone. If a pit is dug and then filled in, an archaeologist can see the clear edges where the pit was cut into the soil. If a timber post is left to rot *in situ*, you see a parallel-sided 'pipe' within the pit, where the timber has decayed. If an upright is pulled out of a pit, however, it changes the shape of the pit's sides, because of the movement of soil caused by levering it out. These differences can be hard to spot for someone with little experience of digging postholes and stoneholes.

To work out what happened at Stonehenge we needed to know more about the Aubrey Holes, to find out both what they were for and when they were dug. Everyone agrees that the construction sequence at Stonehenge begins with the ditch and bank. These were constructed at some point within 3000–2920 BC, on the basis of Bayesian-modelled radiocarbon dates. Some archaeologists reckoned that the Aubrey Holes belonged to this earliest phase, because they are set in a ring just inside the circles of the bank and ditch; others thought they must be part of a later phase.

To date the Aubrey Holes we turned to Salisbury and South Wiltshire Museum again, which has responsibility for many of the prehistoric finds from Wessex. Given the amount of archaeological investigation that has been carried out at Stonehenge, and the huge amount of effort that has gone into unravelling the construction sequence, it is truly surprising that there is material still waiting to be dated. The curators in Salisbury take care of three cremation burials excavated by Atkinson and gave us permission to take samples for radiocarbon dating.

One of these cremation burials was found in Aubrey Hole 32,

excavated during Atkinson's very first Stonehenge season in 1950. Piggott's impeccably drawn section shows that the bone fragments were found scattered within the layer of compacted chalk rubble packed into the bottom sides of the hole; these bones were therefore deposited in the initial 'fill' of the hole, and not inserted later.

We sent a small sample of cremated bone off to the lab. Material for radiocarbon dating (C14 dating) has to go to one of a handful of specialist labs with accelerator mass spectrometers. The two labs that we use are in Glasgow and Oxford. Radiocarbon dating is a slow process that takes many months. On completion the results are sent to the excavator by letter – until it arrives you don't know the date of your sample. When our result finally came back we learned that this Aubrey Hole cremation burial dates to 3030–2880 cal BC, the same period as the antler picks found at the bottom of the Stonehenge ditch, so we were confident that the Aubrey Holes did belong to Stonehenge's initial phase of construction.[7]

We also sent for radiocarbon dating two other cremations found by Atkinson, not from Aubrey Holes but from different layers within the ditch. These dated to around 2900 BC and around 2500–2300 BC. As well as carefully buried cremated bones, loose human bones were also being scattered at Stonehenge: two fragments of unburnt human skulls from the ditch date to 2800–2600 BC.

We now had some new dates to add to the existing chronology for Stonehenge's construction and use. The 1995 book *Stonehenge in Its Landscape* by Ros Cleal and her team had finally provided the 'full and definitive' account that Atkinson, Piggott and Stone had envisaged, though only Piggott lived long enough to see it. Cleal's team had examined all the existing radiocarbon dates, working out whether they were from secure contexts or not, and English Heritage had paid for a new suite of dates from antler picks and animal bones. There was a solid framework for Stonehenge's chronology, but there were still some problems to be ironed out. How did our new dates for the Aubrey Hole and for the other human bones fit into the chronology?

The new dates affected the chronology in two ways. Firstly, the orthodox view, that Stonehenge was used as a cemetery for just a short period of time around 2600 BC, was wrong. The new radiocarbon dates showed that Stonehenge had started as a place of burial since the Aubrey Hole cremation dates to the moment of Stonehenge's construction and initial use. Secondly, the new date showed that the Aubrey Holes were definitely some of the first constructions at Stonehenge. If we were right that they once held bluestones, this had significant implications for the sequence of construction and the dates of the different stages of the monument. If Stonehenge had actually started as a bluestone circle shortly after 3000 BC, these stones must have arrived more than 500 years earlier than anyone had previously reckoned.

13

DIGGING AT STONEHENGE

The dig to retrieve the 1935 deposit of cremated bones from Aubrey Hole 7 began and all except a small handful of Druids went away. Now we could start trying to find out who those people buried at Stonehenge were. Hawley had stripped the entire area around Aubrey Hole 7 and its neighbours, and Newall and Young had dug it out for a second time, so we didn't expect to find very much in the hole other than the reburied bones.

This Aubrey Hole is one of the largest and it was one of the most prolific in finds. Hawley recovered fifty-five sarsen hammerstones from this one hole, together with more than eighty bluestone and sarsen chips, and an axe-shaped bluestone. The bones of a disturbed cremation (of what he thought was a young adult) were scattered from top to bottom through the layers filling the southeast side of the pit. On the bottom of the pit, among chalk rubble, he found a small deposit of wood ash. Apart from three sherds of Roman and Bronze Age pottery and a single worked flint, Hawley did not bother to collect the smaller finds. In 1935 Newall and Young found an unfinished oblique arrowhead in his backfill. This was just the tip of the iceberg in terms of what he either missed or deliberately left behind: we found more than thirty worked flints, more chippings of sarsen and bluestone and more sherds of Roman and prehistoric pottery.

In the thirty-two Aubrey Holes that he excavated, Hawley found thirty cremations, more than four hundred hammerstones and more than a thousand chips of bluestone and sarsen. Just like in the Q and R Holes, there was not a single antler pick. He noticed that most of the cremation burials had been disturbed by the removal of what he reckoned were standing stones, but he also recorded that one or two cremations had been inserted after stone removal, because they remained intact and had not been crushed or otherwise disturbed. Cremation burials had also been placed around the edges of some of the holes.

Why all the hammerstones, stone chippings and cremations? Atkinson believed the Aubrey Holes were neither structural nor sepulchral in their primary purpose. He thought that the cremations were introduced to the holes during their re-filling, in the same way that ritual libations were made in pits as entrances to the underworld in Classical Greece. Yet Hawley was very clear that most of the burials had been included in the initial filling of the pits, and then disturbed later.

Hammerstones are fist-sized cobbles that have been used for pounding the surfaces of the sarsens. They are often used subsequently as packing for standing stones – Gowland found twenty-two of them slipped into the south side of the great trilithon upright to help fix it in place. Perhaps they were used for a similar purpose in the Aubrey Holes, or perhaps they were introduced after the stones were pulled out, to fill in the consequent depressions.

At the bottom of the loose soil tipped back in by Newall and Young in January 1935, we found the lead plaque that they had left there for us, the archaeologists of the future. It reads:

MOST OF THESE BONES WERE DUG UP IN THE YEARS
1921 1922 1923 FROM THOSE HOLES JUST INSIDE THE
BANK OF THIS MONUMENT AND CALLED AUBREY HOLES
BY THE SOCIETY OF ANTIQUARIES OF LONDON IN
CONNECTION WITH HIS MAJESTYS OFFICE OF WORKS
SOME BONES WERE FOUND IN THE DITCH   THE HOLES
WERE CALLED AFTER AUBREY BECAUSE HE SUGGESTED
THEIR EXISTENCE IN THE YEAR 1666
REBURIED 1935

We were all a bit disappointed with this truly prosaic inscription – we'd secretly wished for something more archaeologically informative, or even more poetic. And it's got a spelling mistake.

Once we'd carefully lifted the plaque we could see a mass of cremated bones beneath. Scraping away the last of the loose soil on top of them, it was obvious that they had been dumped in a single heap. Young had written in his diary of their having been laid in four separate sandbags but there was no sign of any such division. It looked more likely that the bones had been poured into the hole, perhaps simply to keep the sand-bags for re-use.

All of us had hoped that these archaeologists of the 1920s and 1930s had understood the value of context – and might therefore have appre-ciated the need to keep the bones from each burial separate. In the months before starting work we'd been hoping that the bones from each burial had been kept separate in tins, paper bags, cloth wrappings – any-thing that could allow us to distinguish between the separate burials. We'd even fantasized that Newell and Young might have written indeli-ble labels detailing from which context – or at least which Aubrey Hole – each burial had originally come.

Jacqui McKinley (top) and Julian Richards (right) excavating the undifferentiated mass of prehistoric cremated bones deposited in Aubrey Hole 7 in 1935.

The lead plaque left on top of the cremated bones in Aubrey Hole 7
by Robert Newall and William Young.

Instead everything was mixed together. It was possible that the whole lot had not been utterly shaken up before being put in the ground, and that the bones from one burial might be packed next to the bones from another. If we took them out of the ground using a very precise three-dimensional grid of 5cm blocks, it was just possible that specialist laboratory analysis could determine which bones belonged to which burials. The gloom induced by this archaeological carelessness was lifted by the optimism of Jacqui McKinley. Jacqui is the osteoarchaeologist (human bone specialist) for Wessex Archaeology and has probably analysed more cremation burials than anyone else in the world.[1] Not only were there far more bones than we had anticipated, but she was very pleased to see that they were generally large pieces in good condition.

When a body is cremated on a pyre, the fat and flesh burn away over a period of four to eight hours (depending on fuel and the tending of the fire) so that only the bones remain. These become calcined, turning blue and white, shrinking, warping, cracking and splintering. Once the fire cools they can be gathered off the pyre surface, which has become a mass of charcoal, ash and calcined bones. Colin has seen the whole process on an open-air pyre at a cremation ceremony on the Indonesian island of Bali. Many years ago, when I was doing some research on modern British funerary practices, I spent some time with the staff at a British crematorium, peering through the furnace spy-hole to watch the flaming bubbling fat and flesh burning off to leave a glowing red skeleton. The crematorium operator then takes a long iron tool and pokes the bones so that they fall in chunks down a chute, to be collected in a metal container. After they've cooled, the burnt bone fragments are put into a 'cremulator' (a machine that looks rather like a tumble-drier) to be reduced to tiny dust-sized particles.

Of course, the cremulator is a twentieth-century invention and prehistoric cremated bones never received this kind of final treatment. That said, archaeologists sometimes find that the bones from a cremation have broken into very small pieces and have been heavily weathered and eroded. Jacqui has also found out that the average archaeological cremation weighs less than a kilogram, whereas the weight of an adult's burnt bones should be around 2 kilograms. Most prehistoric cremation burials have lost some of the bones along the way – partly, she thinks, because retrieval from the pyre would not have been particularly efficient, and partly because bones could well have been divided up so that not all were buried. For example, the three cremation burials excavated by Atkinson from Stonehenge vary in weight from 77 grams to 150 grams to 1546 grams, with only the last one likely to comprise most of the recoverable bone.

With the last of the cremated bones removed from the bottom of Aubrey Hole 7, we trowelled around the edges of the pit to find out whether there were other features – postholes and stakeholes – in its vicinity. There was a small stakehole on its west side and, to our surprise, a completely unexpected cremation burial close to the western edge of the hole. We'd seen the dark spread of its surface as soon as we had taken off the turf but had straightaway assumed that it was something already investigated – two previous groups of very competent archaeologists had already dug here, after all.

It seems strange that both William Hawley and Newall and Young missed this cremation burial. Capped by a small sarsen chipping, this was a small collection of cremated bones placed in a neat little hole cut just 10 centimetres into the chalk. The tidy, circular distribution of the bones indicated that they had been placed there within an organic container, most likely a leather bag but possibly a birch-bark box or some other form of circular wooden container. Hawley had indeed noted other burials as having been deposited in what he too thought had been leather bags. Having disturbed this unexpected cremation burial, we couldn't leave it in the ground, so its fragile fragments were lifted and taken back to the laboratory with the mass of bones from Hawley's excavations. This burial has produced a radiocarbon date of 3330–2910 BC, indicating that it was buried next to Aubrey Hole 7 right at the beginning of Stonehenge's construction.

To Mike, Julian and me it seemed extraordinary that this find had been overlooked. How many more such cremation deposits had Hawley failed to find within Stonehenge? Perhaps we should revise our estimates for the number of people buried at Stonehenge, since Hawley's work had perhaps not been as thorough as everyone thought. Might the stakehole next to the burial have held a grave marker? How many more stakeholes had Hawley missed? He recorded only postholes, and perhaps his ability to recognize these ephemeral features across the ground surface of Stonehenge was not great. Maybe it's no wonder that it's difficult for archaeologists today to make sense of the arrangements of postholes recorded by Hawley: he may well have missed a lot of them.

The first cremated bones to be visible after our team lifted the lead plaque.

We could see that Hawley had failed to thoroughly clean out Aubrey Hole 7: he'd left a thin spread of chalk rubble undisturbed in the bottom. Here was a fortuitous opportunity to see if any evidence remained to show us at first-hand what had once stood, or had been put, in this hole. The chalk rubble was solid, so hard that I had to remove it with a hand-pick; someone in prehistory had worked hard to ram and pack this chalk as firmly as they could. There was one spot without rubble, about 40 centimetres across, where a thin layer of chalk on the bottom of the pit had been crushed. We called Josh over to confirm what those of us who had previously dug stoneholes suspected. The majority of us agreed that we knew exactly what this was – the crushing of a chalk pit base by the weight of a standing stone.*

It seems very likely that Stonehenge was a stone circle from its very beginning. From the sizes of the Aubrey Holes it is evident that the stones they once held were small and narrow. This rules out the sarsens, so we're confident that Stonehenge most likely started as a circle of 56 bluestones. Judging by the number of known empty stoneholes in the bluestone circle and Q and R Holes, from Atkinson onwards archaeologists have reckoned that around 80 bluestones were once here, employed in these later constructions.[2] If the first installation of bluestones was a circle of 56 in the Aubrey Holes, by the time that the bluestone circle and bluestone oval were erected in the period 2280–2030 BC, another 24 or so bluestones had to be added to Stonehenge to reach a total of 80. Many of these have been destroyed and removed; today just 43 bluestones remain at the site.

It always surprises people when I explain to them that Stonehenge is Britain's biggest cemetery from the third millennium BC, with a known total of 63 cremation burials (59 found by Hawley, three by Atkinson and one by ourselves) and an estimated likely total of 150 or more, given that only about half of Stonehenge has been excavated and that Hawley didn't always manage to spot cremation burials where he was digging.

---

* Julian Richards remained unconvinced, by the way. It is a disagreement in which we think we are right, based on our greater experience of excavating stoneholes. Without casting any doubt on Julian's skill as a field archaeologist, we would argue that interpretation of features like this is not easy but a matter of experience and repeated exposure. We've simply dug a lot of very similar stoneholes and, purely by chance, Julian's sites have never contained features like this one.

Through a combination of radiocarbon dating and stratigraphic analysis, we now know that Stonehenge was used for burial for most of that millennium. Burials were definitely placed in the Aubrey Holes, in close association with Welsh bluestones. In at least one case the cremated bones were added to the chalk packing that held the stone in place.[3]

In addition to the cremations, scattered pieces of unburnt human bone were also left at Stonehenge. Many that Hawley recorded cannot be located in any museum, and only about 30 fragments survive.[4] Of these, eight have been radiocarbon-dated. Three of these – fragments of skull and teeth – date to the third millennium BC and we can extrapolate from this 3:5 proportion to estimate that about a dozen of the remaining 30 bones are likely to date to this broad period. Scattering and disarticulating human bodies may seem like something that people would do only to their very worst enemies. Yet it was a common practice in Neolithic Britain in the fourth and third millennia BC, and does not seem to indicate any sort of disrespect.[5] Long barrows and chambered tombs include complete, partial and disarticulated skeletons. Causewayed enclosures were also places where bodies were left to decay and turn into loose bones. Anthropologists have known for over a century of traditional societies in many times and places – from southeast and south Asia to North America and Africa – where the process of rotting and disaggregation down to clean bones must occur in order for the spirit to be freed from the corpse.[6]

Funerary practices in prehistoric Britain changed radically through time. We know very little about what happened to the dead during the Mesolithic period – it seems these hunter-gatherers did not usually bury the corpse, or bury deposits of cremated bone. Their mortuary rites are mostly invisible archaeologically (in the same way as the majority of our own dead will vanish from the archaeological record, since today we generally scatter ashes after cremation). In the Early Neolithic, the time of the first farmers, the bodies of the dead were placed inside long barrows and chambered tombs, and in caves, between about 3800–3400 BC.[7] Between 3600 and 3000 BC individual inhumation burial (that is, burial of the body in the ground), sometimes with grave goods, was common in different parts of the country. Some of these burials were marked by round mounds, over a thousand years before the Bronze Age round barrows.[8] None are known from the Stonehenge area. The most dramatic is from the western end of the Yorkshire Wolds at Duggleby Howe where a group of adult males were buried with grave goods under a huge mound set within its own henge ditch.[9] One of the burials seems to have been accompanied by the skull of a woman who had been hit on the head with a heavy club.

After 3000 BC and before 2400 BC, people in Britain appear to have renounced inhumation burial. Disarticulated bones, bodies thrown into rivers and cremations are all that we find. These seem to have been the only forms of mortuary treatment that have left any trace. There are just a handful of inhumed skeletons from this period: for example, a child buried in a henge at Dorchester, Dorset, a woman buried next to a small henge at Horton in the Calne valley, and an adult with severe injuries found at the bottom of a vertical pothole at North End Pot in North Yorkshire.[10] It is likely that this poor chap fell down the hole, so this is probably a Neolithic fatal accident rather than a burial.

After 2400 BC, the inhumation rite returned.[11] It was not a British innovation but the arrival or adoption of a Continental tradition. In these burials, the corpse was normally accompanied by a pottery Beaker and other grave goods. The last burial at Stonehenge during the third millennium BC, probably after the cremations had ceased, was the inhumation of a young man in the outer ditch close to the northeast entrance.[12] This burial took place at some point during the period 2400–2140 BC. This young man was buried with an archer's wristguard but no Beaker. Remarkably, he had been shot three times or more from different directions. There are marks on his bones where they have been grazed and punctured by arrows, and three barbed-and-tanged arrowheads were found in the area of his body cavity. Known as the Stonehenge Archer, he was a local man according to his isotope signature.

Archaeologists have long speculated whether the Stonehenge Archer was a human sacrifice, a clandestine murder victim, or an executed criminal. He might have been a prehistoric Julius Caesar, assassinated in a bloody coup, a ruler toppled and executed by an angry mob, or even a war leader, surrounded in battle and filled full of arrows. When we put the Stonehenge Archer in the wider perspective of Stonehenge as a place of burial – a cemetery in use for hundreds of years – it is enough to describe him simply as the last person to have been buried at Stonehenge during its heyday.

By the time that the Stonehenge Archer was buried in the Stonehenge ditch, the landscape surrounding the great stone circle was beginning to become a place of burial. Within about three hundred years, by 1800 BC, Early Bronze Age round barrows were everywhere, forming lines and clusters or dotted around the higher ground.[13] Before 3000 BC, too, the dead had been similarly prominent in this landscape, occupying the long barrows and the causewayed enclosure of Robin Hood's Ball. Yet between 3000 BC and the building of the first round barrows around 2400 BC, there is almost no trace of the dead outside Stonehenge itself.

Our excavations at Durrington Walls uncovered just three loose human bones and a single tooth. The human bones from Geoff Wainwright's previous dig there have all turned out to date to later periods. Percy Farrer claimed in 1917 to have seen cremated bones beneath the henge bank but they do not survive for verification of his report. Maud Cunnington found two cremations, one at Woodhenge and one in the large timber structure south of Woodhenge.[14] The latter turned out to be Bronze Age, associated with the later round barrow that was constructed on top of the site of the Neolithic 'tower' structure, but the Woodhenge cremation is earlier, dating to 2580–2470 BC, during the Chalcolithic period.

Cunnington describes how this Woodhenge cremation looked as if it had fallen in from the side of a narrow pit, since the bones were found against one side of the pit, from the top to the bottom. She noted that the post pipe was very indistinct in this, compared to what was recorded in all the other Woodhenge postholes. She also noted that the base of this pit was filled with unusually hard-packed chalk rubble, to a depth of 30 centimetres above the bottom; none of the other postholes at Woodhenge had this sort of packing and Cunnington could only explain it as being there to raise the bottom of a post, so that it stood taller in the ground.

Josh was suspicious – why was this feature labelled as a posthole at all when it was so unlike any of the others? Cunnington's section drawing of this pit shows the characteristic shape produced by an upright having been withdrawn from a pit. Josh realized that not only was Mrs Cunnington describing a stonehole, but that the stone pulled out of it was very narrow, too thin to have been a sarsen like those that had formed the stone 'cove' at Woodhenge. Perhaps a bluestone pillar once stood here, together with a cremation buried at its foot, just like the Aubrey Holes. The cremated bones were those of an adult but there are no indications to determine whether male or female.

In terms of burials and human remains, the contrast between Stonehenge and Durrington Walls could hardly be stronger. At Stonehenge, the most numerous species represented among all the bones ever found is *Homo sapiens* with something in excess of 50,000 bone fragments. There are just 1000 animal bone fragments, most of which are from cattle, and then pig.[15] This is the complete reverse of the pattern at Durrington Walls, where pigs predominate and human bones consist of just three fragments among an assemblage of 80,000 bones. Durrington has produced a handful of bones from less common species: red deer, roe deer, dog, bird, fox, wild cat and wolf. Curiously, more than a third of the antler picks used to dig the Stonehenge ditch had been taken from dead deer, with the antler being cut out of the skull rather than being collected after shedding.[16] At Durrington Walls, only around one in ten of the antlers was taken from slain deer.

There is little doubt that the place for a good party was Durrington Walls and not Stonehenge. The animal bones found at Stonehenge are really not the debris of multiple, enormous feasts, whereas those at Durrington Walls most certainly are. Added to that, some of those very few bones deposited at Stonehenge probably had no meat on them – it seems that they might have been already ancient when they were brought to Stonehenge. Hawley found carefully placed deposits of animal bones lying on the bottom of the ditch, along with the antler picks. Four of these have been radiocarbon-dated – a cattle skull and two jaws, and a red deer leg bone – and the results indicate that these bones are likely to date to before 3000 BC.[17] If so, then these animal bones were curated for a long time before being brought to Stonehenge.

Large numbers of people staying in one place for even half a day can leave enormous quantities of waste. Those attending the overnight midsummer solstice festival at Stonehenge – for example – leave behind them a small mountain of rubbish, every scrap of which, in these eco-friendly days, has to be picked up and taken away in refuse lorries after the solstice-celebrators go home. In 2007 while looking for bluestone chippings, Josh, California Dave and I excavated, by accident rather than design, a small part of the 1977 Stonehenge festival site. I was there myself, among the thousands of people and a small city of tents. Nothing of it survives above ground – nor do traces of any of the solstice festivals – but 100 square metres of archaeological test pits laid out across a field near Fargo Plantation produced plenty of tent pegs, crushed beer cans, bottle glass and even a drug dealer's kit of halfpennies used as weights.

The overall impression from the findings of every archaeological dig at Stonehenge is that the place was a cemetery and a building site, with chippings, hammerstones and broken flints strewn about underfoot, and not a party venue.

THE PEOPLE OF STONEHENGE AND THE BEAKER PEOPLE

Our dig into Aubrey Hole 7 in 2008 salvaged burnt bones from fifty-nine separate cremation burials deposited within Stonehenge more than 4000 years ago. William Hawley had first encountered these burials in the ditch around Stonehenge and in and around the Aubrey Holes, and had excavated them during the 1920s. Although these fifty-nine together with the four cremations found by Atkinson and ourselves probably represent fewer than half of the Neolithic people buried in the monument, they are our only tangible remains of the actual people of Stonehenge. Even reduced to burnt fragments of bone there is much they can tell us about their ancient lives. Christie Cox Willis, an osteoarchaeologist at Sheffield University, has the long task of patiently examining each and every fragment of cremated bone and is still sorting through the 300 bags of material that we recovered from the hole.

In the coming months and years Christie will be helped by Jacqui McKinley of Wessex Archaeology as well as by Sheffield biological anthropologists Andrew Chamberlain and Pia Nystrom to catalogue and identify all the bones, looking for indicators of age, sex, pathology and trauma. Certain bones, notably parts of the skull, jaw and pelvis, can provide indications of whether they come from a man or a woman. Age can be estimated from bones and teeth. Pathologies on bone provide indications about health, in the form of tumours and other growths, arthritic alteration of joints, and bone alterations such as *cribra orbitalia*, a condition caused by iron-deficiency anaemia.[1] Archaeologists are also interested in trauma, such as the marks of arrow wounds found on the human femur from Durrington Walls. All these things are much more difficult to detect on cremated bone than on a complete skeleton, so careful and lengthy study is required.

Only ten years before our excavation nuclear scientists came up with a method for radiocarbon dating cremated human bones. The problem they had to solve was that radiocarbon-dating dates the substance in a bone called collagen, which contains carbon, and bone collagen is destroyed by burning. Scientists finally worked out that combustion over 600°C causes the inorganic components within collagen (known as bio-apatite) to re-crystallize, and that the carbonate in these crystals can be extracted from cremated bone and radiocarbon-dated.[2] As a result of this new science, the cremation burials from British prehistory can now be dated. Previously cremations could be dated only if there was associated wood charcoal from the pyre or if there was, say, a grave good of unburnt bone buried with the cremated bones. There are thousands of previously undated cremations, many without any grave goods at all, that can now be re-studied.

With unburnt human bones it's possible to learn about diet and patterns of mobility from study of various isotopes in the collagen and in tooth enamel.[3] With the collagen burnt away and tooth enamel shattered into minute fragments, though, it's not possible to employ the available study techniques on cremated bone. DNA does not survive the heat of a pyre, for example. However, the range of scientific methods that we can apply has expanded dramatically in recent years, and who knows what may be possible in years to come? In the meantime we can at least get some idea of who these people were – their age, sex, pathology and trauma – and when they lived and died.

Christie was already getting results soon after she began work. The complete cremation burial, missed by Hawley but found by us in 2008 in the side of Aubrey Hole 7, was that of an adult woman in her thirties who died in the period when Stonehenge was first built (3000–2920 BC) or in the century before. One of the cremations found by Atkinson in the Stonehenge ditch is also that of a woman, aged about twenty-five,[4] who died about 500 years later, when the sarsen circle and trilithons were put up, or even a century after that. Although these two burials were of women, Christie has so far found that all of the bones with identifiable sex traits from the mixed mass in the Aubrey Hole are those of men.

As for the age of the individuals, Hawley remarks in his records that he reckoned that only two of the cremations he found were those of children[5] and Christie's findings reveal no more than four or five children of various ages. Jacqui had been very sceptical of Hawley's ability to distinguish men, women and children among the cremations – he had no training in anatomy – but he may not have been too far wrong in simply attributing clusters of very small bones to children as opposed to adults.

The picture that Christie is beginning to reveal is of a burial ground reserved predominantly for adult men. This is not a normal demographic picture. Before modern medicine, childhood mortality was very high and most deaths in any population would have been those of children.[6] Thus if all members of a community were buried at Stonehenge, without discrimination, most of them should be children. Furthermore, half of the people should be women but, according to the identifiable sex traits among the adult bones, they are not there. In other words, there were strong biases at work in selecting people to be buried (as cremated remains) at Stonehenge.

Might the men whose remains were buried there have been sacrificial victims? We can look at the comparative examples of Neolithic and other prehistoric bog bodies from Scandinavia and northwest Europe; many of these show good evidence for having suffered a violent death and archaeological opinion is very strongly in favour of their having been human sacrifices.[7] In contrast to the Stonehenge people, the bog bodies include a high proportion of women and children as well as men. Our overall knowledge of cremation across Britain during the Neolithic indicates that this was the standard burial practice for everybody, with some burials being provided occasionally with grave goods.[8]

The most likely explanation is that the people buried at Stonehenge were drawn from an elite. They could have been rulers, born into the office or chosen by their peers, or even ritual specialists who mediated between the living and the supernatural. The presence of a macehead and an incense burner in two of the burials gives weight to the idea that some sort of power, political and religious, was held by at least two of them.

The good preservation of the burnt bone fragments has allowed Christie to find out about Neolithic illnesses and diseases. While none of the bones have produced evidence for violent trauma, several individuals had arthritis. This was not of the rheumatoid form (a disease that seems to have developed much later in human history) but was osteoarthritis. Christie has so far found it in the lower backs of some individuals, visible as patches of wear on the spine caused by degeneration of the cartilage between the vertebrae. One individual suffered from a soft-tissue tumour behind the knee. It was so large that it affected the growth of the tibia (the larger of the two lower leg bones) but it was benign; it might well have caused a limp but not premature death.

The selection of samples from the Aubrey Hole cremations for dating is a mathematical puzzle. We know that there are fifty-nine burials (although some of these may contain more than one individual) in the form of 50,000 fragments of human bone. How many bones need to be radiocarbon-dated to get a representative sample? We have to be sure that we don't date the same individual twice. To avoid this Christie and Jacqui must establish the minimum number of individuals (MNI) present and select one bone from each. This standard technique used to analyse all archaeological bone – human and animal – means finding out which anatomical part of the skeleton is most regularly represented; we will then radiocarbon-date each example of that.

Jacqui reckoned that the petrous bone (the outside of the ear cavity) is the one most easily identifiable, but we'd have to be careful not to destroy the actual cavity structure itself when sampling from the skull around it. So, if Christie finds 25 left petrous bones and 20 right petrous bones, our MNI will be 25. If every one of these bones came from a different individual, there *might* be as many as 45 individuals represented but archaeologists have to ignore this number and work with what can be proved – in this example, the left-side bones would definitely come from 25 different people, so we would radiocarbon-date all the left-side petrous bones, and none of the right-side bones (which could be 'duplicates', belonging to the same people). The dates from these 25 individuals would give us a range for their deaths, and we would have to hope that this was a representative sample of the dates of death of each of the 59 people.

We already have an inkling of how the burials should be distributed though time, so we know broadly what their numbers should look like from 3000 BC, the beginning of Stonehenge, to around 2400 BC, the latest date of Atkinson's three cremations. This is because Hawley recorded not only where but at what depth he found each cremation burial within the Stonehenge ditch. Thanks to English Heritage's dating of the ditch's layers in 1994, we know the rate at which the ditch filled up over time. Our radiocarbon specialist Pete Marshall has been able to refine their chronology still further, by fine-tuning the statistical model. The cremation burial found by Hawley on the bottom of the ditch is likely to date to soon after its digging, around 2950 BC. Just two cremations were buried in the intermediate, secondary fills of the ditch; these ought to date to 2900–2600 BC. Fifteen were dug into the top of the ditch and can be expected to date to 2600–2300 BC.

A similar statistical exercise is also possible, but less certain, for the cremations from the fills of the Aubrey Holes. Up to eleven cremations (like the one found by Atkinson in Aubrey Hole 32) are probably primary burials from around 2950 BC. These deposits of cremated bone were later disturbed by the removal of small standing stones from these pits. Another twelve cremations are likely to have been inserted after the stones had been withdrawn and the pits filled in, perhaps around 2600–2300 BC. Thirteen of the cremations found by Hawley had been put into isolated pits that are impossible to date within the Stonehenge sequence, so no estimates of their dates can be made.

We also have to bear in mind the likely number of people buried at Stonehenge. Extrapolating from the number of known burials, Mike Pitts estimated in 2000 that it could be as many as 240. Although previous excavators have investigated about 50 per cent of the area of Stonehenge, Mike reckoned that many undiscovered burials may lie under the outer bank and even outside the ditch. These are areas that have never been excavated, so there is no existing sample of burials to work with. My guess for the total number is slightly lower than Mike's, at around 150.

The Stonehenge stratigraphy shows that very few people were buried there at the beginning of the sequence of construction, and lots were buried there towards the end of the monument's use as a cemetery, about 500 years later. The overall pattern of this stratigraphic dating of the cremations suggests that only a minority of the Stonehenge dead (around 10 out of 150) were buried at the beginning, with the numbers growing exponentially to around 90 cremation burials in the centuries around 2500–2300 BC.

Andrew Chamberlain, an expert in human osteology and ancient demography, estimates that this pattern of burials at Stonehenge could be created by a small kin group burying their dead over a 500-year period. The cemetery starts with a small number of founder graves. As the living offspring increase in number over about twenty generations, what started as a small family becomes a large number of families, or a lineage, descended from common ancestors. This may sound like a lot of people but, at a uniform rate of mortality, the number of burials at Stonehenge would derive from only one death every three or four years.

This gives us a model for what to expect from the results of the radiocarbon dating: we should find very few early cremations and a lot of later ones. If that is not the pattern, then there has to be something we have not accounted for – the unstratified burials may all belong to the early period of use, for example, or there may have been more primary burials in the Aubrey Holes than Hawley recognized.

If Andrew is right about Stonehenge being a place of burial for a lineage, who were these people whose burial place was so illustrious? They were provided with no grave goods, except in one or two special cases. Hawley found one burial with a stone macehead, near the south entrance. Maceheads are ground and polished stones, drilled through the centre for mounting on top of a wooden handle or staff.[9] The British Isles' most beautiful example of a Neolithic macehead is an ornately carved specimen from the eastern chamber of the great tomb at Knowth in Ireland.[10] Another dates to about 1900 BC, probably some 500 years later than the Stonehenge example, and was found just half a mile away from Stonehenge, in the richest prehistoric burial known from Britain. It came from Bush Barrow, a burial mound that lies on the skyline to the south of Stonehenge, and was excavated by Colt Hoare in 1808.[11] For many years until Stonehenge's re-dating in 1995, archaeologists wondered if the man buried in Bush Barrow had been responsible for the building of Stonehenge, since his grave goods were so rich and rare.[12] As well as

The polished stone macehead found with one of the cremation burials at Stonehenge by William Hawley. It would have been attached to a wooden handle through the shaft-hole.

a gold lozenge-shaped ornament, a gold buckle, and bronze daggers with gold handles, he was provided with a macehead that had once been mounted on a staff decorated with chevron-shaped rings of bone.

Maces could have been used as stone clubs but there are good reasons for thinking that their role was primarily ceremonial. Even today in Britain we recognize the mace as a symbol of power. The British parliament, local councils and the Lord Mayor of London all have maces to proclaim institutional authority. Perhaps the Stonehenge mace had a similar purpose.

There is another peculiar grave good from among the Stonehenge cremations. This is a ceramic 'incense burner'[13] – a small circular disc with concave surfaces on top and bottom. Holes on the sides show where it was suspended by string, and whatever substance was burned in it has left a sooty stain. Such items are known from all around the world as the paraphernalia of shamans and other ritual specialists. Ramilisonina and I have excavated such items, in use until a hundred years ago, that were once used by Malagasy medicine men and diviners.[14] The Stonehenge 'incense burner' is almost unique – only one other is known from the British Neolithic. Perhaps it tells us that some of the people buried at Stonehenge were ritual specialists as well as political leaders.

We might be tempted to ask why most of the burials had no grave goods – does this mean that these were not important people? But putting grave goods in the burial of an important individual is far from universal, across cultures and across time. Anthropological studies of traditional societies around the world have found that only in 5 per cent to 40 per cent of cases was social status signified by grave goods.[15] A lack of grave goods in a prehistoric burial is not an indication of lack of status; it all depends what the cultural traditions meant. On balance, given the small number of burials and their extraordinary location in this dramatic monument, it seems most likely that the people buried at Stonehenge were the elite of their day – rulers and shamans, perhaps forming a succession of powerful dynasties.

The Beaker people

At the same time as Christie began to examine the cremated remains from the Stonehenge Aubrey Hole, I was co-ordinating a team exploring the lives of the people buried in the period afterwards, from 2400 to 1800 BC. This project was not focused on the Stonehenge area but covered the whole of Britain.[16] Many of the skeletons from this period of the Copper Age and the Early Bronze Age were found with the distinctive form of pottery known as Beakers.[17]

Ever since the nineteenth century, archaeologists have thought that the Beaker people were probably immigrants to Britain. Anatomists measured their skulls, pronouncing them to be round-headed (brachycephalic) in contrast to the long-headed (dolichocephalic) skulls from the Early Neolithic long barrows and, therefore, according to some, members of a different 'race'.[18] Archaeologists saw these immigrants as the bringers of knowledge: it was in the Beaker period that metallurgy, horse-riding and brewing all first occur in Britain, spreading from the Continent.[19] The well-appointed Beaker burials often include not only the characteristic pottery but also archery equipment in the form of barbed-and-tanged arrowheads and stone wrist-guards.

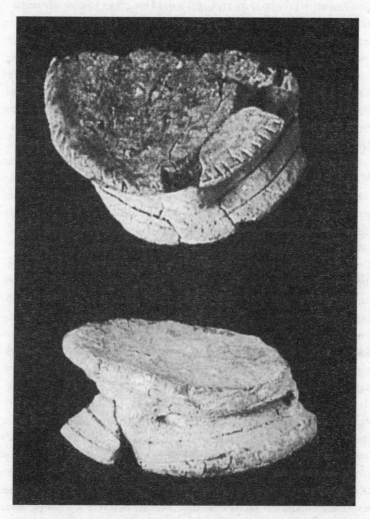

The unique, drum-shaped, small pottery object found with one of the cremation
burials at Stonehenge and interpreted as an 'incense burner'.

Beakers were used by communities across Europe, from Spain and Morocco to northern Denmark and from Hungary to eastern Ireland.[20] They seem to have first appeared in Spain around 2800 BC, and there are also early dates from the Netherlands.[21] Their distribution across northern Europe, however, was patchy rather than uniform. Certain areas, such as much of France and southern Denmark, have never produced evidence for Beakers. In Britain, their footprint is similarly partial. Very few Beakers are known from Wales, for example, but certain areas such as eastern Scotland, Yorkshire, the Peak District, Wessex, East Anglia and Kent were densely occupied by Beaker-using communities.

All of these areas are well-known for Beaker funerary sites, where the dead were buried either under round mounds or in 'flat' burials with no earthen monument to mark them. It seems that the earliest burials, around 2400 BC, were placed in flat graves or within small circular, discontinuous ditches like miniature henges.[22] Only later, around 2000 BC, were large earthen mounds – round barrows – built over a grave.

For years archaeologists have argued about the Beaker people. Were they really a tribe or tribes of migrants sweeping across Europe, perhaps forced westwards into the Netherlands and Britain by other groups expanding out of the east? Or were archery equipment and the distinctive Beaker itself – items so often found in burials – some of the trappings of a lifestyle that cut across ethnic boundaries, part of a 'package' of material culture that was adopted enthusiastically by those aspiring to the Beaker way of life?[23]

Arguments based on the shape of prehistoric skulls subsided many years ago. There is no way to tell if the apparent difference between the shapes of skulls found in long barrows (dating to around 3800–3400 BC) and skulls from burials dating to the beginning of the Beaker period (from 2400 BC) is the result of the invasion of Britain by a large number of people with a different genetic heritage. The long period between the long barrows and the Beaker burials – a time when very few people were buried and thus lacking in unburnt human remains – makes it impossible to judge whether the preponderance of more rounded skulls is the result of gradual physiological change (known as genetic drift) in an existing population, or the result of a new migration.[24]

The arguments about migrants and 'the Beaker package' had

quietened down when a remarkable discovery was made in 2002 by
Wessex Archaeology during the development of a new housing estate in
Amesbury, just three miles east of Stonehenge on the other side of the
Avon. The skeleton of an adult man lay in a grave with more than a hundred grave goods, including five Beakers, a dozen barbed-and-tanged
arrowheads, three copper daggers, a boar's tusk, a small stone anvil for
fine metalworking, two gold 'earrings' (perhaps twists for braided hair)
and two wrist-guards.[25] This is the largest collection of grave goods ever
found in a Beaker burial anywhere in Europe. The 'Amesbury Archer',
or at least the people who organized his funeral, had considerable means
and social standing. Nearby, a second flat grave contained the skeleton
of another man, equipped with a pair of gold earrings.

The discovery of the Amesbury Archer couldn't have happened at a
more awkward time, late on a Friday before a Bank Holiday weekend.
Andrew Fitzpatrick, in charge of the excavation, had to decide whether
to leave the grave open to potential weekend plunderers or to dig
through the night. He couldn't take the risk of leaving the site so, working by the illumination of car headlights, his team pressed on for hours,
patiently recording, plotting and removing every single item on and
around the skeleton.

Radiocarbon dating has revealed that the Amesbury Archer died in
the period 2470–2280 BC. Analysis in the laboratory of his teeth tells a
fascinating story: from the evidence of the strontium and oxygen isotope
values of his molars' dental enamel, we know that this man spent his
childhood years (between the ages of about ten and fourteen) far away
from Britain, somewhere on the Continent and possibly as far east as the
foothills of the Alps.[26] Andrew Fitzpatrick suggested that the region
around Bavaria might have been his homeland. The tabloids had a field
day – Stonehenge built by the Germans! For a while, the Amesbury
Archer was dubbed the King of Stonehenge, ousting the inhabitant of
Bush Barrow from this ever-popular title. Some archaeologists wondered
if he might have been the architect behind the building of the sarsen
circle and trilithons, until it was pointed out that these had been erected
before his time.

The discovery of the Amesbury Archer reignited interest in the
Beaker people's origins. DNA was not going to help answer the question.

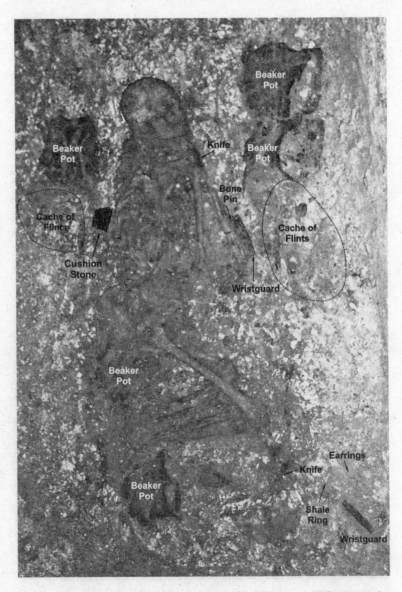

The Amesbury Archer and the artefacts buried with him as grave goods, excavated
by Andrew Fitzpatrick of Wessex Archaeology.

There are too few available skeletons from which ancient DNA could ever be extracted and there are no skeletons from the centuries before the Beaker period to form a control group of 'resident British citizens' with which to compare the DNA of the possible immigrants. The only way to find out if the 'Beaker people' were migrants or just local residents adopting new technology is to analyse strontium and oxygen isotopes to see where people came from. Are there others like the Amesbury Archer, definitely immigrants from Europe?

In 2004 I put together a team of scientists to find out not just where the Beaker people had come from but also what their diet, their health and their geographical mobility had been like. My co-directors were Andrew Chamberlain and Mike Richards. Andrew is an expert in biological anthropology, especially the study of human bones; Mike is an expert in isotope analysis. We recruited our team and talked to museums across Britain to track down Beaker skeletons. Our researchers identified over 400 Beaker skeletons in various collections, but only 360 of them were suitable for our work. Children are too young for the isotope analyses on teeth to be worth doing and we also had to exclude many of the elderly – sadly, the old folk didn't have enough dental enamel left on the surfaces of their teeth.

Scientific projects in archaeology have none of the glamour and immediacy of discoveries made during excavations: television documentary makers just don't know how to make a good story out of people looking at computer printouts. The work is slow and it takes a very long time to obtain results from the various labs. Only six years after the beginning of this project on the Beaker people are we beginning to get enough results to be able to see the full picture. The diet in the Beaker period – as reconstructed from values of carbon and nitrogen isotopes in the bones – was surprisingly uniform from Scotland to Kent.[27] No one was eating marine fish or seafood in detectable quantities, even though lots of the burials analysed were from coastal areas of Scotland, Yorkshire and Kent. Animal protein – either as meat, milk or blood – was a central part of the diet but not massively predominant.

The wear-marks visible microscopically on the Beaker people's teeth can also tell us about their food.[28] These marks are minute scratches and pits on the teeth's grinding surfaces that are constantly being erased and renewed, and show what a dead person's diet was like in the last few months of their life. Interestingly, the Beaker teeth show no sign of the characteristic wear-marks caused by eating stone-ground flour. Plenty have microscopic pitting of the sort most likely to be caused by the tiny grits that lurk inside green vegetables when they're not thoroughly washed. Finally, Lucija Šoberl's separate study of the lipids or fatty acids in the Beaker pots shows that these mostly contained dairy products – whether milk, cheese or curds and whey, we cannot say.[29]

Like the results so far from the Aubrey Hole bones, the Beaker skeletons have revealed that most individuals led lives of good health. Only a handful, like the Stonehenge Archer, buried in the ditch with arrow wounds all over his body, died violently. In fact, the number of woundings that have left traces on the body is far greater among the burials in the Early Neolithic long barrows, more than a thousand years earlier than the Beaker burials.[30] The low level of violent injury on Beaker-period bones belies the archer's equipment frequently found in Beaker graves. One man in eastern Scotland had had his arm broken from being sharply twisted but it had healed long before he died. Arthritis was common at a low level, like the cases seen on some of the Aubrey Hole remains. There was no evidence for malnutrition; had there been episodes of famine these would have shown up as enamel hypoplasia, ridges in the teeth relating to periods of starvation in an individual's life.[31]

One of the completely unexpected discoveries was that a small number – fewer than half a dozen – of the Beaker skulls show evidence of head-binding during childhood. The human head can be easily distorted into a chosen, socially preferred shape by wrapping an infant's skull very tightly to constrain its growth. Archaeologists are familiar with this practice elsewhere (it occurred frequently among the ancient Maya and the Huns, for example) but it has rarely been documented for prehistoric Britain.

The answers to questions about mobility and migration are to be found in the isotope levels within people's tooth enamel. As well as using strontium and oxygen isotopes, the project also developed the study of sulphur isotopes. The value in the human body of sulphur isotopes varies with exposure to sea spray: the further inland people live, the lower the value. Using this technique we hoped to see if people buried inland had ever lived nearer the sea. Overall, the isotope results show that about half the Beaker people studied grew up in an area different to that in which they were buried. Fewer than seven people from Britain (including the Amesbury Archer) had isotope values indicating that they could have grown up outside Britain. This was not a population that had moved lock, stock and barrel from mainland Europe, yet nor are we looking at a population of completely sedentary farmers, growing up to marry the boy next door and never leaving their home village.

It was slightly disappointing to discover how few of these Beaker people were likely to have been immigrants to Britain. For the Amesbury Archer, it is his unusual oxygen isotope value that shows he is likely to have grown up on the Continent. Unfortunately, anyone growing up on the Continent within a couple of hundred miles or so of the English Channel would have an oxygen isotope value no different from someone growing up on the British side. Two burials from Kent may well be those of immigrants, because their dietary isotope values are different to others in Britain, but we cannot be certain that they were incomers. Three burials from the Peak District have strontium isotope values higher than expected for Britain. Quite possibly these could also be immigrants.

When we think about migrations, we often envisage successive waves of incomers whose second, third and successive generations would have been born on British soil but continued the traditions of their immigrant ancestors. The results of this project suggest that a small number of immigrants from Europe arrived in Britain at the beginning of this new cultural phase, around 2400 BC, but that they were not followed by a series of subsequent migrations over the next five centuries. The Amesbury Archer is perhaps a 'founder' burial from that initial phase of migration. These arrivals might well have been very few in number, in contrast to their many descendants born in Britain. Equally, many of indigenous British ancestry would have adopted Beaker fashions of lifestyle and burial rites. There is certainly very little evidence for successive waves of immigrants during the Beaker period, except for the small group who ended up in the Peak District a century or two after the initial Beaker arrival, having left a homeland (as yet unidentified) very different from that of the Amesbury Archer.

The analyses have also highlighted unforeseen problems with the techniques. The oxygen isotope results show that current theories about certain Beaker individuals having travelled very long distances from the Continent must be revised. Development of a new method of calibrating oxygen isotope values places the Amesbury Archer's origins not in the Alpine foothills but somewhere further west. He is more likely to have come from eastern France or western Germany; the middle Rhine is a good possibility, since cultural links in Beaker styles between this area and Wessex have been recognized by archaeologists for more than fifty years.

Another Early Bronze Age skeleton – the 'boy with the amber necklace' – has a local origin in Britain even though he has an unusual oxygen isotope signature, comparable to people living in the Mediterranean. This fourteen-to-fifteen-year-old, wearing ninety beads of Baltic amber, was buried on Boscombe Down, not far from the Amesbury Archer, and at first glance his oxygen isotope values are much higher than would be expected for anyone living east of Land's End in Cornwall. Yet, when the archaeological scientists compared the results of *all* his isotopes with those of the Beaker People Project's individuals from Wessex, it became clear that he was actually a local, one of many whose origins were on the Wessex chalk. The mystery is why the Wessex chalk-dwellers, and indeed all of the Beaker people in the study, have such high oxygen values relative to the regions where they had grown up. The project has clearly discovered a problem with the calibration. A likely explanation for the unusual values can be traced to what these people were drinking.

Oxygen isotope values are mapped geographically from aquifers – below-ground water that appears as rivers and streams. If we were to measure oxygen isotope values of rainwater or 'processed' water (i.e., milk, beer or boiled food) from those same areas, we would find that these values are significantly higher than ordinary 'drinking' water. If people were deriving their liquid intake mostly from cows' milk, beer, boiled foods and even dew ponds when their molars were forming, then their oxygen isotope values would be correspondingly higher. We have to take into account the fact that people's liquid diet has a major effect on their oxygen isotopes.

Putting all the evidence together we can see that we are looking at people who were probably descendants of both a single and perhaps small wave of immigration and of indigenous inhabitants who adopted Beaker ways. Their culture and economy centred on cattle and on the products provided by them. They were semi-mobile, often moving long distances with their herds and settling far from where they grew up. We know from what is found on their settlements that people of the Beaker period did grow cereal crops but they must have consumed them either as boiled porridge or as an alcoholic beverage (or both) – the lack of microscopic scratches on their teeth indicates that they had no querns (grinding stones) so could not have made flour for bread.

15

BLUESTONEHENGE: BACK TO THE RIVER

One of the Stonehenge Riverside Project's key objectives was to investigate the end of the Stonehenge avenue – or, rather, the area where we thought the avenue should meet the River Avon, if indeed it extended that far. When we started work, the avenue was certainly known to stretch as far as today's riverside village of West Amesbury, but there it possibly petered out. In the 1920s the archaeologist O. G. S. Crawford saw in an aerial photograph of West Amesbury some earthworks that he thought might be the avenue's banks continuing right to the river.[1] Survey on the ground during the 1980s showed that these earthworks are actually later land boundaries, probably associated with the remains of West Amesbury's Medieval village.[2] One of the avenue's ditches was located 170 metres from the river in 1972 by George Smith, digging in advance of new housing in the village.[3]

Some archaeologists reckoned that the avenue never actually went as far as the river but came to a stop on the high ground to the west, just beyond the 1972 dig. If they were right then our theory about places of the living/places of the ancestors was wrong: if the avenue didn't link Stonehenge to the river, then the Avon didn't link this landscape of the dead to the wooden circles of the living upstream. This was a key area to explore. The land by the river here at the end of the avenue in West Amesbury is a grassy field but there was no guarantee that we would get permission to survey and dig.

The riverside field has not only been scheduled as an ancient monument, on the off-chance that the avenue really did extend this far, but is also owned by Sir Edward Antrobus, a descendant of Sir Edmund Antrobus – a former owner of Stonehenge who had prevented Flinders Petrie and various other senior archaeologists from digging at Stonehenge during the nineteenth century. To our considerable relief, however, today's Antrobus family was happy to let us see whether there was anything on their land.

We threw everything we'd got at trying to detect the avenue and any other likely prehistoric remains beneath the riverside field. The first resistivity survey produced such poor results, largely on account of the dry ground, that we had to do it again. Even then nothing showed up that could be considered a likely candidate for the avenue. The only intriguing feature was an area of high resistance that, we wondered, might be an area of hard-standing, perhaps a cobbled ramp, leading down to the river.

The magnetometer and radar surveys were no more informative. The field was full of the remains of banks, ditches and levelled platforms from Medieval times when this area was occupied as part of the village, but there was no way we could put hands on hearts and swear that any of it looked promisingly prehistoric. Perhaps the avenue never reached this far; if it ever did, it could have been destroyed by the Medieval houses and ditches.

An auger survey was more hopeful. We located a pair of ditches in roughly the right place for the avenue ditches but only an excavation would reveal whether they were prehistoric or Medieval. In 2007 we opened a long, thin trench near the river to examine these ditches. To our disappointment one of them was Medieval. This could not be the Stonehenge avenue.

We could have given up then and there; the weather was atrocious and the clay sub-soil turned to mud, making digging extremely difficult. Sieving the excavated soil to extract any finds was a nasty job: the diggers had to push and squeeze the mud to try to get it through the perpetually clogged mesh of the sieves. In such circumstances one often wet-sieves the soil, running water through the sieves to wash away the mud, but this process was out of the question at West Amesbury because of the problem of what to do with the muddy run-off involved. The River Avon is a Site of Special Scientific Interest and the Environment Agency is very firm about not allowing water to enter the river.

Our two supervisors on this trench, Jim Rylatt and Bob Nunn, are made of strong stuff and weren't going to stop until the job was done. They located the second ditch indicated by the auger survey and saw from its alignment that this could not be part of the avenue either. It was, however, curving rather than straight, a good sign that it might be pre-historic. A curving ditch could be the remains of anything from a Bronze Age barrow ditch to a gully surrounding an Iron Age roundhouse.

As they dug into the curving ditch Jim and Bob started to find pre-historic worked flints, but there were also small pieces of Medieval pottery. Earthworms were clearly the culprits for the mixing of material of different dates in this layer at the top of the ditch. Lower down, the thick clay layers contained virtually nothing except the occasional cattle bone.

The last day of digging arrived and we weren't much the wiser: per-haps this was the ditch of an Early Bronze Age barrow. On the resistivity plots we could see a faint outline of a circular feature; it was fairly uncon-vincing and only the benefit of hindsight made it at all visible. The problem with interpreting geophysics plots is that the features they show aren't usually clear-cut; it's always easier to fully understand what the geo-physics shows *after* you have dug the features. In this instance it was only after we'd found the curving ditch in the ground that we could see that this faint circular area on the printout wasn't our imagination but was really there. It was the right size for a barrow and Jim reckoned that a platform of natural flints he'd found inside the ditch was possibly the last remains of its destroyed mound.

We really needed something dateable but we had run out of time. Reg Jury, the helpful and interested local contractor who provided mechan-ical diggers from the very first season of our project, had by lunchtime arrived with his machine to fill in our trench. I had resigned myself to disappointment – there would be no dating evidence for the ditch – and went off to fry up an egg sandwich in a spare wheelbarrow, ready to feed it to Jim as soon as he'd laboured through the very last of the sticky clay in the ditch bottom. Then, over the noise of Reg revving his engine, I heard Jim yell – he'd found the broken-off tip of an antler pick right in the bottom of the ditch, literally in his last shovel-full.

When, after months of waiting, the radiocarbon date for this pick came back from the lab, we were delighted to find that it was too early for a Bronze Age round barrow. Our ditch was part of an undiscovered henge dating to 2460–2190 BC, the same date range as the Stonehenge avenue. Jim and Bob's perseverance had paid off.

We'd planned to finish all excavation work in 2008, in order to give ourselves maximum time in which to analyse and write up the project's results over the next four to five years, but it was clear to everyone that we needed another, final season of excavation. A ditch wasn't enough – we needed to know what was in the centre of this henge. Jim had noticed that an ornamental bridge crossing a small leat next to the Avon's main channel has piers constructed from broken-up sarsens. There's no sarsen in the area, so there is a possibility that these bridge pillars came from a destroyed standing stone. Going back to the second resistivity survey we could see four almost circular patches of high resistance arranged in a square inside the henge ditch. We wanted to find out whether these were pits that once held standing stones.

In August 2009 we were back. Ramilisonina came too, on a six-week visit from Madagascar, to see what his insight more than ten years before had led to. This was the longest time he'd spent in the UK and he was fascinated by all aspects of British life. Some of his observations were unexpected and instructive. There were no poor people living in Britain, he concluded, because no one was trapping and eating the squirrels in London's parks. When told that there were indeed poor people and that many of them suffered from obesity, he patently thought such an idea was quite ridiculous. He marvelled at Britain's wildlife, so rich in contrast to Madagascar where anything outside a nature reserve gets eaten. The sight of autumnal elderberries, blackberries, crab apples, sloes and many other fruits lying ungathered in hedgerows left him saddened by the waste of good food. He thought that there couldn't be many people actually living in Britain – the roads that we drove along weren't lined by shanty towns of hawkers selling fast food to passing motorists, nor did we pass through any sprawling towns or cities: the bypass and the motorway are not elements of Madagascar's infrastructure. On one of the few occasions that we bypassed a town visible from the road – in this case Northampton, with a population of 200,000 people – Ramil remarked that it was interesting to see a big village in the distance.

It was sometimes startling to see England through Ramil's eyes, and we wondered what he would make of the archaeology at West Amesbury, and of the project team. Even though the project's directors had not worked together in the same trench since 2004, we discovered that we could still all get along in a confined space without too much arguing. There were also many more professional archaeologists than students in the team for this final year. Over the years, our students had graduated and gone off to jobs in commercial archaeology – this was now their busman's holiday, spending time on the research excavation where they'd first learnt to dig. The weather was fine, the campsite dry and the excavation site was one of the most beautiful spots in Wiltshire, sheltered by riverbank trees beside the gently flowing Avon. We even discovered a swimming hole, halfway between West Amesbury and our campsite, where we could wash away the daily dirt before going home for supper.

We decided to dig two trenches within the henge, a large one in its northeast quadrant and a smaller one on its west side. As Reg's mechanical excavator gently stripped away the topsoil of the larger trench inside the henge it was hard to make out anything distinct in the ground. Then Josh spotted an antler pick sticking out of the grey fill of a large pit.

In the northern part of the field, away from the river, Reg cut two more trenches to see if we would have better luck finding the avenue's ditches. The trench furthest from the river was full of Medieval ditches and pits and it seemed very unlikely that anything prehistoric could have survived all this later construction. We needed to fully excavate and record these features first, and then see if there were any earlier traces. Initial expectations of prehistoric avenue ditches were dashed as all the features turned out to be boundary ditches for twelfth-century tenements.

There was enough worked flint, including a couple of chisel arrowheads, to show that there had been prehistoric activity – but where was it? One of the ditches started to look promising; there was lots of worked flint in it and here Denise Allen found an exquisite Neolithic oblique arrowhead, pressure-flaked to give it a finely rippled appearance. Denise now works for Andante Travels, an archaeological tour company which had been one of the project's sponsors in 2008, and as a very young student at Cardiff University she'd dug for Richard Atkinson and John Evans at Stonehenge in 1978. As she dug to the bottom of the trench we could see that this was indeed the avenue's eastern ditch, dated by her arrowhead find to the mid to late third millennium BC.

A little later, this eastern avenue ditch was located in the other trench nearer the river, lining up with the spot further north where George Smith had last seen it in 1972. Yet it did not extend as far as the trench further south, inside the henge. Somewhere under our spoilheap, within a space of less than 10 metres, the avenue ended. The henge had once had an external bank, now entirely flattened, and the avenue ditch must have reached to the outer edge of this bank or nearly so. We realized how lucky we'd been the year before with the positioning of our trench. Had it been 2 metres to the north, we would have missed both henge and avenue; even further north and we might have found the ends of the east and west ditches of the avenue but wouldn't have had a clue that there was a henge in the vicinity.

In the trench where Denise found the arrowhead the western avenue ditch took longer to find than the eastern ditch. It proved to be under the bank of a Medieval tenement boundary; presumably it had survived as a visible feature that was incorporated into the twelfth-century land boundaries as a useful line of demarcation between two properties. The avenue here at its riverside end is 18 metres wide, just a couple of metres narrower than it is nearer Stonehenge. Both ditches had contained rows of small posts.

We could see that there was a complicated sequence inside the henge. A Medieval drainage ditch had cut through a small, circular Bronze Age ditch at the henge's centre. This Bronze Age ditch was part of an arrangement that included postholes of various sizes, and all of these were cut into an earlier circle of interlinked holes. As the excavation progressed we found nine of these earlier holes, six in the main trench and three others in the western trench, forming a curving or circular cutting. Each had its own ramp leading into it from the outside of the circle.

Gradually it dawned on us that these pits once held standing stones. The ramps enabled the builders to lower each stone into position, and the later removal of each stone left a V-shaped void, filled in with later material, where each stone had been pulled out from its packing of flint nodules and chalk. The antler pick that Josh had found right at the beginning of the excavation was lying on one of the ramps.

Diggers stand in the holes where standing stones once stood at Bluestonehenge
on the bank of the River Avon at West Amesbury.

The traces left by these upright stones were very different from those
left by the narrower and deeper Bronze Age posts that came after them.
And the holes themselves were wider and shallower than any of the holes
for Neolithic posts at nearby Woodhenge and Durrington Walls. From
the shape and size of the holes, we know that the stones they once held
could not have been slab-shaped sarsens.

The standing stones had been placed on individually tailored cushions of river clay and pads of packed flint nodules. Each pit base was
different, suggesting that the co-operative activity of erecting a stone
circle had been carried out by separate teams responsible for each stone.
One stone had sat on a carefully constructed nest of nodules, while
others merely had a thin cushion of clay between their bases and the
chalk. Another sat on a rock-solid pad of nodules and rammed clay.

The bottoms of five of the holes contained imprints of their stones,
pressed through the clay cushions into the soft chalk beneath. The 'profiles' (the shape in section) of the robbed-out holes had already
indicated that they'd contained neither posts nor sarsens. It now became

clear from the imprints in their bases that these holes had once held stones whose pillar-like shapes closely match the Stonehenge bluestones, with their variously curved, indented and straight edges. We had to think of a name for this unknown site, and called it Bluestonehenge. Extrapolating from the curvature of the nine excavated stoneholes, we calculated that, if the stone arrangement continued to form a circle, it had consisted of twenty-five monoliths.

Radiocarbon dates from antler picks told us when the stones were removed from the stoneholes. Josh's first find, the pick from the ramp, produced a radiocarbon date of 2469–2286 BC. A second antler pick, found right at the bottom of one of the robbed-out stoneholes, dated to 2460–2270 BC. The stones had been extracted during the Copper Age, around the same time as the henge ditch was dug, and at the same time as the Stonehenge avenue ditches were dug.

Working out when this bluestone circle was first erected is a more difficult question. No antler picks were deposited in the stoneholes when the circle was built. This absence of picks at Bluestonehenge mirrors their absence in other bluestoneholes – no picks have ever been found in any of the Aubrey Holes or the Q and R Holes at Stonehenge and there are only two antler fragments from the bluestone circle and oval. Archaeologists all accept that the depositing of antler picks in pits, stoneholes and ditches was done with deliberation by Neolithic builders, and was not the accidental abandonment of perfectly serviceable building tools; it looks as if it just wasn't the practice to leave such objects in these holes for bluestones.

We did initially hope that the pick found at the bottom of a stonehole had been put there when the stones were put up, because it seemed to be sticking out of the packing layer, but we later realized it had been stuck *into* that primary layer. Even without radiocarbon dates, however, the circle's construction can be broadly dated by two objects: chisel arrowheads were found in the packing of two of the stoneholes. Such arrowheads date to before 2600 BC, and they first appeared around 3400 BC. They'd therefore already gone out of use by the time of the village of Durrington Walls, so we hadn't seen this type of arrowhead during our excavations there in previous years, but Colin had found one in a pit by the Cuckoo Stone, dating to 2900 BC.

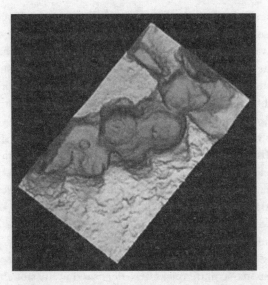

A laser scan of the Bluestonehenge stoneholes. Laser-scanning is used to record
objects and features in three dimensions.

One of the things puzzling me was why we had no chippings from the
stones themselves, either from dressing them or from breaking them up
on removal. The areas of high resistance on the geophysics plot weren't
caused by spreads of stone debris but turned out to be concentrations of
natural flint nodules; the circle of stoneholes was completely invisible to
geophysics.

Going back to the numbers of bluestones and numbers of bluestoneholes at Stonehenge, I realized that Stonehenge seems to have taken
delivery of a second batch of bluestones at some point. We know that the
final circular and oval arrangement within the sarsen circle required
about eighty bluestones. Fifty-six of these would have come from their
first arrangement in the Aubrey Holes. Someone must have brought an
extra twenty-four or so stones to the site to make up the numbers.

The similarity of the dates for dismantling Bluestonehenge and for
digging the henge ditch at West Amesbury made me realize that the
stones had probably been moved before the ditch was dug. There is a
sound practical reason why this was so – the restricted access in and out

of the henge after the ditch was dug would have made it awkward to move the stones. Once the ditch was in place, the henge was accessible only by a causeway across the ditch on its east side. Our trench did not extend quite as far as the causeway, but we can see that the causeway existed because the henge ditch narrows on its east side to form a 'terminal'.

Archaeologists always expect prehistoric ditch ends or 'terminals' to produce finds. A ditch terminal seems to have been an important place, where the builders deliberately left collections of various items at the bottom of the ditch. At Bluestonehenge, where the ditch heads towards its eastern terminal, we found a classic example of such a special deposit of placed artefacts, just as expected. The bottom of the ditch terminal was covered with a spread of finds – antler, stone and bone tools probably for flint-knapping, an antler pick and knapped flints.

As we reflected on just how the Copper Age engineers had managed to extract the stones from their pits, we noticed another reason why the henge ditch has to have been dug after the stone removal had taken place. Using antler picks, the demolition crew dug out just enough chalk packing from around eight of the stones to tilt them outwards at an angle of about 20° from vertical. We could deduce this angle from the crushing in the pits' edges. The ninth stone, one of the stones on the west side, was an exception: here the workers dug out most of the stone's exterior packing and undermined its base. For the majority of the stones, though, they somehow pulled them out of the ground at this steep angle of 70° from horizontal. Some form of equipment such as a wooden A-frame must have been needed and having a newly dug ditch in the way would have caused difficulties.

Here was another example, like Durrington Walls and the two mini-henges inside it, in which the construction of a henge enclosure, with the bank outside the ditch, marked the end of whatever had gone on previously at the site. Henges, with their inward-facing earthworks, were built as memorials to something that had already happened rather than to signal what might still be to come. They are backwards-looking and commemorative.

To have taken stones from this point on the bank of the Avon to Stonehenge on the chalk plain, the lie of the land suggests that at least the first stretch of the route would have followed the route now occupied by the avenue. At this, its eastern end, the avenue runs along a narrow spur of chalk bedrock flanked by lower-lying areas of clay. For anyone trying to land on the riverbank this chalk spur would have offered a perfect landing spot on solid, dry ground.

There has always been discussion about why the avenue takes such a roundabout and indirect path between its eastern end near the Avon and Stonehenge at its western end. It doesn't cut across the landscape in the most direct line between the two points, but instead follows the gentlest contours. Perhaps this was the route taken by the bluestones from Bluestonehenge to Stonehenge. The avenue's ditches and banks may memorialize such an event, constructed after it happened, turning a remembered route into a formalized avenue in the same way that henges and cursuses commemorate places and pathways.

The shortest route on foot from Bluestonehenge to Stonehenge climbs the valley that leads to Coneybury henge and then follows the dry valleys to Stonehenge, to approach either Stonehenge's south entrance or its more grandiose northeast entrance. Coneybury henge, close to the Early Neolithic pit full of feasting debris known as the Coneybury anomaly, may be another example of a henge ditch constructed around an earlier installation. In this case, bones on the bottom of the ditch, including half a dead dog, date to around 2800–2600 BC, while bones from one of a group of pits inside the henge date to before 2900 BC.[4] This pit inside the henge at Coneybury was part of a setting of holes, possibly forming a four-post structure and its approach, like the three found by Josh south of Woodhenge. Julian Richards found evidence for uprights having been pulled out of two of these holes, but without further excavation there's no way of knowing for sure whether these were wooden posts or standing stones.

The addition of Bluestonehenge to our map of Neolithic and Copper Age Wessex helps us understand old discoveries. It now seems likely that Coneybury henge occupied a stopping-point at the top of the ridge, looking back towards the River Avon and forward to Stonehenge, for anyone taking the direct route between the two sites. Perhaps it was a staging point – a 'station', in the traditional sense of the word – from which celebrants got their first view of Stonehenge after leaving the river.

There have been other finds that show the importance of this ridge, which runs north from Coneybury and continues as far as the high ground immediately east of Stonehenge known as King Barrow ridge. In 1967 the Vatchers found a small pit on King Barrow ridge's west side, beside what is now the A303 main road.[5] Within this pit lay two peculiar carved chalk 'plaques' and an antler pick dating to 2900–2580 BC. Fragments of similar plaques have been found within the Neolithic and Copper Age village at Durrington Walls. The pit finds are earlier than the finds from the Durrington settlement, and are decorated with unusual and elaborately carved Grooved Ware-style designs. One has chevrons and criss-cross motifs bordered by horizontal lines and more chevrons. The other has rectilinear meanders bordered by dotted lines. The meaning and purpose of such carved chalk plaques is entirely unknown. Such objects are extremely quick and easy to make, and the raw material is ubiquitous throughout the region. Yet these decorated pieces of chalk are surprisingly rare; they must have had some special value which we can only guess at.

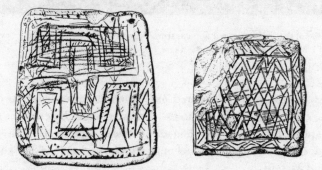

The chalk plaques found in a pit east of Stonehenge, during road-widening in 1968. The small plaque is 56mm across.

On the east side of King Barrow ridge, not far from the Stonehenge avenue, Julian Richards found an area of pits and stakeholes that may be the remains of Neolithic houses, associated with lots of chisel arrowheads lying on the surface of the ploughed field.[6] Radiocarbon dates from animal bones indicate that the area was in use around the same time as the cursuses (before the building of the village or henge at Durrington

One of the chalk plaque fragments from Durrington Walls. This was the most
elaborately decorated artefact found in the Neolithic village.

Walls), though sherds of Grooved Ware also hint at later activity, perhaps
in the earlier third millennium BC. This area might have been a gath-
ering-place for people building the cursuses around 3500 BC and,
perhaps, for building Bluestonehenge and the first stage of Stonehenge
around 2950 BC.

One of the major lessons of finding Bluestonehenge was the realization that there are probably still plenty of sites around Stonehenge
waiting to be found. Some, like a pit circle found by Wessex Archaeology
off the west end of the Lesser Cursus in 2009, will turn up during conventional geophysical survey or aerial reconnaissance. To locate others
will take some real detective work as well as luck, in much the same way
as our own efforts eventually resulted in the discovery of this unknown
henge.

Colin has plotted the distribution of bluestone chippings across the

Stonehenge landscape and wonders if some relate to other lost stone circles. As well as the concentration at Fargo, he has noted various pieces at Coneybury henge, and in the fields north of the Cursus, and at a site called North Kite. North Kite is very peculiar; it is a large three-sided enclosure built in the Beaker period (around 2400–2000 BC), about a mile southwest of Stonehenge.[7] When Julian Richards dug a trench through its west bank he found three chips of spotted dolerite on its buried ground surface. Julian has never thought much of them but Colin is not so sure that North Kite should be dismissed without a closer look. Any fragments of bluestone found in this landscape are of great importance: since the bluestones came from Wales, and do not occur naturally on Salisbury Plain, such fragments indicate nearby prehistoric human activity.

Finding Bluestonehenge not only opened our eyes to the potential for future discoveries around Stonehenge but also demonstrated that the Stonehenge Riverside Project was on the right lines. It certainly justified the project's title and confirmed that any interpretation of Stonehenge must take into account the River Avon and its relationship with sites upstream such as Durrington Walls and Woodhenge.

What was the purpose of Bluestonehenge? Was it just a stone circle where people gathered, or were other activities happening here? The almost complete absence of pottery and animal bones from the henge shows that this was not a place where people lived, despite its attractive location beside the river. Our excavations showed that erosion of the henge surface has left no buried ground intact from the time of its use, but there was one way of finding out what went on here when the stone circle was in use.

After the stones of the Bluestonehenge stone circle were extracted, the voids left behind then filled up with topsoil and turf, collapsing in from the uppermost edges of the stoneholes. As well as providing evidence for the riverside environment this soil filling the stoneholes contains further clues about the activities performed on the ground surface among the stones. There is a lot of wood charcoal, from tiny pieces to a fist-sized lump: fires must have been lit in the vicinity of the stones, perhaps inside the circle.

Perhaps the fires were pyres for cremating the corpses whose ashes were buried at Stonehenge – but we've found no cremated bones among the charcoal. In one of the stoneholes we did find a fragment of an unburnt pig humerus (bone from the upper front leg) dating to 2670–2470 BC. This is particularly interesting because this is the same period as Durrington Walls village and the sarsen phase at Stonehenge. It probably fell into the hole from the ground surface where, by the look of the pitting and cracking of the bone's surface, it must have been lying around for years if not decades.

Once upon a time the site of Bluestonehenge was a settlement, but this was long before the people of the Neolithic came here. In the mud underneath where the henge bank had been, Jim and Bob found a dense spread of flints. These were all mixed together in a single layer but they include microlithic flint blades from the Late Mesolithic and larger blades from the Early Mesolithic, the periods before the Neolithic. Thousands of years before Stonehenge, this riverside spot was a campsite for hunter-gatherers living off the resources of the river and its margins.

Today a spring rises north of the chalk promontory at West Amesbury on which Mesolithic people once camped and on which Bluestonehenge once stood. Back then, when the water table was higher, the springhead was probably much further up the valley – perhaps not far from the Neolithic settlement on the slope of King Barrow ridge – so a stream would have flowed here. On its north bank, our test pits found more Mesolithic flints. We had located one of the campsites that could have been used by the people who put up those pine posts nearly 10,000 years ago.

By the time our excavations finished in 2009 we had come a long way. After seven years of searching we'd found out a lot about Stonehenge, mostly by looking at its context – its landscape – as well as by re-evaluating what had already been found within Stonehenge itself.

WHY STONEHENGE IS WHERE IT IS

One of the most incongruous aspects of Stonehenge today is the presence of a major road, the A303, running within 150 metres of its southern edge. At the point where it passes Stonehenge this busy road is not a dual carriageway, and on Fridays it is packed with long queues of drivers escaping London to spend the weekend in the southwest of England. And they must all come back again on Sunday night, for a second wait in the traffic jam.

Since 1992 the British government has been wondering what to do about this. As well as the 'economic cost' of the traffic jams (there are formulae used to work such things out), this road is seen as a blight on one of the United Kingdom's very few World Heritage Sites. New routes involving moving the road to the north or south of the monument have all been considered and all ultimately rejected. In the late 1990s the Highways Agency proposed that the A303 beside Stonehenge should be hidden in a tunnel, constructed by the 'cut-and-cover' method in which a broad corridor of land would be stripped away and a tunnel created by covering a new, sunken roadway with a grassed-over concrete roof.

The costing for this method looked relatively inexpensive – much cheaper than boring a tunnel – but it would require a very large swathe of land close to Stonehenge to be archaeologically excavated and then entirely removed in advance of construction. There was much opposition to the proposal, from a range of interest groups ranging from local residents to those concerned with the wildlife of Salisbury Plain. Many archaeologists worldwide objected to the scheme because it would utterly destroy a huge slice of archaeological remains within the World Heritage Site, over an area so large that it would make the 1968 new road cut through Durrington Walls look tiny.

The government backed down and agreed to pursue the less damaging but far more expensive option of a bored tunnel. In 2004 the Highways Agency presented their proposal at a public inquiry in Salisbury. Archaeologists and conservation bodies were divided in their views. English Heritage backed the scheme strongly but the National Trust and many others thought the planned tunnel was too short: the proposal on the table was for a 2.1-kilometre tunnel through the 5-kilometre-wide World Heritage Site, which would require long and deeply embanked approaches leading into it; in addition the ground level in Stonehenge Bottom would need to be artificially raised to accommodate its height. Feelings ran high among archaeologists: for some, this deal – albeit imperfect – was the best that Stonehenge would ever get; for others, it was a half-baked solution and the road problem was best left alone until the job could be done properly.

In his report the planning inspector gave the green light for the short tunnel. By that point, though, the cost of implementing the scheme had doubled, to around £500 million. A particular cause for concern was the state of the chalk deep below Stonehenge – it appeared to be unstable and expensive techniques would be required for its safe removal. Even at the height of the noughties' economic boom the British government couldn't afford it. For those who like to know the price of everything, this was more than Stonehenge's scenery was worth. It is reckoned that the government had to spend more than £30 million on consultants and lawyers' fees in order for us all to end up exactly where we started. Fortunately, a tiny proportion of that money did go into something of lasting value.

As part of their proposal the Highways Agency commissioned archaeological contractors to carry out field evaluations along the proposed road line. A huge strip of land immediately to the south of Stonehenge, from one end of the World Heritage Site to the other and even beyond, was given a magnetometer survey and also trial-trenched. Even though the long, thin, machine-dug trenches only represented about 2 per cent of the proposed road corridor, the total area excavated by these 200 or so trenches was vast – the greatest area ever excavated within the World Heritage Site except for the 1967 dig at Durrington Walls. The results were an almost total blank.[1] The only new prehistoric feature of any significance was one Beaker burial.

There is an absolute rule in archaeology that absence of evidence is not evidence of absence. There could once have been prehistoric remains here, since destroyed by ploughing, for example. However, the absence of Neolithic, Copper Age or Early Bronze Age pits – what we now know to have been integral to settlements such as Durrington Walls – makes it likely that nothing of importance was missed by these trial trenches. The excavators concluded that this area to the south of Stonehenge had been largely devoid of activities, monuments or settlement sites in the fourth to second millennia BC.

Years before, archaeologists had noticed that Stonehenge sits at the centre of an area, up to a mile across, that contains far fewer Bronze Age round barrows than the areas slightly further out from the stone circle. The round barrow cemeteries are concentrated in a wide, doughnut-shaped circle on the skyline around Stonehenge.[2] They sit on the edges of a central, empty 'envelope of visibility' immediately around the stone circle, within which there are fewer than forty barrows. Since the trial trenches were within the envelope of visibility, their emptiness supports the existing evidence that this area closely encircling Stonehenge was deliberately avoided both by Neolithic and Copper Age inhabitants of the area as well as by the Early Bronze Age builders of the round barrows.

As our own excavations at Durrington Walls came to an end, our next task was to look at the landscape west and north of Stonehenge for evidence in this area of settlements occupied at the time of Stonehenge. Julian Richards' survey team had recovered lots of worked flints, including Neolithic arrowheads, from a large field on the rising ground immediately to the west of Stonehenge.[3] Here, in fact, was one of the two densest concentrations that he found in the entire survey area.

We also hoped to solve a mystery that had arisen when the visitor centre was installed in 1967. Back then Lance and Faith Vatcher had carried out a small dig and found the end of a long, straight ditch heading off from the car park area southwards, past the west side of Stonehenge, which had held a palisade of closely spaced timber posts.[4] The Vatchers found nothing to date the ditch or the palisade, but they knew that the timber posts were long decayed by the time that a man's corpse was buried in the ditch terminal at some time in the period 780–410 BC (the Early Iron Age). There was a possibility that this timber palisade was part of a huge Neolithic enclosure, like the ones dug by Alasdair Whittle at West Kennet, near Avebury in 1987 and 1990 – Josh had been there too, on the team as a student.[5] If this was a Neolithic enclosure it could have contained a large settlement.

In planning an excavation on this site the work of the Gaffney brothers was important. Quite a few archaeologists have a relative also in the business: second-generation archaeologists are fairly common (archaeological children seem to either love or utterly loathe their summers necessarily spent hanging around excavations) and pairs of siblings aren't unknown. In the case of the Gaffneys, older brother Vince of the University of Birmingham has been interested for many years in the Stonehenge palisade and younger brother Chris of the University of Bradford is a geophysicist. They had just developed the prototype of an improved magnetometer, mounted on a hand-pushed cart with its own on-board GPS. It can cover ground much faster than conventional machines and provides sharper resolution of below-ground anomalies. Wheeling his cart across the field, looking like an ice-cream vendor late for an appointment, Chris was able to track the course of the palisade ditch as it continued southwards up the hill, split into two and headed off to both the south and the west.

In 2008 we set out four trenches in this huge field, using the geophysics plot to decide where to put them. One trench covered the junction where the palisade ditch split in two. The second was positioned south of it, where a recent pipe trench had obscured the magnetometer's plot of the ditch. Both areas were at the heart of Julian Richards' worked-flint concentration, so we hoped that we might pick up traces of a Neolithic village. The third trench was placed by the palisade ditch far along its west fork, beyond a section in which the ditch appeared to have a couple of gaps. The magnetic anomalies here, we thought, might just be pits in a settlement. The fourth trench was further north, closer to the A344 and the visitors' centre; here we wanted to find out whether a line

In the field west of Stonehenge, we dug a number of trenches to explore the enigmatic palisade ditch. Stonehenge is visible to the right beyond the cars.

of magnetic anomalies were more Mesolithic postholes, like those under the nearby car park.

The field is owned by the National Trust, who insisted that we remove the turf and ploughsoil entirely by hand. We were aghast. For Josh and fellow site director Paul Garwood, Vince Gaffney's colleague at Birmingham University, this was a Herculean undertaking. Their team had to lift the turf and sieve all the topsoil across an area half the size of a football pitch – and they had to do it fast. We spent a lot of our grant money building a battle fleet of new sieves and raided the stores of five universities to round up enough shovels, spades and buckets. Even with a small army of students and volunteers it took two whole weeks to get to the point where we could begin to excavate the archaeological features beneath the topsoil. Working conditions on this exposed slope were often miserable and we felt the students were never going to forgive us.

We counted up everything found in the sieves and recorded, grimly, that we could have estimated the total quantity of worked flints in the ploughsoil by sieving just a sample of it. As our geophysics and augering had shown (and as aerial photographs, the tenant farmer and Julian Richards' old Stonehenge Environs team had confirmed many times), this field has been heavily ploughed for centuries. Although the worked flints survive ploughing, more fragile remains like bones and pottery don't.

We felt our hand-digging had been a waste of time and effort (not to mention money); we could have dug an appropriate number of our customary metre-square test pits and then machined the topsoil and come up with the same result. Months later though, as we studied the flints in the lab back in Sheffield, we realized that the laborious sieving of the field's topsoil had been worthwhile: many of the flints recovered were long blades from the Mesolithic. We had discovered the location of a Mesolithic campsite close to the site of Stonehenge and just 400 metres south of the pine posts under the car park. Long before the Neolithic, people had camped in this small valley; perhaps this was where they lived when they erected those gigantic posts.

In terms of Neolithic remains, however, the results were disappointing. The palisade ditch had been cleaned out and re-used in the Middle Bronze Age as a boundary that formed part of a Bronze Age farming landscape of fields. We couldn't find anything to date the palisade ditch but the fact that its line was continued by the Bronze Age ditch makes it pretty likely that it's only a little bit earlier. There was no trace of any Neolithic activity, so the density of flints recovered on the surface was indicative mostly of later activity from the middle and end of the second millennium BC. Even when knowledge of metallurgy spread and bronze tools became available, people continued to work flint. Unfortunately, the vast mass of Bronze Age flint-working looks no different to the worked flints of the previous millennium; it can be impossible to tell them apart unless you find diagnostic tools, such as arrowheads, whose distinctive shapes change through time.

After the field ditch had silted up, around 1250 BC, Late Bronze Age people buried three infants in the top of it, together with a whole pot and a beautiful carved small chalk pig. The 'Stonehenge pig' is an endearing little object that attracted a surprising amount of media inter-est. Someone thought it looked more like a hedgehog, so the British Hedgehog Society was contacted to share its views. On the other hand, most of the diggers agreed that the little figurine's long flat ears left no doubt that the artist had intended to represent a pig.

A carved chalk pig, dating to the Late Bronze Age, was found in the upper layers filling the palisade ditch. The pig has four 'button' feet, a snout and floppy ears.

Paul Garwood found that where he was digging, over in the western-most trench in this field, was part of a Middle Bronze Age settlement. In the lee of a deep ditch was a group of postholes and small pits contain-ing Bronze Age pottery. In the northern, fourth trench our possible line of Mesolithic postholes turned out to be four treeholes of Roman and later date; the fact that there were four in a line was pure coincidence.

We were all disappointed not to find any Neolithic activity in this area west of Stonehenge but we had learned an important lesson. This high chalkland, far from sources of fresh water, was not a place for Neolithic farming even though it had been the site of an earlier hunter-gatherer settlement. Only when people had become fully sedentary farmers, from 1500 BC in the Middle Bronze Age, did they properly colonize this dry landscape, dividing it up into fields for their grazing sheep and plough-ing up the grassland for arable fields of wheat and barley. A good proportion of the huge quantities of worked flints in the topsoil is likely to date to this period, much of it brought on to the fields in rubbish carried from the settlements to be spread as manure.

We now understood that the palisade ditch was the first land boundary to have been laid out across Stonehenge's open grasslands. Although it stopped in the area of the old visitor centre, after a gap of about 400 metres it then continued northwards alongside the Stonehenge avenue before curving westwards across the ruined banks of the Cursus. The northern stretch is called the Gate Ditch; California Dave led a team digging a short section where it runs alongside the avenue and found that it too had held the posts of a timber palisade.

Julian Richards' Stonehenge Environs Project showed that, after the Copper Age, the entire area around Stonehenge was encroached upon by these Bronze Age field systems, visible from aerial photographs.[6] Once known as 'Celtic fields', they have nothing to do with Celts. These lattice arrangements of field ditches mostly date to the Bronze Age but continued in use into the Iron Age.

Interestingly, although the palisade ditch passed close to Stonehenge, the Bronze Age farmers gave Stonehenge itself a wide berth, leaving it untouched within an island of open ground that extended northwards to beyond the avenue's bend, where the avenue changes direction from its solstice axis and heads east towards the river. Stonehenge was evidently still treated as a place of respect at this time, and it was still visited even though construction had ended. In fact, all excavations at Stonehenge put together have recovered nearly as much pottery from the period 1500–700 BC as there is for the period 3000–1500 BC.[7] Most of it comes from the interior of the sarsen circle and from the ditch.

The late summer of 2008 – the year in which we dug both the palisade and the Aubrey Hole – was wet and cold. In previous years our campsite beside the Avon at the Woodbridge Inn in North Newnton had been a happy haven of sunshine and tranquillity but that season it turned into a quagmire of mud and misery. With a team of 160 diggers living there, our feet soon churned up the grass. We tried scattering bales of straw to dry it out but the straw soon rotted into a fetid mess. The floor of the marquee where we ate our supper turned to liquid filth.

Everything was covered in mud – tents, equipment and clothing. The vans and minibuses, perpetually stuck, made things worse spinning their wheels in ever-deepening ruts. Having to push seven heavy vehicles out of the swamp every morning made a bad start to each day. The sewage lorry emptying the Portaloos had to be towed out by a tractor – he wouldn't be coming back. Outbreaks of trench foot were reported. The students either coped – when the going gets tough, the tough have another party – or wimped out. It was crunch time: do you want to be an archaeologist or would it be sensible to consider a rather more indoor career?

Although the campsite was horrible, conditions in the trenches were perfect. Plenty of rain on the free-draining chalk soils brought out the colour contrasts and kept the ground soft. In an entire month we lost only half a day's digging because of the rain. On the north side of Stonehenge our main aim that year was to reopen and extend trenches dug by Richard Atkinson into the Stonehenge avenue, to find out more about its dating and sequence. Atkinson had left barely any records of six of his trenches – just two plans, a single section drawing and two photographs.[8] Half a century later we intended to finish the job of recording his excavations. Two of his trenches, dug in 1978, had been properly recorded, and even published, by John Evans, a colleague of Atkinson's at Cardiff.[9]

I'd known John Evans in his later years when he was a professor of environmental archaeology. He became the leading specialist in land molluscs – 'snail Evans' to distinguish him from lots of other archaeological Evanses – and was one of those people who's interested in everything. He'd had some difficult years when alcohol almost got the better of him, yet his mind was razor-sharp and you never knew what he was going to say next. Conversations with him were always challenging and he never held back, always saying exactly what he thought.

These days mavericks like John don't get jobs in universities – or if they do they don't last long. Gone are the days when a university lecturer can stare at an expectant class and tell them to just clear off (in four-letter words), because he's depressed and really doesn't want to talk to them. Yet John's students adored him – he was a witty, clever and unruly man, hugely enthusiastic and inspirational. A Stonehenge gift-shop coffee mug was John's only audio-visual aid for an excellent lecture he sometimes gave on Stonehenge. Sadly, he succumbed to throat cancer in his early sixties.

When we reopened the trench that John had dug we found in its side the precise spot where, exactly thirty years earlier, he'd taken a snail sample; it may seem strange that this snail sample could be famous but for all the project directors this was a really historic spot, and memories came flooding back. I'd never thought to ask John directly about his work at Stonehenge, having no idea that I'd eventually be reopening his trench. Now it was too late: we'd have to learn what we could from what he and Richard Atkinson had left behind.

The Stonehenge avenue runs dead straight northeastwards for about 500 metres from Stonehenge until it turns sharply east, at its 'elbow'. At this point it dips downward steeply into the dry valley of Stonehenge Bottom, running along the top of a spur before dropping off its end. In Stonehenge Bottom it curves eastwards, but its earthworks are very difficult to see here, disappearing as it climbs the east side of the valley. The top of the slope is called King Barrow ridge; as the avenue crests this ridge it passes through a line of round barrows.

The King Barrows are splendid things to go and see, some of the largest round barrows in Britain. Protected beneath huge old trees, none has ever been investigated. When the 1987 hurricane blew over some of the trees on top of them, Mike Allen got the chance to look inside these newly created tree-holes.[10] He discovered that many of this group of Bronze Age barrows were built not of chalk but of turf and topsoil. To produce enough turf to cover each barrow mound would have required the stripping of six hectares or more of grassland. It must have been a clumsy, difficult job to strip turf with antler picks. This prehistoric turf-stripping would also have put out of use a large area of valuable grazing land, as if the purpose of this part of the funeral ritual was to cut off one's nose to spite one's face, economically speaking.

The avenue then continues down the east side of the King Barrow ridge, curving southeastwards and passing through another two lines of less impressive round barrows. Eventually it reaches the Avon.

We had two main questions we wanted to answer. The avenue is 22 metres wide, with a ditch and internal bank running along each side, parallel to each other. There were originally also external banks but

The Stonehenge Avenue turns sharply eastwards at a point known as the 'elbow'. We re-opened Atkinson's trenches here to check whether the avenue was built in one go or in two stages. Stonehenge is on the horizon (centre).

these are no longer visible. The internal banks are today only 0.3 metres high at their greatest. The ditches are 0.3 metres deep now but were once over a metre deep. As for the avenue's curious 'elbow', it seemed possible to some archaeologists that the part of the avenue that heads off eastwards towards the river was constructed in a second phase, after the section that leads northeastwards from the entrance to Stonehenge. We wanted to find out for sure whether the avenue's ditches had been extended in a second phase of construction, or whether the entire avenue had been built in one go.

The second question was whether there was an earlier, short avenue lying under the present one, running along just the 500-metre-long solstice-aligned length from Stonehenge to Stonehenge Bottom. One of Atkinson's photographs and his section drawing show a series of small gullies within the avenue, running parallel with the avenue ditches but apparently underneath the avenue's banks. These gullies appeared to be generally about 30 centimetres wide and up to half a metre deep, too large to be ancient cart tracks but not big enough for ditches. They were also visible on the geophysics plots, showing up as some seven parallel lines running along the solstice axis of the avenue. We puzzled over them, wondering if they were palisade slots to hold rows of posts, perhaps dividing the celebrants into 'lanes' as they approached Stonehenge.

Down at the avenue elbow, California Dave's team emptied out Atkinson's trenches, and we were allowed to extend them a little to get a better cross-section of the avenue. There were very few finds, just a handful of worked flints from the new trench extension. The stretch of avenue in which we were most interested was where the magnetometer survey had shown a kink in the ditches, suggesting that a new stretch of avenue had possibly been tacked on to the end of the 500-metre-long straight section. In reality, we could see on the ground that there was no such deviation; the bend joined seamlessly with the straight section. It had not been added at a later stage. We also discovered that the avenue ditch, on both sides, had been cleaned out in prehistory after it had silted up. Although the team found nothing to date this event, radio-carbon dates on bones and antler picks from previous excavations date the cleaning-out of other lengths of the avenue ditch to around 2200 BC.

In 1978 one of Atkinson's and Evans' trenches had cut into a small raised feature immediately east of the avenue. This is called Newall's Mound, after Hawley's assistant.[11] It consists of a deposit of heavy clay mixed with natural flints, which continues to a depth of 1.5 metres. It is disgusting stuff to dig out with a pick and shovel – just emptying Atkinson's and Evans' backfill was bad enough – but John Evans must have enjoyed himself immensely while excavating it first time around. It is a periglacial feature, a large solution hole, about 5 metres across, that has filled with a mass of clay-with-flints created in Ice Age conditions not far south of the glaciers' limit. Here was a textbook example of a geo-logical feature of the sort John loved. It contained a buried early post-glacial soil and had been thoroughly bioturbated (that is, the lay-ering had been mixed up by biological action – in this case tree roots).

Mike Allen and Charly French were delighted to see the re-excavated solution hole. Both had been John's students and knew it well from his lecture slides. Then they noticed something that John had missed. Deposits of clay-with-flints, recalcitrant though they are for the digger, are too soft to withstand the forces of natural erosion and normally form flat layers rather than raised mounds. Something had held this deposit together as a raised prominence and the answer lay in the bioturbation. They could see where the roots of long-vanished trees had twisted and inverted the stratigraphy of the clay-with-flints; one or more large trees had stood on this spot in the early post-glacial period, their roots clutching the clay-with-flints like an eagle's talons. This must have been why the deposit survives as a mound. Whether such trees were still standing when Stonehenge was built is anyone's guess, but even treeless the mound would have been a visible natural feature at the end of the straight length of avenue. Maybe its position in relation to the avenue turn is not entirely coincidental.

Closer towards Stonehenge things were going smoothly but not producing what I'd expected. Here we were re-opening another Atkinson trench on the Stonehenge avenue, just 30 metres from the Heel Stone, directly across the road from Stonehenge itself. We had found the outline of the old trench and marked out the 2-metre-wide extension that we had permission to dig adjacent to it. The old backfill was full of finds – flint flakes, sarsen hammerstones, sarsen chippings and bluestone chippings – as if nothing much had been collected during the 1956 excavation.

When we got to the bottom of the old Atkinson trench we found that the gullies we'd seen in the old site photograph were not palisade slots after all. They weren't even man-made. Here were more periglacial features, this time long, thin erosion gullies created by freeze-thaw conditions and filled with sediment formed from the grinding of chalk by ice into a clay 'flour'. The Wessex chalklands are covered in these periglacial stripes and we were not the first archaeologists to be misled by these features of geological origin. Normally they are much shallower and narrower, often resembling ploughmarks. I was disappointed that they weren't man-made, but perfectly happy to change my mind – you always go with what the evidence tells you. We were victims of a geological coincidence. Because these periglacial gullies are aligned on the midsummer sunrise/midwinter sunset solstice axis we'd wrongly assumed that they would *not* be geological.

When Mike and Charly took a look they became very excited. The periglacial stripes are unduly wide for what might be expected here. The reason for their size is that water had been channelled from further up the slope between two low banks of natural chalk bedrock. With a lot of water available for the freeze-thaw processes that formed these gullies, their widths and depths are greater than is usually seen on this geology. Mike and Charly went on to point out that, in the early part of the post-glacial period, these gullies would have been very plain to see; they would have been clearly visible as stripes in the thin grass cover on the slowly developing soil. By the Neolithic period, they would not have been so noticeable, being covered by thicker soil and grass, except in times of drought when the parched chalk of the bedrock would have turned the grass yellow while the damper fill of the sediment-filled gullies remained green, leaving dark stripes on top of the gullies.* Such dry periods would be most likely in summertime.

I had thought that the two natural ridges on either side of the gullies were created by the differential weathering of chalk bedrock: it has remained higher where it has been protected for thousands of years by the avenue's banks. Mike and Charly pointed out that the man-made banks are actually very narrow compared to the widths of the natural chalk ridges beneath them: the presence of the man-made banks cannot account for the creation of such prominent natural features. Looking more carefully at the landscape, we could also see that the natural pair of ridges ran for only about 200 metres whereas the avenue banks continued on well beyond them.

We had stumbled upon the reason why Stonehenge is where it is. The northeast entrance of Stonehenge is positioned at one end of a pair of natural ridges, between which are parallel stripes of sediment-filled gullies and chalk bedrock. It is not particularly unusual for Neolithic monuments to incorporate such aspects of the natural world into their design, but what is exceptional here is that this particular natural feature,

---

* Archaeologists still use such 'parch marks' today to identify sites that are otherwise invisible above ground. They are one of the main reasons for taking aerial photographs. If the ground is sufficiently dry, grass grows less thickly on buried structures. A similar effect is produced in fields of crops, to form 'crop marks'. These are, of course, nothing to do with 'crop circles' which are created by a dedicated band of mathematically inclined enthusiasts, masquerading in the public imagination as aliens.

by sheer coincidence, is aligned on the solstice axis. There is absolutely no doubt that the builders of Stonehenge were aware of the presence of this geological formation, because they enhanced the two natural ridges by digging the avenue's ditches along their outside edges and heaping soil on top of each ridge to form parallel banks.

This explains why the Stonehenge builders were so concerned to mark the solstice alignment of midwinter sunset and midsummer sunrise in the monument's architecture: it was already inscribed in the ground. Perhaps this is also why, in Stonehenge's earliest use, wooden posts were set up to reference major standstills of moonrises and moonsets that would be best seen at midsummer and midwinter full moon.

The natural ridges would have formed what anthropologists call an *axis mundi*, an axis or centre of the world. For Neolithic people this was where the passage of the sun was marked on the land, where heaven and earth came together. Such a place might have been regarded as the centre or origin of the universe. It would certainly have been worthy of celebrations involving the transport of Welsh bluestones and, later on, the huge sarsens.

The presence of these natural ridges may also explain why there are Early Mesolithic postholes under the car park. During that period, ten thousand years ago, the periglacial stripes would have been easier to see under the thin vegetation on shallow soils that had only started forming after the Ice Age, and the ridges would have been more prominent than they are today after millennia of weathering. Perhaps this is why this particular spot was important enough for Mesolithic people to mark its environs with huge pine posts.

Many archaeologists were sceptical about our solstice-aligned natural feature. It was just too good to be true. How could we really prove that these parallel ridges were geological, subsequently enhanced by human construction? Yet this was by no means the first time that archaeologists had noted evidence for the use of natural features by prehistoric people. Almost a decade earlier, archaeologist Richard Bradley had written an entire book on the ways that prehistoric people throughout Europe took natural places – springs, rivers, caves and mountains – to have sacred significance.[12] These appropriations of the natural world could take a number of forms: placing of votive deposits, carving of rock art, extraction of raw materials for tools, and re-sculpting of natural landforms. He had noted that the people of the British Neolithic were no exception to this wider picture. Like other cultures ancient and modern, they invested the world around them with special meanings, singling out certain hills, rivers and other topographic features by leaving human traces that cannot be explained by mere practical activity and expediency alone.

We had already encountered similar re-use of a natural feature at Durrington Walls, with its avenue of rammed flint constructed on top of an entirely natural surface of exposed flint fragments that had formed in the bottom of the dry valley or coombe that ran from the Southern Circle to the River Avon. In that particular case, the avenue builders had added a new surface on top of the existing, natural one, incorporating animal bones, pottery, flint tools and burnt flint amongst the naturally shattered flint that formed the matrix of the avenue's surface. Not only that but Clive Ruggles had also shown that the alignment of this artificially enhanced natural surface was within one degree of the midsummer solstice sunset. Perhaps the very reason for the location of Durrington Walls was this freak of geomorphology, in which a natural bed of broken flints was almost perfectly aligned on the midsummer solstice sunset.

Could a similar natural coincidence also have dictated the placing of Stonehenge? To learn more about the chalk ridges and the deep periglacial gullies between them, Mike Allen consulted a chalk-geologist colleague who came back with the suggestion that we should see if the two ridges showed up on radar mapping. Around the same time, Colin noticed on an aerial photograph of Stonehenge that there was yet another ridge here; a third ridge runs parallel to the other two but further to the east. Kate Welham's geophysics team were sent out to survey it to make sure that there was no trace of associated man-made features: it registered a complete blank. We were then lucky enough to be approached by a Dutch radar company, GT Frontline, who brought their equipment over to Britain and surveyed the avenue. Their results confirmed what we'd hoped: there are indeed three parallel ridges, which show up on the computer plot like a cricket wicket without its bails.

We now had a quite unexpected new interpretation of Stonehenge and an explanation for why it was positioned here. At some point in the very distant past, around 10,000 years ago, hunters in search of game on the grasslands of Salisbury Plain came across a series of ridges and stripes in the ground. Perhaps they already had an understanding of the sun's annual movements and realized that, in this particular place, the axis of midsummer sunrise and midwinter sunset was tracked by ancient marks in the land. Here, heaven and earth were unified by some supernatural force. Around it, they camped, dug pits and erected pine-tree posts, marking the direction of the highest hill on the horizon.

Perhaps the traditions associated with this place continued, though it's more likely that they died out and people forgot. In the intervening millennia, between the end of the Early Mesolithic and the building of Stonehenge around 3000 BC, this location seems not to have attracted interest. Early Neolithic monuments of the fourth millennium BC – long barrows, cursuses and a causewayed enclosure – were built on nearby spots but not here. Rather than there being any continuity of meaning and memory between the Mesolithic posts and the building of Stonehenge 5000 years later, it is more probable that Neolithic people rediscovered this curious geological phenomenon around 3000 BC, perhaps ascribing it to the actions of supernatural beings or a world creator. They might have noticed the prominence that we call Newall's Mound. The large sarsen that we call the Heel Stone was probably lying recumbent at the south end of the stripes in the ground. There, facing the midwinter sunset, they constructed a circular enclosure, whose roundness echoed that of the sun and moon, with a circle of Welsh bluestones and a burial ground for the most illustrious of their dead.

If these natural features were the first phase of the avenue, when were its ditches and banks constructed? Four radiocarbon dates have been obtained from antler picks and a cattle bone found in or near the ditch bottom during previous excavations; but, because the ditches were emptied out at some point in prehistory, and thus all the built-up silt and soil inside them removed, it's difficult to tell whether these picks and bones ended up in the ditch the first or second time that it was dug out.

As we excavated beneath the shallow banks of the avenue we discovered that the Neolithic ground surface had been protected underneath them. It was littered with chippings of sarsen and bluestone. The presence beneath the banks of this stone-dressing waste means that Stonehenge's stones were shaped and put up before the avenue's ditch and bank were constructed. The avenue banks must therefore date to after 2500 BC, confirmed by radiocarbon dates of antler picks on the ditch bottom dating to 2500–2270 BC.

About 70 metres west of our avenue trench, Colin was digging a small square trench just 5 metres across. He was hoping to find evidence for the shaping and dressing of the stones before they were taken the last few hundred yards to the stone circle. His enthusiasm for molehills, generated all those years ago as an evening-class student, has never left him. Every time we stroll around this field in front of Stonehenge he gets everybody to look in the small heaps of loose soil. Immediately east of the visitor centre Colin had found sarsen chippings brought to the surface by those moles. When he returned year after year he was able to see that a very extensive area in front of Stonehenge was producing chippings from the stones. The density of chippings is greatest on the field's west side, where it was ploughed during the 1970s.

Colin consulted the records of the car-park and visitor-centre excavations in 1935 and 1967. Although they had dug carefully, Young and Newall and the Vatchers had found very few stone chippings – though it's clear from their records that they had been looking for them.[13] In contrast, Mike Pitts had found loads in his cable-trench excavation in 1980 on the other side of the road.[14] Kate carried out a resistivity survey in the molehill field, the results of which were great. We could see a skirt-shaped zone of high resistance stretching westwards from the beginning of the avenue to the area ploughed in the 1970s, close to the visitor centre. We were sure that this high resistance was being caused by a pavement-like spread of broken stone. We could hear the crunch of metal hitting sarsen as Mike Allen cored a series of auger holes across the spread, from which we picked out tiny chips.

We were sure that we'd found the stone-dressing area where the sarsens were worked. They must have been dragged here from the quarries, already roughly shaped but awaiting their final smoothing. Perhaps they were also lined up on their wooden cradles and their dimensions checked, to make sure that lintels would fit on top of uprights. Then they would have been hauled on their sledges through the wide northeast entrance into Stonehenge. To demonstrate beyond doubt that this was a stone-dressing area, we needed to put a trench here.

We proposed a 15 × 10-metre area for the trench. This would be just big enough to reveal the silhouette left by the stone debris lying around the edges of at least one sarsen. But the National Trust weren't having it: they would allow only a much smaller hole, 5 x 5 metres. We had no choice – and at least we'd been given permission to open a trench here at all. This was the only completely new area in the avenue field we were allowed to dig; all our other trenches re-opened old excavations.

Beneath the turf in Colin's trench he came down on to a classic worm-sorted topsoil. This had not been ploughed in thousands of years, if ever. Beneath it was a small piece of the Stonehenge Neolithic landscape that had survived the ravages of erosion for four or five millennia. Just as Colin had predicted, there was a carpet of sarsen chippings across the surface of the chalk bedrock. To Mike and Charly's satisfaction, the periglacial stripes here were very narrow and shallow, confirming that the oversized stripes beneath the avenue are unique.

The shape and position of each stone chip as it lay in the ground was drawn on a detailed plan and then the chippings were lifted in half-metre squares for counting, weighing and careful analysis. We needed to establish that this was 'primary refuse' – that the chips lay where they had fallen from the activities of stone-dressing and that these stones had not been collected up from somewhere else and dumped here in heaps at a later date.

Colin's team included Ben Chan and Hugo Anderson-Whymark, who are experts in worked stone – whether flint or sarsen. With all the stone chips laid out across the floor of a giant agricultural barn, they found from patient trial and error that some of the pieces fitted together. The pieces that fitted were found lying close to each other, suggesting that they lay where they had fallen from the stone. One half of the trench had very few chippings in it, with a very obvious and straight north–south line dividing this area from the part of the trench with masses of chippings. We were looking at the silhouetted edge of a stone, where a sarsen had been laid on its back and all its surfaces, apart from its underside, pounded smooth. Had we had been allowed a bigger trench, we could have seen the entire shape of the stone that had been dressed here.

Computer specialists Lawrence Shaw and Mark Dover (standing right) visit Colin
Richards' trench immediately north of Stonehenge. Here the sarsen stones were
dressed (shaped and finished) before they completed the last step
of their journey.

Colin, Ben and Hugo counted and weighed 6500 sarsen chippings
from this one trench. They also found fifty hammerstones, many of which
were fractured and broken. These fist-sized hammers are made of hard
quartzitic sarsen, in contrast to the generally softer stone of the uprights
and lintels of the stone circle. Most of the hammerstones are round but
some have been roughly flaked to make simple hand-axes, their edges
battered from repeated contact with the rock. The process must have
been exceedingly tedious and damaging: anyone could have contributed
to this sort of work – men, women and children – but hour upon hour of
bashing hand-held rocks against the huge stones would surely have
injured their wrists and fingers. Larger hammerstones, termed mauls,
were also used in stone-dressing. Gowland, Hawley and Atkinson all found
examples of these used as packing around the bases of sarsen uprights.
Perhaps these larger hammers were salvaged from the dressing zone
when they were needed to pack the holes of the raised sarsens.

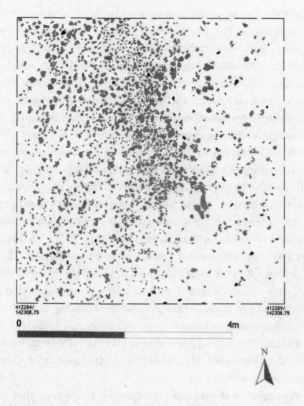

412284/
142308.75

412289/
142308.75

0

4m

N

Colin Richards and his team planned every stone chipping found in the trench. The distribution shows the straight edge where a sarsen once lay while it was being dressed.

Colin has spent a long time during various visits inside Stonehenge looking at the minute details of the finished product. Some surfaces of the sarsens have been hammered smooth, while others are speckled with tiny pockmark-like holes. Some stones have wide grooves separated by low ridges. No stone is dressed exactly the same as another.

A closer look also reveals that the inside faces of the stones in both the outer circle and in the trilithon horseshoe have been dressed, as have their thin sides, whereas their backs (facing outwards) are either unmodified or have been dressed to about head-height only. When the sarsens lay in the dressing zone, the stone-dressers would have been unable to get at the stones' undersides. The sarsens would have then been brought into the construction area, presumably on wooden sledges or cradles, and each manoeuvred to the outside edge of its stonehole before being erected. They would have been raised from the outside of the circle towards the inside, like petals closing on a flower. The back of each stone (on which it had been lying) would have been inaccessible until the stone was raised; final dressing of the back could then be carried out, but only to head height.

This finally explains why the inner faces of the sarsen circle are better dressed than their outer faces, a feature first noted by Stukeley 300 years ago.[15] It may also help to shed light on the curiously small size of one of the sarsens in the stone circle. Stone 11 stands upright but is not much larger than a lintel. It is far too short to have ever been a support for a continuous line of lintels from Stone 10 to Stone 12. In 2005 Mike Pitts was faced with the dilemma of how to reconstruct its lintels. The television company Channel 5 was building a full-sized replica of Stonehenge in polystyrene. Since Stones 10 and 12 have tenons (knobs that project from the top of the stone to fit the cup-shaped mortise holes of lintels), they were definitely designed to support lintels. A double-length stone lintel bridging the gap over Stone 11 would not have been stable but a wooden substitute might. Mike's solution was to use a timber lintel over the top of Stone 11.

Looking again at the surfaces of Stone 11, I could see that its inner face never received the same dressing treatment as the other sarsen uprights. Perhaps this little shorty was not part of the main build. Maybe it was added later, taken from one of the stoneholes of the Station Stones or from one of the two stoneholes next to the Slaughter Stone. Perhaps there never were lintels here. Stone 11 lies on the axis of the south entrance to Stonehenge. Maybe the tenons on all the sarsen uprights were shaped in the quarry or the dressing area in a standardized production-line fashion, before anyone realized that the stones in this part of the circle would not need mortise-and-tenon joints. Interestingly, a former bluestone lintel lies close by (now mostly buried below ground) – perhaps this is the remnant of an entrance through the bluestone circle at this point. Only further excavation can reveal whether Stone 11 is part of the original build or a later addition to the sarsen circle.

Supervisor Chris Casswell stands with a scale behind tiny Stone 11 at Stonehenge. It is clearly too short to have supported a lintel and has not been dressed in a similar fashion to the other stones of the sarsen circle.

In strong contrast to the number of sarsen pieces found (6500), only 40 bluestone chippings were found by Colin in his 5 × 5-metre trench. There were more bluestone chips in the avenue trench but only just over a hundred. Why are there so few fragments of bluestone outside the stone circle, when excavators digging *inside* Stonehenge have found many more bluestone chips than sarsen chips? It is most likely that the dressing of bluestones took place inside Stonehenge. That certainly makes sense if the bluestones were already there, in the Aubrey Holes, ready to be rearranged in the Q and R Holes. Not all the bluestones have been dressed: of the 43 survivors, only 17 have been worked to create smooth surfaces.[16] Although moved around several times, presumably the bluestones have never left the premises since their arrival around 2950 BC.

The builders had to think very carefully about how to position the

dressed sarsens. The lintels had to fit neatly on top of the uprights. The
difficulties of getting a perfect fit would have been compounded by the
slight slope of the site. At Durrington Walls the ground was terraced flat
before the construction of the Southern Circle, but at Stonehenge the
architects chose to retain the natural slope even though they wanted the
lintels on the stone uprights to be horizontal. To compensate for the
slope, the uprights had to be shorter upslope to the southwest and taller
towards the northeast.

The puzzle of how Neolithic people built such a complex structure
has occupied many minds for centuries. Around 1640, Inigo Jones
thought it was so precisely built that it must once have been a completely
symmetrical monument with Classical proportions as set out by the
Roman architect Vitruvius.[17] However, although Jones' stylized portrayal
of Stonehenge's ground plan is accurate to within 5 per cent, his desire
for it to be perfectly symmetrical led to his adding an extra, sixth
trilithon that never actually existed. William Stukeley was the first to try
to work out what unit of measurement had been used.[18] If it was the
Roman foot of 0.96 feet (0.293 metres) then Stonehenge was Roman, as
Jones had thought. Stukeley was convinced that the ancient Britons who
had built it 'knew nothing of Vitruvius' and, after taking 2000 measurements, deduced that Stonehenge's base unit of measurement was
20.8 inches (1.73 feet or 0.528 metres).

One of the reasons why William Flinders Petrie was determined to
make an accurate plan of Stonehenge in 1872 was that he too hoped to
work out the units of measurement used by its builders.[19] He found that
the inner diameter of the sarsen circle amounted to 100 Roman feet (his
calculation of the Roman foot was slightly longer than Stukeley's at 0.973
feet or 0.297 metres). He also deduced that the outer features – the
ditch, bank and Station Stones – were laid out using a completely different unit of 1.873 feet (0.571 metres).

In the 1960s, Alexander Thom stunned the world of archaeology by
claiming that many megaliths, including Stonehenge, had been built by
astronomer priests in order to measure astronomical events. He also
claimed that they had all worked to a common unit of measurement, in
use across the whole of Britain, in order to construct these monuments.
This he called the Megalithic Yard of 2.722 feet (0.830 metres). In 1988

Thom and his son published their finding that the average centre-line diameter of Stonehenge's sarsen circle is 37 Megalithic Yards.[20] Although Thom's work still has something of a following today among the wider public, archaeologists have never accepted wholeheartedly his concept of the Megalithic Yard (although it may be relevant for megalithic monuments in northern Scotland, where he first formulated the idea).

Most recently, archaeologist Tony Johnson proposed in 2008 that Stonehenge could have been planned without a unit of measurement, simply by laying out series of intersecting circles.[21] Using computer-aided design (CAD) methods, he showed how the Aubrey Holes could have been laid out in twelve moves. The positions of the seemingly unsymmetrical trilithons could have been established by marking the intersections of two sets of concentric circles, one centred between Stones 1 and 30 and the other between Stones 15 and 16. These are then combined with circles centred on Stones 1, 11, 20 and 30 of the sarsen circle to arrive at the positions of the trilithons. Johnson is able to show that the inside edges of the ten trilithon uprights (and the external edges of the great trilithon's two uprights) can be plotted at chosen intersections of the six circles. Johnson calls this intersection of the two concentric circles a 'diffraction grating'.

A few months later John Hill, a research student at Liverpool University, demonstrated that Stonehenge could be laid out much more simply using lengths of rope, the sun's shadow and basic counting on fingers.[22] To show how easy it could be he enlisted the help of schoolchildren from Northcote Primary School in Walton to lay out Stonehenge's ground plan at the university sports ground.

I had always kept my distance from the complex issue of Stonehenge's geometry. It was quite clear that there were all kinds of different ways of solving the same problem, and each originator was convinced that his solution was the correct one. How could anyone decide which was the actual solution used by Stonehenge's designers and which were attractive possibilities but no more than that? For John Hill, the principle of Occam's razor applied: they would have been most likely to choose the simplest solution. For Tony Johnson, a decider was the fact that his method could reveal that the great trilithon upright restored under Gowland's direction in 1901 has been re-erected in the wrong place,

60 centimetres from its original position (though this is exaggerated; for the mid-point of the stone's face, the distance by which it is mis-set is actually about 30 centimetres).

Then my colleague Andrew Chamberlain took a look at the problem.[23] As a specialist in human osteology and palaeodemography, Andrew works with mathematical problems all the time. We had worked together some years before on lunar-eclipse cycles and their correlation with the timing of construction of Iron Age timber causeways; Andrew worked out how to compare dendrochronological dates for tree-felling with Saros cycles of full lunar eclipses. Here was a new challenge. Thom's Megalithic Yard value of 37 for the sarsen circle's diameter, for example, did not seem particularly convincing to Andrew. Had Thom come up with not one but a series of whole number measurements, with regular intervals in measurements – such as 40, 50, 60 – for different parts of the Stonehenge plan, then the likelihood of the Megalithic Yard as a base unit would be more persuasive.

Instead of starting where everyone else had, with Stonehenge itself, Andrew looked at the ground plans of all the timber monuments at Durrington Walls, Woodhenge and the other Wessex henges. These could provide an independent test of any concept of a Neolithic base unit of measurement at Stonehenge.

Since we knew that the wooden circles were laid out around the same time as Stonehenge, it should be straightforward to identify shared regularities in design. Andrew started with the Southern Circle, for which we now had a complete circular plan, at least for the larger posts. He employed one key principle from the beginning. When laying out the positions of planned features, people are likely to choose their centres and not their edges. To dig a ditch or raise a bank it's simpler to mark out the mid-line rather than the edges. The issue is even more important for uprights. A simple parallel is the erection of fenceposts in the garden – if you're going to nail trellis to the posts, you must try to get the distances right. You decide where you want the middle of one post to fall, and then measure off to where the middle of the next post will be; if you measure between the edges of the posts it will go wrong, and it's no help at all to measure the distance between the edges of your postholes.

We know from excavations of postholes and stoneholes that it's not always possible to control the erection of an upright so precisely that it fits exactly where it was intended to go. People didn't measure to the edge of an imagined corner of a future post or stone that was going to be put up; they measured to roughly where the centre of the upright would be and could thus mark the centre of the hole to be dug for it.

Measuring the six concentric circles of posts of the Southern Circle's second phase from the centres of the postholes, Andrew found that the diameters of the outer four circles can be matched with regular and incremental multiples of an ancient English unit of measurement called the 'long foot'.

The distances came out as 70 to 90 to 110 to 120 'long feet'. The figures are not precise, with deviations varying from 6 centimetres to 50 centimetres, but Andrew thinks that this can be attributable either to imprecision in construction or, of course, to imprecision in archaeological recording during excavation. Nevertheless, he had identified a possible unit of measurement that could be tried out on other monuments.

The 'long foot' (1.056 feet or 0.32187 metres) was one of the base units used in Medieval England. Andrew had been impressed by some of the research of John Michell and John Neal into ancient metrology and wondered, as they did, whether some of our more recent units of measurement might have great antiquity.[24] He was also aware from their work that ancient measurement systems often made use of multiple values of their base units.

The 'long foot' was so-called because it was longer than the 'short foot' (0.96 feet or 0.2926 metres) – the two units were sometimes used together. For example, 11 short feet make 10 long feet. The ratio of 11:10 is useful when measuring out circles. A diameter of 7 short feet creates a circumference of 22 short feet or 20 long feet (22/7 is a close approximation of the value of π or pi). In the old British system of statute feet, the lengths known as chains, furlongs and miles are based on multiples of 11 statute feet, again reflecting this 11:10 ratio. Andrew and I are old enough to remember running the 110-yards hurdles race and using actual chains for surveying.

Turning to Stonehenge, Andrew examined the dimensions of its first phase. In addition to the Aubrey Holes, henge bank and henge ditch, he looked at the dimensions of a slight bank outside the ditch, called the counterscarp bank. This bank is earlier than the Stonehenge avenue's ditches, which cut through it, and probably belongs to the initial period of construction. The diameters of the four circular features are 270, 300, 330 and 360 long feet, with errors of between 12 centimetres and 45 centimetres. Thus they could have been laid out with a rope running from a centre point, marked with the radius lengths of 135, 150, 165 and 180 long feet.

The fact that these diameters are not only whole numbers but also built on regular intervals of 15 long feet is encouraging. Was 15 long feet a standard unit? Given that there are 56 Aubrey Holes, it is particularly intriguing that the circumference of the Aubrey Hole circle is 847.8 long feet, or 56.52 units when divided by 15. The centres of the Aubrey Holes lie on average just over 15 long feet apart.

Another intriguing measurement employed in Stonehenge's first stage of construction is provided by the distance from the northernmost stonehole (Stonehole 97, found by Mike Pitts in 1980 close to the Heel Stone) to the centre of Stonehenge. This distance measures 250 long feet and provides an alignment on the midsummer solstice sunrise from the centre of the monument. Stonehole 97 might also have been used as a sighting for the rising moon's northerly limit, aligned with Stoneholes B and C. Thus it may have combined both solar and lunar sightings in one.

The distance of 250 long feet was also employed in laying out the four Station Stones on northwest–southeast, northeast–southwest alignments. These stones also have astronomical associations: to the southeast towards the rising moon's southerly limit (full in summer) and, to the northwest, towards the setting moon's northerly limit (full in winter). Although they are essentially undated, the Station Stones were set within the circumference of the circle of Aubrey Holes and are probably later than them.

I asked Andrew to find out if the system of long feet works for the sarsen circle and trilithons, built 500 years after Stonehenge's first stage. The answer was no, not particularly well. The average diameter across the sarsen circle, mid-line to mid-line, is 95 long feet, making a radius of 47½ long feet. We then realized that the circumference of the circle of sarsens is 300 long feet. With 30 uprights, the average spacing between them is 10 long feet. Perhaps this distance of 10 long feet was more important than the radius because the circle's diameter was ultimately determined by the lengths of the lintels: if the lintels could have been longer, the circle could have been wider, but longer lintels would have been less stable because of their necessary curvature. It would have been most sensible for the builders to work out the optimum lengths of the lintels, decide where the uprights had to go and then determine the circumference and radius.

Perhaps the builders had aimed for a standard length of 10 long feet for each lintel. Looking more closely at the measurements for the uprights and surviving lintels, the distance between each pair of lintel mortises is 7 long feet. Several of the lintels are 4 long feet by 2 long feet in width and height, the same proportions as the 'four by two' that carpenters and joiners still buy from timber yards.

Perceiving any regular arrangement of the stones inside the sarsen circle is more problematic. The various diameters of the bluestone circle, the sarsen trilithons and the bluestone oval don't conform to any standard lengths in 'long feet' except that the midline of the great trilithon is about 25 long feet from the centre of the sarsen circle, and the length of its lintel is 15 long feet.

Andrew also found that the 'long foot' unit could have been used at another henge enclosure, Mount Pleasant in Dorchester,[25] where it could be the base measurement for the diameters of a set of concentric timber circles known collectively as Structure IV within this henge enclosure. But it does not work for Woodhenge or the other timber circles at Durrington Walls.

In the 1920s Maud Cunnington discovered that the six oval rings of Woodhenge, when measured along their long axes, had diameters that matched standard lengths in a different unit, which she identified as the 'short foot'.[26] The long diameters of Woodhenge's six rings are close to being a regular series of multiples of ten in short feet. When trying to duplicate Cunnington's measurements from the published plans, however, the errors are large – between 21 centimetres and 88 centimetres. This may reflect inaccuracies of archaeological recording: in 2007 Josh found that one of the Cunnington postholes had quite definitely moved about 30 centimetres from where it was marked on her plan. Closer analysis of Woodhenge's plan reveals that it appears 'oval' because it was, in fact, laid out as a pair of semi-circles whose centres are about 3.8 metres (around 12 short feet) apart.

Turning back to Stonehenge, we recalled that Flinders Petrie estimated the inner diameter of the sarsen circle as 100 Roman feet (0.973 statute feet, very close to the 'short foot').[27] Although we could dismiss this observation – it wasn't a measurement to the midline of the stones and Stonehenge is obviously now known to be pre-Roman – it made us think about the use of the 'short foot' of 0.96 statute feet. The best fit for the radius of the Q and R Holes and bluestone circle on top of them is 40.33 short feet. The bluestone oval at Stonehenge's centre is formed of two semicircles with centres 3.3 metres (10.25 long feet or 11.28 short feet) apart. Their radii are 20.16 short feet. Although not exact, the correspondence of the radii of these two bluestone settings with a 'short foot' distance of 20 is reasonable. Perhaps measurements using short feet were employed at Stonehenge together with long feet.

We have had less success with the trilithons. The two arcs of the sarsen trilithons have centres 4.35 metres (14.87 short feet) apart. The semicircle of the giant trilithon and its two neighbours is 24.78 short feet in radius, while that of the northeast semicircle is 25.8 short feet.

Andrew can find no sign of such a system of measurement being in use among the monuments at Avebury. Although the use of a dual system – long feet and short feet – in the Stonehenge area is intriguing, it is difficult to understand why both systems were used together at Stonehenge itself.

There is plenty more to do on this subject. Were house plans measured out using a standard unit? What dimensions do we have for other timber circles elsewhere in Britain? Plans from archaeological excavations are likely to be more reliable for investigating ancient metrology than survey plans of standing monuments such as stone circles because what we see today may be the result of later phases of rebuilding.

ORIGINS OF THE BLUESTONES

Today archaeologists use a huge range of remote sensing techniques that early excavators such as William Hawley could not have dreamed of. As well as magnetometry, earth resistivity, magnetic susceptibility and ground-penetrating radar, we can use airborne methods such as infra-red photography and LIDAR (laser mapping of micro-variations of the ground surface). We don't have to rely just on our ability to pick up flints while walking across a ploughed field or digging a hole. That said, we're a long way from having any kind of X-ray vision to reveal everything beneath the ground, and we know that many sites simply don't show up using any of these remote sensing methods.

Back in the 1940s, J.F.S. Stone had none of these fancy techniques. Field-walking, excavation and looking in holes in other people's gardens were the ways in which he searched for new sites. One of his interests was in tracking down the distribution of pieces of bluestone around the Stonehenge landscape. In 1938 he dug a trench in the wood known as Fargo Plantation, on the south side of the Cursus about half a mile northwest of Stonehenge. Some Boy Scouts had found bits of Early Bronze Age pottery in a rabbit scrape and Stone wanted to know what else might be there. He excavated a small group of Early Bronze Age inhumation and cremation burials set within a small henge ditch only 7 metres across, and in the ditch he found a chunk of bluestone.[1]

He also knew that bluestone chippings had been found in other spots nearby. Richard Colt Hoare and William Cunnington had found chippings in three round barrows west of Stonehenge, one of them 300 metres west of Stone's small henge. In 1947 Stone picked up eight more pieces from the surface of a ploughed field east of Fargo Plantation, most of them from its northwest corner close to the south ditch of the Cursus, in the same area where William Young had found several bluestone chips on the surface in 1934.[2] Stone's dig into the Cursus ditch here produced a piece of Welsh sandstone.

Stone concluded that, since at least two types of Welsh rock were present – rhyolite and micaceous sandstone – this scatter of bluestones near Fargo Plantation and the south side of the Cursus did not mark the spot where a single stone had been dressed *en route* to Stonehenge. Instead, he wondered if there might once have been a bluestone circle somewhere around the west end of the Cursus. Over the next half-century no one showed any interest in following up Stone's findings; the field in question returned to grass and no further attempts were made to look for what might have been the site of another Stonehenge.

But Colin Richards and I wanted to see if Stone was right. So, in 2006, a small team set out to dig about 150 test pits, each just 1 metre square, in the area where Stone and Young had made their finds. Geophysical survey in advance of the digging had shown no trace of any prehistoric features but we knew that sockets for small bluestone uprights might be too small and shallow to show up as buried features. One of our geological experts is Rob Ixer, a specialist in the identification of bluestones. Colin was looking forward to his visit because the test pits had produced plenty of likely candidates to show him. Unfortunately, Rob was not immediately impressed: most of Colin's suspected bluestones were nineteenth-century railway ballast. However, Rob took the finds away for a closer look and reported back that nine of the stone chippings that Colin found at Fargo Plantation were indeed Welsh rhyolite. We had a result. In 2009 I returned with Josh and California Dave to dig more test pits, and the student team found another three pieces.

Our search for a lost stone circle in this area to the northwest of Stonehenge also included geophysical survey in 2006, resistivity carried out by Kate Welham's students and magnetometry by English Heritage. Survey in Fargo Plantation itself, where Stone had excavated his mini-henge, was out of the question because of the tree-roots, which interfere with the results. The survey therefore covered that half of the field in which we and Stone had found the chips, but we drew a blank. Some years later, however, two separate teams of researchers came up with tantalizing discoveries on either side of Fargo. West of the plantation, a geophysics team from Wessex Archaeology identified in 2009 a circular arrangement of some twenty-two holes, about 30 metres in diameter, on the northern edge of the site of the proposed new Stonehenge visitor centre at Airman's Corner. Because this was a commercial operation (for clients of English Heritage), the results were confidential and the find couldn't be revealed to the public. Is this the site of the missing stone circle or did these holes hold wooden posts? Or is this just a circle of pits?

Without archaeological excavation it's impossible to know when this circle was constructed and whether its pits once held timbers, stones or nothing at all. Only when it is investigated by spade and trowel will we know whether it had anything to do with Stonehenge.

In 2010 a geophysics team from Birmingham University and Vienna's Institute for Archaeological Prospection discovered a similar-sized circle on the east side of Fargo. This one did make the newspapers – 'the first major ceremonial monument near Stonehenge that has been found in the past fifty years' claimed the finders, oblivious of the previous year's discoveries at West Amesbury.[3] Although it was announced as being a timber circle, there is again no way of telling from the geophysical results whether the features recorded by the survey are decayed postholes, former stoneholes or empty pits. Could *this* be our missing stone circle?

This circle encloses an already-known Bronze Age barrow, dating from 500 years or so after Stonehenge, and there is no way of knowing whether it dates to before, during or after the period at which the burial mound was constructed. Geophysics is a tremendously useful science but its results need to be carefully interpreted before conclusions are drawn and, in this particular case, only excavation can decide the matter.

Back on the trail of the possible stone circle at Fargo, Colin asked Rob Ixer to tell him more about the bluestone chippings from the Fargo field. Rob was puzzled that none of them was of dolerite (diabase in American English), the rock type of most of the Stonehenge bluestones. Just as intriguingly, these rhyolite fragments were definitely Welsh but of a slightly different kind to the rhyolite bluestones at Stonehenge. Two pieces of micaceous sandstone from Fargo are, as far as Rob can tell, the same as the stones of this type at Stonehenge. What are these chips of stone doing in Fargo field? Does this mean that there was once a bluestone setting somewhere around the west end of the Cursus? It may well be in the wood, inside Fargo Plantation itself, if it isn't one of the two pit circles revealed by geophysics.

Students digging test pits near Fargo Plantation, south of the Cursus. Colin's team here found small chips of bluestone as well as remains of the 1977 Stonehenge festival.

The Preseli Hills, where the Stonehenge dolerite originates, are an area of upland east of the seaside town of Fishguard and south of Cardigan. As the crow flies they're about 140 miles west-northwest of Stonehenge. Dolerite is a medium-grained igneous rock that forms a series of rocky outcrops on Preseli; despite the 'bluestone' name, it actually has a dark greenish colour. In certain parts of Preseli it appears as an unusual variant called spotted dolerite (also known as preselite) in which the green rock is spotted with groupings of white quartz crystals.

In the early 1920s, Herbert Thomas showed that the Stonehenge spotted dolerite originates in the Preseli Hills.[4] More detailed chemical analysis, published in 1991 by Richard Thorpe and Olwen Williams-Thorpe, narrowed down the geological source to an area about a mile across within the eastern part of the hills.[5] In 2006 Williams-Thorpe and colleagues published more results showing that the closest match for most of the Stonehenge spotted dolerites is an outcrop called Carn Goedog on the northern slopes of Preseli.[6] Other outcrops, notably Carn Menyn (also known as Carn Meini), have chemical signatures close enough to indicate that they may also have been the source.

There are a range of other igneous rocks among the Stonehenge bluestones: rhyolite, rhyolitic ignimbrite (tuff), calcareous ash, volcanic ash and altered volcanic ash. Among the five types of Welsh rhyolite at Stonehenge, Rob Ixer and his colleague Richard Bevins of the National Museum of Wales were able to pin down one of them – in a spectacular piece of geological fingerprinting – to a small outcrop in the Nevern valley, just north of Carn Goedog.[7] They now suspect that three of the other rhyolites come from that same outcrop, and that many or all of the other non-dolerite igneous rocks at Stonehenge derive from nearby out-crops in the valleys of the Nevern catchment, north of Preseli.

There are also two types of micaceous sandstone among the Stonehenge bluestones. The Altar Stone is of one type, and the other is represented by two stumps of former uprights. These stones were thought for a long time to have come from Palaeozoic outcrops of Old Red Sandstone, possibly the Senni Beds around Milford Haven.[8] Scientists reasoned that megalith-movers transporting the bluestones from Preseli to Milford Haven must have picked up these sandstone blocks along the way. From Milford Haven, the stones could then have been floated on rafts or in simple boats around Land's End, along England's south coast and up the River Avon to Stonehenge. Alternatively, the bluestones might have been floated across the Severn estuary to the Somerset Avon, transhipped to the upper waters of the Wiltshire Avon and then to Stonehenge. However, Rob and fellow geol-ogist Peter Turner are sure that the Stonehenge sandstones are Devonian rocks that cannot have come from the Milford Haven area.[9] Instead, they suspect that possible sources for these sandstones may include the Brecon Beacons, about fifty miles due east of Preseli, as well as somewhere within west Wales.

Just how the bluestones got to Stonehenge is a big question. The Welsh stones at Stonehenge are not particularly heavy. The largest, the Altar Stone, is estimated to weigh perhaps 8 to 10 tons but many are likely to be no more than 4 tons. Even so, anthropological studies from different parts of the world show that moving any stone weighing over a ton requires more than just enthusiasm and brute force:[10] there has to be some basic technology involved. Richard Atkinson demonstrated in the 1950s that just thirty-two schoolboys can drag a bluestone on a cradle using wooden rollers.[11]

If the bluestones came from Wales to Wiltshire by sea, just how did Neolithic sailors pilot flimsy boats or rafts made of lashed-together timbers around Land's End through some of the stormiest waters of the British Isles? In 2000, as part of the millennium celebrations, a lottery grant was awarded to a group who intended to use Neolithic technology to bring a bluestone by land and sea from Wales to Stonehenge.[12] The millennium bluestone was moved on wooden rollers and then prepared for embarkation, slung between two boats on the banks of Milford Haven. It didn't even get out of the harbour. Four miles out, the stone slipped into the sea and had to be retrieved by divers and a crane. I think most archaeologists are fairly sceptical now about the likelihood of ocean-going bluestones. If about eighty finally arrived at Stonehenge, how many *didn't* make it? Shouldn't the bottom of Milford Haven be full of bluestones, the results of failed attempts to float them off successfully?

Another possibility, less often considered, is that the bluestones were moved overland for most of their journey. Anthropological studies of megalith-moving confirm that, in traditional societies, people go to great lengths to avoid having to cross water during the transportation of stones – it's just much more difficult than moving them by land.[13] In such societies labour is cheap (and there's no Health and Safety officialdom); in fact, at such events the number of people who can be enticed to help pull the stone is an index of the organizer's social status. In our own society, we're often obsessed with working out the most labour-efficient means when we ponder how the Stonehenge stones could have been moved. Such ergonomic planning is unlikely to have cut much ice in Neolithic societies – the whole point was to have hordes of people involved, not to save labour.

Stone 68, a Stonehenge bluestone of spotted dolerite, has been carefully shaped and has a groove down one side.

If the bluestones were brought overland (with the exception of crossing the River Severn or its estuary), they could have been passed on from one community to the next in a relay involving thousands of people. As I've observed in Madagascar, the problem with moving and lifting megaliths is not in finding enough people but in having to cope with too many. Everybody wants to be involved, especially when there is free alcohol and fresh beef at the end of the day's work. With fifty people on each bluestone, there might have been a task force of 4000 stone-movers if the stones were all brought from Preseli to Wessex in one go. With people dropping in and out as new teams took over at regular intervals, this could have involved an upper limit of as many as 100,000 people – that's a figure possibly close to the total population of southern Britain at that time.[14]

Anyway, the subject of moving the bluestones from Wales to Salisbury Plain is perhaps the aspect of Stonehenge that most intrigues people. There have been all kinds of ingenious ideas. The conventional notion of moving stones on wooden rollers works well for bluestones but we mustn't forget that the builders also had to move the much, much bigger sarsens from the Avebury area. It would probably have been impossible to use rollers for the larger sarsens, which must weigh upwards of 20 tons: such heavy weights would have caused any such rollers to sink into the ground; additional timber rails would have been needed to support the rollers and spread the weight. Derbyshire builder Gordon Pipes came up with an ingenious scheme of 'rowing' the sarsens: using this method the stone sits on its cradle or sledge while lines of people on both sides use wooden poles as levers to lift the stone about 15 centimetres into the air and then forwards the same distance.[15]

There is surely something to be learnt from the solutions found by traditional societies who still move big stones by hand today. On the island of Sumba in Indonesia, the stone is placed on a wooden cradle and moved on wooden rollers pulled by more than 200 men.[16] The sponsor of the event stands on top of the stone, leading the chanting and singing that establishes a rhythm for the stone-pullers. In Madagascar, Ramilisonina has taken part in many stone-pullings and emphasizes the importance of bedding the stone on its cradle in springy materials – shrubs and other vegetation – to act as shock-absorbers.

The idea that the bluestones were brought from Wales by human muscle power is not accepted by everyone. As long ago as 1902 William Judd proposed that the bluestones might have been transported to Stonehenge by glaciers.[17] Herbert Thomas disagreed profoundly with Judd's suggestion, asking where was there evidence for glacial-drift deposits on Salisbury Plain or for glaciation east of the Bristol Channel.[18] In the 1970s, Geoff Kellaway identified glacial sequences deposited on the east side of the Bristol Channel around Bristol and Bath, perhaps during the Anglian glaciation around 450,000 years ago.[19] He also thought that there was an even more extensive glaciation across southern England, which extended from Cornwall as far as Sussex and the English Channel during the Saalian around 300,000 years ago. Kellaway didn't receive much support for his ideas from other geologists but, between 1990 and 2002, he revived his ideas in a modified form.[20] He now thought that the bluestones might have been moved during a glaciation in the Pliocene, 2.47 million years ago, carried southeastwards towards Salisbury Plain in the ice of an ancient river whose surviving trace today is the Solent near Southampton.

There is some evidence of glaciation of southern England, probably in the Anglian period. Rocks picked up by glaciers and dropped far from their source are known as glacial erratics. The distribution of glacial erratics has been plotted over the years by the British Geological Survey and extends across eastern England but not as far west as Salisbury Plain. Rocks from the Scottish midland valley, north Wales and northern England have ended up as far south as Hertfordshire and Buckinghamshire. In the 1970s geomorphologist Christopher Green examined the pebbles of Wiltshire valleys and concluded that there was a complete lack of glacially derived material in these river gravels.[21] No one has been able to find any trace of glaciation on or around Salisbury Plain. When I sought clarification of this point my Sheffield colleague Chris Clark, professor of glaciology, explained that glaciers broadly do not flow uphill. A glacier flows in the direction of slope from the centre of the ice sheet to its margin, so the ice can quite happily move up hills in the glacier's path. However, when very close to the margin where the ice is thin and the surface slope low, a glacier would rather go around a hill than over it.

On the subject of ice, I receive countless emails about the possibility that the bluestones – and sarsens – were dragged to Stonehenge across frozen lakes, along frozen rivers and on specially prepared ice roads. The evidence for climate and temperatures in the third millennium BC shows that, when Stonehenge was built, temperatures were 1°–2° warmer than in later millennia; it was never cold enough for long enough for transport across ice to have been possible.[22]

Since Kellaway's time the glacial-movement hypothesis has been revived and reworked many times. Its chief proponents today are Olwen Williams-Thorpe, a geologist, and Brian John, a glaciologist, who have studied bluestones for more than two decades.[23] They point to sound evidence for glaciation from the Isles of Scilly to south Wales and further north. John thinks that bluestone erratics could have been dumped south of Bristol in the area around Glastonbury where perhaps some remain to be found, buried beneath the peat. Even if this hypothesis were correct, Neolithic people would have had to move the stones forty miles from Glastonbury, or anywhere else in the Severn valley, to Stonehenge.

Yet even this scenario is unlikely on geological grounds alone. Chris Clarke has just carried out a major study of the limits of all previous glaciations in Britain.[24] He notes a distinct lack of any evidence that the ice advanced into southwest England at all. Even at the height of the last glaciation, around 27,000 years ago, the ice sheet seems not to have extended beyond Wales, let alone as far as the area around Bristol and Somerset. No glaciers reached Salisbury Plain or even close to it.

The 'glacial erratics' argument appears to entail our accepting that no Neolithic person in their right mind would have dragged stones further than they had to. This line of reasoning proposes that the most likely Neolithic motivation for using the bluestones is purely pragmatic, that people simply searched for large stones in the closest possible proximity to Stonehenge. Searching over an ever-widening radius from Stonehenge, this argument goes, the Stonehenge builders would have located sarsens to the north and glacially erratic bluestones to the west.

The evidence to which Williams-Thorpe and John point in support of their theory and the questions raised are intriguing. Why are there so many different types of bluestone at Stonehenge? Williams-Thorpe has counted as many as thirteen 'foreign' rocks, many still not identified to source within Wales.[25] She thinks it odd that there was no careful selection to ensure geological consistency. Why are there monoliths of soft easily eroded stone such as the Altar Stone? The harder stones would have been much better suited to long-distance human transport.

Williams-Thorpe also wonders why the bluestone chippings found in round barrows are found only in the soil of the mounds rather than as valuable artefacts placed within the graves under these barrows. In other words, if the bluestone monoliths were worth bringing all the way from Wales, why weren't their chippings treated with a bit more respect a thousand years later?

She has also analysed axes and other prehistoric artefacts made of preselite or spotted dolerite.[26] Although there are only a dozen of these (a very small number in comparison to the thousands of Neolithic stone axes exported from quarries such as Graig Lwyd in north Wales or Langdale in Cumbria), the Preseli-derived stone tools have a very unusual distribution. Some have been found in Wales, but in a wide distribution from Anglesey to the Forest of Dean. There is a concentration of four from Salisbury Plain, with three others from along the south coast between Devon and Hampshire. Might these seven southern English artefacts derive not from long-distance trade but from a local source of glacial erratics? It is certainly possible but the problem with this theory is that no preselite artefacts have been found between Wales and Salisbury Plain: there are none from the English side of the River Severn, the very area where the bluestone erratics are supposed to have been deposited by the glaciers. Instead, the distribution of these spotted-dolerite tools is more suggestive of human transport. It is possible that there was a link between Preseli and Salisbury Plain that began before the building of Stonehenge, back in the Early Neolithic of the fourth millennium BC, when axes were definitely exchanged or traded over long distances all round Britain and Ireland.

Tim and Geoff's excavation at Stonehenge in 2008 recovered a rough-out for a bluestone implement, and others have been found there by previous excavators. It is possible that Stonehenge, in its declining years towards the end of the third millennium BC, became a tool factory, producing objects that were traded within Wessex. After a thousand years, these once-revered standing stones perhaps became little more than useful raw material, miniature quarries for making maces and battle-axes. Of course, such items might have been perceived as imbued with special power – a Stonehenge-derived macehead could have trumped a macehead carved from another type of stone. But whether or not bluestone tools had special value, respect for the monoliths themselves was on the wane by the beginning of the Bronze Age.

No discussion of bluestones is complete without a brief account of the mysterious case of the Boles Barrow bluestone boulder. Boles Barrow is a long barrow at Heytesbury, about eleven miles west of Stonehenge. From its form and style, this barrow probably dates to before 3000 BC, most likely to somewhere within the period 3800–3400 BC. William Cunnington wrote in 1801 that, within a ridge of sarsen boulders (weighing between 13 and 90 kilograms) running down the middle of the barrow, he had found 'the Blue hard Stone also, ye same to some of the upright Stones in ye inner Circle at Stonehenge'.[27] He took away this stone and the sarsens to make a garden feature at his house.

Some people think that this bluestone Cunnington took from Boles Barrow must be the same stone that's now housed in Salisbury Museum, although that stone weighs 611 kilograms, much heavier than anything mentioned by Cunnington, and came to the museum not from Cunnington's garden but from one nearby at Heytesbury House in 1923. Various scholars have tried to unpick the chain of historical events – none more thoroughly than Mike Pitts, who is convinced that the two stones are not one and the same.[28]

Yet the matter is still problematic. Mike has also had a good look at what survives of Boles Barrow; it has been severely damaged by human and animal activity and was definitely reused as a cemetery in periods more recent than the Neolithic. There's no guarantee that the Boles Barrow bluestone was part of the Early Neolithic construction; it could have been brought there later in the barrow's period of use. Even if it was part of the first construction, Mike argues that Cunnington could easily have mistaken another type of igneous rock for a bluestone. Both Colin and I, along with Richard Atkinson before us, have been guilty of such a mistake until corrected by geological experts. The problem of the bluestones is that everybody *wants* to find them, but only identifications by geologists can be relied on.

Even with Mike Pitt's caveats about Cunnington's Boles Barrow bluestone, there is still a chance that bluestones as well as some of the preselite axes were present on Salisbury Plain before 3000 BC. However, I don't think we have to resort to the glacial hypothesis to explain them. As I've argued earlier, we live in a world where the pragmatic and the cost-effective are often the guiding criteria for our actions but this is a culturally specific view of the world. To understand the meaning and practices of stone-moving, we have to fight an innate prejudice that often makes us try to explain prehistoric activities in terms of what we see as 'common sense'.

This is hard because most of the time we don't realize we're doing it. Working in non-Western societies provides the best opportunity to get one's eyes opened to a myriad other possible ways of doing things. During fieldwork with Ramilisonina, we learned from the Tandroy people of southern Madagascar that they prefer to import their standing stones from sixty miles away rather than use what looked to me like perfectly acceptable outcrops of stone just twenty miles away.[29] The nearer quarries are often used but they are not the 'best'. There is nothing more important to Tandroy tomb-builders than showing off – paying the extra to get hold of a more inaccessible stone is part of social competition.

These megaliths have to be hauled in wooden carts over difficult terrain from this distant source at a place called Trañoroa ('two houses'). There are no tarmac roads, and journeys are slow and arduous across a landscape so rocky that even a Land Rover struggles, yet people transport standing stones across it by bullock power alone. Although the Trañoroa stones are of a softer rock than the nearer stone, and are therefore difficult to transport, when properly bedded with shock-absorbing materials, they do survive the journey intact. The Tandroy say that they like the particular colour of the Trañoroa stones, and that they can be cut into pleasingly rectangular monoliths. For the Tandroy, who live in a precarious environment, often on the edge of famine, commemorating the ancestors is the most important aspect of their lives: the goal of life is to honour the dead through monument-building in which no expense is spared. Very little of what they do in their religious and funerary observances is 'practical' in our terms.

Closer to home, we are all well aware that stones can take on powerful spiritual symbolism, as is shown by current mystical notions surrounding Stonehenge itself. The Stone of Scone is a good example of a stone with 'meaning'. Now safely under lock and key with the other treasures of Scottish kingship in Edinburgh Castle, it has had a very eventful life. Originally the throne of Scottish kings, it was captured and brought to Westminster Abbey by Edward I in 1296; during the twentieth century the stone was stolen from London, eventually recovered, and is now back where it started.[30] The Stone of Destiny at Tara in Ireland is another example of a monolith with a special history relating to power and kingship.[31] Fewer people have heard of the London Stone, located in a basement on Cannon Street; its early history is unknown but it has been a London landmark since at least 1198 and is the location where laws were once passed and oaths sworn.[32]

Later I'll explore what I think may have been the reasons for moving stones from west Wales to Salisbury Plain – and why I think it most likely that they were dragged overland, with as few river crossings as possible. For the moment it's worth pointing out two flaws in the logic of the argument for the Stonehenge bluestones having been fetched from a hypothetical location in Somerset.

- At Stanton Drew in north Somerset there is a very impressive group of stone circles and settings, just twenty miles north of Glastonbury.[33] The stones of these circles come from a variety of outcrops in the region. There is not a single bluestone among them. The glacial-erratics hypothesis places the source of the Stonehenge bluestones in exactly this area. If bluestones were present in the area, why did the builders of these stone circles *not* use them, even though other builders were coming all the way from Wiltshire especially to get them?
- Glastonbury, Somerset and the Bristol region are much further from Stonehenge than the sarsen fields of the Marlborough Downs. If proximity of materials was an overriding concern of the Neolithic builders, why go all the way to Somerset to get any stones at all? It makes no sense for the builders of the first stone circle at Stonehenge to have ignored local sarsens less than twenty miles away (or the even closer Cuckoo Stone and Tor Stone), in order to go sixty miles in search of building material.

At this point most readers will have worked out for themselves a convincing answer to what was behind all this: there has to have been something special about bluestones. These are the stones the Neolithic builders of Stonehenge *wanted* to use, and they were prepared to go to great lengths to get hold of them. It wasn't a matter of erecting any old stone that came to hand – it had to be bluestones.

There's plenty of evidence that Neolithic Britain was a place of busy trade routes, with people and objects travelling long distances. Back in the 1970s, archaeologists argued about the movement of stone axes in Neolithic Britain. Axes of Cumbrian, Welsh and Cornish stone turn up all over the country, including Wessex, and some thought this is because Neolithic people exploited local deposits of glacial erratics within southern England. Then archaeologists started finding the actual quarries where the axes had been manufactured.[34] These axes didn't all come from glacial erratics, but from quarries in the mountains from which they were dispersed all over the country.

At the same time, archaeologists discovered that some Neolithic pottery was also being moved more than a hundred miles from the sources of the clay with which it was made. Early Neolithic Britain has turned out to be a pretty sociable place, if sporadically violent. Recent excavations of causewayed enclosures have shown that all kinds of items – from axes and flint to pots and cattle – were moved surprisingly long distances.[35] While there's no denying that some axes might have been made locally from glacial erratics, there was a thriving long-distance network which shows that the Neolithic inhabitants of Wessex, for example, engaged with other communities in distant regions of the country.

Tim Darvill and Geoff Wainwright went back to the source of the bluestones, hoping to dispel the glacial hypothesis once and for all. Just as previous archaeologists had found Neolithic quarries for the axes, perhaps they could find one or more quarries in Preseli for the spotted dolerite monoliths. In 2001 they started a project, the Strumble-Preseli Ancient Communities and Environment Study (SPACES), to begin the search for the bluestone quarries.[36] Carn Goedog, the outcrop with the closest chemical signature to the Stonehenge spotted dolerites, has been used as a quarry in more recent times so they knew it would be difficult to find the ephemeral traces of Neolithic quarrying beneath more modern debris. They selected Carn Menyn as the most promising location at which to start. Here, around the outcrops of dolerite, there are possible prehistoric remains, whereas the area around Carn Goedog was thought to be empty of such sites.

On a cold and wet day Geoff took me to see what he and Tim had found so far. One of the outcrops forms a spectacular group of natural monoliths and Geoff explained that it would require very little effort to detach these pillars from the living rock. They could then be manoeuvred downhill and taken southwards along the Cleddau river and on to Milford Haven. At the bottom of the slope below Carn Menyn we inspected a Stonehenge-sized monolith that had cracked in two after its edges had been roughly shaped. Could this be a quarried stone that had broken and been abandoned? At the top of the outcrop is a small, flat area surrounded by a low stone wall. Geoff and Tim needed to investigate whether this might be a Neolithic enclosure built by the quarry-workers and, in 2005, they carried out a small excavation. The acidic soils of Preseli are not kind to archaeological remains, however, and there were no finds to give any indication of the period in which this stone wall was built.

Preseli is rich in Neolithic monuments. Bedd yr Afanc is a long cairn containing a gallery grave,* excavated in 1939 but containing few finds.[37] On the western end of Carn Menyn itself there's a stone cairn whose central capstone suggests that this too is a passage grave. Three large cairns on the nearby hilltop of Foel Trigarn (or Drygarn) were probably built in the Early Bronze Age but a Neolithic date cannot be ruled out. To the north is the well-known portal dolmen of Pentre Ifan, from which a flint arrowhead and fragments of carinated bowl pottery were excavated in 1936–37 and 1958–59.[38]† In 2005 Tim and Geoff excavated a small trench across the bank and ditch of a causewayed enclosure at Banc Du, and found that the enclosure bank had a stone-walled outer face with timber posts behind. Charcoal from its ditch dated to around 3550 BC.[39]

Geoff and Tim have also been finding evidence of prehistoric rock art

---

* A passage tomb is a stone chamber and entrance passage, covered by a mound; a gallery grave is a particular type of passage tomb with a long, gallery-like chamber. Passage tombs are not of the same construction as long barrows (their mounds are not so long); they are mostly found in Ireland and western Britain whereas long barrows have a more easterly distribution.

† A portal dolmen (also known as a cromlech in Wales only) is an arrangement of two or more upright stones with a capstone or lintel on top. Some archaeologists think that portal dolmens were covered by mounds of soil, like passage tombs, but it is more likely the stone structures were free-standing. Carinated bowls have a steeply angled belly; this style was in use around 3800 BC (the Early Neolithic) and examples of it have been found throughout Britain including the Stonehenge area (at Coneybury and beneath Woodhenge).

in the area. This takes the form of cup-marks, with examples from the springheads below Carn Menyn and from St David's Head where the Preseli Hills meet the sea. Of course, such remains are impossible to date beyond being loosely Neolithic or Early Bronze Age. It is generally thought that cup-marked stones are most likely to be Neolithic in date.

As well as standing stones, set up either singly or in pairs, there are also six stone circles in Preseli, only one of which has been excavated and whose dates we can therefore only guess at, although small circles such as these sometimes date as late as the Bronze Age; the only circle excavated – Meini Gwyr in 1938 – produced only a few sherds of Middle Bronze Age pottery.[40] The stones of these six circles are rather stumpy, nothing like the taller bluestones of Stonehenge, some of which stand as high as 2 metres.

The stone circle of Gors Fawr, south of Carn Menyn, is an egg-shaped arrangement of sixteen widely spaced monoliths, eight of which are of spotted dolerite. Tim and Geoff's geophysical survey did not reveal any features beneath it. They were luckier with the circle of Meini Gwyr, set within a circular bank. Here the geophysics showed that there had never been a ditch to go with the bank. The survey results also picked out a series of anomalies underneath the bank that may be the holes for an outer ring of standing stones.

Another circle is Bedd Arthur, a sub-rectangular arrangement of bluestones that Geoff compares with the bluestone oval in the centre of Stonehenge, although it is longer and thinner in shape than the Stonehenge setting. The thirteen stones are backed by a low bank and surround a levelled area. Other archaeologists have previously considered the stones at Bedd Arthur to be part of a walled enclosure of the Bronze Age or later, rather than a true stone circle.

There is no denying the richness of Neolithic remains from Preseli but incontrovertible evidence for bluestone quarrying has eluded the SPACES team. Frustratingly, the stone-walled enclosure on Carn Menyn could be any date, as could the several pillar stones seemingly broken in transit. Bluestones have been used as gateposts and other structures for centuries and it's impossible to say whether any of the worked pillar stones are prehistoric. That said, the shapes and sizes of the abandoned pillar stones recorded by Geoff and Tim compare well with the smaller bluestones at Stonehenge.

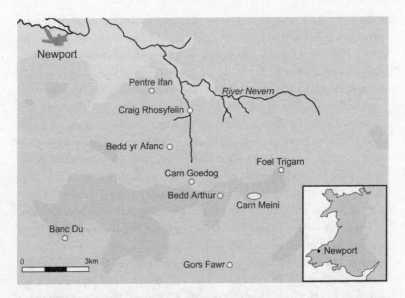

In the Preseli Hills there are several outcrops of dolerite and rhyolite from which the Stonehenge bluestones derive. This landscape also contains Neolithic tombs and other prehistoric monuments.

Other finds include spotted dolerite hammerstones, just like those from Stonehenge, which were found at a small quarry for extracting metamorphosed mudstone. No rock of this type has been found at Stonehenge so this quarry cannot be linked to the extraction of bluestones.

Tim and Geoff have developed their own ideas about why bluestones were brought to Stonehenge. For them the reason is revealed by Geoffrey of Monmouth's *History of the Kings of Britain (Historia Regum Britanniae)*, written in 1136.[41] Geoffrey of Monmouth was not what we'd call a real historian – his work is described as pseudo-history by scholars today, and is full of fantastical stories mixed with matters of fact. His highly embroidered history, like similar fanciful tales today, sold very well.

In one passage Geoffrey of Monmouth describes Stonehenge as a cenotaph put up by the Britons to commemorate the massacre of 460 Britons by the treacherous Saxons during peace talks at 'the Cloister of Ambrius' (an old name for Amesbury). Merlin the magician decides that

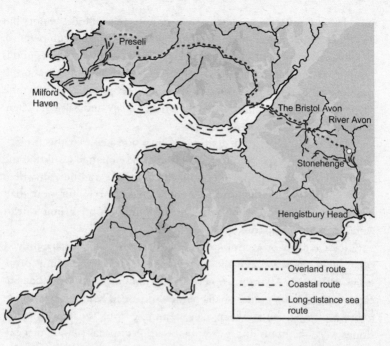

Proposed routes by which the bluestones were taken from Preseli to Stonehenge.
I favour the more northerly route because it avoids difficult sea crossings.

the stones for this memorial have to come from a magical stone circle –
the Giants' Ring or Giants' Dance – erected on Mount Killaurus in
Ireland by a race of giants. He takes thousands of men with him to cap-
ture the Irish circle and bring the stones to England. The reason that
only these stones will do is that they have healing powers. The giants
throw water against the stones and then bathe in it to be cured of mal-
adies. Of course, Geoffrey's account of this magical episode doesn't
distinguish between bluestones and sarsens.

Is it possible that a Neolithic myth survived as oral tradition for over
4000 years, to be eventually written down by Geoffrey of Monmouth?
Tim and Geoff think so but others are less than convinced. Aubrey Burl,
doyen of stone-circle studies, considers that the story was developed to
explain the presence of standing stones that monks had noted in Kildare

in Ireland: 'Geoffrey's Stonehenge story is not a relic of folk memory but an early twelfth-century attempt, blemished by geological incompetence, to explain how the ponderous sarsens had been erected. The legend is no more than a monkish mixture of Merlin, magic and imagination. It has nothing to do with the bluestones, but by geographical misfortune the Preselis happened to lie midway between Kildare and Salisbury Plain. Archaeological gullibility did the rest.'[42]

It has to be pointed out that any connection between this twelfth-century story and the Neolithic building of Stonehenge would be the most outstanding example of the survival of mythic tradition anywhere in the entire world. Oral history generally doesn't survive for more than 500 years so the chances of Geoffrey of Monmouth recording a myth with Neolithic origins are exceedingly remote.

Since Geoffrey of Monmouth's time, however, people have indeed occasionally believed that the Stonehenge stones have healing properties. Richard Atkinson noted in his book *Stonehenge* that an eighteenth-century guidebook lamented the use of hammers by visitors to break off fragments as keepsakes, stemming from 'the belief that the stones were factitious and were possessed of unusual powers of healing'.[43] Hammers could be bought for the purpose in nearby Amesbury. Geoff and Tim have drawn attention to the preferential selection of bluestones for this treatment, but this is not really evidence that people believed that it was only these stones, and not the sarsens, that were supposed to heal. The problem here is that sarsen is desperately resistant to chipping with a hammer whereas dolerite flakes more easily.

Geoff and Tim have also pointed to the large number of bluestones removed from Stonehenge. Yet, when the proportion of missing bluestones is compared to the proportion of missing sarsen uprights and lintels, there is no evidence for selective bias in choosing bluestones to take away. Even if there were a bias, it would not be evidence for a long-standing belief in healing properties. I would argue that the bluestones had a particular meaning in the Neolithic (and only then), which is why they were brought here, and that that meaning no longer exists. We are left with the pragmatic historical reality that the bluestones are smaller than the sarsens, and therefore may have been easier for subsequent inhabitants of Salisbury Plain to 'quarry' for making stone tools or to heave off the site to reuse as building stone for barns, walls, churches, houses and so on.

Support for the 'healing stones' hypothesis is also gleaned from historical accounts of certain of the springheads of Preseli as being holy wells. There is some Pembrokeshire folklore about stones and healing, too. Geoff and Tim have identified a few 'enhanced springheads' where stones have been removed from around the water source to create a small pool, sometimes by also constructing a dry-stone wall. In their view, the presence of occasional cup-marked stones, small stone cairns and standing stones at springheads around Carn Menyn is proof that these folkloric traditions of holiness and healing date back to prehistory.

Finally, Tim has looked for any evidence from the Stonehenge area that people might have come there to be healed of illnesses – as though it were a prehistoric place of pilgrimage something like Lourdes. The argument goes that if this particular place attracted lots of very sick people, there should perhaps be a large number of previously sick dead people buried nearby (readers will of course bear in mind that 'bluestone healing' doesn't actually work, and Geoff and Tim have never suggested that it does).

Tim points to indications of trauma in three skeletons from burials in this part of Salisbury Plain.[44] The most spectacular of these is the Amesbury Archer, the long-distance traveller from the Continent.[45] When Jacqui McKinley examined the Amesbury Archer's skeleton she noticed a couple of bones were missing: one of his ribs (which might have been removed before burial) and his right patella (kneecap). On closer inspection Jacqui also saw that the top of his right tibia (the larger of the two leg bones below the knee) has a deep lesion caused by an unhealed wound. At some point in his youth, many years before his death, this man suffered a knee injury that destroyed his patella; this wound would have festered for the rest of his life, exuding pus continually, and would have caused great pain.

Tim also points out that two skeletons, dating to around 2000 BC, are examples of healing. These have evidence of trepanation or trephination, and are from two round barrows, Amesbury G51 and Amesbury G71, both east of the River Avon near Bulford.[46] Trepanation is the practice of removing a piece of bone from the skull to expose the surface of the brain, known as the *dura mater*. Trepanation has been practised in modern times, in East Africa and Britain, for example.[47] Guides to self-trepanation are today available on the web (carrying it out on another person is illegal). It is thought to have been used in prehistory as a means of releasing evil spirits, curing epilepsy or alleviating headaches; with luck the patient could survive.[48] In one case in Germany, a Neolithic skull was trepanned to treat a depressed fracture of the skull caused by blunt-force trauma. Trepanation was practised across Europe from the Mesolithic to at least the Bronze Age and there are about ten examples known from Neolithic and Bronze Age Britain. Unfortunately for the healing theory, they are widely scattered across Britain but two of the ten *are* from round barrows three miles from Stonehenge, so it could mean something.

Thus, out of more than fifty skeletons of the Copper Age and Early Bronze Age from the Stonehenge environs, three individuals have evidence for healing. This is not a particularly convincing number. If Stonehenge really were a sort of hospital, it seems not to have served a very large clientele. Most people buried in the area have no visible traces of long-term illness (although, of course, not many illnesses leave traces on the human skeleton). More importantly, these three that Tim uses as evidence of trauma/surgery, were all buried here some 700–1000 years after the bluestones came to Stonehenge.

The healing hypothesis is alluring but it has a number of difficulties and contradictions. If the bluestones were brought from Preseli because of their healing powers, why are they all concentrated at Stonehenge, and not more widely distributed in contemporary monument complexes such as Avebury and Stanton Drew? None of the Avebury standing stones are of bluestone. Six small chippings of bluestones have, admittedly, been found near Avebury,[49] four on the top of Silbury Hill, one in the top of a ditch of the Windmill Hill causewayed enclosure and the sixth from the surface of a field 'near Avebury' – all could have ended up in these places long after the Neolithic, maybe even deposited as recently as the last few centuries. Why also were bluestone chippings not treasured as, for example, grave goods? Prehistoric objects made of spotted dolerite include axes, axe-hammers, battle-axes and a mace but they are very rare compared to those made of other rock types. Might we not expect something with healing powers to be more widely disseminated?

The theory also suffers from anachronism. One may be able to identify modern or Medieval stories and attributions linking bluestones and their Preseli source with healing, but to then force on to these a link 4000 to 5000 years back into the past requires some convincing evidence of continuity through the ages. It's not enough to simply show that a spring described as a holy well today also has a prehistoric standing stone or cup-marked stone nearby. As Aubrey Burl has pointed out, the healing story is likely to have arisen within the historical circumstances of the Christian Church during the early Medieval period, when there were plenty of stories about healing involving water and stones. Holy wells are found throughout Britain and Europe but there's no way to find out whether they were considered to have special properties before the start of Christianity, let alone as early as the Neolithic.

In the summer of 2010 the Stonehenge Riverside Project team found time to visit Preseli together and take a look for ourselves. The most recent geological work had pinpointed a spotted dolerite outcrop at Carn Goedog as a likely source of many of the Stonehenge dolerite orthostats and, at Craig Rhosyfelin in a small valley to the north, a rhyolite source for many of the Stonehenge chippings. The position of these outcrops on the northern slopes of Preseli suggested to us that the route from Preseli that is usually proposed – southwards to Milford Haven – might be completely wrong. A northern emphasis for the bluestone sources would also run counter to the local evidence supporting the healing hypothesis, since the holy wells and springs are principally on the southern flanks of Preseli.

My Sheffield colleague Andrew Chamberlain focused on four standing stones on the hill of Waun Mawn, also on the northern slopes of Preseli. Previous archaeologists have wondered if this arc of dolerite stones is all that remains of a stone circle that has been dismantled.[50] If so, are the stones that once stood here now among the bluestones standing at Stonehenge? To drive home the possibility, Andrew pointed out that the diameter and spacing of this possible former circle at Waun Mawn would have been almost exactly the same as that of the Aubrey Hole circle at Stonehenge.

On a sunny summer's day the team walked out to Waun Mawn. One of the stones still stands upright but the other three have fallen. Unlike the stones of the six stone circles elsewhere in Preseli, these are proper Stonehenge-sized monoliths and not 'Spinal Tap' miniatures.[51] They occupy a commanding position on a natural saddle with views to the sea in two directions, across the Gwaun and Nevern valleys. Would geophysical survey reveal whether Waun Mawn was once a stone circle?

The hill on which Waun Mawn stands slopes down to the village of Brynberian, not far from the cromlech of Pentre Ifan. Nearby lies the rhyolite outcrop of Craig Rhosyfelin, a mass of pillar-shaped bluestones, rising vertically from the valley floor, and just waiting to be detached and taken away.

Colin has excavated a standing-stone quarry at Vestra Fjold in Orkney so he knows a fair bit about what a Neolithic megalith quarry should look like.[52] He has discovered that Neolithic quarry workers did not need stone mauls and pounders and nor did they leave much in the way of stone waste. Instead they split natural pillars away from the bedrock by following existing fault lines, presumably using wooden wedges that were hammered into cracks and left in the rain to swell, thereby detaching the monoliths from the living rock. Neolithic quarry workers would then dig a rough trench at the base of the outcrop, within which the monoliths could be propped on stones before being set on to wooden cradles and hauled away.

On our first visit to Carn Goedog we were joined by Louise Austin, a senior archaeologist at Dyfed Archaeological Trust. Her colleagues had recently carried out a survey of the area and she pointed out prehistoric field boundaries and settlements; this rough moorland was once farmland, before the development of the blanket bog that now envelops Preseli's lower slopes. Carn Goedog is an impressive outcrop of spotted dolerite, clinging to the side of the hill rather than sitting on the true summit. Broken boulders from the outcrop litter the hillside but, on its uphill side, the rock forms pillars reaching skywards. Heaps of broken stones here are evidence of more recent quarrying but Colin recognized a narrow depression, about 5 metres wide, running close to the edge of the outcrop along this upper side. It would have been easy to detach the pillars, and to set them up on props within this gully. There are even

The maximum extent of the British–Irish Ice Sheet *c.* 27,000 years ago. The glaciers from this and previous glaciations never reached Salisbury Plain.

three long stones lying within the depression, far enough away from the rock face to be something more than chance rock-falls. Might these be monoliths abandoned within the quarry? There is even an excellent natural ramp, completely free of stones or boulders, running from here down the side of the hill towards the low ground of the valley in which Craig Rhosyfelin sits.

The biggest surprise awaited us just below Carn Goedog. Set on two natural terraces are 15 prehistoric houses.[53] They were first identified in the 1970s by Peter Drewett, coincidentally one of Geoff's supervisors at Durrington Walls in 1967. Their official description is 'Bronze Age hut circles' but, when we looked closer, we could see that nine are actually rectangular in plan. Such architecture is not found in the Bronze Age or even in the Iron Age, when houses were uniformly round throughout Britain. These houses could well be Neolithic in date, and are slightly smaller than the houses at Durrington Walls. Might these be the quarry workers' houses? If so, could they give us a date for when the spotted dolerite bluestones were being quarried? Once again there's only one way to find out, and that is by archaeological excavation. Perhaps one day archaeologists will be allowed to carry out a dig here within the National Park.

Traces of Neolithic quarries are impossible to verify without digging, so in 2011 our Stonehenge team moved to Preseli. Four days before we left for west Wales, Richard Bevins contacted me to say that he and Rob Ixer had pinpointed the geological match for one of the Stonehenge rhyolites. Thanks to its unique geology – called 'Jovian' by Rob because under the microscope its swirls and blobs look like the weather system on Jupiter – it could be located to a precise part of the Craig Rhosyfelin outcrop, the very same spot we reckoned was a Neolithic quarry. We carried out geophysical surveys on the ground next to the outcrop but the results were inconclusive. Only digging would provide an answer. The farmer and his neighbours were enthusiastic about our plans and soon we had the use of a mechanical mini-digger to open up a good-sized area next to the outcrop. It wasn't long before we discovered that the ancient ground surface had been protected under layers of soil washed down from higher up the valley. When we started finding hammerstones on that ground surface, we realized that we had not just a prehistoric quarry but a perfectly preserved one – the Pompeii of prehistoric stone quarries. If that wasn't enough, Josh's expert use of the mini-digger unearthed a long slab of rhyolite lying on the quarry floor. At 13 feet long and weighing about four tons, it is the same size as the larger bluestones at Stonehenge. Someone had left behind a monolith when the quarrying had ended. We could hardly believe our luck. This was a smoking gun; the game was up for anyone still trying to argue that the bluestones were not quarried in Preseli during the Neolithic, and then taken to Wiltshire.

Our small trench also yielded tantalising glimpses of what we may learn in future years. I'd always assumed that archaeology could never answer questions about how the stones were moved, but here is a monolith abandoned in transit. It lies at the end of what appear to be three parallel 'rails' of stones set on edge, leading to that part of the outcrop about 15 metres away from which it has been detached. These 'rails' could have provided a fulcrum for moving the stones with wooden levers in just the way that Gordon Pipes predicted. The monolith's position at the end of the rails and just in front of a drop in the ground level also suggests that it was about to be transferred to a new means of transport. Was this the point where monoliths were lifted onto a wooden sledge and rollers? Or might they have been carried on wheeled sledges? Future excavation of the prehistoric track leading out of the quarry will tell.

Richard and Rob had been busy with geological identifications. As well as Carn Goedog, they had identified other Stonehenge bluestones as coming from the northern edge of Preseli: spotted dolerite from Carn Breseb and plain dolerite from Carn Ddafad-las. It was beginning to look as if the bluestones had been quarried from outcrops of the upper Nevern valley, and not from the top of Preseli or its southern flanks. On our last day of fieldwork in 2011, Colin and I went in search of other quarries where the River Nevern forms a deep gorge with rapids and a waterfall. Rob and Richard suspect that the other types of igneous rock from Stonehenge might be found here, and a local farmer pointed us to the gorge's dramatic outcrops. Wading through torrents, hacking through brambles and scaling steep cliffs, Colin and I not only had a rare opportunity to behave like Indiana Jones but also found two likely quarry sites beside the cacophonous waters.

If the bluestone sources were concentrated in the valleys of the upper Nevern, then not only have we all been looking in the wrong places on top of Preseli but we need to see if there is any evidence of Neolithic occupation that might provide a social context for the bluestones. Apart from the local portal dolmens such as Pentre Ifan, very little is known about Neolithic settlement remains in this area. My eye is drawn to Castell Mawr, one of the many Iron Age hillforts in the area, because its geometrically oval plan looks remarkably like a henge. With its large outer bank seemingly without an outer ditch, and its small inner bank next to a wide inner ditch, Castell Mawr looks like a Neolithic henge whose outer bank and inner ditch have later been modified by Iron Age people into a hilltop fort. The same conclusion was reached in the 1980s by archaeologists carrying out a partial geophysical survey.[54] Future investigation should allow us to find out if our suspicion is right. If so, this would be the largest henge in Wales, a fitting social and political centre for the people of the bluestones.

Our geophysical survey of Waun Mawn failed to reveal any evidence that its four stones were once part of a larger stone circle. If the bluestones were set up as one or more circles, and then dismantled and moved to Stonehenge, a more likely proposition is that any such dismantled circle would have been located in or around the potential henge at Castell Mawr. With two likely quarries in the Nevern gorge directly below Castell Mawr, there is a good chance that the bluestone sources were all providing stones for a local ritual centre. From Craig Rhosyfelin, for example, stone-movers were confined to the steep-sided valley floor until reaching the gentle incline that leads out of the Nevern valley to Castell Mawr a mile away.

Our fieldwork in 2011 opened up an entirely new hypothesis that can be followed up in future years through geological sampling and archaeological excavation. If we can demonstrate that the bluestone quarries were on the north side of Preseli, within the Nevern valley and focused on a large henge, then the healing theory, which relies on the supporting evidence of springhead sites on top of Preseli and its southern flanks, can be rejected. Our find at Craig Rhosyfelin also raises the likelihood that the link between Preseli and Stonehenge was not to do with a 'magic mountain' or any intrinsic properties of its bluestones but involved a powerful polity within the Nevern valley, a people whose earliest Neolithic ancestors had brought traditions of megalith construction to this part of Britain. Perhaps they had celebrated their power and their ancestry by erecting one or more stone circles with monoliths taken from a range of nearby quarries. Then later, for one reason or another, the momentous decision was taken to dismantle these circles and move them over 180 miles to Stonehenge. If these now-vanished stone circles are there, one day archaeologists will find the emptied holes where bluestones once stood.

The Neolithic people of the Nevern had potentially excellent transport links. The glaciated valleys of Preseli have U-shaped profiles, with wide, flat, stone-free bottoms. There is plenty of room for moving megaliths along a valley bottom without having to negotiate its stream. Even where water may have to be crossed, the streambeds are shallow and firm so are no great impediment.

North of Carn Goedog and Craig Rhosyfelin, the Brynberian valley joins the much larger valley of the River Nevern (Nyfer in Welsh) which flows westwards to meet the sea at Newport. This is one of the hotspots of Britain's Early Neolithic. The Nevern valley is dotted with portal dolmens, both on its slopes like Pentre Ifan and in its valley bottom at Carreg Coetan. Little has yet been found of these earliest farmers' settlements but they probably lived along the valley sides. The valley's slopes would have been densely forested, so the open and lightly wooded moorland pastures of the Preseli Hills would have been reached by following the Nevern valley's tributaries, such as the Brynberian valley. These wide-bottomed valleys would have formed ideal droveways for taking the cattle on to the high pastures, past Craig Rhosyfelin and on to Waun Mawn and Carn Goedog. These two bluestone outcrops were probably well-known landmarks to generations of Neolithic farmers long before Stonehenge was built.

As the team explored the ancient landscape of Pembrokeshire, Andrew Chamberlain and I were convinced that Newport, where the River Nevern meets the sea, was the embarkation point for the bluestones' sea voyage along the Welsh coast but Colin was thinking otherwise. He reminded us of the pageantry and display involved in megalith-moving around the world today; these Neolithic stone-moving events were surely great social spectacles involving thousands of people, the sacrifice of animals, and plenty of feasting, not simply labouring tasks to be performed as quickly as possible. Taking stones by sea would have limited the renown of such feats; dragging the stones in long-distance relays overland, handing them on from one community to the next, was surely a more likely proposition.

What has persuaded me to Colin's point of view is the distribution of Neolithic polished-stone axes in south Wales. Somewhere not yet located within west Wales, probably not far from St David's Head, lies a source of rhyolite that was used to make stone axes in the fourth millennium

BC, during the centuries before Stonehenge was built. These axes are of a different type of rhyolite to the four types of rhyolite identified at Stonehenge; geologists can identify this specific rock under the microscope. The St David's source is known as Group VIII and its products are distributed all over south Wales.[55] Axes were also imported from Cornwall into Wales but these all have a coastal distribution, whereas the Group VIII axes are found mostly at inland locations east of Preseli. In other words, unlike the Cornish imports these objects were not being moved by sea but were traded overland. Long before the bluestones were dragged off the hills there had been an established network of routeways leading eastwards from Preseli.

Recent archaeological investigations in advance of new pipelines have found evidence of many Neolithic sites in south Wales' valleys.[56] Neolithic traders would have used these glaciated valleys not only to avoid the thickly wooded hillsides but also to pass through the many settlements. The principal routeways would have followed the valleys of rivers such as the Taf, the Towey and the Usk. These flat-bottomed valleys were the Neolithic equivalent of motorways, cleared of forest by the earliest Neolithic farmers and facilitating long-distance movement of people and their goods. For movers of bluestones, the route was relatively straightforward through south Wales – eastwards along the Nevern valley, across its low watershed into the Taf valley, following that valley southwards to what is now Carmarthen, then joining the Towey valley heading northeast into the Brecon Beacons. After the gentle incline of the pass leading into the Usk valley, the route was downhill past Brecon as far as the deepening waters of the River Usk. Today most of this route is followed by the A40, and the many ancient sites – Roman camps and Medieval castles – along the way are testament to its enduring importance for access in and out of Wales.

On reaching the lower Usk valley, travel by water would have been difficult to avoid but the calm waters of the Severn estuary are at least easier to navigate than the ocean swells of the Irish Sea. If the stones were shipped by boat from somewhere around what is now the town of Usk, they could have been taken across the estuary to Avonmouth, where the Somerset Avon reaches the sea after winding its way from the edge of Salisbury Plain. Somewhere around Bradford-on-Avon the bluestones could have been landed and pulled the last twenty miles to Stonehenge.

I doubt whether archaeologists will ever be able to prove beyond doubt that this was the route taken by the bluestone-movers. If the source of the Altar Stone and the other sandstone monoliths at Stonehenge can be found (these could be from the Brecon Beacons or from west Wales), it may just help to confirm or negate this theory. Finding the sources of all the other types of bluestone – rhyolitic ignimbrite (tuff), calcareous ash, volcanic ash and altered volcanic ash, unspotted dolerite, and one other type of rhyolite – will also help to identify whether all or just some of the stones were taken from the northern edges of Preseli, and which route was taken. There is much for archaeologists and geologists to look for in the years to come.

18

ORIGINS OF THE SARSENS

The Stonehenge sarsens never attract as much interest as the bluestones, and discussions about their origin have been much less heated. The sarsens really ought to be the centre of attention because they're so big. The extraction, transport and shaping of these giants would have been an engineering project on a scale never before seen in prehistoric Britain. Sarsen occurs naturally in Kent as well as in central England, but it is best known from the deposits on the Marlborough Downs in north Wiltshire. Even today, fields around Fyfield Down and Piggledean are littered with large grey lumps of sarsen, and it's easy to see how they acquired the name of 'greywethers' or sheep. They are scattered in stony flocks across the grasslands.

Since John Aubrey's time, almost 400 years ago, these downs have been thought to be the source of the Stonehenge sarsens. Yet none of the stones lying around today is anywhere near as big as those used for the Stonehenge uprights. The largest uprights are those of the great trilithon; the stone still standing (Stone 56) is more than 9 metres tall and the fallen one (Stone 55) is 10 metres long. Each of these must weigh around 35 tons and, together with their lintel, once formed the largest single megalithic structure in Britain.

The uprights of the sarsen circle are generally around 5 metres tall and each weighs around 20 tons. The squared-off appearance of the stones above ground (they look to me like a set of dominoes) belies their irregular bases: the buried parts of the stones, as Hawley discovered, are often irregular in shape.[1] The builders were keen to present an image of symmetry and rectangularity above ground, so any awkwardly shaped ends are underground. The problem with this strategy is that it compromised the stability of many of the uprights, and is why so many have fallen down or have had to be restored in the twentieth century. During our last trip to Stonehenge, Ramilisonina noticed straightaway – drawing on his own knowledge of stone-erecting – that many of the fallen sarsens have toppled because of their inadequate bottom ends.

The lintels are much smaller than the uprights. All five of the trilithon lintels survive, three of them still in position on the tall uprights and two on the ground nearby. The lintel that once lay across the tops of Stones 59 and 60 (the north trilithon) has been broken into three lumps that no longer fit together; it has evidently been chipped and quarried at in more recent centuries. The trilithon lintels are 5 metres to 6 metres long and most of the still-complete examples of the surviving seven lintels in the outer circle of sarsens are each just over 3 metres in length.

In all, the builders of Stonehenge had to look for sarsen stone to create ten trilithon uprights, five trilithon lintels, thirty circle uprights, thirty circle lintels, four Station Stones and three Slaughter Stones, a total of eighty-two stones. The Heel Stone may be a naturally occurring sarsen, and therefore already present when building work began, and the three empty stoneholes between it and the Slaughter Stone could have once been filled by an earlier arrangement of the Heel Stone and the two accompaniments to the Slaughter Stone. If two of the three Slaughter Stones were already on site when the major building work began, in an earlier alignment with the Heel Stone, that would have made eighty sarsens to go out and find – about the same number as the bluestones.

Weathered natural sarsens develop a thick, hard crust that makes this rock extremely difficult to shape. Some sarsen has an iron-hard quartzitic surface that is resistant to stone tools, even in the hands of skilled masons. This quartzitic sarsen was only of interest to Stonehenge's builders in its pebble and boulder form because these tough rocks could be used as hammerstones and mauls. Mauls were boulders that could be used to pound by hand but were probably more efficient if suspended from a rope and swung at the sarsen block. By hitting it at the right angle, the stone-worker could detach a large flake, thereby gradually shaping the block into the desired form. The softest sarsen has a sugary, crystalline texture, though there is much variation in texture and hardness.[2]

It's highly likely that the sarsens sought by the Stonehenge builders were buried below ground, because buried stone surfaces are crust-free and relatively easy to flake and pound. While digging test pits along the Kennet valley at Avebury, John Evans found buried sarsens.[3] They probably survive all over that part of north Wiltshire and one just has to know where to look for them.

As researchers realized many years ago, the current distribution of above-ground sarsens has only the weakest link to their former distribution thanks to millennia of quarrying and removal.[4] The limits of today's distributions are like high-tide marks; a human wave of stone-removers has taken everything from below this line. So where can we look to find the Neolithic sarsen quarries?

Richard Atkinson suggested that Avebury was a marshalling area for the stones: he thought that the larger slabs now at Stonehenge were previously erected there, although no one knows exactly when the stone circles at Avebury were constructed.[5] Today most of Avebury's original standing stones are missing; many were broken up in historical times but it's possible that others were taken down much earlier to be moved to Stonehenge. Atkinson reckoned that here, near Avebury, was the lowest point on the River Kennet and that the large sarsens could have been simply dragged across a shallow ford; crossing this river any further downstream to the east would have required the construction of a substantial wooden causeway. Atkinson also recognized that the symbolism of dragging stones through and from Avebury, the former greatest stone circle, might have played a part in events.

Atkinson's preferred history for the sarsen stones was:

- They were quarried at unknown locations on the Marlborough Downs.
- Then dragged to Avebury to be erected.
- At a later date, some of these were dismantled and, together with newly quarried stones, these were dragged southwest from Avebury towards Devizes.

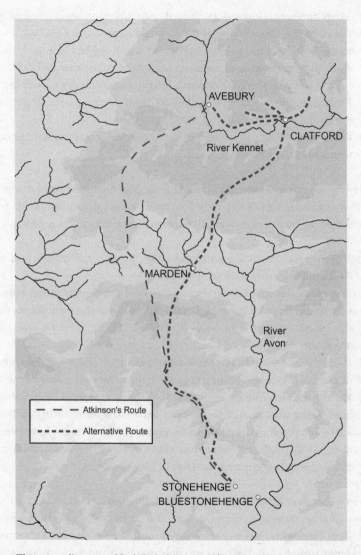

The recent discovery of Stukeley's drawing of 1723 raised the possibility of an undiscovered route by which the sarsens were brought from Avebury and Clatford to Stonehenge.

- Then they were dragged southwards past Bishops Cannings to avoid the steep downward slope of the Vale of Pewsey.
- In the bottom of the Vale's western end, south of Etchilhampton, the stone-pullers could have avoided the streams to the east and headed for the steep slope rising upwards to the northern edge of Salisbury Plain at Redhorn Hill; this would have been the most difficult part of the route, perhaps requiring a dog-leg ascent.
- Once on the Plain, it would have been easy pulling along a ridgeway with a minimum of rise and fall.

In 1961 a geologist named Patrick Hill suggested an alternative route.[6] He thought Atkinson's route was four miles longer than it needed to be and that the ascent of Redhorn Hill was unnecessary and too steep:

- Hill's preferred starting point was at Lockeridge, three miles east of Avebury in the direction of Marlborough.
- From here, his route climbs gradually to the saddle next to the causewayed enclosure of Knap Hill, then drops down the escarpment on the north side of the Vale of Pewsey, where it skirts east of Woodborough Hill.
- It then heads south to the Avon valley, eventually following the route of the Stonehenge avenue from West Amesbury into Stonehenge. Within the Avon valley, Hill reckoned the stones were dragged on land rather than floated on the river because of the shallow depth of water. He did think it possible, however, that they might have been dragged through the water over short distances to avoid riverside bluffs, and when crossing the river at various points.

Since then very little has been published on quarries and routes for the Stonehenge sarsens, though I'm sure that many enthusiasts have given it a lot of thought. I'd never really dwelt on the question until I received an email from Josh in 2008. He was finishing his project on Avebury and his researcher Rick Peterson had turned up a forgotten manuscript in Oxford's Bodleian Library. It is a sketch by William Stukeley of some sarsen stones that he'd noticed on the roadside in 1723 between Avebury and Marlborough, near the villages of Clatford and Preshute, north of

Lockeridge. Three frock-coated gentlemen, one of them on a horse, are depicted next to a group of eleven recumbent sarsens, the largest of which is annotated as being '5 yds long 7 foot broad'. Not only do these dimensions match those of the sarsen circle uprights but Stukeley also depicts this largest stone and seven others as distinctly rectangular, as if they'd been shaped.[7] John Aubrey saw these particular stones at Clatford and described them as 'rudely hewen'.

The last time I'd seen a picture this much fun – 'X marks the spot' – was when someone sent me a pirate's map showing Captain Kidd's stronghold on an island off the coast of Madagascar. Stukeley's drawing is potentially a treasure map in terms of locating the source of the sarsens. Josh and I mulled over the possibilities. This place could have been a marshalling point where partly shaped sarsens were brought prior to being sent on the final leg of the journey to Stonehenge. The stones Stukeley saw could also have been the products of a single quarry, one among many, all working to make the Stonehenge sarsens. Finally, we could not rule out these stones having being quarried many centuries later – leftovers from Medieval or later stonemasons – although the Medieval masons' technique was to break stones into smaller, more manageable blocks before hauling them away. Indeed, someone did later take away the stones Stukeley saw: nothing remains at this spot today.

I visited the place first with Peter Dunn (the reconstruction artist who has provided many of the images for this book) and later identified the exact spot with Kate Welham's survey team in 2011. Our geophysical survey failed to reveal holes for standing stones so the shaped sarsens were probably never erected here but had lain prone. Close by, we detected the ditch and external bank of an unrecorded small henge. Perhaps the stones were brought to this marshalling point from the higher ground to the north, in which direction sarsens still lie in the upper parts of the dry valleys that descend from the Marlborough Downs. In the valley below Stukeley's stones at Clatford ('the ford of the marsh marigold'), a ford crosses the River Kennet. In August 2011, our team hand-drilled cores into the river mud here to reveal what could be the remains of a buried causeway of sarsen boulders and river flints; future excavation should reveal whether this crossing was used to transport stones to Stonehenge.

William Stukeley drew the abandoned but shaped sarsens at Clatford in 1723. The
stones have gone and the road has moved but we have identified the precise spot from
the positions of the round barrow and the windmill.

North-East View of the Kist-Vaen in Clatford bottom. 1 July. 1723.

Stukeley's drawing of the Devil's Den at Clatford in 1723. The stone structure of this
type of tomb, probably a portal dolmen, was never covered by a mound.

Kate's team also carried out a geophysical survey in the next valley to the west, around the Devil's Den, one of the lesser-known megalithic monuments of Britain.[8] It consists of a pair of squat uprights supporting a partly slumped lintel or capstone; other, smaller sarsens lie within the monument and at least three more have been hauled away and dumped in the nearby hedge. Reading the antiquarian literature (or a Google search) will reveal some bizarre folk-tales associated with this odd structure. For example, at midnight the devil may appear driving a coach and horses. My favourite is the apparition of a giant rabbit with eyes that blaze like fiery coals – what an unthreatening natural world Britain is, if the worst creature that the Medieval mind could conjure up was a big scary bunny.

The Devil's Den has been thought to be the chamber of a Neolithic long barrow, though Atkinson and Piggott carried out a small excavation here in 1960 and found nothing. Stukeley drew a particularly fine illustration of it, showing the unworked stones of the trilithon-shaped stone structure and three other unworked slabs lying next to it. What grabs my attention in his drawing is that the monument sits on top of a mound and not within one. This was surely never a chambered tomb beneath a mound. It is more likely to be the remains of an Early Neolithic portal dolmen sat upon a mound. Our geophysical survey revealed remains of a second mound immediately north of it.

Given the likelihood that Stukeley's stones at Clatford had been assembled from nearby quarry sites prior to being taken across the river, Hill's route – at least its initial stretch – seems more plausible than Atkinson's. I would certainly agree with it as far as Knap Hill and the descent into the Vale of Pewsey. Thereafter I'm not convinced that the Avon valley was the easiest route for dragging the stones. There's also no particular reason to think that the avenue has to mark the direction from which the sarsen-dragging teams approached Stonehenge; the avenue's banks and ditches were created *after* the arrival of the sarsens so it wasn't a marked-out routeway at that time.

Colin's and Kate's work on the north side of Stonehenge has shown that the sarsen-dressing area was not centred on Stonehenge's main entrance but was slightly further west, suggesting that the stones were not dragged here from the northeast (along the line of the avenue) but from the north, as Atkinson thought. Coming from that direction, the teams of stone-movers would have skirted to the east of Robin Hood's Ball causewayed enclosure and the Lesser Cursus and passed by the west end of the Greater Cursus.

How did they get from the Vale of Pewsey below Knap Hill to Salisbury Plain next to Robin Hood's Ball? The northern escarpment of Salisbury Plain is extremely steep. I needed to explore the area below that northern edge and find the more gentle inclines, to see if anywhere looked even slightly promising as a suitable route to the top. Driving from west to east, I'd covered most of the ground and nothing looked good. Then, there it was – a long, narrow spur leading gently uphill from the bottom of the valley. Where was I? The nearest road sign pointed to the small village of Marden, a bridging point across a small stream in the bottom of the Vale that flows eastwards into the Avon. The name made me laugh out loud – it was all so obvious.

Marden was a really important place during the Neolithic. In fact, it is one of the five great henge enclosures of Wessex, almost as large as Durrington Walls but rarely mentioned in popular books about Wessex and seldom visited except by archaeologists. There's very little to see on the ground and it lacks the number and density of surrounding Neolithic and Early Bronze Age monuments found in the vicinity of all the other Wessex henges, from Dorchester in the south to Avebury in the north. Unlike the other henge enclosures, Marden's henge bank and ditch do not extend around the entire circuit, leaving the southern side of the henge open to the stream that flows close to it.

In 2010 a team from English Heritage, led by Jim Leary, carried out excavations inside the Marden henge.[9] One of its entrances was excavated back in 1971, by Geoff Wainwright's Central Unit.[10] They found the postholes of a timber circle and plenty of Grooved Ware. Radiocarbon dates from finds at the bottom of the ditch put its construction in the period 2570–2290 BC, so this henge is likely to have been contemporary with Durrington Walls and Stonehenge's sarsen phase.

Antiquarians recorded the presence of an enormous mound within the Marden henge enclosure. It's now completely flattened but its position was pinpointed by the English Heritage team, and one of the research aims of the 2010 excavations was to find the undisturbed basal

Landscape archaeologist Dave Field (left) discusses the excavations at Marden in 2010 with site director Jim Leary (centre) and colleague. They are standing on a layer of soil on top of the chalk floor of a Neolithic house. The edge of the circular hearth is visible in front of them.

layers of this vanished mound. Jim Leary's team also investigated a smaller henge within the main henge. Under its bank they found the chalk-plaster floor of a rectangular house, similar to those from Durrington Walls except that its central area was slightly sunk below ground level. Within the henge's southeast entrance, Jim discovered the remains of a gravel roadway leading towards the River Avon.

If the Stonehenge sarsens came this way, their route up the incline on to Salisbury Plain would have involved crossing the stream at Marden. Was this why the henge was here, to mark or signal the crossing-point where the stones had to be taken across the stream and its surrounding boggy ground? In order to cross here the stone-pullers would have needed to build a substantial causeway. It's just possible that remains of piled timbers to support a causeway might survive here and at Clatford,

deep in the bed of the stream and its wider floodplain. A future archaeologist finding them would be able to date the tree-rings to the very year
in which the trees were felled to build the causeway. One day, we may be
lucky enough to date Stonehenge's sarsen construction to within less
than a decade.

19

EARTHWORMS AND DATES

The wet summer of 2008 had at times made our excavations a miserable experience that none of us wanted to repeat. Getting the campsite evacuated at the end of the dig that year took on the dimensions of a military operation. Nonetheless, we still had enough energy for an end-of-dig party – even though the marquee was unusable and guests had to put up with standing in ankle-deep mud. It took the best part of a week to pack up and move out and, once back in Sheffield, another month to clean the equipment.

During this time, Tim and Geoff were gearing up for a big press announcement on the dating of the bluestones in the Q and R holes at Stonehenge: they now had the results of fourteen radiocarbon dates. It was announced on the BBC's six o'clock news that Stonehenge had finally been dated with certainty – the sarsens were put up around 2300 BC.

I was not the only archaeologist to raise an eyebrow at this surprising announcement: all the existing evidence indicated that the sarsens were put up around 2620–2480 BC. Where did this new date – placing the sarsens several hundred years later – come from? The same evening a BBC *Timewatch* documentary on Stonehenge explained that a carbonized cereal grain from the 2008 excavation of a Q Hole had provided a date of 2300 BC. From what he'd found in his excavations in the 1950s, Richard Atkinson believed that the bluestone Q Holes date to before the erection of the sarsen circle. If a Q Hole has a date of around 2300 BC, therefore, then Stonehenge's sarsen phase cannot be any earlier than this date: the sarsens had to be later than the Q Holes, so must have been put up around or after 2300 BC.

The programme went on to examine the argument for the healing properties of the bluestones. Tim and Geoff had found more chips of bluestones than chips of sarsens in their trench. This indicated – so they argued – that the bluestones were sought out by prehistoric people who chipped bits off them. The documentary didn't try and explain the logical problem of why all these bluestone chips had been left lying around. If the chips were valuable, why hadn't people taken them all away? If bluestones had magical powers of healing, why didn't prehistoric people use these stones to build lots of other stone circles all over Britain?

Maybe the Stonehenge Archer – the man with arrow-wounds who was the last person to be buried at Stonehenge – was shot because he'd tried to steal some of the valuable bluestone chips; three of these were found by John Evans in the soil filling the man's grave[1] and Tim wondered if these were deliberately placed grave goods. The argument against this is that the upper layers of the Stonehenge ditch in which the Archer is buried contain plenty of bluestone chips, any number of which could have ended up in the filling of the grave by accident. John also observed that the three pieces in the grave were not in any special position, which indicates that they were not deliberately placed in the grave.

I struggled to see how the new date for the Q Hole (and therefore the building of the sarsen circle) could make sense. This proposed date of 2300 BC was about 200 years later than the existing radiocarbon dates that come from two antler picks, one from the sarsen circle and one from the south trilithon. The implications were considerable. Not only did the new date suggest these two antlers, from secure contexts, had somehow produced incorrect dates, but it also meant that the bluestones and sarsens had all been erected after Stonehenge had been in use as a cemetery, and also long after the village at Durrington Walls had been abandoned. Could the existing radiocarbon dates be wrong? If this new date was right, it meant that Stonehenge and Durrington Walls were not contemporary with each other after all, and that the timber circles were built long before the sarsens were erected at Stonehenge.

Did Tim and Geoff's excavation results really lead to such a dramatic new conclusion? We suspected that the new date was wrong and that the stories in the press were garbled.

Geoff and Tim soon delivered a lecture for specialists at the Society of Antiquaries in London and the hall was packed to the rafters. Dates are more important to archaeologists than treasure because they provide the framework for investigating the past. Without them we cannot investigate long-term evolution and change. So it was standing room only to hear what Tim and Geoff had to say. To the audience's surprise (and relief), they explained that their dating was extremely tentative.[2] The date for the cereal grain from the Q Hole wasn't 2300 BC: it was actually AD 780–990. The other dates from pieces of charcoal found in this feature ranged from 3370–3090 BC to AD 1480–1640. A pig bone from its bottom layer had dated to AD 1430–1620. Of six radiocarbon dates from this bluestonehole, only two were prehistoric – of these, one dated to before anything was built at Stonehenge (before 3000 BC) and the other was the date that the press had lapped up, 2460–2200 BC.

Of the other dates from the excavation, four were from AD 1600 onwards. The remainder were from the Early Mesolithic (7330–7070 BC), the Neolithic (3090–2900 BC and 2880–2620 BC) and the end of the Neolithic (a human tooth from the turf line, dating to 2470–2230 BC).

This is all quite a lot to digest. Put simply, Tim and Geoff were wrestling with a sequence of dates that was completely scrambled. By the rules of stratigraphy, you have to date a layer by the latest thing in it. If we accepted the new dates, that would mean that the sarsen circle dated to AD 1670–1960 (that's somewhere between King Charles II and the Beatles) and the Q and R Holes to AD 1480–1640. Even the most bizarre theories about Stonehenge don't advocate that sort of date.* The problem that Geoff and Tim had encountered was bioturbation: not only have people been digging around in Stonehenge since the Roman period, but animals have as well.

Charles Darwin knew about the processes of bioturbation, which was why he went to Stonehenge to find out more.[3] Earthworms can move very big things like huge sarsen blocks down through the topsoil by

---

* That said, an internet hoax on 28 December 2008 (Spanish practical joke day; 'el día de los Santos Inocentes') claimed that Stonehenge was built by the Victorians.

several centimetres. They can also move very small things like pieces of charcoal, cereal grains and small pieces of pottery and bone to much deeper depths. The reason is very obvious, and very annoying for archaeologists. Worms burrow through the soil, leaving worm holes behind them. Small things fall down into the worm holes – they change position in the soil. It's also possible for worms to move small objects sideways and even upwards, against gravity.

In 1995 two animal bone experts published the results of a simple experiment that they'd carried out using a glass fish tank.[4] They had filled it with soil and earthworms and then placed the corpses of two voles and a mouse on its surface. Within twenty-four weeks, the earthworms had scattered the little bones throughout the soil, with most bones at a depth of 10 centimetres below the surface and some already at depths of more than 20 centimetres.

Richard Atkinson was also well aware of the power of earthworms to move small objects, not only from reading Darwin and others on the subject but also from his own experiences of digging at Stonehenge. In a famous paper on 'Worms and weathering', published in 1957, he declared that: 'the excavator who ignores the capacity of worms to displace small objects downwards, either through ignorance or wilfully, does so at his peril'.[5]

It was clear that the criteria that Mike Allen had set for establishing reliable dates from the small pieces of charcoal in Geoff and Tim's trench could not be met (see Chapter 11 if you want to remind yourself of the detailed rules). Unfortunately explaining radiocarbon dating is difficult, and the BBC's reporters just hadn't understood what was (and what was not) a secure and reliable date. Certainly each piece of charcoal had a date – we knew how old every piece was – but this didn't tell us anything about the layers of soil in which they'd ended up. Without knowing about the dates of the soil layers, we can't say anything about the construction sequence at Stonehenge. At very best these dates were simply evidence that charcoal was dropped on the ground at that time, or formed in a small fire. Nobody really cared that someone had burnt a bit of wood at Stonehenge in 2300 BC – we were all trying to find out when they built the place! So the BBC were wrong and Stonehenge didn't date to 2300 BC after all.

The one really interesting date from Tim and Geoff's samples is a piece of charcoal from 7330–7070 BC, the Mesolithic period. This coincides nicely with the date of the later of the two pine postholes in the Stonehenge car park. It may mean that somewhere very near Stonehenge – even closer to it than the Mesolithic campsite we have identified in the field to the west – there lie further as-yet-undiscovered traces of Early Mesolithic activity. It's certainly a possibility but caution is needed because single small pieces of charcoal can be moved about on people's shoes or in clods of transported earth, or even by being blown from place to place.

A year later, after all the Stonehenge hype had died down, Geoff, Tim and I together worked out a new chronology that accounted for all the Stonehenge radiocarbon dates ever obtained. The previous scheme had ignored one of the dates because it didn't seem to fit, but now we had a chronology that worked.

The first stage of Stonehenge (in the period 3000–2920 BC) was undoubtedly the construction of its ditch and bank and the digging of the Aubrey Holes, which I believe held a circle of bluestones. Then, apart from various cremation burials, there was no major building work until around 2500 BC. And at this point, Geoff and Tim had a radical proposal. A tremendous result of their excavation in the interior of the stone circle is that they're now certain that Atkinson was wrong about the Q and R Holes: he had said they were earlier than the sarsen trilithons and circle; everybody believed this interpretation and it was all a mistake.

This seemed, at first, to be impossible – there is even a photograph taken by Atkinson that we all thought showed the hole for Stone 3 of the sarsen circle definitely cutting Q Hole 4.[6] Tim and Geoff explained that the most important new information to come out of their excavation is that many of these stoneholes had been cut into, dug out and re-filled again millennia after they had been originally dug by the Neolithic builders, with this later interference taking place mostly in the Roman, Medieval and early modern periods. As a result, none of the stratigraphic observations from Atkinson's excavations – in which he said which stonehole cut which other stonehole – could be trusted.

I cast my mind back to the contradictory section that Tim had showed me when I visited his team in their first week of digging at Stonehenge.

Their trench had uncovered a Q Hole that actually cut the hole for a fallen stone of the sarsen circle, the complete opposite of what Atkinson thought he saw. It's clear from Atkinson's photograph that Sarsen Hole 3 cut Q Hole 4 – but what no one had asked themselves was whether this cutting of one hole by another could be dated. It was just assumed to be prehistoric but we actually don't know when it happened. That particular sarsen's hole is uncharacteristically large, so it's likely that this enlargement was made much later: it's most likely not a Neolithic intersection between the two holes at all. Furthermore, Tim and Geoff's findings show that the Q Holes have been placed at the wrong point in the construction sequence.

Geoff explained that one of the problems with studying Stonehenge is that it can be so difficult to put aside our taken-for-granted assumptions. We cling on to what we think are certainties and it can be difficult to recognize when a mistake has been made earlier, back down the line, because it has taken on the status of an incontrovertible fact. Atkinson's stratigraphic observation of the relationship between bluestone arc and sarsen circle was precisely one of those apparently unchallengeable facts, until new information revealed that we could no longer assume that this stratigraphy had been formed in prehistory. Tim and Geoff found out that the interior of Stonehenge had been hacked about very badly before modern times.

Geoff and Tim suggested that the Q and R Holes belong in the main phase of construction, the same phase as the sarsen trilithons and circle. Both spatially and architecturally they fit within this stage dating to 2620–2480 BC. It then makes sense that the bluestones in the Q and R Holes were later rearranged into the bluestone circle of Stage 4.

20

THE NEW SEQUENCE FOR STONEHENGE

The new work at Stonehenge – in terms of both excavations and the examination of old records – has produced a sequence of construction that takes into account, for the first time ever, all the spatial relationships between the different stoneholes, and all the radiocarbon dates that have been acquired over the years. We don't all agree on every detail, but these are the main stages that we can identify.

First stage 3000–2920 BC (Middle Neolithic)

The first features to be constructed were the *outer bank, ditch, inner bank, and Aubrey Holes with bluestones* in them. *Cremation burials* accompanied these early features. Arrangements of *posts* and perhaps three or more *standing stones* were set up within the central area of the circular enclosure; some of these post settings were aligned roughly on the southern major moonrise to the southeast. To the south there was an entrance through the banks and across the ditch. A post-lined passageway led from this south entrance to the centre. There was a wider entrance to the northeast. In this northeast entrance and just beyond there were two settings of posts aligned approximately on the northern major moonrise. On the same axis, beyond the entrance and running southwest–northeast, was a line of standing stones (surviving as Stoneholes B, C and 97). The most distant of these (97) provided a sightline on the midsummer solstice sunrise from the centre of the circle. Together with stones B and C it provided a second approximate alignment towards the northern major moonrise.

Second stage 2620–2480 BC (Late Neolithic)

It seems most likely that the five *trilithons* were the next element to be erected. For engineering reasons the trilithons must have gone up before the sarsen circle around them. The building of the trilithons was followed by a rearrangement of the bluestones into the double arc of *Q and R Holes* and the construction of the *sarsen circle*.

Beyond the northeast entrance the erection of the *Heel Stone* may belong to this stage (moved from its former position in Stonehole 97), as may the putting-up of the *Slaughter Stone and its two partners* within that entrance. *Two D-shaped buildings* were constructed (beneath the North and South Barrows) against the inner bank and two of the four *Station Stones* were erected within them. English Heritage's survey team have suggested that the northern D-shaped structure was built before Stage 1 because the bank and ditch appear to kink around it, but the Aubrey Hole ring shows no such deviation. Only future excavation will reveal for certain which construction stage this D-shaped building belongs to.

While the axis of the trilithons was northeast–southwest, on midsummer sunrise/midwinter sunset, the rectangular plan of the Station Stones provided approximate alignments both on this same axis and on another, on its southeast–northwest axis, to the southern major moonrise as well as the northern major moonset.

Third stage 2480–2280 BC (Copper Age)

The *avenue*, running from the northeast entrance along the natural, solstice-aligned periglacial ridges, was built by digging out two parallel ditches with inner and outer banks, in 2500–2270 BC. Stonehenge's circular *ditch was cleaned out* in 2560–2140 BC but *cremation deposits* continued to be buried in the ditch even after it subsequently filled up. In the centre of Stonehenge, there may have been a circular arrangement of *bluestones* inside the trilithons, indicated by an arc of four stoneholes on the west side of the interior.

Then a *large pit* was dug into the north side of the great trilithon, cutting this bluestone arc as well as the outer circle of Q and R Holes. This is the pit that Atkinson mistakenly identified as a 'ramp' and it can be dated to the period 2470–2210 BC. The Slaughter Stone's two companions (*Stoneholes D and E*) were probably taken down, to widen the northeast entrance. The *avenue ditch filled up and was cleaned out* at some time in 2290–2120 BC. *Mounds* were raised to form the North and South Barrows, on top of the D-shaped buildings.

Fourth stage 2280–2020 BC (Early Bronze Age)

The bluestones in the Q and R Holes were rearranged into an outer *bluestone circle* (2270–2020 BC) and the central arc/circle of bluestones was remodelled into a *bluestone oval* (2210–1930 BC). Atkinson thought that the bluestone oval was later modified by the removal of four of its northeastern monoliths, leaving a horseshoe-shaped arrangement of stones. Geoff and Tim now know that Atkinson was unaware of the full extent of Roman and later destruction and removal wreaked on the monument. He made a fair assumption that the removal of four bluestones from the oval to create a horseshoe was an event planned and carried out in prehistory but, in light of the 2008 excavation, it's more likely that this happened millennia later. Out goes the bluestone horseshoe – there is no archaeological justification for regarding it as a separate prehistoric entity: it is more probably simply the degraded remains of the bluestone oval.

Fifth stage 1680–1520 BC (Middle Bronze Age)

Two rings of rectangular holes were dug outside the sarsen circle. These pits are known as the Y and Z Holes and they appear to be arranged in a double circle. As well as antler picks, some of these holes contained other antlers that were antiques – perhaps centuries old – when they were put in the holes. Atkinson suggested that the Y and Z Holes were dug to hold some of the bluestones but were never used, and no one has ever come up with a better idea. The holes were left open and filled in gradually with fine silt blown in from surrounding fields. Two circular, low ridges outside each ring have been tentatively identified as being the remains of prehistoric hedges – 'Stonehedge' – but they may just be the spread remnants of the heaps of chalk produced when the pits were dug, and then just left lying outside the holes.[1]

This period of 1680–1520 BC, in the middle of the Bronze Age, was a turning point in prehistory. No more major monuments were constructed in Britain and it seems that collective labour switched from tomb-building to the laying-out of field boundaries all over the country. Labouring for the ancestors gave way to labouring for the living. The abandonment of the Y and Z Holes and their filling-up with soil blown in from newly opened, nearby fields encapsulates this transition very neatly. This was the last time that any attempt was made to modify Stonehenge's form other than by robbing its stones. Thereafter, it was a relic of a bygone age, surrounded by a landscape of fields laid out around the cemeteries of Early Bronze Age round barrows.

Pottery sherds found in excavations at Stonehenge span the period from the Middle Bronze Age to the modern era. There is pottery of the Middle and Late Bronze Age, Iron Age, Roman, Saxon, Medieval and early modern periods from various parts of the site. Certain moments of activity stand out. The many sherds of pottery and occasional coin from the third to fourth centuries AD indicate a marked degree of interest in the site during the Late Roman period, shortly before the departure of the Romans in AD 410. After that date, there is little evidence for any centralized authority in Wessex during the Dark Ages until the rise of the West Saxon kingdom in the early seventh century.[2] A piece of human skull found at Stonehenge dates to AD 340–510, on the cusp of the Dark Ages.

Geoffrey of Monmouth's twelfth-century 'history' of Britain says that the British king Aurelius Ambrosius (elsewhere referred to as Ambrosius Aurelianus) and his brother Uther Pendragon (the father of King Arthur) were buried at Stonehenge, at a date that can be estimated around AD 500. Ambrosius Aurelianus is named as a Romano-British war leader of the fifth century by the Dark Age historian Gildas.[3] Gildas was a cleric writing in the early sixth century whose *De Excidio et Conquestu Britanniae* (*On the Ruin and Conquest of Britain*) is the most reliable of our few written sources from the Dark Ages; despite its shortcomings – it was written as a sermon and not a history – it is certainly more reliable than what was written by Geoffrey of Monmouth, who seems to have fabricated other aspects of Ambrosius' life, including quite probably his place of burial. The imaginative reader could fantasize that this fragment of skull is all that is left of Ambrosius Aurelianus but this is very unlikely.

The Medieval period shows up at Stonehenge in a decapitated burial and two human teeth, two dates from charcoal (AD 720–990), and other

Medieval finds. This may have been the time when Stonehenge acquired its name: 'Stone Hangings' could mean a place of execution. It is possible that early churches built in the area used stones from Stonehenge. Amesbury Abbey dates back to a Benedictine foundation in AD 979 and the church at Durrington was probably built by AD 1150.[4] Excavations along the Stonehenge avenue and on the Cursus have identified cart tracks, probably from this period and later, leading from Stonehenge towards Amesbury and Durrington.

There is also plenty of debris from the early modern period of the sixteenth to eighteenth centuries, represented by six radiocarbon dates and by quantities of broken pottery, glass and other artefacts. This was the period in which the earliest recorded 'excavations' were carried out. Behind one of the trilithons (Stones 53–54), a slight rise in the ground is probably the remnants of the Duke of Buckingham's spoil heap of 1620, though without excavation we cannot rule out the possibility that a prehistoric mound stood here.

Stone-robbing probably also continued until the seventeenth century. In the eighteenth century the area next to Stonehenge was turned into a racecourse and the monument itself seems to have been a handy spot for race-goers to dispose of empty bottles and other rubbish.

21

STONEHENGE: THE VIEW FROM AFAR

Stonehenge is, in various ways, unique. Its dressed stonework, its lintels and the remarkable distances travelled by sarsens and bluestones (even people who support the glacial-erratics hypothesis have to agree that these have come at least forty miles) are all aspects that make this a very unusual monument for Late Neolithic Britain. This might justify one considering it as a solitary edifice in splendid isolation but, to misquote John Donne, no monument is an island, entire of itself.

In the context of the surrounding landscape, the Stonehenge Riverside Project has attempted to show how Stonehenge was part of a long-lived and larger complex of monuments, settlements and landforms. We must also examine how it compares with monuments built elsewhere in Britain, to see what light these may shed on its nature and purpose.

As an example of such a comparison we can look briefly at a distinctive piece of modern architecture, the 'Gherkin' (or 30 St Mary Axe) in central London. We know that this was not beamed down from outer space or built at the command of an alien master-race (bankers are, apparently, human), because we know who designed it and how. We also know what preceded it, what were the fashions of the time, and the financial and technological limits for such a building project. Yet the Gherkin stands out because of its curvilinear shape, contrasting strikingly with the standard rectilinear architecture of the City.

To understand why Norman Foster designed this unique structure we need to see what influenced him. We don't have access to his private imagination but we do have various examples worldwide of other

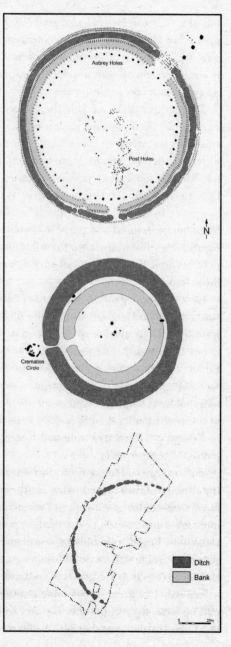

Stonehenge (in its Stage 1; top), Llandegai Henge A (middle) and Flagstones (bottom) had many features in common, including burials and large stones.

buildings (Frank Gehry's Guggenheim Museum in Bilbao, say, which opened in 1997) that mark the emergence of a new architectural fashion. Innovation is a constant process of comparison and contrast, reworking tradition with novelty, and expanding the resources and technology to turn dream into reality.

The earliest phase of Stonehenge, with its circular enclosure, cremation burials and standing stones, is actually just one example of a type of monument – a cremation enclosure – that we know well from different parts of Britain. Stonehenge is, in fact, quite late in the fashion for this particular type of structure. Those who accept that the bluestones were fetched from west Wales (rather than moved to Somerset by glaciers) may not be entirely surprised to learn that Stonehenge's closest comparison was built perhaps a century earlier, in north Wales 140 miles from Preseli. Outside the town of Bangor, and now covered by an industrial estate, was one of Britain's other two Stonehenges.

Here at Llandegai (also written as Llandygai) were two henge enclosures, known as Henge A and Henge B.[1] The earlier of these, Henge A, was excavated in advance of development in 1966–1967: we have to write about Llandegai in the past tense now because it has all disappeared under concrete and survives only in the excavation records. Like Stonehenge, Henge A at Llandegai was circular and also had a ditch external to its bank. At 90 metres in diameter, this henge enclosure was only slightly smaller than Stonehenge. Its ditch, however, was both wider and deeper – 10 metres wide and 3 metres deep – and its bank was a colossal 7 metres wide.

The interior of Henge A produced very few traces of Neolithic activity, although it was reused many centuries later. The henge's entrance faced west-southwest (though not towards the midwinter solstice sunset) and, against the inside of the bank opposite this entrance, there was a cremation burial, probably of a woman. Next to her ashes someone placed a rhyolite slab for polishing stone axes and a cobble of crystallized tuff, probably as grave goods. Geologists cannot tell for certain from where either of these stones came but they did travel some distance to end up here; the axe-polisher is either from just west of Preseli or from the Lake District. Another pit on the west side of the henge interior contained no burial, just a complete and unused polished axe from the Langdale quarry in the Lake District. Curiously the bank covered a shallow pit containing Early Mesolithic pine charcoal dating to 7000 BC: was this just a treehole of a lightning-struck tree, or a man-made 'fire-pit', as it is described by the excavators?

There was a smaller ditched circle, just 9 metres across, immediately in front of the entrance to Henge A. It was cut by five causeways, and all five of its ditch segments contained cremated human bones and quantities of charcoal, some of which may have come from burnt planks. The burials were those of at least five adults (one of them a woman), a child, an infant and a newborn baby. Some of these remains came from small pits inside and around the circular ditch.

A large block of hornfels (a metamorphic rock) lay within one of the cremation circle's ditches, pushed over from a standing position. This was evidently the stump of a broken-off standing stone but was not recognized as such by the excavators. We don't know if more stones had been removed intact from the ditch circle without leaving evidence of their former presence.

This small circle was very similar in size to Bluestonehenge. Together with the larger henge, the site at Llandegai contained all the major elements found at Stonehenge and Bluestonehenge, just in a different pattern and without bluestones. Seven radiocarbon dates show that this proto-Stonehenge dated to somewhere within the period 3300–2900 BC, having been started before 3000 BC.

The other prototype for Stonehenge lies closer to Salisbury Plain, underneath the house of a famous Wessex author. Thomas Hardy lived in a large house named Max Gate on the eastern outskirts of Dorchester, the county town he made famous under the fictional name of Casterbridge. During building works on the house, workmen found a human burial. Although Hardy reported this discovery in the local archaeological journal, he would have had no idea that he was living on top of Wessex's other Stonehenge.[2]

Named after the other house that stood on its site, Flagstones, this henge was not found until 1987 when Wessex Archaeology excavated its western half in advance of a new bypass road.[3] Today, half of 'Flagstonehenge' has been destroyed by the bypass and the rest is under

Max Gate's garden. It is a bit sad that our other two Stonehenges have been largely destroyed.

Flagstones's ditch, with its gang-dug segments and diameter of 100 metres, was almost identical to that of Stonehenge. A cremated adult, an adult's leg bone and the incomplete skeletons of three children were found in the ditch, most of them covered by stone slabs in the same fashion as the burial found at Thomas Hardy's house. The slabs were of sarsen and local sandstone, presumably part of a setting of standing stones that might have been demolished shortly after the ditch was dug out. Fragments of sarsen, sandstone and limestone in the fill of the ditch hinted at other stones having been broken up or taken away. Three cremation burials were found inside the henge enclosure but none have been dated.

There is one other tie-up with Stonehenge. Thomas Hardy's neighbours in Wareham House, just northwest of Max Gate, found a small circular pottery disc in their garden.[4] This is an incense burner, almost identical to the one accompanying one of Stonehenge's cremation burials. They are the only two of this type ever found in Britain.

The Flagstones henge ditch was dug in the period 3300–3000 BC. Whether it had an inner bank and external counterscarp like Stonehenge or an outer bank like other henges is difficult to say since nothing survives above ground. Flagstones had one thing that Stonehenge does not: using flint flakes, someone in the Neolithic carved pictures into the vertical chalk sides of its ditch segments in four separate places. This art was very basic: concentric circles, a meander motif, criss-cross lines and parallel lines – exactly the same motifs as were used on chalk plaques and Grooved Ware pottery. Unlike the peoples of other parts of Europe, Britain's Neolithic artists seem to have been very restricted in what they could portray.

Flagstones lies at the heart of a Neolithic ritual landscape, surrounded by remains of burial mounds and three large monuments. To the east lies the henge enclosure of Mount Pleasant with a timber circle and a newly discovered avenue leading northwards to the River Frome.[5] To the west is a large pit circle at Maumbury Rings, reused as a Roman amphitheatre.[6] To the northwest at Greyhound Yard, under

Dorchester's Roman town centre, archaeologists discovered a line of holes for Neolithic timber posts that formed a large enclosure.[7]

Stonehenge, Llandegai A and Flagstones are at the top of the scale for burial enclosures in terms of size and grandeur. Archaeologists have found another sixteen such sites in other parts of Britain. Most are now destroyed, having been found in advance of development, but enough evidence was recovered for us to know that they were in use around the same time as Stonehenge.

One group of burial sites, rivalling Stonehenge in terms of numbers of cremations, lies north of Stonehenge on the River Thames at the other Dorchester. Sitting in and around a cursus, the Dorchester-on-Thames complex of circular monuments includes six pit circles and a ditched circular enclosure, all with cremations.[8] It was here that Richard Atkinson cut his archaeological teeth in the 1940s, excavating some of these pit circles before working at Stonehenge. About 170 cremations were found in these seven small cemeteries. Although none of the cremations have ever been radiocarbon-dated, long bone skewer pins and a broken stone macehead among the grave goods are identical to similar items found with burials at Stonehenge.

Since Atkinson's discoveries at Dorchester-on-Thames, more Neolithic cremation cemetery enclosures have been found in midland England. A pit circle within a small henge ditch at Barford in Warwickshire contained cremated bones.[9] At West Stow in Suffolk, archaeologists digging a Saxon village also found a Neolithic cremation circle with a central burial and forty-nine cremations.[10] Just recently, seven cremation burials dating to 3300–3000 BC were found in two circular enclosures beneath Imperial College's sports ground in the Colne valley, west of London.[11] Nearby at Horton, the skeleton of a woman, dating to around 2700 BC, lay buried next to a similar enclosure.

Within Wessex there are another two Neolithic enclosures with burials. Farmer and archaeologist Martin Green found a curious circle of fourteen pits enclosing a large central hole at Monkton Up Wimborne on Cranborne Chase in Dorset.[12] In the edge of this hole, a woman and three children had been buried in a communal grave around 3300 BC. From their DNA it seems that the woman was probably the mother of one of the children, a girl. The other children were brother and sister but unrelated to the woman with whom they were buried. Isotope analysis of tooth enamel shows that the mother grew up about forty miles away on the Mendip Hills, moved to Cranborne Chase, returned to Mendip where she gave birth to her daughter, and then returned again to the area of Dorset where all four met an untimely death. Martin Green also found a small pit-circle henge on his farm. Known as Wyke Down, it has

Middle–Late Neolithic cremation enclosures and related sites of the same date as Stonehenge occur throughout Britain.

cremation deposits around its entrance, dating to around 2700 BC, as well as Grooved Ware pottery and a stone axe of rhyolite from just west of Preseli.[13]

In 1890 the antiquarian J. R. Mortimer dug into the Neolithic barrow of Duggleby Howe, on the chalk wolds of North Yorkshire.[14] This enormous mound measures 37 metres across and stands more than 6 metres high. As mentioned in an earlier chapter, Mortimer found at the bottom of it an impressive group of fourteen skeletons of adults, children and infants and a woman's bashed-in skull, recently dated to around 3400 BC.[15] These inhumation burials were followed by fifty-three or more cremation burials, three of which were accompanied by Stonehenge-style bone skewer pins. Unfortunately Mortimer made the same mistake as Hawley: he didn't know what to do with cremation burials either, so he poured all the Duggleby bones into a single big box.

Many years later, in 1983, archaeologists discovered that the Duggleby mound was surrounded by a circular, segmented ditch.[16] At 370 metres in diameter it is even bigger than the ditched enclosures at Flagstones, Llandegai and Stonehenge, although incomplete on its south side. Only in 2009 was this ditch finally investigated, by Neolithic expert Alex Gibson.

As far away as Scotland, archaeologists have also found a cremation cemetery of this period.[17] It is near Edinburgh at Cairnpapple, West Lothian, where an arc of seven pits was associated with eleven cremations in and around them. A skewer pin from one of these cremations dates them to just before 3000 BC. This Neolithic cemetery was later covered by an Early Bronze Age cairn.

Llandegai, Flagstones and the other sixteen enclosures have largely escaped the notice of archaeologists and others interested in Stonehenge. Some have been wrongly assumed to be later in date or, as in the case of Llandegai, the full account of their excavations languished unpublished for years. Only now is it possible to pull together the records of all these excavated sites and see the broader picture. What they show is that, throughout Britain during the centuries immediately before and during Stonehenge's use, many other circular enclosures were being used for burial. Stonehenge was in the upper stratum as regards size and complexity, on a par with the slightly earlier burial enclosures at Llandegai, Flagstones and Duggleby Howe.

In the vast majority of cases, the burials within these circles were cremations. Stonehenge, Duggleby Howe, West Stow and the Dorchester-on-Thames circles were the most densely used for burial, yet none of these contains enough cremated individuals to have been serving each site's whole local community. It seems that most of Britain's population during the period 3300–2400 BC was disposed of in other ways, with no lasting memorial. Who were these happy few buried in these prominent places? As with Stonehenge, I suspect that by and large we are looking at the burials of members of prominent local families, a pattern of use of these sites only by an elite that continued, at the larger cemeteries, over many generations.

Other burials are more mysterious. The Monkton Up Wimborne burial site is earlier than most of the others and that burial of a woman with a group of children speaks more of violence or tragedy than dynastic memorialization. Duggleby Howe's group of skeletons has also been considered, by Mortimer as well as others, to be a mass sacrifice on the death of a leader. However, new radiocarbon dates indicate that this was not a single mass deposit but a long-term sequence of burials, more in line with being a dynastic burial ground.

Another question concerns the shape of these cremation burial cemeteries – why do so many of them employ circular geometry in their plans? Archaeologists have been aware for some years that the digging of enclosures with perfectly circular plans started only after about 3400 BC, thereafter diversifying into a wide range of ellipses, ovals and sub-circular shapes. It is also a peculiarly British phenomenon. There are very few perfectly circular Neolithic enclosures of the late fourth and early third millennia elsewhere in Europe, which is odd because marking out a circle with a rope and peg is so very simple.

Perfect circles are present in nature in various forms: the iris of the human eye, ripples in still water, the sun and the full moon, for example. We will probably never know whether any or all of these were perceived by Neolithic people as sharing the same geometric property, but it seems reasonable to suggest that the sun and the moon were the two principal entities symbolized in circular enclosures. Elsewhere in the ancient world at this time, other cultures expressed less equivocal materializations of their religious attitudes towards the sun. Examples of these, from very different times and places, are the sun symbols of ancient Egypt and the many 'sun motif' carvings on flat stones found among former wooden-post circles at the Neolithic Rispebjerg complex on Bornholm in the Baltic Sea.[18]

Some of the most enigmatic circular sites are the four Priddy Circles in the Mendips. These circular enclosures, each about 160 metres in diameter, have often been compared with Stonehenge because they have external ditches. Re-excavation in 2008 of a 1950s excavation yielded charcoal from within the ditch of Circle 1, dating the beginning of the ditch's filling-in to 2930–2870 BC, close to the date of Stonehenge's first stage.[19] Only further excavations will reveal whether these circles too are burial enclosures from that time.

Some archaeologists have talked of a religious reformation around 3300 BC, on a par with the sixteenth-century upheavals of early modern Europe.[20] There is no doubt that choosing to bury the dead within these enclosures was very different to burying people inside long barrows and causewayed enclosures, the latter never being properly circular. The Duggleby Howe mound and ditch – with their similarities to Early Neolithic mounds and causewayed enclosures – are something of a hybrid, on the cusp between two mortuary styles, past and present.

There seems to have been an intervening period between causewayed enclosures and circular burial enclosures, from 3600 BC to 3300 BC, when cursuses were fashionable. Although our interpretations favour cursuses having a funerary dimension, linking the living and the dead, we have little idea where the actual remains of the dead went during that period. There is no evidence at all of anyone being buried within the cursuses. As we found at Amesbury 42, the long barrow at the east end of the Stonehenge Cursus, only a very few people were buried in the long barrows associated with the cursuses.

After 3300 BC there was an explosion of stone circle construction. In Orkney, off the northern tip of Scotland, people built one of the largest circular monuments of the age – the great stone circle of the Ring of Brodgar. With probably more than sixty standing stones arranged in a single circle inside a 123-metre-diameter ditch, it is one of Britain's most impressive stone circles. In 2008, Colin and Orkney archaeologist Jane Downes dug a trench into its massive 3.5-metre-deep ditch to try and get

The Ring of Brodgar is one of Orkney's many Neolithic monuments. In its first stage,
Stonehenge would have looked very much like this with its bank and ditch and ring
of bluestones in the Aubrey Holes.

samples for dating.[21] Though they were ultimately unsuccessful, they
think the Ring of Brodgar was built shortly before 3000 BC. To the east
of it, along a narrow peninsula half a mile away, lie the newly discovered
Neolithic settlement complex of the Ness of Brodgar and the settlement
of Barnhouse, excavated by Colin in the 1980s.[22] Beyond these is
another, smaller stone circle from this period, the Stones of Stenness, set
within a henge ditch and bank.[23] Colin thinks that a central fireplace and
other structural features found within the Stones of Stenness were once
part of a large house that was turned into a stone monument.

At the Ring of Brodgar archaeologists have tried to explain the
absence of a bank to go with the ditch as being the result of the ditch's
contents being used for the circle's standing stones. Colin can tell that
the rock here would not have been solid enough to work into megaliths – and, anyway, he has found one of the quarries for the Brodgar

standing stones a couple of miles away. He also suspects that the stones dug out by the Neolithic builders from the Ring of Brodgar's ditch went into building the masonry walls of the Ness of Brodgar houses.

There is no doubt from Nick Card's recent excavations at the Ness of Brodgar that thousands of tons of stone were required to build the houses and halls of this enormous village.[24] Colin thinks that the copious use of stone in Orcadian Neolithic houses was more than just the result of a shortage of timbers on these treeless islands. Working on the stone circles at Calanais (Callanish) on the Isle of Lewis in the Outer Hebrides, he came to appreciate that these two similar environments, both rendered treeless in the Neolithic, gave rise to two entirely different types of house and settlement. The Neolithic communities of Orkney and the Hebrides developed along very different pathways after the arrival of farming.

In the Outer Hebrides, habitation was transient and people used turf as well as whatever wood they could find – driftwood and small timbers – to build their houses. Stones were used in the foundation layers but the superstructures were built of perishable materials. In Orkney, Colin reckons, habitation was sedentary, with stone providing a potent metaphor for permanence and a material manifestation of attachment to place. Perhaps Orcadian Neolithic people's identity was rooted in their relationships to particular places and expressed through stone architecture. Whereas the places of the living within the rest of Britain were constructed in metaphors of impermanence, Orkney was different – tombs as well as places of the living were made of stone.

We can now see that Stonehenge incorporated elements of design and use that were current across Britain. Its Aubrey Hole bluestone circle is similar to the Ring of Brodgar, its various elements can be found in a different configuration at Llandegai, and it shares many similarities with other cremation cemeteries. The distance travelled by the bluestones, however, is truly remarkable and requires explanation.

If we accept the role of human agency in moving the stones from Preseli and other parts of Wales, we need to explain why people did this. One of the interesting aspects of west Wales' archaeology – and the Brecon Beacons – is the presence here of a significant concentration of Early Neolithic monuments: portal dolmens, long cairns and a causewayed enclosure. Between 3800 and 3600 BC this was a thriving Neolithic society. Recent research by Alison Sheridan of the National Museums of Scotland has shown that the west coast of Britain may have provided favoured landfalls for Continental farming groups arriving in Britain as early as 4000 BC.[25]

We normally think of invaders and immigrants to Britain coming across the shortest route from Calais to Dover, and there is evidence for some very early Neolithic people here, including a megalithic sarsen tomb at Coldrum in Kent.[26] Otherwise, however, the closed chamber tombs and short passage tombs – thought to be among the very earliest Neolithic monuments in Britain – have a distinctly westerly distribution, from Pembrokeshire and northwest Wales to the west of Scotland. Alison has also looked at the pottery of these earliest farmers. It is in some west coast sites in Britain that the styles of pots are closest to those used in northern France and Brittany. For example, she is certain that a pot from the burial chamber of Carreg Samson closed chamber tomb is of a style identical to that made in Brittany before 4000 BC. She reckons that, in large measure, the Neolithic way of life was brought by migrating Continental farmers as a 'package' rather than just its separate components being imported by the indigenous hunter-gatherers. Once farming had arrived in Britain, it was adopted by the locals. Two 'hotspots' of surviving Breton-style tombs within Britain are in north Wales and in Pembrokeshire.[27] These areas might well have been points of origin for the earliest immigrant farmers who colonized the valleys that run down to the coast and exploited the adjacent uplands for grazing.

There are no radiocarbon dates for the beginning of the Neolithic in Wales earlier than about 3700 BC, but the evidence from Carreg Samson indicates that farmers probably lived here before then. Unfortunately the acidic soils of the region do not preserve human bones or antler picks, so there is nothing suitable to date the use of the earliest tombs. Archaeologists recovered a few tiny fragments of cremated human bone from the burial chamber within Carreg Samson but these are too small for radiocarbon dating.[28]

The most interesting point when thinking about Stonehenge is that areas such as Salisbury Plain were not densely inhabited until around 3600 BC, although there was some initial settlement around 3900–3800

BC (as well as that enigmatic date of 4360–3990 BC on a cow bone from Stonehenge itself). All of the area's long barrows so far dated were built after 3600 BC and many of the undated ones are of styles likely to be similarly late in date. This was good, open grazing land, however, and access to these chalk grasslands would have been strongly contested by arriving groups making claims to the land. Did early farmers move in large numbers from Wales to Salisbury Plain during the fourth millennium BC, between 3600 and 3000 BC?

Such a mass migration would certainly explain the apparent absence of Late Neolithic monuments in southwest Wales. There is not a single cursus or henge in Preseli or its environs. There are henges further south around Carmarthen – one has recently been excavated – but otherwise, to find monuments of that date, you have to go as far east as the Walton Basin in Clwyd–Powys, 30 miles northeast of the Brecon Beacons, where Alex Gibson has excavated a 34ha palisaded enclosure at Hindwell dating to around 2700 BC.[29] Further north, near Welshpool, he also found a cursus, a small cremation enclosure dating to around 3300 BC and a timber circle dating to about 2100 BC.[30]

It may be that the eastern part of Wales, around the Severn valley, flourished while west Wales stagnated. There is, however, no sign in the pollen diagrams of regenerating woodland – such a change in vegetation would hint at a mass exodus – nor is there any evidence of a climatic downturn that made Wales' uplands any more inhospitable than usual at this time. Even if there were no migration out of west Wales, it may be that many descendants of the earliest farmers headed east in search of new pastures. It is highly unlikely that they packed their Neolithic suitcases with bluestone monoliths, but perhaps they came back for them a few generations later.

As anthropologists have observed, immigrant communities drop their heaviest cultural anchors in second, third or even later generations, when links to former homelands and traditions may be re-forged. I have seen something of this at first-hand during my fieldwork in the Outer Hebrides, the ancestral homeland of many Scottish Americans and Canadians; the descendants of nineteenth-century emigrants feel a powerful emotional link to their Hebridean origins, not only visiting the islands but reviving music, language and folk customs thousands of miles away.

A perhaps more likely scenario is that Preseli was considered to have ancestral significance for the descendants of immigrant farmers who had landed on the coast of west Wales and brought farming to Britain shortly before 4000 BC. Perhaps people could recall that this was a place of origin after 30 or so generations (or, more likely, re-invented it as such); the existence of the now ancient closed chamber tombs and portal dolmens would certainly have served to remind them of an ancestral presence in this region.[31] Preseli and Stonehenge could have been considered as the two most sacred places of origin of the British people, one as the place where the first farming settlers built their portal dolmens and the other as the place where indigenous hunter-gatherers and, later on, early farmers celebrated the axis of the world, where lines in the land marked the sun's solstices.

Stonehenge was a monument of unification, bringing together groups with different ancestries in a coalition that encompassed the entirety of southern Britain, if not the entire island. Its design embodied cosmic unity, geometrical harmony and inter-connectedness.

Extrapolating from the evidence of modern DNA, the earliest communities of farmers in Britain were probably genetically diverse, composed of groups from Iberia and the French coast as well as indigenous hunter-gatherers already inhabiting Britain when the farmers arrived. Similarly, the styles of pottery and tombs in use during the fourth millennium BC hint at a marked degree of regionalism: tombs in the Cotswolds and Severn valley are different to those in Wessex, for example. And there is evidence that certain groups did not always get along with each other. Within southwest Britain, for example, archaeologists have found defended enclosures whose encircling distributions of arrowheads indicate that these strongholds were attacked.[32]

One such site is Hambledon Hill in Dorset. Any thoughts that this was merely a ritual enclosure were dispelled when archaeologists discovered that parts of this complex had been turned into fortifications which had been attacked and burned around 3400 BC, probably entailing the deaths of two young men. One was found in the bottom of a ditch with an arrowhead in his ribs, and the other's body, similarly shot, had been covered over with a layer of loose chalk. Further north in Gloucestershire at Crickley Hill, another causewayed enclosure's encircling banks were

In 2010 I went to Orkney to work as a volunteer digger for archaeologist Nick Card who had been excavating a Neolithic village at the Ness of Brodgar in Orkney, west of the Ring of Brodgar. The buildings are very large, more like halls than domestic houses, and have well-preserved stone walls.

turned into fortifications in the same period; the positions of hundreds of flint arrowheads showed that the defended entrances had been attacked and that arrows had rained down upon the defenders.

Other enclosures further west, at Hembury in Devon and Carn Brea in Cornwall, may also have been attacked, and tombs in Dorset, Gloucestershire, Wiltshire, Somerset and south Wales contain many casualties of violence, with the skeletons bearing wounds caused by clubbing and shooting. It seems odd to think of areas such as Gloucestershire and Dorset as war zones but that is what they appear to have been in the fourth millennium BC. Such warfare was probably endemic in Neolithic society at that time but it might have had a regional and tribal dimension – the evidence for violence in this part of Britain is not matched elsewhere and it may indicate that these were borderlands where the western British fought the eastern British.

Towards the end of the fourth millennium BC, the evidence for violence drops away. At the same time, fashions of pottery and monument-building began to take on wider currencies. Cursus monuments were built from Scotland to the south coast. The use of a particular style of pottery decorated with impressed, abstract motifs (known as Peterborough Ware) extended from eastern England to Wales. After 3000 BC, people across Britain became ever more uniform in their tastes for pottery styles, funerary practices, domestic architecture and the new monumental forms of henges. The new pottery was Grooved Ware, with its flat-bottomed pots with external decoration. The new funerary practice involved cremation. Houses were now small and square rather than rectangular, and almost identical in form from Wessex to Orkney to Wales. Archaeologists have been used to looking beyond Britain for the origins of new styles. We know that farming had to be imported, so it is possible that subsequent forms of pottery and architecture were brought by later waves of immigrants. Yet it's clear that there are no Continental precursors for these material styles of the British Neolithic – they appear to be indigenous innovations within Britain. In fact, they represent a growing divide between Britain and the rest of Europe, manifestations of an essentially British way of life diverging from its European origins.

Certain of these innovations – Grooved Ware and henges – may have originated in Scotland, most likely in the islands of Orkney. By 2800 BC, Grooved Ware had spread to Wessex, as Britain's inhabitants enjoyed the first sharing of fashions across the entire land mass. Early archaeologists used to consider such uniformity of material culture as the product of a single tribe or ethnicity – were these the 'Grooved Ware people'? Given what we know about the likely diversity of their genetic ancestries, the people of Britain were anything but a single tribe. It's far more likely that the widespread sharing of material styles served to create a sense of unity for an ethnically diverse population. People could now travel the length and breadth of the land and feel 'at home' among people who had previously been strangers or even enemies with unfamiliar ways and habits.

The first stage of Stonehenge was built in that pivotal period around 3000 BC when this pan-island solidarity was gathering momentum. Within this wider context it's possible to understand how Stonehenge might have been designed as a monument for unity, embodying the spirit of the age. The designers of that first Stonehenge had big plans: it wasn't just a unification of people and places, drawing bluestones from an ancestral place of power in Wales, but also a unification of the entire cosmos – the earth, the sun and the moon.

Those who brought the stones from Wales were not simply laying claim to some good grazing land here on Salisbury Plain; they were also taking control of something akin to the *omphalos*, the navel of the world, or the birthplace of gods – the place where the movement of the sun was marked in the land. The work of moving the bluestones was not that of a small, devoted sect but entailed the mobilization of an entire society, possibly a growing political domain or kingdom.

If Stonehenge in its first phase, shortly after 3000 BC, was a monument to herald unity and unification in cosmic as well as human terms, its dramatic transformation around 2500 BC into the Stonehenge we see today with its huge megaliths may have had slightly different meanings. Its builders were making an even more grandiose gesture to mark this centre of the earth and heavens; the sarsens were even joined together to symbolise unification. Was the reworked Stonehenge a triumphal celebration of the actual attainment of political unity – no longer a vision but a reality? Or was this a moment when unity was threatened by the end of Britain's long isolation from the Continent, with the arrival of metalworking and the imminent immigration of the Beaker people? After 500 years, the site had also taken on an ancestral significance as a place of the revered dead commemorated by huge stones. Although megalith-building continued in various pockets around Britain on a smaller scale, Stonehenge was the last great stone monument of the megalithic age.

From earlier periods there are larger megaliths, both in Britain and northern France. In Pembrokeshire, south of Preseli, a collapsed portal dolmen at Garn Turne supports a massive capstone weighing about 60 tons;[33] it may actually have collapsed the tomb's chamber when it was hauled on top of it from its quarry about 100 metres away. Near the Yorkshire coast the Rudston monolith stands 7.6 metres high – more than half a metre higher than the top of Stonehenge's great trilithon – and was probably quarried ten miles away to the north.[34] All three are minnows in comparison to the Menhir Brisé at Locmariaquer in Brittany, which is 20.3 metres long and weighs perhaps 280 tons; it probably came from a quarry two miles away.[35] The Rudston monolith is undated but may well be Neolithic, given its location close to a group of cursuses, and the Menhir Brisé dates to probably more than a thousand years before Stonehenge.

Further afield, from around the same time as Stonehenge, the Cueva de Menga at Antequera in southern Spain is the largest megalithic tomb in Europe.[36] The biggest of its four huge capstones weighs an estimated 250 tons. Its lintelled entrance leads into a chamber in which the roof slabs are supported along the central axis on two dressed uprights. Although the large stones came from nearby, their massive size would have made them more difficult to move and lift into position than the Stonehenge sarsens.

The question that many people have asked is whether there was a link between the culture that built Stonehenge and the civilizations of the eastern Mediterranean and ancient Egypt. It was in 1956 that Richard Atkinson seriously proposed that there had been influences on Stonehenge from Mycenae and Minoan Crete, two ancient Greek civilizations. Ten years later, the journal *Antiquity* rejected as unsuitable for publication an academic paper entitled 'Wessex without Mycenae', written by Colin Renfrew, then a very young scholar and now one of Britain's most eminent archaeologists.[37]

Renfrew eventually published this paper, which turned out to be a crucial study of Stonehenge, in the rather obscure Annals of the British School at Athens. He demolished every claim that the building of Stonehenge was influenced by ancient Greece, and it's worth remembering that he worked out all the arguments at a time when radiocarbon dating was only in its infancy. Much later, in 1995, when high-precision radiocarbon dates were finally obtained for Stonehenge, Renfrew was proved completely right: Stonehenge is far older than Mycenae.

In spite of Renfrew's impeccable refutation of the Mycenae theory, we do still have to ask whether some distant civilization, flourishing at an earlier date, could have influenced the building of Stonehenge. It seems that many people are intrigued by the possibility of a link between Stonehenge and some other culture, being apparently reluctant to accept that a group of Stone Age British farmers could have come up with either the idea or the engineering skills without outside help. We therefore need to look at ancient Egypt (although I'm not going to waste any space discussing the 'built by aliens' nonsense).

The first of the three great pyramids of Giza, the pyramid of Khufu or Cheops, was built during the first half of the twenty-sixth century BC.[38] It would have been a brand-new, state-of-the-art structure when the sarsens went up at Stonehenge probably at the end of that century. Each pyramid at Giza had an associated mortuary temple that was connected by a causeway to a 'valley temple' beside the Nile. Although Stonehenge has nothing in common with the form of the Giza pyramids' construction, it does have a vague similarity to the architecture of the valley temple of Khafra (or Chephren), who reigned in the second half of the twenty-sixth century BC and built the second Giza pyramid. Although Khufu's valley temple can no longer be seen, Khafra's has a rectangular arrangement of pillars and lintels.

The arrangement of valley temple, linking causeway and mortuary temple (placed next to the pyramid) also strikes a faint chord with the relationship between Bluestonehenge, the avenue and Stonehenge. Unfortunately for the enthusiasts for 'foreign intervention' arguments, this slight similarity is entirely fortuitous. Construction at Stonehenge started long before the great pyramids were built, and the juxtaposition of Stonehenge and Bluestonehenge is probably many centuries earlier than Khufu's pyramid and valley temple. To claim any direct link is pushing interpretation of similarities much too far, especially in the total absence of any other evidence for contact between Britain and ancient Egypt at that date.

The Amesbury Archer's long-distance movement does, however, prove that some individuals travelled more than 400 miles in a lifetime. We cannot rule out the possibility of garbled stories about distant splendours passing from ear to ear over a distance of 2000 miles or more and over many lifetimes. Yet we shouldn't lose sight of the fact that Stonehenge and the contemporary wooden circles at Durrington Walls were built in geometrical styles whose ancestry was definitely British. There never were any Egyptian or Mediterranean missionaries, architects or builders.

Ultimately, we don't need to look for the source of the ideas behind

Stonehenge by going any further than Britain. Putting really big stones on top of each other had long been practiced, since the fourth millennium. All around western Britain the simple megalithic structures called portal dolmens were built hundreds of years before Stonehenge, around 3800 BC and after. In the case of Pentre Ifan in Preseli, the capstone, perched on three uprights, weighs around 16 tons.[39] Closer to Stonehenge, the long barrow of West Kennet near Avebury contains a stone chamber, built around 3650 BC, whose entrance consists of a large slab supported by upright sarsens.[40] Although access to West Kennet was blocked off around 2400 BC, constructions like these were visitable ancient monuments for Stonehenge's designers around 2500 BC.

It is possible that these old tombs provided food for thought for the Stonehenge builders. The only problem is that, having been built more than a thousand years earlier, their style would have been rather 'retro'. There might have been another, more current source of architectural ideas, albeit in another material. Josh has sometimes said that Stonehenge is our most impressive example of a timber circle. What he means by this curious (and at first glance contradictory) statement is that Stonehenge was built to look as if it were made of wood. The stonemasons used the techniques of wood-working, as archaeologists have known for decades. The dressing of the faces of the stones, the mortise-and-tenon joints, and the tongue-and-groove jointing of the lintels all derive from carpentry.

Neolithic builders would have been completely familiar with the appearance and construction of house doorways, in which a horizontal lintel rests on two upright jambs. In addition, they probably used lintels in monumental wooden architecture. Over the previous century or three, Neolithic people had been building timber circles throughout Britain and Ireland with regularly spaced uprights whose tops could have been spanned by wooden lintels.[41] We cannot prove that lintels were added to these timber circles, since we only ever see where the bases of the posts stood, but it seems more likely than not. Stonehenge was something of a *trompe l'oeil*, a timber circle made of stone.

The interiors of many timber circles had central posts arranged in a square. The Northern Circle and the Southern Circle at Durrington Walls are both good examples of this use of a square within a circle. The structure inside Coneybury henge is probably another, earlier example.[42] This format of a circle with an interior square arrangement can be found as far away as Ireland, where similar post circles are known at Ballynahatty near Belfast and at Knowth on the Bend in the Boyne near Dublin.[43]

Josh has also spotted that the houses at Durrington Walls have the opposite arrangement – a circle within a square. In domestic architecture, a circular hearth pit was set within a square-walled house with rounded corners. The two houses excavated by Julian Thomas within the western half of Durrington Walls are a variation on a theme. These had four interior postholes forming a square around the circular central hearth, as well as being enclosed within square walls. Both houses were enclosed by circular palisades.

Does this juxtaposition of circles and squares provide a clue for understanding why there was a horseshoe-shaped setting of five trilithons within the centre of Stonehenge? It is possible that the four shorter trilithons are a representation of the corners of a stylized house, in which the great trilithon is the doorway. The problem with this idea is that the trilithons' horseshoe arrangement is more of a curve than a square. We might also expect corners to be marked by single uprights rather than pairs.

Of course, not all houses were square in plan. The largest ones in southern Britain, around 12 to 13 metres by 11 metres, had D-shaped or horseshoe-shaped plans. Ephemeral traces of one of these D-shaped structures were found next to the Southern Circle at Durrington Walls in 1967, although at the time of excavation it was thought to be just a hollowed-out midden or rubbish heap. Another is located just inside the south entrance through the ditch at Stonehenge and was later covered by the South Barrow. Stonehenge's North Barrow may hide a third example. With no obvious hearth, these may have been public buildings or meeting houses.

Such D-shaped houses are known from one other location in Britain, from the charmingly named village of Upper Ninepence in Powys, Wales.[44] In 1994 archaeologist Alex Gibson was excavating a Bronze Age barrow near the village and discovered Neolithic remains preserved underneath this burial mound. Among the various pits were three semicircular settings of stakeholes. Alex was sure these had to be the remains of circular houses but there were no traces of stakeholes to form full circles despite the excellent preservation of the ground surface beneath the barrow. In hindsight, these structures can be interpreted as D-shaped houses. The two smaller ones had hearths but the largest, at 12 metres by 9 metres, had no fireplace. Radiocarbon dates put their construction in the period 2900–2500 BC, probably slightly earlier than the Durrington Walls D-shaped house.

The plan of the Durrington Walls D-shaped house, located next to the Southern Circle, can be fitted snugly within a horseshoe setting of ten large posts at the centre of the Southern Circle's second phase. Given that the D-shaped house probably belongs with the circle's first phase, it could have been the model for this horseshoe setting. This horseshoe of posts replaced an earlier square of posts at the centre of the circle. Thus the horseshoe setting in the Southern Circle may represent in monumental form the D-shaped meeting house, a new architectural design to replace the traditional format of a square of posts that repre-sented the rectangular domestic house. This would also explain the shape and size of the trilithon setting at Stonehenge, or at least its south-western arc formed by the great trilithon and its two neighbouring trilithons. Yet there is an additional form in which the D-shaped meet-ing house was represented monumentally.

Turning to Woodhenge, the arrangement here of six concentric rings of posts has conventionally been perceived as an oval. Even allow-ing for minor inaccuracies in excavator Maud Cunnington's plan, it is better understood as a pair of concentric semicircles of posts facing each other across the middle of the monument. Look carefully at the plan in Chapter 5 and it is apparent that the two half-circles do not meet precisely along the structure's northwest–southeast axis. The builders of the two halves also positioned the ramps of the largest post circle in two different ways. In the northeast D-shape, the posts were erected from ramps inside the semicircle. The southeast D-shape is dis-tinctly different because the posts were erected from outside the semicircle. Perhaps Woodhenge represents the joining of two monu-mental representations of the D-shaped house.

Such a 'double D' form is also found in the bluestone oval at the centre of Stonehenge. Although it, too, has been considered as an oval, it may in fact be formed of two semicircles. The clue to this is the position of one particular bluestone (Stone 61a), now reduced to a stump. It is off the line of a proper oval (which may explain why it is even some-

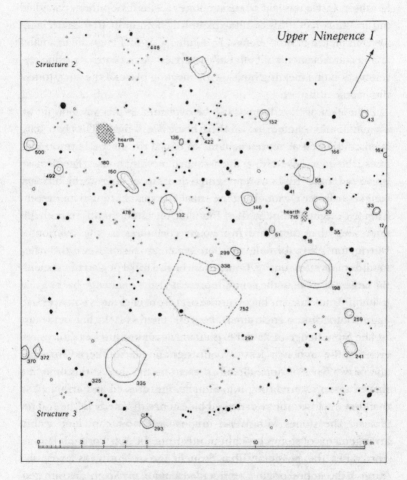

On this plan of the pits and stakeholes excavated by Alex Gibson at Upper Ninepence in Wales, one can trace the outlines of two D-shaped buildings. The larger (Structure 3) appears to have had no hearth; the smaller (Structure 2) does.

times left off plans of the bluestone oval) and lies at the intersection of the two semicircles formed by the two halves of the 'oval'.

We may conclude that Stonehenge incorporates constructional principles also found in the Southern Circle – the horseshoe plan of uprights – and from Woodhenge – the 'double D' plan. Since the Southern Circle was laid out using 'long feet' and Woodhenge was laid out in 'short feet', this could explain why both units of measurement were employed at Stonehenge. In summary, Stonehenge amalgamates architectural elements of both timber 'circles'. At its centre is a stone representation of a meeting house – the meeting place of the ancestors of the people of Britain.

If the plan of the trilithons can be explained in this way, how do we account for their lintels and for there being five of them? They have long been considered as representations of doorways, but we have no idea where the doorways were on the D-shaped meeting houses. People have wondered if the trilithons represented doors to another world, but they could equally have symbolized five tribal lineages charting their descent from five original households or founding ancestors. In this respect, it is interesting that there are five house enclosures in the interior of Durrington Walls, forming an approximate arc facing down the valley towards midwinter sunrise. Could these be five tribal or clan houses, with the largest of them in the centre represented at Stonehenge by the great trilithon? Unfortunately the otherwise neat arc of enclosures is not perfect, as the southernmost enclosure is about 100 metres off the line of the arc.

The Stonehenge of 2500 BC is an amalgam not just of features referencing the timber circles of Woodhenge and the Southern Circle, but also of two types of stone already present on the site. At this time, the shaped sarsens were brought to Stonehenge, dressed and arranged so that they enclosed the re-arranged bluestones (formerly in the Aubrey Holes). The stones with Welsh origins were now contained within arrangements of stones brought mostly from the Marlborough Downs. This raises the possibility that Stonehenge's identity, as expressed through the stones' origins, represented a union of two groups with geographically diverse ancestries – the people of the bluestones and the people of the sarsens.

One of the problems with which we've been wrestling at Durrington

Walls is why there were two wooden versions of Stonehenge – the Southern Circle and Woodhenge – and why Woodhenge was placed in a location marginal to the Southern Circle and its avenue. We did think that the two timber circles might have been built and used at different times, with Woodhenge replacing the Southern Circle, but the dates of the two structures suggest that this is not a good explanation. Although Woodhenge's henge ditch was not dug until 2400–2280 BC, the person whose cremated bones were buried in hole C14 of Woodhenge died around the same time as the Southern Circle was constructed, more than a century earlier.

Josh has noticed that the timber structures he excavated immediately south of Woodhenge are different in plan to the post settings within the house enclosures and of the Northern Circle within Durrington Walls. Instead of having circular perimeters, the structures south of Woodhenge are oval and slightly irregular. The holes for the large central posts in the structures south of Woodhenge are also anomalous; although they are the same size as other large posts at Durrington Walls, they have no ramps with which to ease the posts into their holes.

Perhaps the two groups of timber monuments – the Woodhenge set and the Durrington Walls set – were constructed by two different groups of people. If so, there may be a clue as to which group was which. The sarsens that stood along the Durrington avenue may be associated with the Southern Circle, showing a local ancestry for the builders and users of these sites. One of the stoneholes at Woodhenge probably held a bluestone rather than a sarsen, so perhaps the Woodhenge complex of structures indicates an association with Welsh ancestry for a second, separate group of people. There is no way of knowing for sure but we should learn more in the coming years from aspects such as the origins of the cattle brought to Durrington Walls and Woodhenge.

We now know a lot more about Stonehenge. We know that it was a place of burial for a long period of its use, that it was built on the end of a geological feature coincidentally aligned on the solstice axis, and that its first two stages date to around 3000 BC and 2500 BC. Around the same time as that second stage of construction, when the trilithons and then the sarsen circle were erected, people were building comparable circles in timber at Durrington Walls, within a large settlement to which people and their herds came from many miles away for seasonal feasting in winter and summer. While Stonehenge was a place for the dead, Durrington Walls was occupied by the living, whose houses reveal many aspects of their daily lives. This short-lived and seasonal settlement may well have been the builders' camp for Stonehenge.

Ultimately, the Stonehenge of 2500 BC is unique, without any evident predecessors in northern Europe. But could the people of Neolithic Wessex have built it without outside help? Previous generations of archaeologists, including Richard Atkinson, had a pretty low opinion of the Stonehenge people. As far as Atkinson was concerned, 'these men were essentially barbarians'.[45] Since this society had no architecture (as distinct from mere construction), he claimed, they would not have been able to build Stonehenge without the assistance of a superior civilization. A lot has happened since 1956 and our knowledge of these 'barbarians' and their abilities has mushroomed. Atkinson knew very little about the sophisticated timber architecture of the many British henge complexes, since most of them have been found since his time. He also belonged to an era when people talked about 'primitive societies' rather than 'societies with primitive technologies'.

Stonehenge's architectural plan and design owe nothing to very distant lands and cultures. Yet the scale of moving, shaping and lifting its sarsens puts it in a league of its own, beyond anything else in Britain at that time. Only Avebury comes close but even that major achievement in stone lacks the elements of dressing uprights and raising lintels.

THE END OF STONEHENGE

Stonehenge is not one monument, built at one moment in history, but many monuments built over many centuries. To try to study the stone circle in isolation is to be doomed to failure and error. Understanding Stonehenge requires knowledge of the Early Mesolithic use of Salisbury Plain, the subsequent arrival of farming communities there as well as across Britain, and the wider developments in Late Neolithic society.

Long-distance patterns of mobility and trade, and widespread architectural developments and funerary customs are an essential key to making sense of the development of the first Stonehenge as a stone circle and cremation cemetery. Understanding its transformation around 2500 BC requires knowledge of its landscape context, to grasp how it formed part of a larger complex centred on the River Avon. We can also now consider the social and economic forces that led to Stonehenge's decline.

Before doing so, it is worth summarizing how the discoveries of the Stonehenge Riverside Project have changed the way that we think about Stonehenge.

- Firstly, we now have several instances where prehistoric people adapted pre-existing natural features into their cultural designs. The most significant of these is the series of three chalk ridges aligned by geological accident on the midsummer sunrise/midwinter sunset axis. On top of these, Neolithic people constructed the first stretch of the Stonehenge avenue. This natural landform's solstitial alignment, on the end of which Stonehenge was constructed just after 3000 BC, seems to have set the blueprint for solstitial alignments in the monuments of the immediate locality, not only at Stonehenge but at four of the timber circles at Durrington Walls and Woodhenge as well. It's interesting that no certain solstitial alignments have been identified at the other great henges of Wessex, such as Avebury, Marden or Dorchester. Maybe this was a particular feature of celebrations at Stonehenge.

- Stonehenge was inspired by fashions of building monuments and houses locally within Britain, not by distant civilizations in the Mediterranean. Its first two stages were, in fact, constructed during a period of cultural isolation from the Continent, when the people of Britain were increasingly unified by sharing pan-island styles of material culture (pots, houses, burial practices) despite their diverse genetic ancestries. Stonehenge can be understood as a monument of unification, integrating the cosmological aspects of earth, sun and moon into a single entity which also united the ancestors of the people of Britain in the form of Welsh bluestones and English sarsens.

- The Durrington Walls avenue is a Neolithic structure whose existence was entirely unknown and unsuspected. We went out to look for it on the basis of a theory, not because of any evidence on the ground. Not only does the newly discovered Durrington avenue link the Southern Circle to the River Avon but this solstice-aligned feature also sits on top of a natural precursor, in this case a geologically formed surface of broken flint that had collected in the bottom of the valley. The Durrington Walls avenue's midsummer sunset orientation provides a counterpoint to the Stonehenge avenue's midsummer sunrise axis, while the Southern Circle's view towards midwinter sunrise contrasts with Stonehenge's midwinter sunset axis.

- What started as a hypothesis – that Durrington Walls was a place of the living – has now become something we recognize as fact. When we started work nobody knew that Durrington Walls was a Neolithic settlement. We found evidence for a large village, with the remains of many houses being well-preserved beneath the henge banks. The discovery of just three human bones among 80,000 animal bones found at Durrington shows that the activities that took place here were the complete opposite of what was happening at Stonehenge, where the bones of *Homo sapiens* are more common than those of any other species.

- Our identification of Stonehenge as a place of the dead has also been confirmed, not only by dating some of its sixty-three cremation burials to show that they span the monument's use during the third millennium BC but also by showing how Stonehenge started not as a unique site but rather as one of several enclosed cremation cemeteries well known across Britain.

- The animal bones from Durrington Walls and the lipids from within the pots point to midwinter and summertime gatherings, suggesting that the solstitial and lunar alignments at Stonehenge are not part of an abstract astronomical calendar but marked key moments of the year when people gathered here and celebrated.

- Within Stonehenge, the identification of mistakes made by Richard Atkinson has enabled us to refine the monument's chronology and phasing. Drawing from the analysis of existing records and from Tim Darvill and Geoff Wainwright's new excavation results, we can place the sarsen trilithons, bluestone Q and R Holes and sarsen circle in a single phase. We can also date that stage to around 2500 BC, about 500 years after the initial construction. In that initial stage, we can now confidently place the Aubrey Holes and identify them as stoneholes for bluestone monoliths.

- Our review of old excavations at Durrington Walls and Stonehenge has identified a previously unrecognized type of Neolithic building with a D-shaped or horseshoe-shaped plan. These large houses were probably for public gatherings. Their D-shaped plan formed the model for the central settings of the Southern Circle's Phase 2 and the Stonehenge trilithons. Woodhenge and Stonehenge's bluestone oval appear to be modelled on face-to-face pairings of opposed D-shaped structures.

- Finally, down by the River Avon, at the end of the Stonehenge avenue at West Amesbury, we have found a previously unknown henge. Its small circle contained about twenty-five bluestones that were removed around 2400 BC, perhaps to be taken to Stonehenge. Just when this

stone circle was constructed is not certain but it was well before 2500
BC. The discovery of Bluestonehenge, together with new timber monuments upstream south of Woodhenge, has established the central
importance of this stretch of the Avon.

By 2500 BC, the Avon had come to link two separate but contemporary
monument clusters, each with an avenue leading to and from the river.
Upstream to the northeast were the timber circles of Durrington Walls,
surrounded by the houses of the living. Downstream to the southwest
were the stone circles of Stonehenge and Bluestonehenge, set within an
area largely or entirely devoid of settlement.

Just what happened in the next few centuries after 2500 BC is of crucial importance for understanding the decline of Stonehenge, or rather
the decline of the Stonehenge–Durrington Walls complex. One of the
big problems we face in trying to understand the changes is how to date
events within the period 2470–2280 BC. The calibration curve flattens
out at this point in time, so it is generally impossible to get a single date
any more precise than this broad 190-year period. This makes understanding this period – the Copper Age, or transition from the Neolithic
to the Bronze Age –very difficult: although we know a lot happened, we
cannot be certain of the order in which it happened. It's the equivalent
of trying to work out the sequence of events of the last two centuries
without knowing any precise dates.

In a rare instance, it is possible to be more precise. Where we have a
stratigraphic sequence of dated layers, we can apply Bayesian statistics to
narrow the probable date range. This has been achieved for Silbury Hill,
at Avebury, with its construction now dated to within fifty years either
side of 2400 BC.[1] We still don't know what this giant mound was for but
we do know when it was built.

The biggest event after 2470 BC was the arrival of the Beaker people
and the gradual increase in their numbers. Beaker pottery may have
been in use in Britain before this date but the distinctive burial rite in
which a Beaker accompanied the corpse did not appear until after 2470
BC. Similarly, copper metallurgy might have arrived before the Beaker
burial tradition; many such burials contain equipment for working gold
as well as copper. A Beaker in a grave at Ashgrove in Scotland contained

pollen indicative of a mead-like drink;[2] archaeologists have thought that the Beaker people also introduced alcohol to Britain, although it was probably already widely in use in the form of beer and possibly cider. So far, the earliest bones of domesticated horses in Britain are from the Beaker period,[3] so these people may have introduced horse-riding. They certainly brought entirely new attitudes to monuments and to the dead.

The Beaker people came from parts of continental Europe – the Rhine valley from the Netherlands to the Alps – that had no traditions of large-scale monument-building. There are a few small standing stones and stone monuments from Switzerland and the Alps during the third millennium BC but they are on nowhere near the same scale as Stonehenge, Avebury and the many other monuments found in Britain. The Beaker people brought to Britain a new funerary rite, burying the dead in graves within small cemeteries. There was no strong sense of separating the dead from the living in a geographical or topographical sense. The living might occupy the same spaces as the dead, except that the dead were below the ground.

The Beaker people were similar in economic lifestyle to the indigenous population of Britain, being semi-mobile cattle pastoralists and cereal cultivators. It's likely that indigenous Britons adopted the new way of life from a small number of immigrants, learning to make the fine Beaker pots and acquiring the new trinkets in gold and copper, adorning themselves with these and other personal ornaments.

Monuments were still built during this period, but they seem to have been something of a swan-song, or a final attempt at a statement of power. At Stonehenge, a large and unexplained pit was dug against the inside edge of the great trilithon and was then filled back in. Its avenue ditches and banks were constructed, while Bluestonehenge was dismantled and enclosed within a henge ditch. Woodhenge's decaying posts were enclosed within a henge ditch at this time. At Durrington Walls the avenue continued in use but the henge ditch was constructed over the ruins of the village by 2460 BC. The Southern Circle's timbers decayed, and pits were dug into them around or after 2300 BC. All of these pits, ditches and boundaries give a sense that these places were being cut off and closed down, marked as separate from everyday life.

Most of the Avebury monuments are not closely dated but the two events in that area that definitely fall within this period of the Copper Age at the very end of the Neolithic are the building of Silbury Hill around 2400 BC and the blocking with large sarsen slabs of the entrance to the filled-in chamber of West Kennet long barrow. The settlement at the West Kennet palisade enclosures might also have been occupied in this period. Building Silbury was a massive project, moving many thousands of tons of chalk from huge quarries around the base of the hill. Back in 1967 when Richard Atkinson excavated a shaft into the centre of the mound, the scale of its building was compared to every person living in the UK in the 1960s each carrying a bucket of chalk.

Elsewhere in Britain, some monuments were modified. One example of such re-modelling is a long barrow at Skendleby in north Lincolnshire whose ditches were re-dug in this period, many hundreds of years after the barrow was first constructed, and its mound rebuilt.[4] Otherwise, there was no great funerary monument-building. The early Beaker burials were not marked by round barrows; these did not appear until after the start of the Bronze Age in 2200 BC.

Britain was open to new influences from the Continent. Things were done differently there – no overlords told the people how much earth to move or how many stones to lift. Personal identity was emphasized and expressed through the wearing of ornaments by both men and women. The dead were still treated with ceremony but in ways that quickly removed them from the living; they were no longer a constant presence. The old regime was in danger of being undermined and, ultimately, it would fall. Rather like Saddam Hussein's Iraq, the greatest monumental spectacles preceded the regime's demise. Silbury Hill was that last great monument. After that, no one had the will or ability to work for the authorities on any grand scale.

By 2000 BC the world of Stonehenge had changed. The avenue ditches had been cleaned out and the bluestones rearranged in an outer bluestone circle and an inner bluestone oval. This would be the last time that any stones were moved until stone-robbers came to dismantle the structure. Activities had largely ceased on the other Wessex henges. At Mount Pleasant, however, the henge's interior was enclosed within a huge palisade wall of timber posts around 2100 BC.[5] Whether the single entrance through this palisade led into a ceremonial space or whether this was a fortification is unknown. One or more of the West Kennet palisaded enclosures might also have been occupied around this time.

By now, monument-building had picked up but in a quite different form. From 2200 BC, round barrows started to appear across the landscapes of Britain. Particular concentrations have been noted around the great henges of Wessex, and today more than 350 of these Bronze Age burial mounds are protected within the Stonehenge World Heritage Site alone. Between 2200 and 1500 BC both sides of the River Avon, in an area centred on Durrington Walls, were covered with more than 1000 round barrows. The only locations left empty were the 'envelope' around Stonehenge (though not entirely so) and the ridge of hills that includes Beacon Hill. Whether these were too sacred to occupy is anyone's guess.

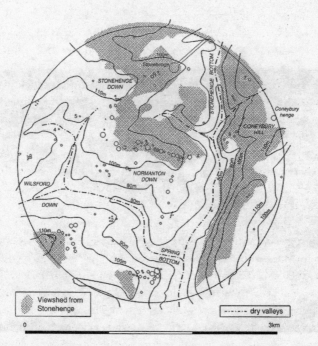

Visible from Stonehenge to its south are the Early Bronze Age round barrows on Normanton Down, including the rich burial under Bush Barrow. A viewshed is those areas of landscape visible from any particular point, in this case Stonehenge.

These round barrows were monuments on a much more personal scale. People were now building only for their own family's ancestors. To construct an average-sized round barrow would have needed only the labour of the extended family of a small lineage. If any one of us were to assemble all the descendants of one great-grandfather, such a group would be easily big enough to build a round barrow. Even so, the work would have been hard and must have taken months. During one of our excavation seasons, we took a day off to visit a team from Bournemouth University excavating a round barrow near Cranborne Chase. Using a team of around twenty diggers over three summer seasons, their director John Gale has meticulously unpicked the entire construction

John Gale's team of Bournemouth University students excavating a round barrow at High Lea Farm, Dorset in 2008. The central baulk preserves the last remnants of the turf which once formed the mound, capped by chalk from the ditch.

sequence.[6] To put it in 'rewind' gives us some idea of the scale of the process.

The building of this Cranborne Chase barrow began with the erection of a circular wooden fence around the chosen spot for the grave. Other fences were erected around this in a series of concentric rings. Then the grave was dug out and the cremated bones were buried within a Collared Urn. John Gale has so far found no trace of the site of the funeral pyre itself. The grave was filled in but some or all of the soil for this was brought from elsewhere, leaving the chalk that originally came from the hole lying around it on the surface.

The hardest job of all then began. Turfs were cut from surrounding grassland, presumably with antler picks, and then piled up to form a mound 30 metres in diameter, centred on the grave. This tedious and difficult labour must have hurt, physically, emotionally and economically. Perfectly good grassland for the herds was being removed; the area of ground stripped of its turf was thereby taken out of productive use for years afterwards. Some of the denuded area could later have been ploughed up but no evidence has been found for this.

Finally, a circular ditch just over 1.5 metres deep and 30 metres in diameter was dug around the perimeter of the turf mound. This ditch was deep and wide enough to prevent any casual visitor from climbing on to the barrow, which was now capped with a layer of gleaming white chalk. This reversed world – in which grass lay beneath chalk – was separated from the everyday world by this ditch with no entrances.

Not everybody who died between 2200–1500 BC was buried under a round barrow, though it clearly became the fashionable style for those who had enough land to provide the turf, enough family to provide the labour and a big enough food surplus to feed the numbers needed to build the mound and dig its ditch. There was a wealth divide, also apparent in the grave goods, and it started widening. By 1900 BC some burials were lavishly equipped – notably those within the barrow cemetery of Normanton Down, overlooking Stonehenge from the south. The most dramatic of these 'rich burials' is the man buried beneath Bush Barrow.[7] Other men and women buried in nearby barrows were also provided with ornaments of gold, amber and jet.

Similarly 'rich' graves have been found all over Wessex. In 1938, Stuart

Piggott declared them to be the Wessex Culture, a group of aristocratic burials centred on Wessex but with outliers in East Anglia, and also occurring elsewhere in England, Wales, Scotland and Brittany.[8] The name has stuck and these barrows appear to have been a first wave of fancy burials. As a result they are known as 'Wessex I', to distinguish them from a later sequence of burials (around 1700–1500 BC) known as 'Wessex II'. We have recently obtained the first radiocarbon date for a Wessex I burial and it confirms the date as being around 1900 BC.[9] By now, Stonehenge's stones had received their final modification.

We will never know just how much gold was owned by the families burying these individuals in the Wessex I barrows but, given the amounts that they could evidently afford to leave in the ground with the corpse, it is likely to have been a lot. To get an idea of the quantities of gold in circulation by this time, it's worth visiting the National Museum of Ireland in Dublin. Five minutes in the 'gold hall', packed with Bronze Age gold ornaments, is enough to get an impression of the sheer scale of Bronze Age bling.

With no Bronze Age banks or safety-deposit boxes, this jewellery must have been worn more frequently than just on special occasions. These people wanted to show off their wealth. Burying this amount of gold-work with a dead relative was an extraordinarily ostentatious thing to do; the people who arranged these funerals were able to show that they were so rich that they could easily spare large quantities of gold.

Overall, the picture we have of Stonehenge's decline suggests a gradual process. It appears to have ended not with a bang but with a whimper. Even though the main construction work had finished by the time that the Amesbury Archer and his fellow immigrants arrived in Britain, Stonehenge remained a focus for them, as demonstrated by the hundreds of Beaker pottery sherds from in and around the monument. Yet the area in which it stood was now treated very differently. The hitherto empty space on all sides of Stonehenge, especially north of the stone circle and south of the Cursus, started to fill with burials and settlements. Beaker sherds from small temporary settlements have been found in many areas around Stonehenge, particularly the enigmatic Beaker-period North Kite enclosure and further north next to the Fargo bluestone scatter.

As communal public-works projects tailed off in Wessex, ceasing with
the construction of Silbury Hill around 2400 BC, Stonehenge was no
longer at the centre of the people's world – or, rather, their afterworld.
The dead remained just as important as they ever were, except that the

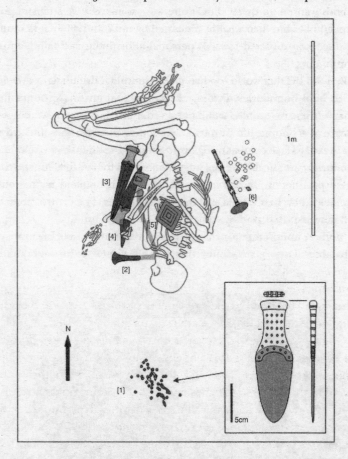

Bush Barrow was excavated by Richard Colt Hoare in 1808. A plan of this Early Bronze
Age grave, dating to about 1900 BC, has been reconstructed by Stuart Needham and
colleagues from Hoare's description of where the many grave goods lay in relation to
the skeleton. The objects include bronze studs from the handle of a dagger or knife (1),
a bronze axe (2), a pair of bronze daggers and a gold belt-hook (3), a small bronze
dagger (4), a gold lozenge (5), and a stone macehead and its bone and gold fittings (6).

focus was now on family and close kin. By 2000 BC the fashion for monument-building had returned but it was now channelled towards the
family-sized round barrows. Perhaps nobody could recruit the labour any
more for building on the scale of Stonehenge or Silbury Hill, or perhaps
nobody wanted to. By 1900 BC there were some very wealthy and powerful families but their wealth, generated by cattle and other agricultural
produce, was directed towards personal adornment and family burial
monuments.

By 1500 BC that world too had gone. Southern Britain was parcelled
up by land boundaries dividing the communal grazing grounds into
plots.[10] Intensive arable farming and sedentary farmsteads were now a
feature of economic life. Disputes were settled not with bows and arrows
but in face-to-face combat using bronze rapiers, leather shields and body
armour. Economically, Wessex was out-matched for soil fertility, and thus
cereal production, by the farmlands of eastern England in the lower
Thames valley, East Anglia and the east Midlands. The centre of wealth
and power shifted, and Stonehenge was left high and dry.

Just how important Stonehenge remained for the rest of prehistory is
debatable. There's no doubt that people visited it throughout the

Silbury Hill has been excavated twice in modern times, by Atkinson in 1968–1970
and by English Heritage in 2007–2008. It dates to 2490–2340 BC, broadly
contemporary with Stage 3 at Stonehenge.

following millennia, judging by the sherds of pottery from the Bronze Age, Iron Age and later. Just over a mile to the east, the construction of a hillfort called Vespasian's Camp (though it has absolutely nothing to do with Claudius' general Vespasian who invaded Britain in AD 43) shows that this landscape was occupied and farmed in the Iron Age (750 BC–AD 43). Durrington Walls too was being used at this time, being the site of a large agricultural settlement during the Iron Age. This brings us to another disputed interpretation of Stonehenge: that it was internationally renowned during the Iron Age.

In the first century BC the Roman historian Diodorus Siculus (Diodorus of Sicily) recorded in Book II of his *Library of History* that, on an island in the far north of Europe in the land of the Hyperboreans, there was a temple where the god Apollo was said to reside during the summer months, returning to his temple at Delphi for the rest of the year. The Hyperborean temple was associated, he said, with the vernal equinox and the Pleiades constellation. He obtained this story from a late-fourth-century BC writer Hecateus of Abdera, who, in turn, had found it in the writings of the Greek seafarer and explorer Pytheas of Marseilles. Diodorus described this building as 'a temple of a spherical form', which has been taken to mean a round temple.

Even if we discount the possibility that Diodorus was referring to one of any number of circular Iron Age wooden structures in Britain or Ireland – and we have no idea how many might still remain to be discovered – the prehistorian Aubrey Burl has highlighted an important reason why this temple could not have been Stonehenge. According to Diodorus, the moon as viewed from the island in question appears closer to the earth.[11] Burl points out that, if this was an attempt to describe a particular astronomical phenomenon, it cannot be a description of southern Britain. Rather, Diodorus may be describing a lunar phenomenon that can only be seen much further north, at 58° north, at least 500 miles from Salisbury Plain. Burl thinks that the temple in question is the Neolithic stone circle at Calanais on the Isle of Lewis in the Outer Hebrides.

If we discount Diodorus' story as having nothing to do with Stonehenge, as I think we should, Stonehenge's first appearance in written records was in AD 1129. In his *Historia Anglorum*, Henry of Huntingdon, archdeacon of Huntingdon in the diocese of Lincoln, described Stonehenge as one of four wonders of Britain. Of it, he wrote, 'no one has been able to discover by what mechanism such vast masses of stone were elevated, nor for what purpose they were designed.'[12]

For nearly 900 years people have puzzled over the same questions. Stonehenge still keeps many of its secrets but we now know a little more about when, how and why it was built. Although further excavation at Stonehenge itself is unlikely in the near future, new survey and excavation projects in the area – some already underway – will continue to add to our knowledge in years to come. It seems perverse that Stonehenge has become a focus of conflict and disagreement when the purpose of its construction was to symbolize social unity and cultural cohesion.

NOTES

CHAPTER 1

1 Wim van Es, cited in Bakker 1999: 9.

CHAPTER 2

1 Cleal *et al.* 1995: 154–5, 451–61.
2 Wainwright with Longworth 1971.
3 Cleal *et al.* 1995: 291–329.
4 Burl 2002; Gillings *et al.* 2008; Pollard and Gillings 2004.
5 Whittle 1997a.
6 Parker Pearson and Ramilisonina 1998a.
7 Durrani 2009.
8 Flinders Petrie 1880: 31.
9 Evans 1885.
10 Burl 1987.
11 Bender 1998; Whittle 1997b.
12 Barrett and Fewster 1998; Whitley 2002.
13 Parker Pearson and Ramilisonina 1998b.
14 Spindler 1995; Walton and Wild 1990.
15 Barker 2009.
16 Larson *et al.* 2007; Edwards *et al.* 2010.
17 Whittle and Cummings 2007.
18 Sykes 2006; Oppenheimer 2006.
19 Haak *et al.* 2005; Zvelebil and Pettitt 2008.
20 Sykes 2006: 330; Oppenheimer 2006: 243.
21 Sahlins 1972.a
22 Sheridan 2003; 2004.
23 Sheridan 2010.
24 Hammond 2009.
25 Coles and Coles 1986.
26 Cleal *et al.* 1995: 188–90, 441, 522.
27 Richards 1990: 40–61.

CHAPTER 3

1 Burl 2006: 42–9.
2 Field *et al.* 2010.
3 Cleal *et al.* 1995: plan 1.
4 Burl 2006: 42.
5 Stukeley 1740.
6 Stukeley 1724: 67, cited in Burl 2006: 45.
7 Burl 2006: 47.
8 Chippindale 1994: 161.
9 Flinders Petrie 1880.
10 Darwin 1881: 154–6.
11 Gowland 1902.
12 Chippindale 1994: 176.
13 Hawley 1921; 1922; 1923; 1924; 1925; 1926; 1928.
14 Atkinson 1956.
15 Hawley 1928.
16 Cleal *et al.* 1995: table 2.
17 Atkinson 1946.
18 Atkinson 1956; 1979.
19 Atkinson 1979: 196.
20 Atkinson 1956.
21 Pitts 1982.
22 Cleal *et al.* 1995: 270–1.
23 Pitts 2008.
24 Cleal *et al.* 1995.
25 Chippindale 1994: 139–40.
26 Hawkins with White 1965.
27 Hoyle 1977.
28 North 1996.
29 Thom 1967.
30 Thom *et al.* 1974.
31 Ruggles 1997; Pollard and Ruggles 2001.

CHAPTER 4

1 Richards 2005.
2 Childe 1931.
3 Wainwright with Longworth 1971.
4 Cleal and MacSween 1999.
5 Thomas 1999.
6 Wainwright with Longworth 1971.
7 Richards and Thomas 1984.
8 Tilley 1994.
9 Gillings *et al.* 2008.

10 Cunnington 1931.
11 Leary and Field 2010.
12 Schulting and Wysocki 2005.
13 Mercer 1999.
14 Passmore 1942.
15 Teather 2007.

CHAPTER 5

1 Reynolds 1977.
2 Wainwright with Longworth 1971: 41–4.
3 *Ibid.*: 23–38.
4 *Ibid.*: 38–41.
5 Cunnington 1929.
6 Pollard 1995a.

CHAPTER 6

1 Gibson 1998a.
2 Richards 1990: 40–61.
3 Atkinson 1956: 14–16.
4 Richards 2005.
5 Richards 1991.
6 Parker Pearson 2005: 63.
7 Gibson 2008.
8 Farrer 1918.
9 Stone *et al.* 1954.
10 Wainwright with Longworth 1971: 14–18.
11 *Ibid.*: 19–21.
12 *Ibid.*: 21.
13 *Ibid.*: figs 6–8.
14 *Ibid.*: 38–41.
15 Richards 2005; 2010.
16 Hawley 1923: 14–15.
17 Parker Pearson *et al.* 2009.

CHAPTER 7

1 Parker Pearson 2007; Thomas 2007.
2 Booth and Stone 1952.
3 Thom and Thom 1974. This small mound is located at OS grid reference 14334 43967.
4 Buck *et al.* 1996.

5 Stone *et al.* 1954.

6 Parker Pearson *et al.* 2009: table 3.

7 Wainwright with Longworth 1971: 22.

8 Cleal *et al.* 2004.

9 Mukherjee 2004; Mukherjee *et al.* 2008.

10 Jay and Richards 2007; Mahoney 2007; Montgomery *et al.* 2007.

11 Parker Pearson *et al.* 2009: table 3.

12 Albarella and Serjeantson 2002.

13 Viner *et al.* 2010.

14 Cleal *et al.* 2004.

15 Parker Pearson 2003.

16 Entwistle and Grant 1989.

17 Jones and Rowley-Conwy 2007.

18 Wainwright with Longworth 1971: 156–81.

19 Allen *et al.* 2011.

20 Parker Pearson 2008.

21 Gibson 1998b: fig. 6.6.

CHAPTER 8

1 Atkinson 1979: 207.

2 Parker Pearson *et al.* 2007.

CHAPTER 9

1 Richards 1990.

2 Vatcher and Vatcher 1973.

3 Cleal *et al.* 1995: 43–7.

4 Kenyon 1957.

5 Schmidt 2005.

6 Lawson 2007: 50–60.

7 *Ibid.*: 62–7.

8 Mercer and Healey 2008; Whittle *et al.* 1999.

9 Farrer 1917.

10 Stone 1947.

11 Christie 1963.

12 Richards 1990: 93–6.

13 *Ibid.*: 72–93.

14 Thomas *et al.* 2009.

15 Richards 1990: 96–109.

16 Barclay and Harding 1999.

17 Green 2000: 57–63.

18 Stone 1947: 19.

19 Thurnham 1869.

20 Burl 2006: 92–3.
21 Bowen and Smith 1977.
22 Johnson 2008: fig. 62.
23 Parker Pearson 1999.
24 Annable and Simpson 1964: 49–50, 104.

CHAPTER 10

1 Hunter-Mann 1999; Jacques 2010.
2 Metcalf and Huntington 1991.
3 Parker Pearson *et al.* 2010: 29–41.
4 Stone 1935.
5 Green 2000: 70; Rosamund Cleal pers. comm.
6 Stone and Young 1948.
7 Stone 1949.
8 Parker Pearson 2007.
9 Wainwright with Longworth 1971: 235–306.
10 Cunnington 1929.
11 Pollard 1995b.
12 Parker Pearson *et al.* 2009.
13 Scaife in Cleal *et al.* 2004.
14 Allen 1997.

CHAPTER 11

1 Darvill and Wainwright 2002; Darvill *et al.* 2003; 2004; 2005.
2 Darvill and Wainwright 2009.
3 Richards 1990.
4 Pitts 1982.
5 Young 1935a.
6 Darvill and Wainwright 2009.
7 Cleal *et al.* 1995: fig. 85.
8 Atkinson 1956: 46–50.
9 Atkinson 1956: 63.
10 Richardson 1988.
11 Sayer 2010.
12 Thackray and Payne 2010.
13 Piggott 1968.
14 Julius Caesar [1951].
15 Field and Parker Pearson 2004: 144–8.
16 *Ibid.*: 31–3.
17 Ross 1999.
18 Tierney 1960.
19 Tacitus [2003]. *Annals*, Book 14: 30.

20 Pliny the Elder [1945]. *Natural History, Librum XVI.*
21 Parker Pearson *et al.* 2009; Pitts *et al.* 2002.

CHAPTER 12

1 Atkinson *et al.* 1951.
2 Atkinson 1956: 13.
3 Hawley 1921: 30–1.
4 Hawley 1928: 156.
5 Parker Pearson *et al.* 2009: fig. 8.
6 Cleal *et al.* 1995: fig. 55; Parker Pearson *et al.* 2009: fig. 4.
7 Parker Pearson *et al.* 2009: table 2.

CHAPTER 13

1 McKinley 1993; 1994; 1997; 2000; McKinley and Bond 2001.
2 Atkinson 1956: 49.
3 Cleal *et al.* 1995: 101, fig. 55.
4 Cleal *et al.* 1995: tables 57 and 58.
5 Thomas 1999: 131–51.
6 Metcalf and Huntington 1991: 33–5.
7 Whittle *et al.* 2007.
8 Kinnes 1979.
9 Gibson and Bayliss 2009.
10 Healey 1997; Barclay *et al.* 2009; Stephany Leach pers. comm. (North End Pot).
11 Needham 2005.
12 Evans 1984.
13 Woodward and Woodward 1996.
14 Cunnington 1929.
15 Cleal *et al.* 1995: 437–51.
16 *Ibid.*: 421–2.
17 *Ibid.*: table 64.

CHAPTER 14

1 Roberts and Cox 2003.
2 Lanting and Brindley 1998.
3 Montgomery *et al.* 2000; Richards *et al.* 2003.
4 Cleal *et al.* 1995: 456.
5 Hawley 1924: 33; Cleal *et al.* 1995: table 57.
6 Roberts and Cox 2003.
7 Van der Sanden 1996.

8 Atkinson *et al.* 1951; Healy 1997; Lynch and Musson 2004; Piggott 1948b; West 1990.
9 Roe 1968; 1979.
10 Fenwick 1995.
11 Colt Hoare 1812; Needham *et al.* 2010.
12 Needham *et al.* 2010: 2.
13 Cleal *et al.* 1995: 360–1.
14 Parker Pearson *et al.* 2010: 426–8.
15 Carr 1995; Tainter 1978.
16 Parker Pearson 2006.
17 Case 2004; Gibson 2007.
18 Thurnham 1863.
19 Clarke 1976; Mercer 1977.
20 Harrison 1980.
21 Muller and van Willigen 2001.
22 Barclay and Halpin 1998.
23 Burgess and Shennan 1976.
24 Brodie 1994.
25 Fitzpatrick 2002.
26 Evans *et al.* 2006.
27 Jay *et al.* 2011.
28 Mahoney 2007.
29 Šoberl *et al.* 2009.
30 Smith and Brickley 2009.
31 Roberts and Cox 2003.

CHAPTER 15

1 Crawford 1924.
2 Earthwork survey carried out by Desmond Bonney, and later by Carenza Lewis, of the former Royal Commission on Historic Monuments for England (subsequently assimilated into English Heritage).
3 Smith 1973.
4 Richards 1990: 123–58.
5 Harding 1988.
6 Richards 1990: 109–23.
7 *Ibid.*: 184–92.

CHAPTER 16

1 Leivers and Moore 2008.
2 Woodward and Woodward 1996.
3 Richards 1990: figs 12–14.
4 Cleal *et al.* 1995: 154–61.

5 Whittle 1997a.
6 Richards 1990: fig. 2.
7 Cleal *et al.* 1995: 356–9.
8 *Ibid.*: 301, 309–11.
9 Evans 1984.
10 Cleal and Allen 1994.
11 Newall's Mound is not to be confused with Peter's Mound (named after the astronomer 'Peter' Newham) on Larkhill.
12 Bradley 2000.
13 Young 1935b; Vatcher and Vatcher 1973.
14 Pitts 1982.
15 Stukeley 1724: 43.
16 Atkinson 1956: 39, 42; Cleal *et al.* 1995: fig. 15.
17 Jones 1655.
18 Stukeley 1740; Piggott 1985.
19 Flinders Petrie 1880.
20 Thom and Thom 1988.
21 Johnson 2008: 186–250.
22 Hill 2008.
23 Chamberlain and Parker Pearson 2007.
24 Michell 1981; Neal 2000.
25 Wainwright 1979.
26 Cunnington 1929.
27 Flinders Petrie 1880.

CHAPTER 17

1 Stone 1938.
2 Stone 1947.
3 BBC 2010.
4 Thomas 1923.
5 Thorpe *et al.* 1991.
6 Williams-Thorpe *et al.* 2006.
7 Ixer and Bevins 2011.
8 Atkinson 1956: 46.
9 Ixer and Turner 2006.
10 Van Tilburg 1994.
11 Atkinson 1956: 109.
12 John 2008: 47–53.
13 Hoskins 1986; Parker Pearson *et al.* 2010: 36–9, 490–510.
14 Pryor 2003: 160.
15 Pipes 2004.
16 Hoskins 1986.
17 Judd 1902.
18 Thomas 1923.

19 Kellaway 1971.
20 Kellaway 1991; 2002.
21 Green 1973.
22 Bell and Walker 1992: 72. My research in the Western Isles of Scotland has revealed that it was warm enough at that time to grow wheat, a crop which cannot be grown there today; Parker Pearson *et al.* 2004.
23 John 2008; Williams-Thorpe *et al.* 1997.
24 Clark *et al.* 2011; Gibbard and Clark in press.
25 Williams-Thorpe *et al.* 1997.
26 Williams-Thorpe *et al.* 2006.
27 Cunnington 1924.
28 Pitts 2001: 198–203.
29 Parker Pearson *et al.* 2010: 36–9.
30 Breeze and Munro 1997.
31 Campbell 2003.
32 Wikipedia 2010.
33 Morgan 1887; Burl 1976: 104–6.
34 Bradley and Edmonds 1993.
35 Whittle *et al.* 1999; Mercer and Healy 2008.
36 Darvill and Wainwright 2002.
37 Grimes 1936; 1939.
38 Grimes 1949; 1960.
39 Darvill *et al.* 2005: 22.
40 Grimes 1963; Darvill and Wainwright 2003.
41 Wright 2007.
42 Burl 2006: 136.
43 Atkinson 1956: 190–1.
44 Darvill 2006.
45 Fitzpatrick 2002.
46 Ashbee 1978; Christie 1967.
47 Pia Bennike pers. comm.; Sundem 2010.
48 Smith and Brickley 2009: 134.
49 Leary and Field 2010; Thorpe *et al.* 1991: 109, 112.
50 Grimes 1963: 150.
51 Spinal Tap are a fictional heavy metal band whose 1984 comedy rock musical 'mocumentary' featured a laughably small Stonehenge megalith only 18 inches high, due to a mistake made in the design stage about its dimensions.
52 Parker Pearson 2005: fig. 49.
53 Murphy *et al.* 2010: 17.
54 Mytum and Webster 2003.
55 Cummins 1979.
56 Louise Austin pers. comm.

CHAPTER 18

1 Hawley 1921; 1922.
2 Howard in Pitts 1982.
3 Evans *et al.* 1988.
4 Bowen and Smith 1977.
5 Atkinson 1956: 110–17.
6 Hill 1961.
7 Piggott 1948a.
8 *Ibid.*
9 Leary *et al.* 2010.
10 Wainwright *et al.* 1971.

CHAPTER 19

1 Evans 1984.
2 Darvill and Wainwright 2009.
3 Darwin 1881: 154–6.
4 Armour-Chelu and Andrews 1994; Canti 2003.
5 Atkinson 1957.
6 Cleal *et al.* 1995: fig. 92.

CHAPTER 20

1 Field *et al.* 2010.
2 Hinton 1977.
3 Wright 2007; Giles 1841.
4 Crowley *et al.* 1995.

CHAPTER 21

1 Lynch and Musson 2004.
2 Hardy 1928.
3 Healy 1997.
4 Cleal *et al.* 1995: 361; Piggott 1938.
5 Wainwright 1979; Barber 2009.
6 Bradley 1975.
7 Woodward *et al.* 1993.
8 Atkinson *et al.* 1951; Whittle *et al.* 1992.
9 Oswald 1969.
10 West 1990.
11 Barclay *et al.* 2009.
12 Green 2000: 77–84; Montgomery *et al.* 2000.

13 Green 2000: 69–76.
14 Mortimer 1905.
15 Gibson and Bayliss 2009.
16 Kinnes *et al.* 1983.
17 Piggott 1948b.
18 SNS-Bornholm n.d.
19 Lewis and Mullin 2010.
20 Harding 2003.
21 Towrie 2008.
22 Richards 2005.
23 Ritchie 1976.
24 Towrie 2010.
25 Sheridan 2003; 2004.
26 Ashbee 1993; Healy 2008.
27 Cummings and Whittle 2004.
28 Lynch 1975.
29 Gibson 1999.
30 Gibson 1992.
31 As well as Carreg Samson, the other two closed chamber tombs in Pembrokeshire are Hanging Stone and Parc y Llyn; Sheridan 2010, and see Barker 1992.
32 Mercer 1999.
33 Barker 1992: 28–30; V. Cummings and C. Richards pers. comm.
34 Wikipedia 2010.
35 Burl 1993; Cassen 2009.
36 Márquez-Romero and Fernández Ruiz 2009; Ruiz González 2009.
37 Renfrew 1968.
38 Taylor 2001: 142–3.
39 Grimes 1949.
40 Piggott 1962.
41 Gibson 1998a & b.
42 Richards 1990: fig. 97.
43 Hartwell 1998; Eogan and Roche 1997.
44 Gibson 1999.
45 Atkinson 1956: 163.

CHAPTER 22

1 Leary and Field 2010.
2 Dickson and Dickson 2000: 79–81.
3 O'Kelly 1982.
4 Phillips 1936.
5 Wainwright 1979.
6 Gale *et al.* 2008.
7 Needham *et al.* 2010.

8 Piggott 1938.
9 Needham *et al.* 2010.
10 Yates 2007.
11 Burl 2006: 20.
12 Henry of Huntingdon 1129–1154 [1991].

BIBLIOGRAPHY

Albarella, U. and Serjeantson, D. 2002. A passion for pork: meat consumption at the British Late Neolithic site of Durrington Walls. In P. Miracle and N. Milner (eds) *Consuming Passions and Patterns of Consumption*. Cambridge: Cambridge University Press. 33–49.

Allen, M.J. 1997. Environment and land-use: the economic development of the communities who built Stonehenge (an economy to support the stones). In B. Cunliffe and C. Renfrew (eds) *Science and Stonehenge*. London: British Academy & Oxford University Press. 115–44.

Allen, M.J., Gardiner, J., Sheridan, A. and McOmish, D. (eds) 2011. *The British Chalcolithic: people, place and polity in the later 3rd millennium*. Prehistoric Society Research Paper 4. Oxford: Oxbow.

Annable, F.K. and Simpson, D.D.A. 1964. *Guide Catalogue of the Neolithic and Bronze Age Collections in Devizes Museum*. Devizes: Wiltshire Archaeological and Natural History Society.

Armour-Chelu, M. and Andrews, P. 1994. Some effects of bioturbation by earthworms (Oligochaeta) on archaeological sites. *Journal of Archaeological Science* 21: 433–43.

Ashbee, P. 1978. Amesbury Barrow 51: excavation 1960. *Wiltshire Archaeological and Natural History Magazine* 70/71 (1975–76): 1–60.

Ashbee, P. 1993. The Medway megaliths in perspective. *Archaeologia Cantiana* 111: 57–111.

Ashbee, P. 1998. Stonehenge: its possible non-completion, slighting and dilapidation. *Wiltshire Archaeological and Natural History Magazine* 91: 139–42.

Atkinson, R.J.C. 1946. *Field Archaeology*. London: Methuen & Co.

Atkinson, R.J.C. 1956. *Stonehenge*. London: Hamish Hamilton.

Atkinson, R.J.C. 1957. Worms and weathering. *Antiquity* 33: 219–33.

Atkinson, R.J.C. 1979. *Stonehenge*. Third edition. Harmondsworth: Penguin.

Atkinson, R.J.C., Piggott, C.M. and Sandars, N. 1951. *Excavations at Dorchester, Oxon*. Oxford: Ashmolean Museum.

Bakker, J.A. 1999. Two drawings of Stonehenge from 1662 by Willem Schellinks. In H. Sarfatij, W.J.H. Verwers and P.J. Woltering (eds) *In Discussion with the Past. Archaeological studies presented to W.A. van Es*. Zwolle/Amersfoort: SPA/ROB. 9–22.

Barber, M. 2009. *Mount Pleasant, Dorset: a survey of the Neolithic 'henge enclosure' and associated features as seen on aerial photographs*. London: English Heritage Research Department Report Series.

Barclay, A. and Halpin, C. 1998. *Excavations at Barrow Hills, Radley, Oxfordshire*.

Volume I: The Neolithic and Bronze Age monument complex. Oxford: Oxford Archaeological Unit.

Barclay, A. and Harding, J. (eds) 1999. *Pathways and Ceremonies: the cursus monuments of Britain and Ireland.* Oxford: Oxbow.

Barclay, A., Beacan, N., Bradley, P., Chaffey, G., Challinor, D., McKinley, J.I., Powell, A. and Marshall, P. 2009. New evidence for mid-late Neolithic burial from the Colne valley, west London. *Past* 63: 4–6.

Barker, C.T. 1992. *The Chambered Tombs of South-West Wales: a re-assessment of the Neolithic burial monuments of Carmarthenshire and Pembrokeshire.* Oxford: Oxbow.

Barker, G. 2009. *The Agricultural Revolution in Prehistory: why did foragers become farmers?* Oxford: Oxford University Press.

Barrett, J. and Fewster, K. 1998. Is the medium the message? *Antiquity* 72: 847–51.

BBC. 2010. Archaeologists unearth Neolithic henge at Stonehenge. http://www.bbc.co.uk/news/uk-england-10718522

Bell, M. and Walker, M.J.C. 1992. *Late Quaternary Environmental Change: physical and human perspectives.* Harlow: Longman.

Bender, B. 1998. *Stonehenge: making space.* London: Berg.

Booth, A.St.J. and Stone, J.F.S. 1952. A trial flint mine at Durrington, Wiltshire. *Wiltshire Archaeological and Natural History Magazine* 54: 381–8.

Bowen, H.C. and Smith, I.F. 1977. Sarsen stones in Wessex: the Society's first investigations in the Evolution of the Landscape Project. *Antiquaries Journal* 57: 185–96.

Bradley, R. 1975. Maumbury Rings, Dorchester: the excavations of 1908–1913. *Archaeologia* 105: 1–98.

Bradley, R. 2000. *The Archaeology of Natural Places.* London: Routledge.

Bradley, R. and Edmonds, M. 1993. *Interpreting the Axe Trade: production and exchange in Neolithic Britain.* Cambridge: Cambridge University Press.

Breeze, D and Munro, G. 1997. *The Stone of Destiny: symbol of nationhood.* Edinburgh: Historic Scotland.

Brodie, N. 1994. *The Neolithic-Bronze Age Transition in Britain.* Oxford: BAR (British Series) 238.

Buck, C.E., Cavanagh, W.G. and Litton, C.D. 1996. *The Bayesian Approach to Interpreting Archaeological Data.* Chichester: Wiley.

Burgess, C. 2003. *The Age of Stonehenge.* London: Orion.

Burgess, C. and Shennan, S. 1976. The Beaker phenomenon: some suggestions. In C. Burgess and R. Miket (eds) *Settlement and Economy in the Third and Second Millennia B.C.* Oxford: BAR (British Series) 33. 309–31.

Burl, A. 1976. *The Stone Circles of the British Isles.* New Haven & London: Yale University Press.

Burl, A. 1987. *The Stonehenge People.* London: J.M. Dent.

Burl, A. 1993. *From Carnac to Callanish: the prehistoric stone rows and avenues of Britain, Ireland, and Brittany.* New Haven & London: Yale University Press.

Burl, A. 2002. *Prehistoric Avebury.* Second edition. New Haven & London: Yale University Press.

Burl, A. 2006. *Stonehenge: a new history of the world's greatest stone circle.* London: Constable & Robinson Ltd.

Caesar, J. [1951] *The Conquest of Gaul.* Trans. by S.A. Handford. Harmondsworth: Penguin.

Campbell, E. 2003. Royal inauguration in Dál Riata and the Stone of Destiny. In R. Welander, D. Breeze and T. Owen Clancy (eds) *The Stone of Destiny: artefact and icon.* Edinburgh: Society of Antiquaries of Scotland. 43–59.

Canti, M. 2003. Earthworm activity and archaeological stratigraphy: a review of products and processes. *Journal of Archaeological Science* 30: 135–48.

Carr, C. 1995. Mortuary practices: their social, philosophical-religious, circumstantial, and physical determinants. *Journal of Archaeological Method and Theory* 2: 105–200.

Case, H. 2004. Beakers and the Beaker culture. In J. Czebreszuk (ed.) *Similar but Different: Bell Beakers in Europe.* Poznan: Adam Mickiewicz University. 11–34.

Cassen, S. 2009. *Exercice de Stèle: une archéologie des pierres dressées, refléxion autour des menhirs de Carnac.* Paris: Errance.

Chamberlain, A. and Parker Pearson, M. 2007. Units of measurement in Late Neolithic southern Britain. In M. Larsson and M. Parker Pearson (eds) *From Stonehenge to the Baltic: cultural diversity in the third millennium BC.* Oxford: BAR (International Series) 1692. 169–74.

Childe, V.G. 1931. *Skara Brae: a Pictish village in Orkney.* London: Kegan Paul.

Childe, V.G. 1957. *The Dawn of European Civilization.* Sixth edition. London: Routledge & Kegan Paul.

Chippindale, C. 1994. *Stonehenge Complete.* Revised edition. London: Thames & Hudson.

Christie, P.M. 1963 The Stonehenge Cursus. *Wiltshire Archaeological Magazine* 58: 370–82.

Christie, P.M. 1967. A barrow cemetery of the second millennium BC in Wiltshire, England. *Proceedings of the Prehistoric Society* 33: 336–66.

Clark, C.D., Hughes, A.L.C., Greenwood, S.L., Jordan, C.J. and Sejrup, H.P. 2010. Pattern and timing of retreat of the last British-Irish Ice Sheet. *Quaternary Science Reviews.* doi:1016/j.quascirev.2010.07.019

Clarke, D.L. 1976. *Beaker Pottery of Great Britain and Ireland.* Cambridge: Cambridge University Press.

Cleal, R.M.J. and Allen, M.J. 1994. Investigation of tree-damaged barrows on King Barrow Ridge and Luxenborough Plantation, Amesbury. *Wiltshire Archaeological and Natural History Magazine* 87: 54–84.

Cleal, R.M.J., Allen, M. and Newman, C. 2004. An archaeological and environmental study of the Neolithic and later prehistoric landscape of the Avon valley and Durrington Walls environs. *Wiltshire Archaeological and Natural History Magazine* 97: 218–48.

Cleal, R.M.J. and MacSween, A. (eds) 1999. *Grooved Ware in Great Britain and Ireland.* Oxford: Oxbow.

Cleal, R.M.J., Walker, K.E. and Montague, R. 1995. *Stonehenge in its Landscape: twentieth-century excavations.* London: English Heritage.

Coles, B. and Coles, J.M. 1986. *Sweet Track to Glastonbury: the Somerset Levels in prehistory.* London: Thames & Hudson.

Colt Hoare, R. 1812. *The Ancient History of South Wiltshire.* London: William Miller.

Crawford, O.G.S. 1924. The Stonehenge Avenue. *Antiquaries Journal* 4: 57–8.

Crowley, D.A., Pugh, R.B. and Stevenson, J.H. 1995. *A History of Amesbury, Bulford and Durrington.* Trowbridge: Wiltshire County Council.

Cummings, V. and Whittle, A.W.R. 2004. *Places of Special Virtue: megaliths in the Neolithic landscapes of Wales.* Oxford: Oxbow.

Cummins, W.A. 1979. Neolithic stone axes: distribution and trade in England and Wales. In T.H.McK. Clough and W.A. Cummins (eds) *Stone Axe Studies: archaeological, petrological, experimental and ethnographic.* London: CBA Research Report 23. 5–12.

Cunnington, B.H. 1924. The 'blue stone' from Boles Barrow. *Wiltshire Archaeological and Natural History Magazine* 42: 431–7.

Cunnington, M.E. 1929. *Woodhenge.* Devizes: Simpson.

Cunnington, M.E. 1931. The Sanctuary on Overton Hill near Avebury. *Wiltshire Archaeological and Natural History Magazine* 45: 300–35.

Darvill, T.C. 2005. *Stonehenge World Heritage Site: an archaeological research framework.* London & Bournemouth: English Heritage & Bournemouth University.

Darvill, T.C. 2006. *Stonehenge: the biography of a landscape.* Stroud: Tempus.

Darvill, T.C. and Wainwright, G.J. 2002. Strumble-Preseli Ancient Communities and Environment Study (SPACES): first report 2002. *Archaeology in Wales* 42: 17–28.

Darvill, T.C. and Wainwright, G.J. 2003. Stone circles, oval settings and henges in south-west Wales and beyond. *Antiquaries Journal* 83: 9–45.

Darvill, T.C. and Wainwright, G.J. 2009. Stonehenge excavations 2008. *Antiquaries Journal* 89: 1–19.

Darvill, T.C., Morgan Evans, D. and Wainwright, G.J. 2003. Strumble-Preseli Ancient Communities and Environment Study (SPACES): second report 2003. *Archaeology in Wales* 43: 3–12.

Darvill, T.C., Morgan Evans, D. and Wainwright, G.J. 2004. Strumble-Preseli Ancient Communities and Environment Study (SPACES): third report 2004. *Archaeology in Wales* 44: 104–9.

Darvill, T.C., Morgan Evans, D., Fyfe, R. and Wainwright, G.J. 2005. Strumble-Preseli Ancient Communities and Environment Study (SPACES): fourth report 2005. *Archaeology in Wales* 45: 17–23.

Darwin, C. 1881. *The Formation of Vegetable Mould Through the Action of Worms, with observations on their habits.* London: John Murray.

Dickson, C. and Dickson, J. 2000. *Plants and People in Ancient Scotland.* Stroud: Tempus.

Durrani, N. 2009. First written reference to soul. *Current World Archaeology* 33: 12.

Edwards, C.J., Magee, D.A., Park, S.D., McGettigan, P.A., Lohan, A.J., Murphy, A., Finlay, E.K., Shapiro, B., Chamberlain, A.T., Richards, M.B., Bradley, D.G., Loftus, B.J. and MacHugh, D.E. 2010. A complete mitochondrial genome sequence from a Mesolithic wild aurochs (*Bos primigenius*). *Public Library of Science One* 5: e9255.

Entwistle, R. and Grant, A. 1989. The evidence for cereal cultivation and animal husbandry in the southern British Neolithic and Bronze Age. In A. Milles, D. Williams and N. Gardner (eds) *The Beginnings of Agriculture.* Oxford: BAR (International Series) 496. 203–15.

Eogan, G. and Roche, H. 1997. *Excavations at Knowth. Volume 2.* Dublin: Royal Irish Academy.

Evans, A. 1885. *Megalithic Monuments* (i–v). Oxford: Ashmolean Museum, Arthur Evans Archive.

Evans, J.A., Chenery, C. and Fitzpatrick, A.P. 2006. Bronze Age childhood migration of individuals near Stonehenge, revealed by strontium and oxygen isotope tooth enamel analysis. *Archaeometry* 48: 309–21.

Evans, J.G. 1984. Stonehenge – the environment in the Late Neolithic and Early Bronze Age and a Beaker-Age burial. *Wiltshire Archaeological and Natural History Magazine* 78: 7–30.

Evans, J.G., Limbrey, S., Maté, I. and Mount, R.J. 1988. Environmental change and land use history in a Wiltshire river valley in the last 14,000 years. In J.C. Barrett and I. Kinnes (eds) *The Archaeology of Context in the Neolithic and Bronze Age: recent trends.* Sheffield: Department of Archaeology, Sheffield University. 97–103.

Farrer, P. 1917. Excavations in 'The Cursus', July 1917. Unpublished manuscript.

Farrer, P. 1918. Durrington Walls, or Long Walls. *Wiltshire Archaeological and Natural History Magazine* 40: 95–103.

Fenwick, J. 1995. The manufacture of the decorated macehead from Knowth, County Meath. *Journal of the Royal Society of Antiquaries of Ireland* 125: 51–60.

Field, D., Pearson, T., Barber, M. and Payne, A. 2010. Introducing 'Stonehedge' (and other curious earthworks). *British Archaeology* 111: 32–5.

Field, N. and Parker Pearson, M. 2004. *Fiskerton: an Iron Age timber causeway with Iron Age and Roman votive offerings. The 1981 excavations.* Oxford: Oxbow.

Fitzpatrick, A. 2002. 'The Amesbury Archer': a well-furnished Early Bronze Age burial in southern England. *Antiquity* 76: 629–30.

Flinders Petrie, W.M. 1880. *Stonehenge: plans, description, and theories.* London: Edward Stanford.

Gale, J., Hewitt, I. and Russell, M. 2008. Excavations at High Lea Farm, Hinton Martell, Dorset: an interim report on fieldwork undertaken during 2006–7. *Proceedings of the Dorset Natural History and Archaeology Society* 129: 105–14.

Gibbard, P.L. and Clark, C.D. 2011. Pleistocene glaciation limits in Great Britain. In J. Ehlers, P.L. Gibbard and P.D. Hughes (eds) *Quaternary Glaciations – extent and chronology – a closer look.* Developments in Quaternary Science 15. Cambridge MA: Elsevier. 75–93.

Gibson, A. 1992. The timber circle at Sarn-y-Bryn-Caled, Welshpool, Powys: ritual and sacrifice in Bronze Age mid-Wales. *Antiquity* 66: 84–92.

Gibson, A. 1998a. *Stonehenge and Timber Circles.* Stroud: Tempus.

Gibson, A. 1998b. Hindwell and the Neolithic palisaded sites of Britain and Ireland. In A. Gibson and D.D.A. Simpson (eds) *Prehistoric Ritual and Religion: essays in honour of Aubrey Burl.* Stroud: Sutton. 68–79.

Gibson, A. 1999. *The Walton Basin project: excavation and survey in a prehistoric landscape 1993–7.* York: Council for British Archaeology.

Gibson, A. 2007. A Beaker veneer? Some evidence from the burial record. In M. Larsson and M. Parker Pearson (eds) *From Stonehenge to the Baltic: cultural diversity in the third millennium BC.* Oxford: BAR (International Series) 1692. 47–64.

Gibson, A. 2008. Were henges ghost-traps? *Current Archaeology* 214: 34–9.

Gibson, A. and Bayliss, A. 2009. Recent research at Duggleby Howe, North Yorkshire. *Archaeological Journal* 166: 39–78.

Giles, J.A. (ed.) 1841. *The Works of Gildas and Nennius*. London: James Bohn.

Gillings, M., Pollard, J., Wheatley, D. and Peterson, R. 2008. *Landscape of the Megaliths: excavation and fieldwork on the Avebury monuments, 1997–2003*. Oxford: Oxbow.

Gowland, W. 1902. Recent excavations at Stonehenge. *Archaeologia* 58: 37–105.

Green, C.P. 1973. Pleistocene river gravels and the Stonehenge problem. *Nature* 243: 214–16.

Green, M. 2000. *A Landscape Revealed: 10,000 years on a chalkland farm*. Stroud: Tempus.

Grimes, W.F. 1936. The megalithic monuments of Wales. *Proceedings of the Prehistoric Society* 2: 106–39.

Grimes, W.F. 1939. Bedd yr Afanc, Pembrokeshire. *Proceedings of the Prehistoric Society* 5: 258.

Grimes, W.F. 1949. Pentre-ifan burial chamber, Pembrokeshire. *Archaeologia Cambrensis* 100: 3–23.

Grimes, W.F. 1960. *Pentre-ifan Burial Chamber, Nevern, Pembrokeshire*. London: HMSO.

Grimes, W.F. 1963. The stone circles and related monuments of Wales. In I. Foster and L. Alcock (eds) *Culture and Environment: essays in honour of Sir Cyril Fox*. London: Routledge & Kegan Paul. 93–152.

Haak, W., Forster, P., Bramanti, B., Matsumura, S., Brandt, G., Tänzer, M., Villems, R., Renfrew, C., Gronenborn, D., Alt, K.W. and Burger, J. 2005. Ancient DNA from the first European farmers in 7500-year-old Neolithic sites. *Science* 310: 1016–18.

Hammond, N. 2009. Magic mountain yields jade axes. *Times Online*. http://www.timesonline.co.uk/tol/life_and_style/court_and_social/article6497835.ece

Harding, J. 2003. *Henge Monuments of the British Isles*. Stroud: Tempus.

Harding, P. 1988. The chalk plaque pit, Amesbury. *Proceedings of the Prehistoric Society* 54: 320–7.

Hardy, F. 1928. *The Early Life of Thomas Hardy, 1840–91*. London: Macmillan.

Harrison, R. 1980. *The Beaker Folk*. London: Thames & Hudson.

Hartwell, B. 1998. The Ballynahatty complex. In A. Gibson and D.D.A. Simpson (eds) *Prehistoric Ritual and Religion: essays in honour of Aubrey Burl*. Stroud: Sutton. 32–44.

Hawkins, G.S. with White, J.B. 1965. *Stonehenge Decoded*. Garden City NY: Doubleday.

Hawley, W. 1921. The excavations at Stonehenge. *Antiquaries Journal* 1: 19–39.

Hawley, W. 1922. Second report on the excavations at Stonehenge. *Antiquaries Journal* 2: 36–51.

Hawley, W. 1923. Third report on the excavations at Stonehenge. *Antiquaries Journal* 3: 13–20.

Hawley, W. 1924. Fourth report on the excavations at Stonehenge. *Antiquaries Journal* 4: 30–9.

Hawley, W. 1925. Report of the excavations at Stonehenge during the season of 1923. *Antiquaries Journal* 5: 21–50.

Hawley, W. 1926. Report on the excavations at Stonehenge during the season of 1924. *Antiquaries Journal* 6: 1–25.

Hawley, W. 1928. Report on the excavations at Stonehenge during 1925 and 1926. *Antiquaries Journal* 8: 149–76.

Healy, F. 1997. Site 3. Flagstones. In R.J.C. Smith, F. Healy, M.J. Allen, E.L. Morris, I. Barnes and P.J. Woodward, *Excavations along the Route of the Dorchester By-pass, Dorset, 1986–8* (Report No. 11). Salisbury: Wessex Archaeology. 27–48.

Healy, F. 2008. Causewayed enclosures and the Early Neolithic: the chronology and character of monument building and settlement in Kent, Surrey and Sussex in the early to mid-4th millennium cal BC. *South East Research Framework Resource Assessment.* 1–29. https://shareweb.kent.gov.uk/Documents/Leisure_and_Culture/Heritage/frances-healy.pdf

Henry of Huntingdon. 1129–1154 [1991]. *Historia Anglorum.* Felinfach: Llanerch Press.

Hill, J. 2008. The secret measurement of Stonehenge. http://www.johnhillma.co.uk/press_release.php

Hill, P. 1961. Sarsen stones of Stonehenge. *Science* 133: 1216–22.

Hinton, D.A. 1977. *Alfred's Kingdom: Wessex and the South, 800–1500.* London: Book Club Associates.

Hoskins, J. 1986. So my name shall live: stone-dragging and grave-building in Kodi, West Sumba. *Bijdragen tot de Taal-, Land- en Volkenkunde* 142: 31–51.

Hoyle, F. 1977. *On Stonehenge.* San Francisco: W.H. Freeman.

Hunter-Mann, K. 1999. Excavations at Vespasian's Camp Iron Age hillfort, 1987. *Wiltshire Archaeological and Natural History Magazine* 92: 39–52.

Ixer, R.A. and Bevins, R.E. 2011. The detailed petrography of six orthostats from the bluestone circle, Stonehenge. *Wiltshire Archaeological and Natural History Magazine* 104: 1–14.

Ixer, R.A. and Turner, P. 2006. A detailed re-examination of the petrography of the Altar Stone and other non-sarsen sandstones from Stonehenge as a guide to their provenance. *Wiltshire Archaeological and Natural History Magazine* 99: 1–9.

Jacques, D. 2010. Amesbury excavation: summary of AA309 students' field work at Vespasian's Camp, near Stonehenge, Wiltshire, 2005–2009. http://www.open.ac.uk/Arts/classical-studies/amesbury/index.shtml

Jay, M. and Richards, M. 2007. The Beaker People Project: progress and prospects for the carbon, nitrogen and sulphur isotope analysis of collagen. In M. Larsson and M. Parker Pearson (eds) *From Stonehenge to the Baltic: cultural diversity in the third millennium BC.* Oxford: BAR (International Series) 1692. 77–82.

Jay, M., Parker Pearson, M., Richards, M.P., Nehlich, O., Montgomery, J., Chamberlain, A. and Sheridan, A. 2011. The Beaker People Project: an interim report on the progress of the isotopic analysis of the organic skeletal material. In M.J. Allen, J. Gardiner, A. Sheridan and D. McOmish (eds) *The British*

Chalcolithic: people, place and polity in the later 3rd millennium. Prehistoric Society Research Paper 4. Oxford: Oxbow.

John, B. 2008. *The Bluestone Enigma: Stonehenge, Preseli and the Ice Age.* Newport: Greencroft Books.

Johnson, A. 2008. *Solving Stonehenge: the new key to an ancient enigma.* London: Thames & Hudson.

Jones, G. and Rowley-Conwy, P. 2007. On the importance of cereal cultivation in the British Neolithic. In S. Colledge and J. Conolly (eds) *The Origins and Spread of Domestic Plants in Southwest Asia and Europe.* Walnut Creek CA: Left Coast Press. 391–419.

Jones, I. 1655. *The Most Notable Antiquity of Great Britain, vulgarly called Stone-Heng.* London: Daniel Pakeman.

Judd, J.W. 1902. Note on the nature and origin of the rock-fragments found in the excavations made at Stonehenge by Mr Gowland in 1901. In W. Gowland, Recent excavations at Stonehenge. *Archaeologia* 58: 106–18.

Kellaway, G.A. 1971. Glaciation and the stones of Stonehenge. *Nature* 232: 30–5.

Kellaway, G.A. (ed.) 1991. *The Hot Springs of Bath: investigations of the thermal waters of the Avon Valley.* Bath: Bath City Council.

Kellaway, G.A. 2002. Glacial and tectonic factors in the emplacement of the bluestones on Salisbury Plain. In M. Chapman and E. Holland (eds) *The Survey of Bath and District, No. 17.* Bath: British Geological Survey. 57–71.

Kenyon, K. 1957. *Digging up Jericho.* London: E. Benn.

Kinnes, I. 1979. *Round Barrows and Ring-ditches in the British Neolithic.* London: British Museum Occasional Paper 7.

Kinnes, I.A, Schadla-Hall, T., Chadwick, P. and Dean P. 1983. Duggleby Howe reconsidered. *Archaeological Journal* 140: 83–108.

Lanting, J.N. and Brindley, A.L. 1998. Dating cremated bone: the dawn of a new era. *Journal of Irish Archaeology* 9: 1–7.

Larson, G., Albarella, U., Dobney, K., Rowley-Conwy, P., Schibler, J., Tresset, A., Vigne, J.D., Edwards, C.J., Schlumbaum, A., Dinu, A., Balaçsescu, A., Dolman, G., Tagliacozzo, A., Manaseryan, N., Miracle, P., Van Wijngaarden-Bakker, L., Masseti, M., Bradley, D.G. and Cooper, A. 2007. Ancient DNA, pig domestication, and the spread of the Neolithic into Europe. *Proceedings of the National Academy of Sciences* 104 (39): 15276–81.

Lawson, A.J. 2007. *Chalkland: an archaeology of Stonehenge and its region.* Salisbury: Hobnob Press.

Leary, J. and Field, D. 2010. *The Story of Silbury Hill.* London: English Heritage.

Leary, J., Field, D. and Russell, M. 2010. Marvels at Marden henge. *Past* 66: 13–14.

Leivers, M. and Moore, C. 2008. *Archaeology on the A303 Stonehenge Improvement.* Salisbury: Wessex Archaeology.

Lewis, J. and Mullin, D. 2010. Dating the Priddy Circles, Somerset. *Past* 64: 4–5.

Lynch, F. 1975. Excavations at Carreg Samson, Mathry, Pembrokeshire. *Archaeologia Cambrensis* 124: 15–35.

Lynch, F. and Musson, C. 2004. A prehistoric and early medieval complex at Llandegai, near Bangor, north Wales. *Archaeologia Cambrensis* 150: 17–142.

Mahoney, P. 2007. Microwear studies of diet in Early Bronze Age burials from Scotland. In M. Larsson and M. Parker Pearson (eds) *From Stonehenge to the Baltic: cultural diversity in the third millennium BC.* Oxford: BAR (International Series) 1692. 83–9.

Márquez-Romero, J.E. and Fernández Ruiz, J. 2009. *The Dolmens of Antequera: official guide to the archaeological complex.* Malaga: Junta de Andalucia, Consejería de Cultura.

McKinley, J.I. 1993. Bone fragment size and weights of bone from modern British cremations and the implications for the interpretation of archaeological cremations. *International Journal of Osteoarchaeology* 3: 283–7.

McKinley, J.I. 1994. Bone fragment size in British cremation burials and its implications for pyre technology and ritual. *Journal of Archaeological Science* 21: 339–42.

McKinley, J.I. 1997. Bronze Age 'barrows' and the funerary rites and rituals of cremation. *Proceedings of the Prehistoric Society* 63: 129–45.

McKinley, J.I. 2000. The analysis of cremated bone. In M. Cox and S. Mays (eds) *Human Osteology.* London: Greenwich Medical Media. 403–21.

McKinley, J.I. and Bond, J.M. 2001. Cremated bone. In D.R. Brothwell and A.M. Pollard (eds) *Handbook of Archaeological Science.* London: Wiley. 281–92.

Mercer, R. (ed.) 1977. *Beakers in Britain and Europe.* Oxford: BAR (International Series) 331.

Mercer, R. 1999. The origins of warfare in the British Isles. In J. Carman and A. Harding (eds) *Ancient Warfare: archaeological perspectives.* Stroud: Sutton. 143–56.

Mercer, R. and Healy, F. 2008. *Hambledon Hill, Dorset, England: excavation and survey of a Neolithic monument complex and its surrounding landscape.* 2 vols. London: English Heritage.

Metcalf, P. and Huntington, R. 1991. *Celebrations of Death: the anthropology of mortuary ritual.* Cambridge: Cambridge University Press.

Michell, J. 1981. *Ancient Metrology.* Bristol: Pentacle Books.

Montgomery, J., Budd, P. and Evans, J. 2000. Reconstructing the lifetime movements of ancient people: a Neolithic case study from southern England. *European Journal of Archaeology* 3: 407–22.

Montgomery, J., Cooper, R. and Evans, J. 2007. Foragers, farmers or foreigners? An assessment of dietary strontium isotope variation in Middle Neolithic and Early Bronze Age East Yorkshire. In M. Larsson and M. Parker Pearson (eds) *From Stonehenge to the Baltic: cultural diversity in the third millennium BC.* Oxford: BAR (International Series) 1692. 65–75.

Morgan, C.L. 1887. The stones of Stanton Drew: their source and origin. *Proceedings of the Somerset Archaeological and Natural History Society* 33: 37–50.

Mortimer, J.R. 1905. *Fifty Years' Researches in British and Saxon Burial Mounds of East Yorkshire.* London: A. Brown & Sons.

Mukherjee, A.J. 2004. The importance of pigs in the later British Neolithic: integrating stable isotope evidence from lipid residues in archaeological potsherds, animal bone, and modern animal tissues. Unpublished PhD thesis, University of Bristol.

Mukherjee, A.J., Gibson, A.M. and Evershed, R.P. 2008. Trends in pig product processing at British Neolithic Grooved Ware sites traced through organic residues in potsherds. *Journal of Archaeological Science* 35: 2059–73.

Muller, J. and van Willigen, S. 2001. New radiocarbon evidence for European Bell Beakers and the consequences for the diffusion of the Bell Beaker phenomenon. In F. Nicolis (ed.) *Bell Beakers Today: pottery, people, culture, symbols in prehistoric Europe.* Torento: Servizio Beni Culturali, Ufficio Beni Archeologici. 59–75.

Murphy, F., Page, M., Ramsey, R. and Wilson, H. 2010. *Scheduling Enhancement Project 2010: prehistoric sites fieldwork – Pembrokeshire.* http://www.dyfed archaeology.org.uk/projects/schedulepembroke2010.pdf. Llandeilo: Dyfed Archaeological Trust.

Mytum, H. and Webster, C. 2003. Geophysical surveys at defended enclosures in the neighbourhood of Castell Henllys, Pembrokeshire. http://www.coflein. gov.uk/pdf/AENT17_06/

Neal, J. 2000. *All Done with Mirrors.* London: The Secret Academy.

Needham, S. 2005. Transforming Beaker culture in north-west Europe: processes of fusion and fission. *Proceedings of the Prehistoric Society* 71: 171–217.

Needham, S., Lawson, A.J. and Woodward, A. 2010. 'A noble group of barrows': Bush Barrow and the Normanton Down Early Bronze Age cemetery two centuries on. *Antiquaries Journal* 90: 1–39.

Needham, S., Parker Pearson, M., Tyler, A., Richards, M. and Jay, M. 2010. A first 'Wessex I' date from Wessex. *Antiquity* 84: 363–73.

North, J. 1996. *Stonehenge: Neolithic man and the cosmos.* London: Harper Collins.

O'Kelly, M.J. 1982. *Newgrange: archaeology, art and legend.* London: Thames & Hudson.

Oppenheimer, S. 2006. *The Origins of the British: a genetic detective story.* London: Constable.

Oswald, A. 1969. Excavations at Barford, Warwickshire. *Transactions of the Birmingham and Warwickshire Archaeological Society* 83: 3–54.

Parker Pearson, M. 1999. The Earlier Bronze Age. In J. Hunter and I. Ralston (eds) *The Archaeology of Britain: an introduction from the Palaeolithic to the Industrial Revolution.* London: Routledge. 77–94.

Parker Pearson, M. 2003. Food, culture and identity in the Neolithic and Early Bronze Age: an introduction and overview. In M. Parker Pearson (ed.) *Food, Identity and Culture in the Neolithic and Early Bronze Age.* Oxford: BAR (International Series) 1117. 1–30.

Parker Pearson, M. 2005. *Bronze Age Britain.* Second edition. London: Batsford & English Heritage.

Parker Pearson, M. 2006. The Beaker people project: mobility and diet in the British Early Bronze Age. *The Archaeologist* 61: 14–15.

Parker Pearson, M. 2007. The Stonehenge Riverside Project: excavations at the east entrance of Durrington Walls. In M. Larsson and M. Parker Pearson (eds) *From Stonehenge to the Baltic: cultural diversity in the third millennium BC.* Oxford: BAR (International Series) 1692. 125–44.

Parker Pearson, M. 2008. When did copper first come to Britain? *British Archaeology* 101: 25.

Parker Pearson, M. and Ramilisonina. 1998a. Stonehenge for the ancestors: the stones pass on the message. *Antiquity* 72: 308–26.

Parker Pearson, M. and Ramilisonina. 1998b. Stonehenge for the ancestors: part two. *Antiquity* 72: 855–6.

Parker Pearson, M. and Richards, C. 1994. Architecture and order: spatial representation and archaeology. In M. Parker Pearson and C. Richards (eds) *Architecture and Order: approaches to social space.* London: Routledge. 38–72.

Parker Pearson, M., Chamberlain, A., Jay, M., Marshall, P., Pollard, J., Richards, C., Thomas, J., Tilley, C. and Welham, K. 2009. Who was buried at Stonehenge? *Antiquity* 83: 23–39.

Parker Pearson, M., Cleal, R., Marshall, P., Needham, S., Pollard, J., Richards, C., Ruggles, C., Sheridan, A., Thomas, J., Tilley, C., Welham, K., Chamberlain, A., Chenery, C., Evans, J., Knüsel, C., Linford N., Martin, L., Montgomery, J., Payne, A. and Richards. M. 2007. The age of Stonehenge. *Antiquity* 81: 617–39.

Parker Pearson, M. with Godden, K., Heurtebize, G., Radimilahy, C., Ramilisonina, Retsihisatse, Schwenninger, J.-L. and Smith, H. 2010. *Pastoralists, Warriors and Colonists: the archaeology of southern Madagascar.* Oxford: BAR (International Series) S2139.

Parker Pearson, M., Sharples, N. and Symonds, J. with Mulville, J., Raven, J., Smith, H. and Woolf, A. 2004. *South Uist: archaeology and history of a Hebridean island.* Stroud: Tempus.

Passmore, A.D. 1942. A disc barrow containing curious flints near Stonehenge. *Wiltshire Archaeological and Natural History Magazine* 49: 238.

Phillips, C.W. 1936. The excavation of the Giants' Hills long barrow, Skendleby, Lincolnshire. *Archaeologia* 85: 37–106.

Piggott, S. 1938. The Early Bronze Age in Wessex. *Proceedings of the Prehistoric Society* 4: 52–106.

Piggott, S. 1948a. Destroyed megaliths in north Wiltshire. *Wiltshire Archaeological and Natural History Magazine* 52: 390–2.

Piggott, S. 1948b. The excavations at Cairnpapple Hill, West Lothian, 1947–8. *Proceedings of the Society of Antiquaries of Scotland* 82: 68–123.

Piggott, S. 1962. *The West Kennet Long Barrow.* London: HMSO.

Piggott, S. 1968. *The Druids.* London: Pelican.

Piggott, S. 1985. *William Stukeley: an eighteenth-century antiquary.* London: Thames & Hudson.

Pipes, G. 2004. A new and unique theory on the movement of heavy stones. http://www.world-mysteries.com/gw_gpipes.htm

Pitts, M.W. 1982. On the road to Stonehenge: report on the investigations beside the A344 in 1968, 1979 and 1980. *Proceedings of the Prehistory Society* 48: 75–132.

Pitts, M.W. 2001. *Hengeworld.* Second edition. London: Arrow Books.

Pitts, M.W. 2008. The big dig: Stonehenge. *British Archaeology* 102: 12–17.

Pitts, M.W., Bayliss, A., McKinley, J., Budd, P., Evans, J., Chenery, C., Reynolds, A. and Semple, S. 2002. An Anglo-Saxon decapitation and burial from Stonehenge. *Wiltshire Archaeological and Natural History Magazine* 95: 131–46.

Pliny the Elder [1945]. *Natural History. Volume 4: Libri XII–XVI.* London: Heinemann.

Pollard, J. 1995a. Inscribing space: formal deposition at the later Neolithic monument of Woodhenge, Wiltshire. *Proceedings of the Prehistoric Society* 61: 137–56.

Pollard, J. 1995b. The Durrington 68 timber circle: a forgotten Late Neolithic monument. *Wiltshire Archaeological and Natural History Magazine* 88: 122–5.

Pollard, J. and Gillings, M. 2004. *Avebury*. London: Duckworth.

Pollard, J. and Ruggles, C. 2001. Shifting perceptions: spatial order, cosmology, and patterns of deposition at Stonehenge. *Cambridge Archaeological Journal* 11: 69–90.

Pryor, F. 2003. *Britain BC: life in Britain and Ireland before the Romans*. London: HarperCollins.

Renfrew, C. 1968. Wessex without Mycenae. *Annals of the British School at Athens*. 63: 277–85.

Reynolds, P.J. 1977. Experimental archaeology and the Butser Ancient Farm Project. In J.R. Collis (ed.) *The Iron Age in Britain: a review*. Sheffield: Sheffield Academic Press. 33–40.

Richards, C. 1991. Skara Brae: revisiting a Neolithic village in Orkney. In W.S. Hanson and E.A. Slater (eds) *Scottish Archaeology: new perspectives*. Aberdeen: Aberdeen University Press.

Richards, C. (ed.) 2005. *Dwelling Among the Monuments: the Neolithic village of Barnhouse, Maeshowe passage grave and surrounding monuments at Stenness, Orkney*. Cambridge: McDonald Institute for Archaeological Research.

Richards, C. 2010. The Ness of Brodgar – a Neolithic tribal meeting place? Kirkwall: Orkneyjar (Orkney Archaeology News). http://www.orkneyjar.com/archaeology/crnessofbrodgar.htm

Richards, C. and Thomas, J.S. 1984. Ritual activity and structured deposition in later Neolithic Wessex. In R. Bradley and J. Gardiner (eds) *Neolithic Studies: a review of some current research*. Oxford: BAR (British Series) 133. 189–218.

Richards, J. 1990. *The Stonehenge Environs Project*. London: English Heritage.

Richards, J. 2004. *Stonehenge: A History in Photographs*. London: English Heritage

Richards, J. 2007. *Stonehenge: the story so far*. Swindon: English Heritage.

Richards, M.P., Schulting, R.J. and Hedges, R.E.M. 2003. Sharp shift in diet at onset of Neolithic. *Nature* 425: 366.

Richardson, R. 1988. *Death, Dissection and the Destitute*. London: Pelican.

Ritchie, J.N.G. 1976. The Stones of Stenness. *Proceedings of the Society of Antiquaries of Scotland* 107: 1–60.

Roberts, C. and Cox, M. 2003. *Health and Disease in Britain: from prehistory to the present day*. Stroud: Sutton.

Roe, F.E.S. 1968. Stone mace-heads and the latest Neolithic cultures of the British Isles. In J.M. Coles and D.D.A. Simpson (eds) *Studies in Ancient Europe: essays presented to Stuart Piggott*. Leicester: Leicester University Press. 145–72.

Roe, F.E.S. 1979. Typology of stone implements with shaftholes. In T.H.McK. Clough and W.A. Cummins (eds) *Stone Axe Studies: archaeological, petrological, experimental and ethnographic*. London: Council for British Archaeology. 23–48.

Ross, A. 1999. *Druids*. Stroud: Tempus.

Ruggles, C. 1997. Astronomy and Stonehenge. In B. Cunliffe and C. Renfrew (eds) *Science and Stonehenge*. London: British Academy and Oxford University Press. 203–29.

Ruiz González, B. (ed.) 2009. *Dólmenes de Antequera: tutela y valorización hoy.* Sevilla: Consejería de Cultura.

Sahlins, M. 1972. *Stone Age Economics.* Chicago: University of Chicago Press.

Sayer, D. 2010. *Ethics and Burial Archaeology.* London: Duckworth.

Schulting, R. and Wysocki, M. 2005. 'In this chambered tumulus were found cleft skulls . . .': an assessment of the evidence for cranial trauma in the British Neolithic. *Proceedings of the Prehistoric Society* 71: 107–38.

Schmidt, K. 2005. 'Ritual centers' and the Neolithicisation of Upper Mesopotamia. *Neo-Lithics* 2: 13–21.

Sheridan, A. 2003. French connections I: spreading the marmites thinly. In I. Armit, E. Murphy, E. Nelis and D.D.A. Simpson (eds) *Neolithic Settlement in Ireland and Western Britain.* Oxford: Oxbow. 3–17.

Sheridan, A. 2004. Neolithic connections along and across the Irish Sea. In V. Cummings and C. Fowler (eds) *The Neolithic of the Irish Sea: materiality and traditions of practice.* Oxford: Oxbow. 9–21.

Sheridan, A. 2010. The Neolithization of Britain and Ireland: the 'big picture'. In B. Finlayson and G. Warren (eds) *Landscapes in Transition.* Oxford: Oxbow. 89–105.

Smith, G. 1973. Excavation of the Stonehenge avenue at West Amesbury, Wiltshire. *Wiltshire Archaeological and Natural History Magazine* 68: 42–56.

Smith, M. and Brickley, M. 2009. *People of the Long Barrows: life, death and burial in the earlier Neolithic.* Stroud: History Press.

SNS-Bornholm. n.d. Rispebjerg. http://www.skovognatur.dk/Ud/Beskrivelser/Bornholm/Rispebjerg

Šoberl, L., Pollard, J. and Evershed, R. 2009. Pots for the afterlife: organic residue analysis of British Bronze Age pottery from funerary contexts. *Past* 63: 6–8.

Spindler, K. 1995. *The Man in the Ice.* London: Weidenfeld & Nicholson.

Stone, J.F.S. 1935. Some discoveries at Ratfyn, Amesbury and their bearing on the date of Woodhenge. *Wiltshire Archaeological and Natural History Magazine* 47: 55–67.

Stone, J.F.S. 1938. An Early Bronze Age grave in Fargo Plantation, near Stonehenge. *Wiltshire Archaeological and Natural History Magazine* 48: 357–70.

Stone, J.F.S. 1947. The Stonehenge Cursus and its affinities. *Archaeological Journal* 104: 7–19.

Stone, J.F.S. 1949. Some Grooved Ware pottery from the Woodhenge area. *Proceedings of the Prehistoric Society* 15: 122–7.

Stone, J.F.S. and Young, W.E.V. 1948. Two pits of Grooved Ware date near Woodhenge. *Wiltshire Archaeological and Natural History Magazine* 52: 287–306.

Stone, J.F.S., Piggott, S. and Booth, A. St. J. 1954. Durrington Walls, Wiltshire: recent excavations at a ceremonial site of the early second millennium BC. *Antiquaries Journal* 34: 155–77.

Stukeley, W. 1724. *The History of the Temples and Religion of the Antient Celts, 1721–4.* MS. 4, 253, Cardiff Public Library.

Stukeley, W. 1740. *Stonehenge: a temple restor'd to the British druids.* London: Innys & Manby.

Sundem, G. 2010. Self-trepanation: a DIY skylight for your brain. *Science 20.*

http://www.science20.com/brain_candyfeed_your_mind/selftrepanation_diy_
skylight_your_brain

Sykes, B. 2006. *Blood of the Isles: exploring the genetic roots of our tribal history*. London:
Transworld Publishers.

Tacitus, C. [2003]. *The Annals and the Histories*. Ed. M. Hadas. New York: Modern
Library.

Tainter, J.R. 1978. Mortuary practices and the study of prehistoric social systems.
Archaeological Method and Theory 1: 105–41.

Taylor, J.H. 2001. *Death and the Afterlife in Ancient Egypt*. London: British Museum
Press.

Teather, A. 2007. Neolithic phallacies: a discussion of some southern British artefacts.
In M. Larsson and M. Parker Pearson (eds) *From Stonehenge to the Baltic: cultural diversity in the third millennium BC*. Oxford: BAR (International Series) 1692. 205–11.

Thackray, D. and Payne, S. 2010. *Avebury Reburial Request: summary report*. English
Heritage & National Trust. http://www.english-heritage.org.uk/content/
imported-docs/a-e/avebury-reburial-request-summary.pdf

Thom, A. 1967. *Megalithic Sites in Britain*. Oxford: Oxford University Press.

Thom, A. 1971. *Megalithic Lunar Observatories*. Oxford: Oxford University Press.

Thom, A. and Thom, A.S. 1974. Stonehenge. *Journal for the History of Astronomy* 5:
71–90.

Thom, A. and Thom, A.S. 1988. The metrology and geometry of megalithic man.
In C. Ruggles (ed.) *Records in Stone: papers in memory of Alexander Thom*.
Cambridge: Cambridge University Press. 132–51.

Thomas, H.H. 1923. The source of the stones of Stonehenge. *Antiquaries Journal*
3: 239–60.

Thomas, J.S. 1999. *Understanding the Neolithic*. London: Routledge.

Thomas, J.S. 2007. The internal features at Durrington Walls: investigations in the
Southern Circle and Western Enclosures 2005–2006. In M. Larsson and M.
Parker Pearson (eds) *From Stonehenge to the Baltic: cultural diversity in the third
millennium BC*. Oxford: BAR (International Series) 1692. 145–57.

Thomas, J.S., Parker Pearson, M., Pollard, J., Richards, C., Tilley, C. and Welham,
K. 2009. The date of the Stonehenge cursus. *Antiquity* 83: 40–53.

Thorpe, R.S., Williams-Thorpe, O., Jenkins, D.G. and Watson, J.S. 1991. The geological sources and transport of the bluestones of Stonehenge, Wiltshire, UK.
Proceedings of the Prehistoric Society 57: 103–57.

Thurnham, J.T. 1863. On the principal forms of ancient British and Gaulish skulls.
Memoirs of the Anthropological Society of London 1: 120–68.

Thurnham, J.T. 1869. On ancient British barrows, especially those of Wiltshire and
the adjoining counties (part I – long barrows). *Archaeologia* 42: 161–244.

Tierney, J.J. 1960. The Celtic ethnography of Posidonius. *Proceedings of the Royal
Irish Academy* 60C: 189–275.

Tilley, C. 1994. *A Phenomenology of Landscape: places, paths and monuments*. London:
Berg.

Towrie, S. 2008. Brodgar excavation ends, but the secrets of the ring becoming
clearer. Kirkwall: Orkneyjar (Orkney Archaeology News) http://www.orkney-
jar.com/archaeology/brodgar2008.htm

Towrie, S. 2010. The Ness of Brodgar – excavation background. Kirkwall: Orkneyjar (Orkney Archaeology News) http://www.orkneyjar.com/archaeology/nessofbrodgar/background.htm

Van der Sanden, W.A.B. 1996. *Through Nature to Eternity: the bog bodies of northwest Europe*. Amsterdam: Batavian Lion.

Van Tilburg, J.A. 1994. *Easter Island: archaeology, ecology and culture*. London & Washington DC: British Museum Press & Smithsonian Institution.

Vatcher, F. de M. and Vatcher, H.L. 1973. Excavation of three post-holes in Stonehenge carpark. *Wiltshire Archaeological and Natural History Magazine* 68: 57–63.

Viner, S., Evans, J., Albarella, U. and Parker Pearson, M. 2010. Cattle mobility in prehistoric Britain: strontium isotope analysis of cattle teeth from Durrington Walls (Wiltshire, Britain). *Journal of Archaeological Science* 37: 2812–20.

Wainwright, G.J. 1979. *Mount Pleasant, Dorset: excavations 1970–1971*. London: Society of Antiquaries.

Wainwright, G.J. with Longworth, I. 1971. *Durrington Walls: excavations 1966–1968*. London: Society of Antiquaries.

Wainwright, G.J., Evans, J.G. and Longworth, I.H. 1971. The excavation of a Late Neolithic enclosure at Marden, Wiltshire. *Antiquaries Journal* 51: 177–239.

Walton, P. and Wild, J.P. (eds) 1990. *Textiles in Northern Archaeology: NESAT III Textile Symposium in York 6–9 May 1987*. London: Archetype Publications.

West, S.E. 1990. *West Stow: the prehistoric and Romano-British occupation*. Bury St Edmunds: East Anglian Archaeology 48.

Whitley, J. 2002. Too many ancestors. *Antiquity* 76: 119–26.

Whittle, A.W.R. 1997a. *Sacred Mound, Holy Rings. Silbury Hill and the West Kennet palisade enclosures: a later Neolithic complex in north Wiltshire*. Oxford: Oxbow.

Whittle, A.W.R. 1997b. Remembered and imagined belongings: Stonehenge in its traditions and structures of meaning. In B. Cunliffe and C. Renfrew (eds) *Science and Stonehenge*. London: British Academy & Oxford University Press. 145–66.

Whittle, A.W.R. and Cummings, V. (eds) 2007. *Going Over: the Mesolithic–Neolithic transition in north-west Europe*. Oxford: British Academy & Oxford University Press.

Whittle, A.W.R., Atkinson, R.J.C., Chambers, R. and Thomas, N. 1992. Excavations in the Neolithic and Bronze Age complex at Dorchester-on-Thames, Oxfordshire, 1947–1952 and 1981. *Proceedings of the Prehistoric Society* 58: 143–201.

Whittle, A.W.R., Barclay, A., Bayliss, A., McFadyen, L., Schulting, R. and Wysocki, M. 2007. Building for the dead: events, processes and changing worldviews from the thirty-eighth to the thirty-fourth centuries cal. BC in southern Britain. *Cambridge Archaeological Journal* 17 (Suppl.): 123–47.

Whittle, A.W.R., Pollard, J. and Grigson, C. 1999. *The Harmony of Symbols: the Windmill Hill causewayed enclosure*. Oxford: Oxbow.

Wikipedia. 2010. London Stone. http://en.wikipedia.org/wiki/London_Stone

Wikipedia. 2010. Rudston monolith. http://en.wikipedia.org/wiki/Rudston_Monolith

Williams-Thorpe, O., Green, C.P. and Scourse, J.D. 1997. The Stonehenge bluestones: discussion. In B. Cunliffe and C. Renfrew (eds) *Science and Stonehenge*. London: British Academy & Oxford University Press. 315–18.

Williams-Thorpe, O., Jones, M.C., Potts, P.J. and Webb, P.C. 2006. Preseli dolerite bluestones: axe-heads, Stonehenge monoliths, and outcrop sources. *Oxford Journal of Archaeology* 25: 29–46.

Woodward, A.B. and Woodward, P.J. 1996. The topography of some barrow cemeteries in Bronze Age Wessex. *Proceedings of the Prehistoric Society* 62: 275–92.

Woodward, P.J., Davies, S.M. and Graham, A.H. 1993. *Excavations at Greyhound Yard, Dorchester 1981–4*. Dorchester: Dorset Natural History and Archaeological Society Monograph 12.

Wright, N. 2007. *Geoffrey of Monmouth, The History of the Kings of Britain* (ed. Michael D. Reeve). An edition and translation of *De gestis Britonum [Historia regum Britanniae]*. (Arthurian Studies 69.) Woodbridge: Boydell and Brewer.

Yates, D.T. 2007. *Land, Power and Prestige: Bronze Age field systems in southern England*. Oxford: Oxbow.

Young, W.E.V. 1935a. *Leaves from My Journal VII*. Manuscript diary, Library of the Wiltshire Archaeological and Natural History Society (Devizes).

Young, W.E.V. 1935b. The Stonehenge car park excavation, 1935. *Leaves from My Journal VII*. Manuscript diary, Library of the Wiltshire Archaeological and Natural History Society (Devizes).

Zvelebil, M. and Pettitt, P. 2008. Human condition, life and death at an Early Neolithic settlement: bioarchaeological analyses of the Vedrovice cemetery and their biosocial implications for the spread of agriculture in central Europe. *Anthropologie* 46: 195–218.

LIST OF ILLUSTRATIONS

Colour Plates

Reconstruction of the Stonehenge Avenue reaching the West Amesbury henge after
   removal of the bluestones and construction of a henge ditch and bank. © Peter Dunn
The busy moments of an excavation. This is Bluestonehenge in 2009. © Aerial-Cam
The periglacial stripes and chalk ridges revealed in our excavation across the Avenue
   close to Stonehenge in 2008. © Aerial-Cam
Colin Richards (left) and Andrew Chamberlain at the closed chamber tomb or cromlech of Carreg Samson in west Wales. © Mike Parker Pearson and the Stonehenge
   Riverside Project
At Craig Rhosyfelin we found the first clear evidence of bluestone quarrying. The
   monolith (lower right) left behind in the quarry was detached by prehistoric stone-
   workers from the outcrop (behind where Ben Chan and I are standing); they then
   moved the monolith from the rock face along stone 'rails' on which it still rests. ©
   Aerial-Cam

Black & White Illustrations

Chapter 4

p. 67 An oblique arrowhead from the ditch of the Stonehenge Avenue. This type of arrowhead was in use in the Late Neolithic/Chalcolithic (2600–2200 BC). © Aerial-Cam

p. 68 The flint phallus (and two flint balls) from a pit beneath the avenue at Durrington Walls. © Mike Parker Pearson and the Stonehenge Riverside Project

Chapter 5

p. 73 The floor of House 547 at Durrington Walls. The white rectangular area is the chalk-plaster floor in the centre of the house. Within it, the dark circular area is the hearth. A line of stakeholes, showing where the wattle-and-daub wall once stood, surrounds the house. © Mike Parker Pearson and the Stonehenge Riverside Project

p. 75 The remains of four Late Neolithic houses are visible in this main trench at Durrington Walls. I am standing outside the doorway of one of the houses in an area of midden (heaps of domestic rubbish). © Mike Parker Pearson and the Stonehenge Riverside Project

p. 78 A plan of the excavation trenches at Durrington Walls, showing some of the house floors and their hearths. The inset (top left) shows the position of the trenches in relation to the henge bank, the river and the modern roads. © Mike Parker Pearson and the Stonehenge Riverside Project, drawn by Mark Dover

p. 79 Computer-generated plots showing the relative density in the northern part of the main trench of animal bones (left), worked flints (centre) and burnt flints (right). The outline plans of the houses are visible, as is the curving line of postholes forming a fence that separated two of the houses. © Mike Parker Pearson and the Stonehenge Riverside Project, drawn by Ben Chan

p. 80 Full plan of the Southern Circle, combining the 1967 and 2005–2006 excavation and geophysics results. The 'cone' shapes are the postholes and their ramps. Julian Thomas' excavation trench is marked to the west. The rest of the circle is now buried beneath the modern road. © Mike Parker Pearson and the Stonehenge Riverside Project, drawn by Lawrence Shaw

p. 81 A plan of the Late Neolithic timber circle of Woodhenge. Today the postholes are marked with small concrete pillars and the bank and ditch are barely visible. The contents of the grave were destroyed during the Blitz but the burial is thought to date to the Early Bronze Age. J040097_Reconstruction drawing by Peter Dunn. © English Heritage

p. 82 A reconstruction of the timber posts at Woodhenge. Reconstruction drawing by Peter Dunn

p. 84 Model of Phase 1 of the Southern Circle as a square-shaped arrangement of posts surrounded by two concentric timber circles, with the D-shaped house to the northeast. © Mike Parker Pearson and the Stonehenge Riverside Project

p. 85 Model of Phase 1/2 of the Southern Circle. In this phase the builders added a timber portal facing the midwinter sunrise. © Mike Parker Pearson and the Stonehenge Riverside Project

p. 87 Model of Phase 2a of the Southern Circle. In this phase, a horseshoe-shaped arrangement of timber posts was erected inside three concentric circles. © Mike Parker Pearson and the Stonehenge Riverside Project

p. 88 Model of Phase 2b of the Southern Circle. In this last phase, a ring of posts was added at the centre of the circle and a final ring was added around the outside. © Mike Parker Pearson and the Stonehenge Riverside Project

lifted from the ground so that its contents could be excavated in the laboratory. © Colin Richards and the Stonehenge Riverside Project

p. 151 The Bulford Stone now lies close to where it once stood, in a field east of the River Avon. © Colin Richards and the Stonehenge Riverside Project

Chapter 11

p. 168 A plan of Stonehenge showing the locations of the excavated cremation burials (black circles) in the Aubrey Holes and ditch. © Mike Parker Pearson and the Stonehenge Riverside Project

p. 171 Tim Darvill (left), Geoff Wainwright (centre) and Miles Russell (right) excavating at Stonehenge in 2008. © Mike Parker Pearson and the Stonehenge Riverside Project

p. 178 William Stukeley's drawing of how he imagined a British druid to have looked.

Chapter 12

p. 182 A section of Aubrey Hole 32, drawn by Stuart Piggott, showing the filled-in void where a bluestone once stood (5) and the chalk packing material for the stone (4, 6, 7) from which bones of a cremation burial were recovered (4). To the left (at 3), the side of the pit has been crushed and the packing layer displaced where the stone was removed. From Cleal *et al.* 'Stonehenge in its Landscape' figure 55. © English Heritage

p. 184 Removing a bluestone from an Aubrey Hole, showing how the shape of a pit is altered when a stone is removed. © Mike Parker Pearson and the Stonehenge Riverside Project

Chapter 13

p. 189 Jacqui McKinley (top) and Julian Richards (right) excavating the undifferentiated mass of prehistoric cremated bones deposited in Aubrey Hole 7 in 1935. © Mike Pitts and the Stonehenge Riverside Project. Photograph by Mike Pitts

p. 190 The lead plaque left on top of the cremated bones in Aubrey Hole 7 by Robert Newall and William Young. © Aerial-Cam

p. 192 The first cremated bones to be visible after our team lifted the lead plaque. © Aerial-Cam

Chapter 14

p. 205 The polished stone macehead found with one of the cremation burials at Stonehenge by William Hawley. It would have been attached to a wooden handle through the shaft-hole. Courtesy of Salisbury and South Wiltshire Museum

p. 207 The unique, drum-shaped, small pottery object found with one of the cremation burials at Stonehenge and interpreted as an 'incense burner'. From Cleal *et al.* 'Stonehenge in its Landscape' plates 8.1 & 8.2 © English Heritage

p. 210 The Amesbury Archer and the artefacts buried with him as grave goods, excavated by Andrew Fitzpatrick of Wessex Archaeology. © Wessex Archaeology

Chapter 15

p. 222 Diggers stand in the holes where standing stones once stood at Bluestonehenge on the bank of the River Avon at West Amesbury. © Aerial-Cam

INDEX

(page numbers in italic type refer to illustrations)